An outline of
the law of agency

Fourth edition

Basil S Markesinis

QC, LLD (Cantab), DCL (Oxon), FBA, D Iur hc mult
Clifford Chance Professor of Law at the University of Oxford

R J C Munday

MA, PhD (Cantab)
Fellow of Peterhouse
Lecturer in Law, University of Cambridge
Barrister of Lincoln's Inn

Butterworths
London, Edinburgh & Dublin
1998

United Kingdom	Butterworths, a Division of Reed Elsevier (UK) Ltd, Halsbury House, 35 Chancery Lane, LONDON WC2A 1EL and 4 Hill Street, EDINBURGH EH2 3JZ
Australia	Butterworths, a Division of Reed International Books Australia Pty Ltd, CHATSWOOD, New South Wales
Canada	Butterworths Canada Ltd, MARKHAM, Ontario
Hong Kong	Butterworths Asia (Hong Kong), HONG KONG
India	Butterworths Asia, NEW DELHI
Ireland	Butterworth (Ireland) Ltd, DUBLIN
Malaysia	Malayan Law Journal Sdn Bhd, KUALA LUMPUR
New Zealand	Butterworths of New Zealand Ltd, WELLINGTON
Singapore	Butterworths Asia, SINGAPORE
South Africa	Butterworths Publishers (Pty) Ltd, DURBAN
USA	Lexis Law Publishing, CHARLOTTESVILLE, Virginia

A CIP Catalogue record for this book is available from the British Library.

ISBN 0 406 90412 X

Printed and bound by William Clowes Ltd, Beccles & London

Visit us at our website: http://www.butterworths.co.uk

Preface to the fourth edition

Much has occurred since the appearance of the third edition of this book a mere six years ago. Within that period, the entry into force in 1994 of the Commercial Agents (Council Directive) Regulations 1993 and, more particularly, the appearance of the first English case law on this distinctive European Directive, represent an obvious and notable legal development. Similarly, within the last few years even a concept as basic as 'apparent authority' has been the subject of judicial decision that could ultimately transform the familiar contours of this area of law. While of course account has been taken of these and other legal changes and while a good deal of the text has also been rewritten, the aim of this fourth edition has remained steadfastly the same as that of its predecessors: to provide a succinct, readable account of a significant and intellectually challenging branch of our law that, we hope, will enable students to acquire a sound and critical understanding of the subject.

I take this opportunity to thank my daughter, Amelia, for all her assistance with the proofreading.

July 1998   R.J.C. MUNDAY

Preface to the first edition

For the academic, the law of agency can present an interest which is both profound and intellectually satisfying. In its rules are to be found frequent variations from the so-called general principles of the law of contract which, often, can only be explained by reference to commercial exigencies. Equally interesting is the fact that the principles of agency have evolved from such disparate sources as the law of contract, equity, tort, restitution and Admiralty cases dealing with the legal powers of shipmasters. However, the practical applications of the law of agency are no less important and, in the circumstances, it is both surprising and a matter for regret that in Britain the subject has not yet managed to attain the status it has achieved in other countries, notably the United States of America.

The fact that the law of agency in this country tends to be incorporated into general courses on mercantile law or the law of contract and to have no independent existence has greatly influenced the size and format of this book. This, then, is a small book with modest aims and with no particular pretensions to be breaking new ground. Indeed, the authors are deeply conscious of their considerable, though not perhaps immediately apparent, debt to the standard textbooks. In writing this book we have striven to produce a text which is readable and concise. But whilst adopting a broad approach to the subject with the intention of sparing the overburdened student its most complex minutiae, we have at the same time set out to make the text sufficiently detailed to be informative. We have also innovated in one sense by combining in one volume both an introductory textbook and a casebook. Our selection of cases, it should be said, has been greatly facilitated by the fact that within this subject judicial statements of law are relatively few, the vast majority of reported decisions being concerned essentially with questions of fact. This phenomenon may serve to explain why the extracts from judgments given in the second part of this book do not evenly cover the entire material discussed in the text.

Our intention has not been to produce a book which will supplant the standard works of reference in the field. Nothing so ambitious. Rather we have sought to complement the existing literature by offering an outline of the law of agency which both stands on its own as an independent, self-contained textbook designed to cater for courses where greater emphasis is laid upon principles than upon matters of technical detail, and which also will serve as an introductory book for more detailed study of the subject. We feel that this novel combination of text and materials fills an important gap in the literature of the law of agency and we hope that it will offer students for the first time a general introduction to the subject which is stimulating, but, most of all, clear and concise.

January 1979   B.S.M.
                                                                 R.J.C.M.

Contents

Part two

Case extracts

Table of statutes

Page references in **bold** type indicate where the section
of the Act is set out in part or in full.

List of cases

Page references in **bold** type indicate where a case is set out.

Part one

The law of agency

Introduction

I THE CONCEPTS OF POWER AND AUTHORITY

Definitions have their undoubted uses. At times, they prove invaluable, for example, when construing contracts or statutory enactments, for in such cases they can help delimit the terms used in these documents. But they are of doubtful validity in books or lecture courses; and they can also be misleading, especially if they attempt to compress an entire subject into a single sentence intended to be both concise and meaningful. This is certainly true of agency, where academics have been quick to criticise each other's definitions and find in them errors and omissions. There is, therefore, little justification for yet another definition which, more likely than not, would prove unsatisfactory.

This is not to overlook the fact that there have been serious disagreements concerning both the scope and nature of this subject. Nor is it to ignore the fact that the law of agency, as it has developed in common law jurisdictions, has acquired some highly distinctive characteristics. To instance the first phenomenon, the highly influential Oliver Wendell Holmes proposed a freestanding and wide-ranging law of agency that would have straddled all areas of law to which the notion *qui facit per alium facit per se* might apply, thereby encompassing portions of the law of contract, the law of tort, company law and so on[1]. Most writers today would reject this melding of tort and contract, and more particularly the idea that *respondeat superior*, embodied in the tortious doctrine of vicarious liability, when the law imposes liability for the activities of those whom one employs, is of a kind with the rights and liabilities generated by the acts of those

---

1   'History of Agency' 4 Harv L Rev, 345 and 5 Harv L Rev 1 (1891). See also Wambaugh *Cases on Agency* (1896).

whom one authorises to conduct business on one's behalf[2]. Clearly, it is possible to debate the boundaries of the discipline. As for the common law vision of agency, the subject is open to a number of analyses. Otto Kahn-Freund, for example, in arguing that the shortcomings of English law can be better seen by those who possess some understanding of foreign law, once observed:

'The most elementary student of law going through his first year course in the law of contract ... will see that much of the law of agency is a remedy for the damage done to the practical operation of the law of contract through the doctrine of consideration.'[3]

Whether or not agency should be seen as substantially a response to conflicting influences within the English law of contract, however, it is indisputable that, unlike its Continental counterparts, English law sometimes seems to lack a fully delineated theory of legal representation[4] which may mean that at a micro-level courts from time to time tolerate conclusions that defy cogent theoretical explanation[5] and at a macro-level the law develops institutions, such as the doctrine of the undisclosed principal[6], which are original and in many respects patently anomalous.

Rather than engage with these issues, however, important as they are, it is probably more profitable in an introductory work to attempt to grasp from the outset both the purpose and the essence of the institution of agency. In a highly commercial and industrialised world the purpose of the law of agency and the need to employ 'agents' to perform certain tasks which their 'principals' have neither the time, knowledge nor expertise to perform themselves scarcely require explanation. Commerce would literally grind to a halt if businessmen and merchants could not employ the services of factors, brokers, forwarding agents, estate agents, auctioneers and the like and were expected to do everything themselves. These specialised 'middle-men', whose main purpose usually is to make contracts on behalf of their principals or to dispose of their principals' property, are to be found in all advanced societies and, howsoever one views certain of the economic consequences of this phenomenon, the fact is that the agent's activities are an inevitable feature of a developed economy.

2   See, eg, Conard 'What's Wrong with Agency?' J Leg Ed 540 (1948–9).
3   'Comparative Law as an Academic Subject (1966) 81 LQR 40, 60.
4   See, eg, remarks of Zweigert & Kötz *An Introduction to Comparative Law* (1992, Oxford), esp pp 460–3.
5   See, eg, *Watteau v Fenwick* [1893] 1 QB 346, discussed at pp 32-36 post, and *First Energy (UK) Ltd v Hungarian International Bank Ltd* [1993] 2 Lloyd's Rep 194, discussed at pp 43-45 post.
6   See post, pp 153-171.

Moreover, the growth of the law of agency, both in volume and sophistication, has sought to keep pace with the expansion and development of comtemporary commerce. This close connection between agency and modern economic life is important, for it can often help to explain some of the divergences of the law of agency from the general principles of the law of contract. The purpose of the law of agency, therefore, is obvious. Its essential *legal* characteristic, however — the ability of one person to affect the legal relations of another in the sense suggested above — is not so easy to explain.

(i) Agency and consent

For many authors *consent* forms the basis of the law of agency and explains why the agent can represent the principal. The editors of *Bowstead* define agency as 'the fiduciary relationship which exists between two persons, one of whom expressly or impliedly *consents* that the other should so act as to affect his relations with third parties, and the other of whom similarly consents so to act or so acts on his behalf'[7]. A broadly similar definition appears in the American *Restatement of the Law of Agency* where agency is described as 'the fiduciary relation which results from the manifestation of *consent* by one person to another that the other shall act on his behalf and subject to his control, and consent by the other so to act'[8]. Too much emphasis on 'consent', however, should be avoided. True, in many cases, consent is the basis of the agent's power and determines its ambit. But there are many cases, notably the cases of apparent and presumed authority, in which the relationship may arise irrespective of or indeed *contrary to* the real wishes of the parties: to speak of consent in such cases is only to distort the real and usual meaning of the word. Too great an emphasis on consent should also be avoided for another reason: namely, that it may suggest that all the courts have to do is to look at the facts before them and mechanically determine whether they are faced with an agency relationship. This is not necessarily the case, for the courts have to look at the facts and construe them in a legal manner. Ultimately, what is and what is not an agency is a question of law. In *Garnac Grain Co Inc v H M F Faure and Fairclough Ltd*[9] Lord Pearson left no doubt about the objective approach adopted by the courts. 'The relationship of principal and agent', he said, 'can only be established by the consent of the

7   *Bowstead and Reynolds on Agency* (16th Edn), §1–001 (emphasis added).
8   *Restatement of the Law of Agency* (2nd Edn, 1958), para 1.
9   [1968] AC 1130n, [1967] 2 All ER 353, HL.

principal and agent'. But, he added, parties will be deemed to have consented 'if they have agreed to what in law amounts to such a relationship, even if they do not recognise it themselves and even if they have, for example, professed to disclaim it'[10]. In *Boardman v Phipps*[11], for example, the House of Lords found that an agency relationship existed even though there was no consent on the part of the principal. Hence, consent will not provide a universal criterion for determining whether there exists an agency relationship. It is important, therefore, to grasp from the outset that often both the existence and the incidents of agency derive from the law and not from the consent of the parties. Once this fact is accepted, it becomes easier to explain many of the incidents of agency. For example, the agent's duty to hand over to the principal money belonging to the latter and received to the principal's use[12], or his duty to exercise due care (even where the agency is gratuitous and unsupported by consideration)[13], stem from the law itself and do not depend on any agreement between the parties. The absence of an agreement is particularly obvious in the so-called 'agency by operation of law' (notably agency of necessity, discussed below, Chapter 1, section 4). Consent and agreement in such cases may be absent altogether.

(ii)   Agency and authority

Other writers have tried to explain agency in terms of the existence of *authority* on the part of the agent to bind his principal. Once again, for reasons similar to those given in the preceding section, one is, in a sense, dealing with an artificial notion. In a variety of situations an 'agent' can, by law, and for various reasons of public or social policy, affect the legal relations of another person even though he has no authority to represent him or has exceeded the authority that was given to him. A good illustration is afforded by the case of *Lloyd v Grace, Smith & Co*[14] in which a widow owned two cottages and a sum of money secured by a mortgage. Since she was dissatisfied with the income she derived from them, she sought the advice of a firm of solicitors. The person she saw was the managing clerk of the firm, who also conducted the conveyancing business without any control

---

10   Ibid, at 358.
11   [1967] 2 AC 46, [1966] 3 All ER 721.
12   Infra, pp 114-115 et seq.
13   Infra, pp 96-97 et seq. From this it follows that an agency relationship may arise out of an agreement which falls short of being a contract.
14   [1912] AC 716: see Extract 1, p 217. See also *United Bank of Kuwait Ltd v Hammoud; City Trust Ltd v Levy* [1988] 3 All ER 418, [1988] 1 WLR 1051; see Extract 2, p 217.

from the one and only partner of the firm. The clerk induced her to give him instructions to sell the property and call in the mortgage money, and for that purpose to give him the title deeds. This she did. He then fraudulently made her sign some documents which she thought were necessary for the sale of the property but which in fact conveyed to him the cottages and transferred to him the mortgage. The House of Lords held that the clerk's principal, the firm of solicitors, was liable for the fraud of its agent, committed by him 'in the course of his employment'. It is obvious that in such cases the agent has no real 'authority' to do the act in question. But for reasons of public policy, as much as anything else, he is nevertheless given the 'power' to affect the legal relations of his 'principal'[15].

Before proceeding further with the analysis of the concept of agency, let us take the opportunity to say something of the relationship or connection between agents, servants and independent contractors. The problem, which will be discussed again in Chapter 4, has exercised many authors and much, at times, unnecessary confusion has arisen. The confusion has resulted from the difficulty of defining the proper interrelationship of agency and vicarious liability, a task which has now been facilitated by the decision in *Armagas Ltd v Mundogas SA, The Ocean Frost*[16].

To understand the problem we must begin by reminding ourselves of a point made earlier, namely, that the agent's primary task is to enter into a contract on behalf of his principal (or to dispose of his principal's property), even though incidentally he may at times also render him liable for harm occasioned to third parties. Agency, therefore, is closely linked with the law of contract. Vicarious liability, on the other hand, is a notion belonging to the law of torts. It deals with the relationship of master and servant, in which the nature of the servant's duties is very different from that of an agent's duties, but which, when discharged, may also render the master liable to third parties. The difficulties will arise where the 'employed' person can be regarded as being both an agent of the employer (principal)

---

15 As Lord Keith pointed out in *Armagas Ltd v Mundogas SA* [1986] AC 717, [1986] 2 All ER 385, 392, the significance of *Lloyd v Grace Smith & Co* is that it 'established that it is not necessary to a master's liability for the fraud of his servant that the fraud should have been committed for the master's benefit.' Moreover, as he spelt out later in his speech, 'in the end of the day the question is whether the circumstances under which a servant has made the fraudulent misrepresentation which has caused loss to an innocent party contracting with him are such as to make it just for the employer to bear the loss' (p 394).

16 [1986] AC 717, [1985] 3 All ER 795, CA, see Extract 3, p 220; affd [1986] AC 717, [1986] 2 All ER 385, HL. See, also, *Kooragang Investments Pty Ltd v Richardson and Wrench Ltd* [1982] AC 462, [1981] 3 All ER 65, PC.

and his servant (where the criteria that determine the master-servant relationship are satisfied). Whenever this is the case, which is the appropriate test? Authority or course of employment? It is easy to see why an act within the ostensible authority of the employed person will also be performed in the course of his employment; but does it also follow that an act that lies outside the scope of ostensible authority cannot be in the course of employment? To put it at its simplest: are the two admittedly indistinct notions of authority and course of employment always coterminous?

The answer would appear to be that in some cases at least — notably, fraud — the employer will be vicariously liable for the employee's fraud only when the latter has acted within his ostensible authority. *Lloyd v Grace, Smith & Co* perfectly illustrates the coincidence of these two concepts. For, in reality, in a case such as this, a decision whether the servant committed a fraud 'in the course of his employment' can only be made after it has been ascertained with what authority, actual or apparent, the servant is clothed. In contrast, in torts which involve no reliance by the plaintiff upon a representation by the servant, but involve other wrongs (eg, intentional or negligent physical acts by the employee (servant/agent)), the ostensible authority of the employee (servant/agent) does not provide the criterion for his employer's possible vicarious liability.

(iii) Agency as a power-liability relationship

If agency cannot be understood solely in terms of authority, how else can it be accounted for?

Agency must be explained in different terms and it is increasingly argued that this can best be done if the concept is analysed as a power-liability relationship between two persons — the principal and the agent. This, however, should not allow the student to forget that agency is a triangular relationship between principal, agent and third party and that the whole concept of agency can never be fully understood if the other two relationships (ie, principal and third party, and agent and third party) are ignored, just as no triangle can be defined in geometry by reference to only one of its sides. But, having said this, one must agree that Professor Dowrick is right in identifying as the *essential* characteristic of agency the fact that the

'agent is ... invested with a *legal power* to alter his principal's legal relations with third persons'

and that

'the principal is under a correlative liability to have his relations altered'[17].

This power must be understood as a *legal concept* whereas authority is a *factual situation*. The two should not therefore be confused. Authority is the sum total of the acts which the principal and the agent have agreed that the latter can do and in so doing bind the principal. In other words, when P confers authority on A, this means that P and A have agreed that certain acts should be done by A on P's behalf. Thus, if P confers authority on A (factual situation) then A will have power to affect P's relations by exercising this authority (legal situation). This should not be taken to mean that the principal has conferred power on the agent. Power is strictly a legal concept. It has been explained, notably by Professor Montrose, in terms of a legal rule:

'The power of an agent is not strictly conferred by the principal but by the law: the principal and agent do the acts which bring the rule into operation, as a result of which the agent acquires a power'[18].

In other words, it is the authority the principal confers on the agent to do certain acts which brings the rule into play and vests the agent with the necessary power to affect the principal's legal relations with third parties. It may be that the agent can sometimes affect his principal's relations even though he has no authority or has exceeded the authority that has been given to him. But when, and to what extent, this can be done is a matter of law and, as such, it is a question not merely of logic but also of social policy[19].

It should be clear from the above that the concept of power differs from that of authority in that power is a legal concept since power may exist where authority is lacking. This can be explained by the fact, already mentioned, that power and authority emanate from different sources. The existence and extent of the power is determined by public policy. Authority, on the other hand, is limited by the expression of the principal's will as contained in the agreement with the agent. As a result, in certain cases an agent who is neither expressly nor apparently authorised to do certain things may nevertheless have power to bind his principal and confer rights on a third party.

---

17 'The Relationship of Principal and Agent' (1954) 17 MLR 24 at 36 (emphasis added).
18 'The Basis of the Power of an Agent in Cases of Actual and Apparent Authority' 16 Can Bar Rev 756, 761 (1938).
19 See generally Seavey 'The Rationale of Agency' 29 Yale LJ 859 (1920).

The editors of *Bowstead* have explained this phenomenon in the following manner:

'Authority, like possession, is thought of as *fact* from which *legal* consequences should arise. In the paradigm case the reason why it seems logical for the agent to have the power is that the principal has conferred something on him from which it stems, called authority. Thus, cases where the agent has the power but cannot be regarded as having been given authority by the principal seem exceptional and it is said that there is only "apparent authority". Yet the power is the same: there is no temptation to talk of "apparent power". "Authority", like "possession", carries the image of a paradigm case justifying a legal result; "power" is neutral and simply states the results regardless of the reasons for them'[20].

This difference between the narrower concept of authority and that of power is clear in cases where the agent lacks *actual* authority but has *apparent or ostensible* authority to act (which is not strictly speaking authority at all). The presence of apparent or ostensible authority may serve to broaden the scope of the relationship of principal and agent and render the former liable for the unauthorised acts of the latter. The case of *Lloyd v Grace, Smith & Co*[1], discussed earlier, neatly illustrates this distinction. The same point emerges from the subsequent decision in *United Bank of Kuwait Ltd v Hammoud*[2], in which it was held that if a solicitor, with actual authority to represent himself as a partner in a firm, gives an undertaking, which the receiver is objectively entitled to assume is given as part of 'solicitorial' services, such undertaking will be enforced against that solicitor's firm as having been given with ostensible authority if it subsequently turns out to be false and worthless.

In agency, therefore, one is concerned with a relationship in which the agent holds in trust for, and subject to the control of, his principal a power to affect the legal relations of the principal. This power-liability relation constitutes the essence of the relationship of principal and agent. But since such power-liability relationships can be found in other parts of the law, the question becomes 'what is the essential characteristic of this particular power-liability relationship?'. It has been aptly pointed out that

---

20   *Bowstead on Agency* (13th Edn, 1968), p 4. In the 16th edition the last five lines of the quotation have been retained virtually verbatim, but the preceding sentences have been enlarged to provide Chapter 1 with a fine summary of some of the basic theoretical problems in the law of agency.

1   [1912] AC 716: see Extract 1, p 217.

2   [1988] 3 All ER 418: see Extract 2, p 217.

'the distinctive feature of the agency power-liability relation is that the power of the one party (the agent) to alter the legal relations of the other party (the principal) is *a reproduction* of the power possessed by the latter to alter his own legal position. In other words, the power conferred by law on the agent is *a facsimile* of the principal's own power. This is to be inferred from the main principles of the law of agency, notably the following: when an agent acts on behalf of his principal in a legal transaction and uses the principal's name, the result in law is that the principal's legal position is altered but the agent drops out of the transaction; persons who are not themselves *sui juris* may nevertheless have the power to act as agents for persons who are; the power of the agent to bind his principal is limited to the power of the principal to bind himself; if the powers of the principal to alter his own legal relations are ended by his death, insanity, or bankruptcy, the agent's powers are terminated automatically'[3].

It is this manifest similarity between the principal's capacity to perform acts in law and his agent's capacity to perform them for him which led Pollock to state that 'by agency the individual's legal personality is multiplied in space'[4]. The necessary consequence of the above is, in the words of Wright J (in *Montgomerie v United Kingdom Mutual SS Association*[5]), that

'the contract is the contract of the principal, not that of the agent, and prima facie at common law the only person who can sue is the principal and the only person who can be sued is the principal'.

This principle will be discussed in greater detail in subsequent chapters. For the present, it is sufficient to note that, although the agent may sometimes be entitled to sue and be sued by the third party on contracts he makes for his principal, as a general rule, where he makes a contract for his principal with a third party, the agent drops out of the transaction and does not himself become a party to the contract[6].

---

3   Dowrick, ante, at 37 (emphasis added).
4   Pollock *Principles of Contract* (ed Winfield, 13th Edn), p 45.
5   [1891] 1 QB 370 at 371; see Extract 4, p 223. For the opposite situation, see *United Kingdom Mutual SS Assurance Association v Nevill* (1887) 19 QBD 110.
6   Eg *Fairlie v Fenton* (1870) LR 5 Exch 169; see Extract 5, p 224. *Universal Steam Navigation Co Ltd v J McKelvie & Co* [1923] AC 492; *Gadd v Houghton & Co* (1876) 1 Ex D 357; see Extract 6, p 225. See generally Chapter 5, post.

2   THE LEGAL USE OF THE TERM 'AGENT'

Three further points may be made by way of introductory comments. First, it should be clear that the law of agency does not come into play every time one person represents another. For example, no rules of agency apply when a husband sends his wife to a wedding to congratulate the newly-weds, for in such cases the representation only serves a social purpose. For the rules of agency to come into play the representation of one person by another must be meant to affect the principal's legal position though, of course, this does not mean that the legal purpose intended to be achieved by the use of an agent need be a complex one. A father who sends his son to the nearby shop to buy him a newspaper is making an agent of him and will be liable to the shopkeeper for the price of the newspaper.

Secondly, for an agency relationship to arise, one person must intend to act on behalf of another. This is a question of fact. But, it is submitted, such an intention is not, in itself, enough; the purpose of the relationship must be for the agent to enter into a contract on behalf of his principal (or to dispose of his principal's property). If this approach is adopted, cases like *Ormrod v Crosville Motor Services Ltd*[7] should be excluded from the ambit of agency textbooks[8]. Since between A and B there is no master-servant relationship (in the traditional sense of the term), it is difficult to bring this factual situation under the heading of vicarious liability. The tendency has thus grown to use agency terminology and to describe B as A's agent. But since B's aim is not to enter into any contract on behalf of A, and since B cannot normally incur any expenses on behalf of A (eg, pledge A's credit to purchase petrol for the journey), it proves equally difficult to describe their relationship as one of true agency. Of course, to recognise the difficulty of classifying this factual situation is not to question the validity of the solution reached by the courts: that is, to impose liability on A for the harm caused by B's negligent driving. This result is equitable and is quite conceivably dictated by the consideration that A, as the owner of the car, is covered by obligatory third party insurance and is consequently in the better position to carry the risk[9].

---

7   [1953] 2 All ER 753, [1953] 1 WLR 1120. (A wishes his car to be taken to the South of France and B, out of friendship, drives it there for him.)

8   But contrast Treitel *The Law of Contract* (9th Edn, 1995), p 623.

9   This insurance reasoning was used by Lord Denning in one case to extend the *Ormrod* rule to cases where the driver of the car was using it with its owner's consent but for his own exclusive purposes. The reasoning was, however, rejected when that case reached the House of Lords. See *Morgans v Launchbury* [1973] AC 127, [1972] 2 All ER 606, HL.

Finally, there is a difference between the legal and commercial use of the term 'agent'. Car dealers, for example, are commonly referred to as 'agents' of particular manufacturers, although this does not mean that the dealer is, by his intervention, concluding a contract between the manufacturer and the purchaser of the car. What normally happens is that the dealer first buys the car from the manufacturer and *then* sells it to the purchaser. Consequently, if the car is defective, the customer's only remedy *under the contract of sale* is against the dealer and the only way he can sue the manufacturer — that is, assuming he wishes to — is by relying on any guarantee that may exist[10] or, possibly, by suing in *tort* for damage or personal injury caused by the product if the manufacturer has been negligent. Similarly, a 'sole agency' agreement, whereby one person grants to another the exclusive selling rights in his products, is not, strictly speaking, an agency relationship. *WT Lamb & Sons v Goring Brick Co Ltd* illustrates this point[11]. The defendants appointed the plaintiffs as sole agents for their goods for a given period of time. Before this period had expired, the defendants began to sell their goods themselves. Had this been a genuine case of agency, there might have been nothing to prevent them from so doing. But it was not. This was a contract giving exclusive sales rights to the plaintiffs, and the defendants' decision to start selling whilst the agreement was still in operation amounted to a breach.

The question, therefore, whether the buying or selling agent is an agent in the technical sense of the word is important as well as

10　Such guarantees, however, are rarely found in English law. An exception can be seen in the well-known case of *Carlill v Carbolic Smoke Ball Co* [1893] 1 QB 256. For a more detailed (comparative) discussion see Beale, Harris, Sharpe and Sayes 'The Distribution of Cars: A Complex Contractual Technique' in *Contract Law Today — Anglo-French Comparisons* (eds Harris and Tallon, 1989), pp 302 et seq, esp pp 312, 318–321.

11　[1932] 1 KB 710. Troublesome relationships are also created by hire purchase contracts. In such cases, does the dealer who sells goods to a finance company (which then hires them out to the hire purchaser) act as the agent of that finance company? For some purposes (eg, the making of representations concerning the goods 'sold' to the hirer) the legislature has provided a positive reply: Consumer Credit Act 1974, ss 56(1),(2), 57(3), 69(6), 102(1), 175. But the question whether the dealer can be regarded *in general* as the agent of the finance company has neither been determined by the legislature nor conclusively decided by the courts. Against the view of an agency relationship: Pearson LJ in *Financings Ltd v Stimson* [1962] 3 All ER 386, [1962] 1 WLR 1184 and *Mercantile Credit Co Ltd v Hamblin* [1965] 2 QB 242 at 269; in agreement Lords Morris, Guest and Upjohn in *Branwhite v Worcester Works Finance Ltd* [1969] 1 AC 552 at 573, 574 and 576. In favour of a kind of presumed agency: Lord Denning and Donovan LJ in the *Financings* case, above, and Lords Wilberforce and Reid in the *Branwhite* case, above, at pp 586–7.

sometimes being difficult to answer. Very often it will depend upon whether the person concerned acts for himself, trying to make the best profit he can, or whether his remuneration has been prearranged. In the first case he is usually regarded as a buyer for sale, although it must be remembered that nowadays prices are commonly fixed by manufacturers in advance and this, by itself, will not make the supplier an agent. It is equally difficult to determine whether the person who has undertaken to procure goods is acting as an agent or seller, for in the first case all he has to do is to use his best endeavours to supply the goods in question. The solution to this and to so many other problems of the law of agency depends on the facts of each case and the ascertainment of the true intention of the parties.

Estate agents, despite their name, are agents *sui generis*. Although they may have the right to make certain representations about the property they have been asked to dispose of, they normally have no power to make a contract between their client and the prospective purchaser[12], and, as we shall see, they are in many respects truly 'independent persons'. Estate agency raises special problems and will be discussed in greater detail in Chapter 3. Similarly, the relationship between a client and a 'professional man' is not always one of principal/agent giving rise to the usual incidents of agency. Thus, solicitors, stockbrokers and architects may often act as agents of their clients. But the hiring of a valuer[13] to make certain valuations or of a painter to paint a mural or a portrait, does not normally make such persons the agents of their employers.

3 THE ADVENT OF THE 'COMMERCIAL AGENT'

Although English law has not in the past differentiated systematically between different categories of agent, creating distinct legal régimes attaching to each division, on 1 January 1994 the Commercial Agents (Council Directive) Regulations 1993, implementing the 1986 EC Directive on Commercial Agents, came into force. Broadly speaking, it singled out a category of agents, hitherto considered undeserving of special protection by English law, and conferred upon them and their principals a legal régime which likens them more to employees

---

12 But they can conclude a contract if, as apparently was the case in *Spiro v Lintern* [1973] 3 All ER 319, CA, they are specifically authorised to do so.

13 On this see *Leicestershire County Council v Michael Faraday & Partners Ltd* [1941] 2 KB 205 at 216 (per MacKinnon LJ).

than the independent commercial traders which in reality they mostly are[14].

A commercial agent is defined in the Regulations as 'a self-employed intermediary having continuing authority to negotiate the sale and purchase of goods on behalf of another person ..., or to negotiate and conclude the sale or purchase of goods on behalf of and in the name of that principal' (para 2(1)). Provided that the agent does not perform these functions in a purely secondary capacity (para 2(3)), the Regulations impose a raft of obligations on both the parties. Some are relatively unproblematical — for instance, each party's right to request from the other a signed and written record of the terms of their contract (para 13), or the agent's duty to look after the principal's interests (para 3(1)), to communicate all necessary information available to him and to comply with the principal's reasonable instructions (para 3(2)), or even the principal's correlative obligation to facilitate the agent's performance of his functions by furnishing the latter with all necessary documentation and information, in particular notifying him within a reasonable period once he anticipates that the volume of commercial transactions will be significantly lower than that which the agent could normally have expected (para 4(2)). Other provisions, however — for instance, the requirement that each party is under a general obligation to act dutifully and in good faith[15] towards the other (paras 3(1) and 4(1)) — will appear relatively unfamiliar to English lawyers.

The Regulations also contain detailed provisions (paras 6–20) governing remuneration of commercial agents — how much an agent is entitled to receive if it has not been agreed inter partes, when such payment falls due, when the principal will be exonerated from such liability, how much notice is required to end a commercial

---

14 See Davis 'The Demise of Commercial Agents' (1994) 144 NLJ 388. As Staughton LJ observed in *Page v Combined Shipping and Trading Co Ltd* [1997] 3 All ER 656, 660, the preamble to these Regulations suggests that it was thought that commercial agents were 'a down-trodden race, and need and should be afforded protection against their principals.'
15 On the problematic nature of a requirement of 'good faith' in English law, see Goode *The Concept of 'Good Faith' in English Law* (1992). English law's omission to require parties to perform their contracts in good faith contrasts sharply with the position obtaining in some other European jurisdictions. Thus, in France art 1134 of the Civil Code stipulates that contracts are to be performed in good faith. In Germany, too, para 242 of the BGB imposes a general requirement of *treu und glauben*. This is not to say that good faith has no part to play in the English law of contract. It may make an *entrée* via the implied term: see, eg, Steyn 'The Role of Good Faith and Fair Dealing in Contract Law: A Hair-Shirt Philosophy' [1991] Denning LJ 131, 133; Clarke, 'The Common Law of Contract in 1993: Is there a General Doctrine of Good Faith?' (1993) 23 HKLJ 318, esp p 330.

agency, and, most importantly, what compensation, over and above damages he may receive for breach of contract in the event of wrongful termination of his agency by the principal, is due to a commercial agent when his agency is terminated. The Regulations also include rules concerning the enforceability of covenants in restraint of trade under which the principal may seek to prevent his former agent from entering into competition with the principal after termination of the agency (para 20). Finally, the Regulations forbid the parties to contract out of a number of the obligations imposed — for instance, the parties may not derogate from the duty to act dutifully and in good faith, nor from the rules governing remuneration, compensation and termination of agencies (paras 5(1) and 19). The 1993 Regulations are far-reaching, particularly in the realms of the payment of commission and compensation following termination of the agency. These latter rules will be referred to with greater particularity when we come to consider commission and termination[16].

16　See pp 124–125 and 208–209, post.

1 The power of the agent to bind his principal

PRELIMINARY REMARKS

An agency relationship may arise from an express or implied agreement between principal and agent. Where this is so, the important question is to determine the scope of the agent's express or implied authority. This will be discussed in the two sections that follow. Agency, however, may arise even in the absence of an agreement between principal and agent. This can happen in the following circumstances: the doctrine of apparent authority (discussed in section 3 of this chapter) may be invoked; alternatively, a person may possess authority of necessity (considered in section 4 of this chapter); or, finally, as a result of the doctrine of ratification (examined in the next chapter), an agency relationship may spring up retroactively.

1 EXPRESS ACTUAL AUTHORITY

In the typical case express actual authority is conferred on an agent by agreement with the principal. This agreement, however, need not technically amount to a contract. As Diplock LJ said in *Freeman and Lockyer v Buckhurst Park Properties (Mangal) Ltd*:

' "actual" authority is a legal relationship between principal and agent created by a consensual agreement to which they alone are parties'.[1]

From the point of view of the law of agency, therefore, there may be a complete agency without a contract. This will for example be the case whenever the agent undertakes to act for his principal

---

1   [1964] 2 QB 480 at 502.

gratuitously. Even in the commercial context one occasionally encounters non-contractual agencies. As Colman J recently pointed out in *Yasuda Fire and Marine Insurance Co of Europe Ltd v Orion Marine Insurance Underwriting Agency Ltd:*

'Although in modern commercial transactions, agencies are almost invariably founded upon a contract between principal and agent, there is no necessity for such a contract to exist. It is sufficient if there is consent by the principal to the exercise by the agent of authority and consent by the agent to his exercising such authority on behalf of the principal.'[2]

It is certainly the case, however, that nowadays in many, if not most cases the agency relationship will derive from a contract between the principal and the agent.

The main differences between the two kinds of agency (contractual and consensual) are, firstly, the presence or absence of consideration and, secondly, the fact that in cases of contractual agency there is, invariably, an *obligation* on the part of the agent to carry out his function accompanied by a corresponding obligation of the principal to remunerate him. This, of course, does not mean that the gratuitous agent has no rights against his principal. We shall see in Chapter 3 that in the absence of a contrary agreement, the agent has the right to be indemnified for any losses he has sustained and expenses he may have incurred in the execution of his duties. However, this indemnity cannot be regarded as consideration moving from the principal; it is a duty which is one of the normal incidents of agency and which exists by operation of law and quite independently of any agreement between the parties. In the words of Lord Wright in *Brook's Wharf v Goodman Bros:*

'The obligation (to indemnify the agent) is imposed by the court simply under the circumstances of the case and on what the court decides is just and reasonable, having regard to the relationship of the parties. It is a debt or obligation constituted by the act of the law, apart from any consent or intention of the parties or any priority of contract'[3].

No formality is required for the appointment of an agent, and this is so even when the agent is expected to make a contract which has to be either executed or evidenced in writing. In *Heard v Pilley*[4] the court held that a contract for the purchase of land made by an

2   [1995] 2 WLR 49 at 57.
3   [1937] 1 KB 534, [1936] 3 All ER 696.
4   (1869) 4 Ch App 548.

agent would be enforced even though the agent was not appointed in writing and the same is, presumably, true of contracts of guarantee, which are the only other kind of contract still within the ambit of the Statute of Frauds. But it is otherwise if an agent has to execute an instrument under seal, in which case he must be appointed by an instrument under seal[5], usually known as power of attorney.

The extent of the agent's actual authority

The extent of the agent's actual authority will depend upon the true construction of the words of his appointment. If the agency agreement is oral, the precise limits of the agent's authority will be a matter of evidence. If, on the other hand, the agreement has been put into writing, then the relevant document will have to be examined. In such cases the scope of the agency agreement is to be ascertained by applying ordinary principles of construction of contracts, including any proper implications from the express words used, the usages of the trade, or the course of previous business between the parties.

Appointment by deed

If the appointment is made under deed, the usual strict rules of construction of deeds will be applied. Thus, the authority will be limited to the purpose for which it was given. In *Midland Bank Ltd v Reckitt*[6] a solicitor was given by power of attorney the right to draw cheques on his client's banking account and to apply the money for the purposes of his client. The power of attorney also contained a ratification clause by which the principal ratified and confirmed in advance whatsoever the attorney should do or purport to do by virtue of the power. The solicitor/agent drew some cheques on his principal's account and paid them into his own seriously overdrawn account with the defendant bank. The bank was found guilty of converting the plaintiff's money to its own use and the House of Lords took the view that the ratification clause could not be extended to include acts done by the agent which were beyond the purposes set out in the deed. Similarly, in *Jonmenjoy Coondoo v Watson*[7] a power of attorney gave the holders authority to act on the principal's behalf and 'from time to time ... negotiate, make sale, dispose of, assign and transfer, or cause to be procured and assigned and transferred

5   *Berkeley v Hardy* (1826) 5 B & C 355.
6   [1933] AC 1.
7   (1884) 9 App Cas 561.

... all or any of the government promissory notes, or bank shares or other stock ...' standing in the principal's name. After a careful examination of the wording of the document, their Lordships concluded that the holders of the power had authority to sell or purchase such notes but no authority to pledge them so as to raise a loan. If the main body of the deed is ambiguous, the limits of the agent's authority may be found in the recitals. Thus, in *Danby v Coutts & Co*[8] the plaintiff appointed X and Y to act as his attorneys without limiting in term the duration of their powers. The operative part of the document, however, was preceded by recitals which stated that it was the plaintiff's desire that agents represent him during his 'absence' from England. It was held that the recitals controlled the operative part of the document and limited the authority of the agents to the period of the plaintiff's absence from England.

The strictness of construction of powers of attorney is illustrated by *Jacobs v Morris*[9] which supports the proposition that if an agent is given authority to do particular acts and this is expressed in general words, the words will be restricted to what is absolutely necessary for the performance of the acts in question. In that case an Australian merchant authorised an English agent to purchase goods 'in connection with his (the principal's) business' and to make, draw, sign etc a bill of exchange. The agent borrowed £4,000 on the security of some bills of exchange and then appropriated the money. In an action against the firm which had advanced the loan it was held that the agent had exceeded his authority and that the principal was not liable.

There is, however, one case where the use of general words or language will not be given a restricted meaning. Under s 10 of the Powers of Attorney Act 1971, if a general power of attorney is drawn up in the statutory form or in a similar manner and expressed to be made under the Act, it confers on the donee of the power authority to do on behalf of the donor, ie the principal, 'anything which he can lawfully do by an attorney'. Hence, if the words used are unqualified, the agent's authority will be restricted only by any incapacity that may affect his principal. In all other cases general words will be restricted to the performance of the particular special duties contained in the deed.

Oral appointment or appointment by writing not under seal

When authority is contained in a document not under seal or has been given orally, the rules of construction are much laxer.

8   (1885) 29 Ch D 500.
9   [1902] 1 Ch 816.

According to the Privy Council in *Ashford Shire Council v Dependable Motors Pty Ltd*[10], 'the extent of an agent's authority, if in doubt, must be determined by inference from the whole circumstances'. *Ireland v Livingston*[11] exemplifies how the courts apply this method. Additionally, it establishes the proposition that if the document giving authority to the agent is vaguely worded and capable of different interpretations and the agent in good faith interprets it in a sense not intended by the principal, then the principal will be bound by the agent's acts. In *Ireland v Livingston* the defendant asked the plaintiff to ship to him from Mauritius a consignment of sugar, suggesting various English ports to which it might be sent. The plaintiff procured four-fifths of the cargo and shipped it in one vessel in accordance with the defendant's specifications, the rest presumably to follow in another vessel. The defendants, however, refused to accept the consignment and wrote to the plaintiff to cancel any further shipment. The question turned on the proper construction of the order document and the House of Lords decided by a majority that it was susceptible of two different interpretations. In the circumstances, therefore, it was unjust to make the plaintiff bear the loss which was occasioned by the defendant's own imprecision[12].

The laxer rules of interpretation which apply in such cases are further exemplified in the proposition that authority given in general terms is interpreted to mean authority to act in the usual way. Thus, in *Wiltshire v Sims*[13] the court held that a stockbroker who is authorised to sell stocks and shares has no authority to sell on credit since this is not the usual thing for a stockbroker to do. Likewise, an agent who is authorised to receive money is not authorised to receive payment by cheque unless it is usual to do so in his particular profession[14].

---

10 [1961] AC 336 at 341.
11 (1872) LR 5 HL 395; see Extract 7, p 225. See also, *Weigall & Co v Runciman & Co* (1916) 85 LJKB 1187.
12 Students of the law of agency will notice that the subject's case law is still dominated by many cases that derive from the age of the stagecoach and the tea clipper. Conditions of trade will often have materially altered since these cases were decided, and some must be viewed with a certain scepticism. In this regard, it is obvious that present day communications will frequently mean that it is easy for an agent to seek clarification of his principal's ambiguous instructions: see, eg, *Woodhouse AC Israel Cocoa Ltd SA v Nigerian Produce Marketing Co Ltd* [1972] AC 741 at 772. Moreover, if the agent realised or ought to have realised that the instructions were ambiguous, he may be under a duty to seek clarification before he acts: *European Asian Bank AG v Punjab and Sind Bank (No 2)* [1983] 2 All ER 508, esp at 517–8 (per Robert Goff LJ).
13 (1808) 1 Camp 258.
14 *Sweeting v Pearce* (1859) 7 CBNS 449.

Having now considered actual authority which has been given expressly to the agent, we now turn to implied actual authority which presents greater difficulties, not least because of the terminological ambiguities which seem endemic to this part of the law.

2　IMPLIED ACTUAL AUTHORITY

Actual authority is the authority which the agent *actually* has pursuant to the consensual agreement which has been reached between himself and his principal. It is, in other words, real authority. But such authority may be conferred upon the agent either (a) *expressly*, that is by express words, in which case the main problem is to determine the limits of his authority by application of the principles discussed in the preceding section; or (b) it may be *implied* authority, which will concern us in the present section. As Lord Denning MR said in *Hely-Hutchinson v Brayhead Ltd*:

'... actual authority may be express or implied. It is express when it is given by words such as when a board of directors pass a resolution which authorises two of their number to sign cheques. It is implied when it is inferred from the conduct of the parties and the circumstances of the case, such as when the board of directors appoint one of their number to be managing director. They thereby impliedly authorise him to do all such things as fall within the usual scope of that office'.[15]

The facts in *Hely-Hutchinson* were as follows: Richards, the second defendant, was the chairman of Brayhead Ltd and also acted as *de facto* managing director of that company with the acquiescence of its board. The plaintiff was the managing director of another company (Perdio Electronics) which was sustaining heavy losses. Brayhead decided to help Perdio through its economic difficulties, and to this end it bought some of Perdio's shares with the ultimate intention of obtaining control of that company. At a later stage the plaintiff (who in the meantime had also become a director of Brayhead) privately discussed with Richards the possibility of injecting more funds into Perdio. The plaintiff agreed to do this after the defendant, Richards, had written to him in his capacity as chairman of Brayhead undertaking to indemnify him for any loss

---

15　[1968] 1 QB 549 at 583; see Extract 8, p 225. It must be noted that here we are talking of *authority* being implied. It is quite a different matter if the agency itself is being implied as a result of a particular conduct or occasion.

which he might incur as a result of lending money to Perdio or guaranteeing any loan made to Perdio. Unfortunately, Perdio went into liquidation and the plaintiff had to pay off a company loan which he had guaranteed. In this action he relied on the defendant's letter of indemnity and sought to make Brayhead liable for the loss he had sustained. One of the main issues was whether the second defendant (Richards) had acted within the scope of his authority when he undertook that Brayhead would indemnify Richards so as to bind Brayhead to that undertaking. We are here solely concerned with this aspect of the case.

At first instance counsel for the plaintiff (Hely-Hutchinson) argued that Richards had both implied *and* apparent authority, although he laid greater emphasis on the former. Roskill J refused to 'hold that there is implied authority in a chairman of a company, *merely* by reason of his office' to do what Richards had done[16], although he later admitted that there may be cases where such an authority can be implied. But he did hold that Richards had ostensible or apparent authority because the board of Brayhead knew of and had acquiesced in Richards' activities as *de facto* managing director of Brayhead and the plaintiff had relied upon the representations made to him, in consequence of which he had sustained loss. When apparent or ostensible authority is discussed, it will be seen that it is based on a representation by the principal to the third party, intended to be and in fact acted upon by that third party. Therefore, unlike actual authority, which is created by a consensual agreement between the principal and the agent, apparent authority is based on the representation made by the principal to *the third party* and relied upon by the latter. Roskill J thus took the view that since the board of Brayhead had allowed Richards to act as managing director, they had represented him as having the normal powers associated with that office and, hence, they could not escape liability to the plaintiff who had relied on this representation.

In the Court of Appeal Lord Denning MR reached the same conclusion, but on slightly different grounds. He took the view that Brayhead was bound because Richards had *implied* authority to act in the way in which he did. Like Roskill J, the Master of the Rolls refused to accept that this authority was automatically implied from the nature of the office. It was rather to be 'implied from the conduct of the parties and the circumstances of the case'[17]. Furthermore, it is noteworthy that the Master of the Rolls did not disagree with Roskill J's judgment — which he described as a '*tour de force*' — in

16 Ibid, at 560.
17 Ibid, at 548.

holding that Richards had ostensible or apparent authority; rather, he said,

'his [Roskill J's] findings carry with it the necessary inference that (Richards) had *also* actual authority, such authority being implied from the circumstances that the board by their conduct ... had acquiesced in his acting as their chief executive and committing Brayhead Ltd to contracts without the necessity of sanction from the board'[18].

This, therefore, was a case in which *both* ostensible and implied authority could be pleaded. We will note in due course, however, that the scope of implied authority may, in some circumstances at least, be less extensive than that of apparent authority.

(i)   Some illustrations

As we have explained, every agent who is given express authority has also the 'right to do all subordinate acts incidental to and necessary for the execution of that authority'. It is important to understand that the principal is taken to have consented (albeit impliedly) to the agent having such authority. The explanation for this is really the desire to make the express actual authority more effective, since actual authority almost invariably includes 'medium powers', which are not expressed, but which consist of 'all the means necessary to be used, in order to attain the accomplishment of the object of the principal power ...'[19]. Two contrasting examples will serve to clarify this concept.

In *Rosenbaum v Belson*[20] it was held that instructions from an owner of a house to an agent to sell the property and to be paid commission on the purchase price accepted was authority to the agent to make a binding contract, including authority to sign an agreement of sale. In *Hamer v Sharp*[1], however, authority was given to an agent to 'find a purchaser' not to 'sell' and the court held that in these circumstances there was no implied authority to conclude a contract. As Buckley J said in *Rosenbaum v Belson*:

'there is substantial difference between those expressions. Authorising a man to sell means an authority to conclude a sale; authorising him to find a purchaser means less than that — it means

---

18   Ibid.
19   *Howard v Baillie* (1796) 2 Hy Bl 618 at 619 per Eyre CJ.
20   [1900] 2 Ch 267.
1   (1874) LR 19 Eq 108.

to find a man willing to become a purchaser, not to find him and also make him a purchaser'[2].

'A sale', it was pointed out, 'prima facie means a sale effectual in point of law, including the execution of a contract where the law requires a contract in writing'. The agent's authority to sign was thus acquired by necessary implication in order to give effect to his express authority. Similar considerations explain why the agent is held not to have implied authority to warrant that the property in question may be suitable for a particular purpose[3], even though he may describe the property to the prospective purchaser and state facts which may affect its value[4].

All these cases show two things. Firstly, the 'additional' authority acquired by the agent is given to him precisely in order to make more effective the execution of his express actual authority. Secondly, they show that in many cases the problem whether 'additional' authority is necessary (and what this should actually be) is one of construction of the relevant agreement between principal and agent. If, therefore, one can infer from the surrounding circumstances that the agent had authority — albeit not express — to sign a binding contract, his principal will be bound to the contract and will be unable to establish that the agent lacked authority. As has already been said, this question will always turn on the facts of each individual case[5].

By way of illustration, it may be helpful at this point to examine a problem which has exercised the courts with some measure of frequency. It is the question as to whether estate agents have implied authority to request and receive earnest money — usually, but erroneously, referred to as a deposit — during the subject-to-contract period. As one can imagine, what has happened in such cases is that the estate agent has absconded with the earnest money and the question before the court is which of the two innocent parties (the would-be purchaser or the vendor who engaged the dishonest agent) should be made liable for the money. What may be conveniently described as the 'old law' can be summarised under three propositions: (i) if the agent signed the receipts expressly 'as agent for the vendor' the proposed purchaser could recover the 'deposit' from the vendor[6]; (ii) if the agent signed the receipt in his own name without qualification, not saying that he signed it on behalf of the vendor or anyone else, the would-be purchaser could, once again,

2 [1900] 2 Ch 267 at 270.
3 *Hill v Harris* [1965] 2 QB 601, [1965] 2 All ER 358.
4 *Mullens v Miller* (1882) 22 Ch D 194.
5 See *Davies v Sweet* [1962] 2 QB 300, [1962] 1 All ER 92, CA.
6 *Ryan v Pilkington* [1959] 1 All ER 689.

recover the 'deposit' from the vendor[7]; (iii) if the agent signed the receipt expressly as 'stakeholder' (a term loosely applied), the would-be purchaser could still recover the 'deposit' from the vendor[8]. To these one could add a fourth proposition which underlay and justified the preceding three: namely, that when someone who wishes to sell his house puts it in the hands of an estate agent, he gives him authority to receive a precontractual 'deposit' on his behalf[9].

In *Sorrell v Finch*[10], when the problem finally reached the House of Lords, the old cases were declared to have been wrongly decided. The grounds for the new departure can be found in the weaknesses of the 'old' view. First and foremost among these were considerations of justice which, apparently, require that the vendor be held liable since it is he 'who has chosen the estate agent, ... has clothed him with the capacity of agent, and ... has enabled him to ask for and receive a deposit'[11]. Prima facie the moral overtones of this argument might seem overwhelming — that is, until one realises that in all these cases the vendor is, in fact, just as innocent as the purchaser. Could it not be said then with equal force that it should be the purchaser who should bear the risk? Indeed, one might even argue that, since both vendor and purchaser are equally innocent, they should share the loss. This, in turn, can be countered by arguing that such a solution would, in fact, be doing injustice rather than justice to both. Pondering over these variations, one soon realises that 'intuitive feelings for justice seem a poor substitute for a rule of law antecedently known'[12].

The old view, which has now been discarded, was also reached under the influence of early auction cases which held the vendor liable for the defaults of the auctioneer[13]. Although prima facie attractive, this analogy is dangerous in that it fails to take into account the fact that, whereas in the estate agency cases the purchaser pays earnest money during the subject-to-contract period, in the auctioneer cases the deposit is paid *in accordance with the terms of the contract which has already been concluded.* The auctioneer, therefore, demands and receives money because he has been authorised to do so. Can such authority be found to exist in favour of an estate agent

---

7   *Burt v Claude Cousins & Co Ltd* [1971] 2 QB 426, [1971] 2 All ER 611.
8   *Barrington v Lee* [1972] 1 QB 326, [1971] 3 All ER 1231.
9   *Ryan v Pilkington*, ante, at 693 per Hodson LJ and at 695 per Morris LJ.
10 [1977] AC 728, [1976] 2 All ER 371, HL; see Extract 9, p 226.
11 *Burt v Claude Cousins & Co Ltd* [1971] 2 QB 426 at 452 per Megaw LJ.
12 *National Insurance Co of New Zealand v Espagne* (1961) 105 CLR 569 at 572.
13 See *Goding v Frazer* [1967] 1 WLR 286 at 290–291 per Sachs LJ and *Burt v Claude Cousins & Co Ltd*, ante, at 449–50 per Sachs LJ.

who collects earnest money? With the exception of *Ryan v Pilkington*[14], the facts of the other cases cannot support the existence of *express* actual authority. Equally, quite apart from their understandable reluctance to imply terms into contracts, there is little justification for courts implying authority in this situation. It is difficult to see how the taking of a precontractual deposit *on such terms as to make the prospective vendor liable* can be regarded as *reasonably* incidental to the simple engaging of an estate agent to find a purchaser. Indeed, expert evidence in *Burt v Claude Cousins*[15] suggested that the practice of collecting earnest money was dying out — an additional reason, one could say, why this should not be regarded as a reasonably incidental activity. Nor, of course, can it be termed *necessarily* incidental for, as already stated, there is no *legal* obligation to pay this money. It is suggested, therefore, that the whole problem can be solved by asserting boldly that estate agents have no implied authority to collect earnest money — a solution which, incidentally, would be entirely in tune with the prevailing attitude in the courts to interpret narrowly the ambit of the estate agent's implied authority.

Such an approach would also avoid the absurd result reached by the 'older view': namely, that even though the deposit is received *in a representative capacity*, the recipient (agent) must nevertheless return it to the depositor at his request, the principal (vendor) having *no* control over it whatsoever. It was, in fact, this weakness more than any other that the House of Lords exploited in deciding to reverse the previous common law rule. For if the vendor never receives the money, and is not entitled to receive it until the contract is concluded, it is difficult to see on what grounds he can be made liable for it. Clearly, he cannot be sued for money had and received, precisely because he never received the money in the first place. Nor can he be sued in contract since he never promised to pay if the agent defaulted (a promise, incidentally, which under the Statute of Frauds would have to have been in writing). Nor can he be sued in trust, as he never had control over the money. It is true that his vicarious liability in tort has been more widely canvassed and in *Sorrell v Finch*[16] itself the respondents did seek to render the vendor vicariously liable for the fraudulent misrepresentation and conversion of the agent. But this argument was dismissed on the grounds that the agent was not 'in the course of his employment', nor was he within the scope of his 'actual or apparent authority'. And, perhaps, a point already

---

14 [1959] 1 All ER 689, [1959] 1 WLR 403, CA and especially Willmer LJ's account of the evidence at 413.
15 See fn 7, ante.
16 See fn 10, ante.

made should be repeated here: in cases where it is sought to hold the principal vicariously liable for the fraud of his agent, the true test of liability is whether the agent possessed actual or apparent authority, not whether he was acting in the course of his employment. In view of what has already been said and the facts of the case, neither of these criteria was satisfied. In the circumstances, therefore, it can only be the estate agent — holding the money until the negotiations are determined or until the purchaser asks for it — who must be taken to promise to return it on either occasion. Indeed, s 13(1)(a) of the Estate Agents Act 1979 now makes it clear that anyone engaged in estate agency work, who has received money from the prospective purchaser, holds it in trust for him and must not pay it over to his client before the contract of sale is concluded. Moreover, this sum is repayable to the purchaser on demand; and, pursuant to regulations made under s 15 of the Act, estate agents are now obliged to ensure that such funds attract legal interest during the period that they are in their hands (SI 1981/1520).

Another interesting illustration of implied authority can be found in the context of solicitors' and barristers' powers to enter into a compromise on behalf of their clients. After some initial hesitation, it became clear by the 1860s that attorneys had such authority. Indeed, by the turn of the century there was no doubt that a solicitor or counsel, retained in an action, had implied authority as between himself and his client to compromise the suit without reference to the client and, similarly, apparent authority, as between himself and the opposing litigant, to enter into such an arrangement provided — in both cases — the compromise did not involve a matter 'collateral to the action'. This position was reaffirmed by the Court of Appeal in *Waugh v HB Clifford & Sons*[17]. The decision presents the additional interest of (a) having stressed that in future a narrow view was likely to be taken as to what matters were collateral; (b) having clearly articulated the policy reason which dictates this result (settlements would be greatly impeded if attorneys were constantly put to proof of their actual authority to effect a compromise)[18]; and (c) having considered the interrelationship between implied and apparent authority in such circumstances. In the view of

17 [1982] Ch 374. [1982] 1 All ER 1095, CA; see Extract 10 p 229. For a general discussion of lawyers' authority to settle or compromise actions, see Fridman 'Lawyers as Agents' [1987] UNBLJ 9, 24–40.
18 The importance attaching to the settlement of disputes was recently further underlined by the decision in *Kelley v Corston* [1997] 4 All ER 466 where Butler-Sloss and Pill LJJ held that the immunity of an advocate from suit in negligence in respect of out of court work extended to the making of a settlement at the door of the court when the trial of the merits was about to begin.

Brightman LJ the two notions were not, in this context at least, coterminous and, therefore, there might well be instances where the attorney, having exceeded his implied authority to enter into a compromise, might nevertheless still be within his apparent authority to do so and thus be able to bind his client. Speaking more generally, however, it may be noted that the courts remain willing to exercise a summary jurisdiction to order solicitors who have acted without authority on behalf of a litigant to pay any costs needlessly incurred by the opposing party[19].

(ii)   Usual and customary authority

Implied authority is sometimes sub-divided into two further categories — usual authority and customary authority. Both categories of case share in common the fact that they deal with *actual* or *real* authority. But they are differentiated on the grounds that whereas implied authority is founded upon the vague notion of 'business efficacy' or upon the possibility of discovering from previous transactions between the parties what their agreement really involved, customary authority 'is based upon the more specific idea of settled and well understood trade, business or professional usages and customs, evidence of which will have to be produced should a dispute arise'[20]. Exponents of this dichotomy argue that it helps explain the notion of authority. This would perhaps be the case, were this area of the law of agency not bedevilled by loose terminology. It is often quite difficult to distinguish between actual, implied, and apparent authority and it would only add to the confusion if one were to add two more terms, especially since there does not seem to be a clear consensus of opinion as to their actual meaning. Treitel, for example, has described as implied, authority what Fridman describes as customary authority. Similar terminological differences have divided Fridman and Bowstead. Judges, too, appear confused by the loose terminology as the *Pilkington* and *Hely-Hutchinson* cases already mentioned clearly reveal. Thus, in view of the fact that even the adherents of the dichotomy acknowledge that in practical terms the distinction is of little or no significance, we shall only employ the one term — implied authority to cover both implied (in the sense of incidental) and customary authority. It suffices to remember that this implication may derive from different sources or be justified by different reasons.

19   See *Babury Ltd v London Industrial plc* [1989] NLJR 1596.
20   Fridman *The Law of Agency* (7th Edn, 1996), p 64.

It has already been said that implied authority empowers the agent to do everything which is necessary for or reasonably incidental to the effective execution of his duties. It must now be added that agents who practise a particular trade, business or profession, are normally authorised to do everything which is usually or ordinarily done in such a trade, business or profession. In *Howard v Sheward*[1], for example, it was held for this reason that an agent for a horse-dealer had implied authority to warrant the soundness of the horses he was selling and if the horse turned out not to be sound, the principal, not the agent, would be liable to the purchaser. In *E Bailey & Co Ltd v Balholm Securities Ltd*[2] brokers in cocoa and sugar were held to be agents even though, in accordance with custom, they had acted in their own name and had rendered themselves personally liable to the third party. Hence, their action to close certain accounts was not unauthorised and did not amount to a breach of contract. Their principals were consequently held liable to the brokers. Similarly, in *Real and Personal Advance Co v Phalempin*[3] it was held that the matron of a hospital had implied authority to pledge the credit of the institution in order to supply it with meat for its ordinary use. And in *Walker v Great Western Rly Co*[4] a station-manager of a railway company was held to have implied authority to order medical attendance for an injured servant of the company. More recently, in *Strover v Harrington*, it was held that 'In all ... normal conveyancing transactions, after there has been a subject to contract agreement the parties hand the matter over to their solicitors who become the normal channel for communication between vendor and purchaser in all matters relating to that transaction. In so doing ... the parties impliedly give actual authority to those solicitors to receive on their behalf all relevant information from the other party relating to that transaction'[5]. Finally, one must take note of the recent trend to treat solicitors as 'men of affairs' and thus accept that nowadays they are likely to perform a rather wider range of commercial activities than in the past. Nevertheless, the giving of an undertaking to pay money by a solicitor will only be held to be within his ordinary authority

1   (1866) LR 2 CP 148.
2   [1973] 2 Lloyd's Rep 404.
3   (1893) 9 TLR 569.
4   (1867) LR 2 Exch 228.
5   [1988] 1 All ER 769 at 779 per Sir Nicolas Browne-Wilkinson. Thus, information concerning the drainage of the property sold, conveyed by the vendor's solicitor to the purchaser's solicitor, will be imputed to the purchaser. But if such information is not passed on to the purchaser, the latter's only remedy may lie against his own solicitor. Note, however, that in *Strover's* case the judge was equally willing to hold solicitors liable on the basis of ostensible authority: ibid, at 780.

under the following conditions: 'First, in the case of an undertaking to pay money, a fund to draw on must be in the hands of, or under the control of, the firm; or at any rate there must be a reasonable expectation that it will come into the firm's hands ... Secondly, the actual or expected fund must come into their hands in the course of some ulterior transaction which is itself the sort of work that solicitors undertake. [For] it is not the ordinary business of solicitors to receive money or a promise from their client, in order that without more they can give an undertaking to a third party. Some other service must be involved'[6].

As one would expect, special customs obtain in the various professions. Factors, for example, are entitled to sell the goods entrusted to their possession in their own names[7], but custom does not allow them to warrant the goods they sell[8]. The activities of auctioneers, too, are governed by customs of the profession. An auctioneer only has implied authority to receive payment from the purchaser in cash[9] and, if the lot in question is advertised subject to a reserve price, the principal will not be bound if the auctioneer sells the goods below the reserve set[10]. Finally, estate agents, who form a category of agent subject to rules that often differ from those generally applying to the conventional relationship of principal and agent, have no implied authority to appoint sub-agents[11]. Nor may estate agents conclude a contract for the sale of property[12] — unless they were held out as having such authority[13], or the circumstances permit such an inference[14].

In addition to any such implied authority, the agent may also acquire authority to do certain things simply because he is operating within a particular locality or market. Such authority emanates from the local custom or usage. A usage is taken to mean:

'a practice which the court will recognise ... For the practice to amount to such a recognised usage, it must be *certain,* in the sense that the practice is clearly established; it must be *notorious,* in the sense that it is so well known in the market in which it is alleged to exist

---

6   *United Bank of Kuwait v Hammoud* [1988] 1 WLR 1051 at 1063 per Staughton LJ; see Extract 2, p 217.
7   *Baring v Corrie* (1818) 2 B & Ald 137.
8   *Payne v Lord Leconfield* (1882) 51 LJQB 642.
9   *Williams v Evans* (1866) LR 1 QB 352.
10 *McManus v Fortescue* [1907] 2 KB 1.
11 *John McCann & Co (a firm) v Pow* [1975] 1 All ER 129, [1974] 1 WLR 1643, followed in *Robert Bruce & Partners v Winyard Developments* (1987) 282 Estates Gazette 1255 at 1261.
12 *Hamer v Sharp* (1874) LR 19 Eq 108.
13 *Walsh v Griffiths-Jones* [1978] 2 All ER 1002.
14 *Davies v Sweet* [1962] 2 QB 300, [1962] 1 All ER 92.

that those who conduct business in that market contract with the usage as an implied term, and it must be *reasonable*[15].

Thus, in *Dingle v Hare*[16] the jury found that it was customary whenever one sold manure to supply a warranty. The agent in that case, who in fact had supplied such a warranty, was therefore held to have had an implied authority to do so. The custom must not be inconsistent with the express authority and instructions given to the agent, nor must it be unreasonable. In *Robinson v Mollett*[17] it was alleged that there was a custom in the London tallow market which allowed agents employed by several principals to buy in bulk in their own name so as to satisfy the needs of all their principals, amongst whom they would subsequently allocate the goods. The custom was held to be unreasonable since, in effect, it turned the agent into a seller. This was held to be incompatible with the principal and agent relationship: an agent must buy as cheaply as he can, whereas a seller sells at the highest possible price.[18] The only circumstances in which a principal will be bound by an unreasonable custom is where he knows of it, for knowledge in this context is taken to amount to assent.

When, unknown to the third party, the principal seeks to circumscribe the usual authority of the agent: the problematical case of Watteau v Fenwick

In all these cases complications may arise when the principal has expressly deprived his agent of powers which are considered 'usual' (in the sense of incidental or typical) in the conduct of the business with which he has been entrusted. Generally speaking, the solution to this problem appears to be that the principal continues to be bound by the acts of his agent even though he has prohibited him from doing them if (a) they can be regarded as incidental to the kind of business he is carrying out, and (b) the person dealing with the agent is not aware of the limitations imposed upon the agent's 'usual' powers. *Daun v Simmins*[19] illustrates the point. In that case the principal, who had employed the agent to manage a 'tied' house

---

15   *Cunliffe-Owen v Teather and Greenwood* [1967] 3 All ER 561 at 572–3 per Ungoed-Thomas J.
16   (1859) 7 CBNS 145.
17   (1875) LR 7 HL 802.
18   For further examples of a custom held unreasonable on the ground that it required the agent to put the interests of the third party before those of his principal, see *Anglo-African Merchants Ltd v Bayley* [1969] 2 All ER 421 and *North and South Trust Co v Berkeley* [1971] 1 All ER 980.
19   (1879) 41 LT 783 (a case of apparent authority).

which was in his name, expressly prohibited the agent from purchasing spirits from X. The agent ignored his principal's instructions, purchased spirits from X and then failed to pay for them. In an action by X against the principal it was held that the latter should *not* be liable for the unauthorised acts of the agent since the third party dealing with the agent was a person involved in the trade and *should have known* that the house was 'tied' and therefore not allowed to purchase spirits from elsewhere. But if the third party does not know, and cannot reasonably be expected to know of the agent's restricted authority, then he will be entitled to assume that the agent's usual authority continues to operate irrespective of the principal's contrary instructions. In the words of Fridman, in such cases 'what would normally be expected to be the situation must be taken as being the situation, unless there are indications to the contrary arising from the conduct of the parties or the external circumstances as appreciated by anyone dealing with the agent'[20].

The situation becomes even more complicated, however, when the *existence* of the principal is not known to the third party. *Edmunds v Bushell and Jones*[1] illustrates this problem. The principal (Jones) employed an agent (Bushell) to manage his business and to carry it on in the name of Bushell & Co. Although drawing and accepting bills of exchange was incidental to carrying on such a business, it was agreed that the agent should not draw or accept bills. Bushell having accepted a bill in the name of Bushell & Co, the court held that the principal could be made liable on the bill in the hands of an indorsee who took it without knowing that the agent's authority had been restricted in this respect. The case itself is curious. Cockburn CJ's language is imprecise; and he makes reference both to 'apparent authority' and also to 'implied authority', by which he means authority 'incidental to carrying on the business' in question. Mellor J holds even more categorically that this is a case concerned with the apparent authority of the agent. The confused terminology hardly helps. And the solution to this problem becomes more difficult since in both this and the next case we shall discuss the courts seem to have paid no attention to the fact that the agency was undisclosed. Jones' name and existence were at no time disclosed by Bushell. Therefore, it must be an error to apply the principles of apparent authority in this case: the principal never represented to the third party that Bushell was his agent although, as we shall see, he may have represented him to be the owner of the business.

---

20 *Fridman*, p 75.
1 (1865) LR 1 QB 97.

This same question assumed an even more acute form in the case of *Watteau v Fenwick*[2]. The owner of a public house employed an agent to act as its manager. The principal, whose name did *not* appear in public, expressly prohibited his manager from purchasing certain kinds of goods from third parties. The manager, however, bought some cigars for the purpose of business and when later the principal was discovered and sued, he was held liable for the purchase money. It is clear from the facts of the case that the principal could not be held liable on the grounds of the apparent authority of the agent because the third party never regarded the agent as an agent but treated him as a principal. Apparent authority, as we shall see, does not apply whenever the third party is ignorant of the agency relationship. Admittedly, the third party in this case did believe that the agent was buying for himself. But it is just as important to note that the agent had no express power to purchase cigars; far from this, he had been deprived of all such power. These troublesome points, however, did not greatly disturb the court. On the contrary, in a surprisingly short judgment, which completely concealed the underlying difficulties, the court held the principal liable on the ground that the agent had acted within the authority usually given to agents of this kind. This decision was followed shortly afterwards in *Kinahan & Co Ltd v Parry*, where Lord Coleridge CJ simply stated that in these circumstances the third party was 'entitled ... to sue the real principal when disclosed, notwithstanding any limitations on the authority given to the agent by the principal.'[3]

Watteau v Fenwick[4] has not 'sired a [long] line of authority'[5]. But a case with such little subsequent judicial history has done remarkably well in exciting the imagination of academic writers who have striven hard to find a theoretical basis for it. As for the decision itself, it has not been followed in all common law jurisdictions (eg, Canada[6]); its binding nature has been questioned by some writers in England[7]; and it has been described (obiter) by one English judge as a 'somewhat puzzling case'. However, since the decision technically has not been overruled, something more must be said about it.

The actual result in *Watteau v Fenwick* has most frequently been justified on the grounds that since in most cases the principal stands to benefit from such contracts (made by his agent) it is only fair that

2   [1893] 1 QB 346; see Extract 11, p 231.
3   [1910] 2 KB 389, 394.
4   See fn 2, ante.
5   *Rhodian River Shipping Co SA and Rhodian Sailor Shipping Co SA v Halla Maritime Corpn, The Rhodian River and The Rhodian Sailor* [1984] 1 Lloyd's Rep 373 at 379 (per Bingham J); see Extract 12, p 231.
6   *McLaughlin v Gentles* (1919) 51 DLR 383.
7   Hornby [1961] CLJ 239, 246.

he should also be liable in those cases where the contract is to his disadvantage. This 'parity of reasoning' argument is not one which invariably finds favour in English law. Moreover, it does not seem to be applicable in this case. For though *Watteau v Fenwick* makes the principal liable for the cost of the merchandise ordered by the agent, it would not allow him to sue the third party for damages for non-delivery. If this reverse situation were to come before the court, the position of the principal would not be a strong one. For, since the agent had no real authority to act, the concept of undisclosed agency could not be invoked to allow the undisclosed principal to intervene (see discussion below, pp 153ff); and since the agent in that case never purported to act on behalf of another person, ratification of his acts would be impossible (see discussion below, pp 64ff). Likewise, in the absence of any empirical evidence, it is dubious to assume that the principal always stands to gain from such transactions entered into by his agent. The fact that he had prohibited the agent from entering into such contracts would, if anything, suggest the opposite.

But even if the actual result can be justified, how is it to be explained from a theoretical point of view? Some have spoken in terms of apparent authority using estoppel language[8]. This, as we have seen, is clearly not applicable in *Watteau v Fenwick*. Others have used the words 'inherent agency power'[9] and others again prefer to treat this as 'an independent type of authority'[10]. Finally, Treitel has argued that the rule in *Watteau v Fenwick* is analogous to the doctrine of vicarious liability[11]. In an earlier edition of this book we argued that though none of these explanations is entirely convincing, probably the best answer can be found in the analogical extension of the doctrine of apparent ownership: the principal has invested the agent with all the external signs of ownership, therefore he should also bear the consequences.[11a] The sheer number of theories, however, made us increasingly doubtful as to the utility of trying to find a theoretical basis for a solution which, on reflection, may not be as just as has been assumed. As has been stated, the principal never wished to be bound by such contracts. Moreover, the third party entered into the contracts in question in the belief that he was dealing only with the agent, and it is only subsequently that he discovers that he may also have another person (the principal) to

8   Goodhart and Hamson [1931] 4 CLJ 320, 336.
9   *Restatement of the Law of Agency* (2nd Edn, 1958), paras 8A, 140.
10   *Bowstead and Reynolds on Agency* (16th Edn), para 3-006.
11   *Law of Contract* (6th Edn), p 634. Cf *The Rhodian River and The Rhodian Sailor* [1984] 1 Lloyd's Rep 373 at 379 (per Bingham J); Collier [1985] 44 CLJ 363.
11a While agreeing that it cannot be supported using orthodox agency principles, Tettenborn has recently defended the decision in *Watteau v Fenwick* on estoppel grounds: see 'Agents, Business Owners and Estoppel' [1998] CLJ 274.

sue. It is, therefore, respectfully submitted that *Watteau v Fenwick* has caused more trouble than justice and that its overruling could rid the law of agency of the independent heading of 'usual authority'[12]. If that were to happen, 'usual authority' would be reduced to (a) an alternative to the term 'implied authority' (agents of a certain type are impliedly authorised to act in the 'usual' way); and (b) to those cases of apparent authority where the principal has not expressly represented to the third party that the agent has authority to bind him but has put the agent in a position that carries with it a 'usual' authority in the sense just described[13].

3   APPARENT AUTHORITY

In *Barrington v Lee*[14] Lord Denning MR remarked on the confusion that has existed between the concepts of implied and apparent authority — a confusion which persisted until at least 30 years ago, and which may not yet have completely died out. For example, in the recent case *Industrie Chimiche Italia Centrale and Cerealfin Co v Alexander G Tsavliris & Sons Maritime Co, The Choko Star*[15] Sheen J clearly proceeded on the assumption that there was a causal connection between implied and apparent authority. The Court of Appeal[16], however, reverted to the orthodoxy of Lord Denning's judgment in *Hely-Hutchinson* (discussed in the text above) according to which implied and apparent authority may co-exist but are not co-extensive[17]. No doubt, this confusion has been partly owing to the fact that in many, if not most cases actual (express or implied) and apparent authority 'co-exist and coincide'. *Hely-Hutchinson*[18] exemplifies the coincidence of the two species of authority. But then,

---

12   This has, in fact, now been done by the British Columbia Court of Appeal in *Sign-o-lite Plastics Ltd v Metropolitan Life Insurance Co* (1990) 73 DLR (4th) 541, a case noted by Fridman in (1991) 70 Can Bar Rev 329; see Extract 13, p 231.

13   Broadly, this view is now advocated by Stone 'Usual and Ostensible Authority — One Concept or Two?' [1993] JBL 325, esp pp 336–7. It does of course found upon an assumption that designated species of agent do have clearly delineated 'usual' powers — a concept which probably works only for some agents (see *The Raffaella* [1985] 2 Lloyd's Rep 36, 45 per Kerr LJ). It is increasingly apparent that 'late twentieth-century business practices do not enable a facile classification of stereotypical agents with concomitant, standardised authorities': Brown, 'The Agent's Apparent Authority: Paradigm or Paradox?' [1995] JBL 360, 367.

14   See fn 8, p 26.

15   [1989] 2 Lloyd's Rep 42 at 45.

16   [1990] 1 Lloyd's Rep 516.

17   For further discussion of this decision, see Munday 'Salvaging the Law of Agency' [1990] LMCLQ 1.

18   [1968] 1 QB 549, discussed at p 22 ante.

'either may exist without the other and their respective scopes may be different'. Even though the two concepts may overlap, they are clearly distinct and one must not lose sight of the differences.

Apparent authority (or ostensible authority, as it is sometimes called) is not really authority at all. In the words of Professor Montrose[19]:

'Apparent authority is really equivalent to the phrase "appearance of authority". There may be an appearance of authority whether in fact or not there is authority'.

It is usually said that the doctrine of apparent authority is, in reality, a particular application of the doctrine of estoppel and writers often refer to it as giving rise to agency by estoppel. Not all authors would agree with this, especially if estoppel is used here in a strict and narrow sense, some conceding that the notion of apparent authority is 'probably better based on the same reasoning as that which holds contracting parties to the objective appearance of intention which they create.'[20] Certainly, ever since the decision in *Freeman & Lockyer v Buckhurst Park Properties*[1], the estoppel view seems to have prevailed in English law.

The doctrine of apparent authority covers a multitude of cases which can, for convenience's sake, be categorised under four different headings:

(1) *Cases in which a person allows another to appear as if he were his agent, whereas in fact he is not.* In *Barrett v Deere*[2] payment of a debt was made to a person who was found in a merchant's counting house and who appeared to be responsible for the conduct of its business. This was held to be good payment to the merchant for, in the words of Lord Tenterden CJ: 'The debtor has a right to suppose that the tradesman has the control of his own premises, and that he will not allow persons to come there and intermeddle in his business without his authority'.

(2) *Cases where a principal allows his agent to give the impression that he has more authority than he actually has.* In *Todd v Robinson*[3] the

---

19 'The Basis of the Power of an Agent in Cases of Actual and Apparent Authority' (1932) 16 Can Bar Rev 756, 764.
20 Reynolds 'The Ultimate Apparent Authority' (1994) 110 LQR at pp 21–22.
1 [1964] 2 QB 480, see Extract 14, p 223; *Metropolitan Police Comr v Charles* [1977] AC 177 at 183; *Ricci Burns Ltd v Toole* [1989] 3 All ER 478 at 489; *Gurtner v Beaton* [1993] 2 Lloyd's Rep 369; Spencer Bower *Estoppel by Representation* (3rd Edn), p 181 et seq. Contra, *Bowstead and Reynolds* (16th Edn), para 8-029 with further references to the relevant literature.
2 (1828) Mood & M 200 at 202.
3 (1825) Ry & M 217.

defendant employed an agent in London to purchase on credit goods belonging to the plaintiff. Whereas his principal had only authorised him to order goods worth £31, during one of these transactions the agent ordered goods worth £45, which he appropriated to his own use. The liability of the defendant was not disputed for the £31. The question was whether the defendant could be made to pay the additional £14 which he had not authorised. The court held that 'the authority actually given in each particular instance to (the agent) can only be known to the defendant himself; the plaintiffs can only look to the appearances, held out by him'. Consequently, the principal was liable to pay the full £45.

(3) *Cases where a principal allows his agent to continue to appear as his agent whereas in fact the agency relationship between them has been terminated.* Unlike (1) above, in this case initially there was an agency relationship but it has come to an end. In *Drew v Nunn*[4] the defendant had appointed his wife as his agent and given her authority to deal with the plaintiff. He later became insane. While his illness lasted his wife ordered goods. The plaintiff was unaware of the defendant's insanity. When the defendant recovered his health he refused to pay for the goods and was sued for their price. We shall see in a subsequent chapter that insanity terminates agency because an insane person cannot validly contract and therefore cannot appoint or act as an agent. Brett LJ declared that, 'where such a change occurs to the principal that he can no longer act for himself, the agent whom he has appointed can no longer act for him'. But although it was held that the agency relationship had come to an end and the agent's (actual) authority had been terminated, the defendant was declared liable on the grounds that representations made by the principal (while he was sane) entitled third persons to act upon them until they heard that these representations had been withdrawn regardless of the fact that, as between the defendant and his wife, the agency expired upon his becoming to her knowledge insane.

(4) *Cases in which the principal limits the agent's actual, implied authority but fails to inform third parties who deal with him of the agent's limited authority.* In *Manchester Trust v Furness, Whity & Co Ltd*[5] a charterparty contained a clause that the captain and the crew, although appointed by the owners of the vessel, should be considered to be servants of the charterers and that in signing all bills of lading the captain was signing them as charterers' agent. The captain, having signed a bill

4   (1879) 4 QBD 661.
5   [1895] 2 QB 539. See also, *The Samah and Lina V* [1981] 1 Lloyd's Rep 40, 43–4.

of lading for delivery of coal at Rio was then misled and deceived and took the coal to Buenos Aires where it was stolen. The question was, who was to bear the loss? The court held that the special clause in the charterparty was binding only as between shipowner and charterer, that the holders of the bill of lading did not have constructive knowledge of the contents of the charterparty, and that therefore they were entitled to assume that the usual situation obtained and to regard the captain as agent for the owners. Another and, perhaps, better example of this kind of authority was given by Lord Denning MR in his judgment in *Hely-Hutchinson v Brayhead Ltd*[6] in the course of showing that on occasion apparent authority may exceed the bounds of actual authority. His Lordship said:

'... when the board (of a company) appoint the managing director, they may expressly limit his authority by saying he is not to order goods worth more than £500 without the sanction of the board. In that case his *actual* authority is subject to the £500 limitation, but his *ostensible* authority includes all the usual authority of a managing director. The company is bound by his ostensible authority in his dealings with those who do not know of the limitation'[7].

Arguably, some of these decisions could be treated as instances of implied authority (in the wide sense used previously) and it could be said that the reason why the principal is bound is not because he held the agent out as being his agent (apparent authority) but because his agent's implied authority had been restricted without the third party being aware of the restriction (implied authority). *Hely-Hutchinson*, once again, serves to illustrate this phenomenon.

The essential elements of apparent authority

It will be apparent from at least some of these instances that there was no agency relationship whereas in others the agent did things which were forbidden to him. In both cases the agent had no *real* authority to represent the principal even though he purported to act for him. Nor had the principal in any way consented to be bound by the so-called agent. Yet, in all these cases, the principal was held liable. The reasons for holding the principal liable in such circumstances have invariably been based on grounds of public policy, business efficacy, or equity. But what should also be clear is that in the end what really brings the rules of apparent authority into

6   [1968] 1 QB 549.
7   Ibid, at 583.

operation is the 'principal's' *own conduct*, to which we must now turn our attention.

In *Rama Corpn v Proved Tin and General Investments Ltd*[8] Slade J declared:

'Ostensible or apparent authority ... is merely a form of estoppel, indeed, it has been termed agency by estoppel, and you cannot call in aid an estoppel unless you have three ingredients: (i) a representation, (ii) a reliance on the representation and (iii) an alteration of your position resulting from such a reliance'.

Let us analyse each of these three ingredients in turn.

(i)   Representation

(a) *The representation can be express (oral or in writing); it may be implied from previous dealings, or, more often, it may be implied from conduct (eg by putting the agent in a position that carries with it 'usual' authority*[9], *or from a given and known relationship of the parties such as a partner in a partnership or a managing director in a company).* In *Summers v Solomon*[10] the defendant employed his nephew as manager to run his jewellery shop in Sussex and regularly paid for jewellery which the nephew ordered from the plaintiff for resale in his shop. The nephew left the shop, thus terminating the agency, without giving notice to the defendant, went to London, obtained goods from the plaintiff in the defendant's name and then absconded with them. The defendant was held liable to pay for the goods. In the words of Crompton J[11]:

'As soon as you have given the agent authority to pledge your credit, you render yourself liable to parties who have acted upon notice of such authority until you find the means of giving them notice that the authority is determined'.

In a brief judgment Coleridge J went on to underline the difference between actual and apparent authority. He said:

'The question is not what was the actual relation between the defendant and his nephew, but whether the defendant had not so conducted himself as to make the plaintiff suppose the nephew to be the defendant's general agent. What passes between the

8   [1952] 2 QB 147 at 149–50; see Extract 15, p 236.
9   *The Ocean Frost* [1986] AC 717 at 777; *United Bank of Kuwait v Hammoud* [1988] 1 WLR 1051; see Extract 2, p 217.
10   (1857) 7 E & B 879. See also, *The Unique Mariner* [1978] 1 Lloyd's Rep 438; *The Samah and Lina V* [1981] 1 Lloyd's Rep 40.
11   Ibid, at 884–5.

defendant and his nephew cannot limit the defendant's liability to the plaintiff'[12].

This issue has great relevance to the law of partnership, which to a large extent is now regulated by statute. Section 14(1) of the Partnership Act 1890 states that:

'Every one who by words spoken or written or by conduct represents himself, or who knowingly suffers himself to be represented, as a partner in a particular firm, is liable as a partner to any one who has on the faith of any such representation given credit to the firm, whether the representation has or has not been made or communicated to the person so giving credit by or with the knowledge of the apparent partner making the representation or suffering it to be made'.

Thus, retired partners will continue to be liable unless and until they give notice of their retirement. Although analogous to the problems of the law of agency at present under discussion, detailed treatment of the law of partnership is more appropriate to the specialised works to which the reader is referred[13].

(b) *The representation must be made by the principal himself or by someone acting in accordance with the law of agency; it cannot normally be made by the agent himself.* This proposition, currently under scrutiny by the courts, has for long been taken as an axiom of apparent authority. As Lord Donaldson MR said in *United Bank of Kuwait v Hammoud*, 'it is trite law that an agent cannot ordinarily confer ostensible authority on himself. He cannot pull himself up by his own shoe-laces'[14]. The case of *A-G for Ceylon v Silva*[15] affords an orthodox example of this proposition of law at work. A Crown agent, who was a customs official, mistakenly treated goods belonging to the Crown as unclaimed goods and advertised their sale by public auction. At the auction the respondent bought some of the goods. As he could not obtain delivery, he sued the Attorney-General for Ceylon as representing the Crown. The question was whether the Crown agent had authority to sell the goods. It was held firstly 'that a public officer has not by reason of the fact that he is in the service of the Crown the right to act for and on behalf of the Crown in all matters which concern the

12 Ibid, at 884.
13 See *Lindley and Banks on Partnership* (17th edn, 1995), Morse *Partnership Law* (3rd edn, 1995).
14 [1988] 3 All ER 418.
15 [1953] AC 461, [1953] 2 WLR 1185. See also *The Rhodian River* [1984] 1 Lloyd's Rep 373; *United Bank of Kuwait v Hammoud* [1988] 1 WLR 1051 at 1064.

Crown'. The right to act for the Crown in any particular matter must be established by reference to statute or otherwise. Secondly, the Crown agent *also* lacked ostensible authority: 'All "ostensible" authority involves a representation by the *principal* as to the extent of the agent's authority. No representation by the agent as to the extent of his authority can amount to a "holding out" by the principal'[16].

This last point can raise delicate issues when the principal is not a physical person but a legal entity, eg a company. The difficulties here stem from the fact that unlike a physical person, a corporation can only make representations through its agents. Consequently,

'in order to create an estoppel between the corporation and the contractor (the third party), the representation as to the authority of the agent which creates his "apparent" authority must be made by some person or persons who have "actual" authority from the corporation to make the representation. Such "actual" authority may be conferred by the constitution of the corporation itself, as, for example, in the case of a company, upon the board of directors, *or* it may be conferred by those who under its constitution have the powers of management upon some other person to whom the constitution permits them to delegate authority to make representations of this kind'[17].

This is what occurred in *Freeman and Lockyer v Buckhurst Park Properties Ltd*[18] where the second defendant, who was a director of the first defendant's company, instructed the plaintiffs, a firm of architects, to apply for planning permission to develop a certain estate. The plaintiffs executed the work and were suing for their fee. The defendant company's main argument was that the second defendant had no authority to bind them to such a contract. The first defendant's articles of association contained a provision for the

---

16   Ibid, at 479 (emphasis added). Unless the agent, *through the principal's conduct*, has 'authority' to make representations or act as if he were entitled to enter into particular transactions. This is a grey area, where different professions may operate under different rules and customs, and where it is therefore necessary to scrutinise all the surrounding circumstances before determining the issue. See *Egyptian International Foreign Trade Co v Soplex Wholesale Supplies Ltd and PS Refson & Co Ltd, The Raffaella* [1985] 2 Lloyd's Rep 36, esp pp 4–43; see Extract 16, p 236. But although an agent *may* in such cases be able to enlarge an *existing* authority he cannot normally, through his own representations, create an apparent authority out of thin air.

17   *Freeman and Lockyer v Buckhurst Park Properties (Mangal) Ltd* [1964] 2 QB 480 at 504–5 per Diplock LJ. See also, *British Bank of the Middle East v Sun Life Assurance Co of Canada (UK) Ltd* [1983] 2 Lloyd's Rep 9, HL; Collier [1984] 43 CLJ 26–7.

18   Ibid.

appointment of a managing director. Although none was finally appointed, it was found as a fact that the other directors were fully aware of the second defendant's activities and had never objected to him acting as de facto managing director. The company was held liable for the acts of its directors, who had actual authority under its constitution to manage the company's business, had permitted one of their number to run the company and had thereby represented to all persons dealing with him that he had authority to enter on behalf of the company into contracts of a kind which an agent authorised to do acts of the kind which he was in fact permitted to do usually enters into in the ordinary course of business[19].

Hitherto, it has been clearly understood that an agent cannot confer authority upon himself and that the representation that he has authority must ultimately emanate from the principal. True, the courts have occasionally strayed slightly beyond this point. In *United Bank of Kuwait Ltd v Hammoud*,[20] for instance, the Court of Appeal held the principal bound by its agent's assertion to the third party that certain background facts were true. A solicitor, in this case, represented that certain funds would become available to his firm. Had this been correct, it would have been normal for such a solicitor to give a guarantee to a bank on behalf of his client. The third party was entitled to rely on the solicitor's representation that these background facts obtained. This line of authority has not traditionally extended to cases where the third party *knows* that the agent does not have authority. In *First Energy (UK) Ltd v Hungarian International Bank Ltd*[1], however, the Court of Appeal took this additional bold step.

In *First Energy*, whilst awaiting the opening of a more permanent facility, a client arranged ad hoc finance through a senior manager of a bank. From an earlier similar dealing with the bank the client was aware both that this particular manager did not have authority to agree such an arrangement and that the bank's decision would normally be communicated to the client by a letter bearing two signatures. The manager wrote and signed a letter to the client indicating that the temporary facility had been approved by the bank. This was not the case, and the bank sought to repudiate the arrangement. The Court of Appeal nevertheless held that the bank was liable on the grounds that the senior manager had apparent authority to inform the client that the ad hoc facility had been

---

19 Ibid, at 505 per Diplock LJ.
20 [1988] 1 WLR 1051.
1 [1993] 2 Lloyd's Rep 194. See generally Reynolds 'The Ultimate Apparent Authority' (1994) 110 LQR 21.

approved by the bank. Previously, in *Armagas Ltd v Mundogas SA*[2], the House of Lords had determined that where a third party relies solely on the agent's false assertion that he has authority, the principal incurs no liability. *First Energy*, therefore, poses a puzzle. Were it to create a general precedent that someone without any authority, and known by the third party not to possess it, could simply confer authority upon himself by misrepresenting his powers, the notion of apparent authority would lose its fundamental characteristic: the representation would no longer need to derive from the principal at all. The case has been described by one commentator as 'exceptional on the facts'[3].

Given how radical the decision would prove if it was felt to embody a general statement of the conditions necessary for the existence of apparent authority, effectively permitting an agent to confer authority upon himself, it might seem wise for the time being to assume that *First Energy* is indeed a decision confined to its own particular facts. However, an alternative thesis is that the case marks a welcome shift in the doctrine of apparent authority that better caters for the needs of modern commerce[4]. The argument runs that, given the impersonal complexity of modern business and the difficulty and embarrassment incidental to making intrusive enquiries into an agent's authority, an approach more favourable to third parties, in the words of Steyn LJ, would fulfil 'the objective which has been and still is the principal moulding force of our law of contract', namely, 'the reasonable expectation of honest men'[5]. While a balance must be struck between protection of the principal and the third party, the courts may have tended in the past to be over-protective of the former at the expense of the latter[6]. Moreover, their characterisation of the agent as a mere passive participant in agency, acting only as a conduit between principal and agent, is an 'outmoded paradigm' for, it is said,

'in most instances the agent's apparent authority emanates from the joint actions of principal and agent: the principal's appointing an agent to a position thereby frequently enabling or necessitating the latter's ability to bolster his authority in dealings with the third party'[7].

2   [1986] AC 717.
3   Reynolds 'The Ultimate Apparent Authority' (1994) 110 LQR 21, 24.
4   Brown 'The Agent's Apparent Authority: Paradigm or Paradox?' [1995] JBL 360.
5   [1993] 2 Lloyd's Rep at p 196.
6   Eg *British Bank of the Middle East v Sun Life Assurance Co of Canada* [1983] 2 Lloyd's Rep 9.
7   [1995] JBL at p 368.

Recognising this fact of commercial life, the *First Energy* case adopts the third party's perspective and judges the scope of the agent's authority according to the manner in which that party would have apprehended the situation. This serves to impose primary responsibility upon the principal for the actions of the agent whom he appointed to a position within his organisation. It also means that the test for apparent authority focuses on the third party's perception of the conduct of the agent rather than upon whether or not the principal has made a representation as to the agent's authority.

Plainly two schools of thought are now developing concerning the exact nature of apparent authority. It remains to be seen if the orthodox doctrine, with its emphasis on the need for a representation emanating from the principal, will survive in the face of an approach more kindly to third parties who are often helpless in the modern corporate context to determine the true scope of an agent's authority, no matter how assiduous their enquiries may have been.

(c) *The representation must be made to the third party.* In *Freeman and Lockyer* Diplock LJ expressed this important requirement, which distinguishes cases of actual authority from cases of apparent authority, in the following terms:

'An "actual" authority is a legal relationship between principal and agent created by a consensual agreement to which *they alone* are parties … To this agreement the contractor (third party) is a stranger; he may be totally ignorant of the existence of any authority on the part of the agent. Nevertheless, if the agent does enter into a contract pursuant to the "actual" authority, it does create contractual rights and liabilities between the principal and the contractor … An "apparent" or "ostensible" authority, on the other hand, is a legal relationship between the principal and the contractor (third party) created by a representation, *made by the principal to the contractor (third party)*, intended to be and in fact acted upon by the contractor (third party), that the agent has authority to enter on behalf of the principal into a contract of a kind within the scope of the "apparent" authority, so as to render the principal liable to perform any obligations imposed upon him by such a contract. *To the relationship so created the agent is a stranger.* He need not be (although he generally is) aware of the existence of the representation *but he must not purport to make the agreement as principal himself.* The representation, when acted upon by the contractor (third party) by entering into a contract with the agent, operates as an estoppel, preventing the principal from asserting that he is not bound by the contract. It is irrelevant whether the agent had actual authority to enter into the contract'[8].

(d) *The representation made by the principal must be one of fact not of law.* Thus, if a third party is shown a power of attorney and misconstrues its contents, he will not be able to recover from the principal since the construction of such a document is a matter of law. In *Chapleo v Brunswick Permanent Building Society*[9] the directors of the defendant building society allowed a firm, who acted as their agents, to continue to accept loans for their society even though they had already exceeded the limit imposed by the rules of the society. In this case it was held that the society was not bound since the representation (to third parties) that it could continue to borrow was contrary to its rules which rendered such loans ultra vires.

(e) *The representation must be that the so-called agent is authorised to act as an agent.* There is therefore no apparent authority to bind the 'principal' if the agent appears to act as a principal and the third party believes that he is acting in this capacity. This is why we observed that no question of apparent authority could arise in *Watteau v Fenwick*[10]. Finally,

(f) *The representation must have been made intentionally or, possibly, negligently.* Clearly an intentional representation will bring estoppel into play. But what if the representation was merely negligent? If there is a contractual or fiduciary relationship between the person making the representation and the person to whom the representation is made, estoppel is likely to be relied upon. Whether the *Hedley Byrne* doctrine can be extended to cover cases such as these remains to be decided[11]. Generally speaking, the answer is likely to be in the affirmative.

(ii)   Reliance

The second requirement which has to be fulfilled in order to bring the doctrine of apparent authority into play is that the third party must have relied on the representation. This requires two things to occur. The first of these has already been noted: there must be a

8   [1964] 2 QB 480 at 502–3 (emphasis added).
9   (1881) 6 QBD 696.
10   [1893] 1 QB 346.
11   *Hedley Byrne & Co Ltd v Heller & Partners Ltd* [1964] AC 465, [1963] 2 All ER 575. Cf *Kooragang Investments Pty Ltd v Richardson & Wrench Ltd* [1982] AC 462, [1981] 3 All ER 65, PC (where this requirement was not satisfied).

representation *to the third party* and it is not sufficient for it to have been made only to the 'agent' (in which case there is no apparent authority) or to the world at large. In the words of Lord Lindley in *Farquharson Bros & Co v King & Co*:

'... the "holding out" must be to the particular individual who says he relied on it, or under such circumstances of publicity as to justify the inference that he knew of it and acted upon it'[12].

The second is that it must be shown that the third party relied on the representation. The third party, therefore, cannot hold the principal liable if no causal link can be shown between the representation and the third party's dealing with the agent. Furthermore, where the 'holding out' is the result of negligence on the part of the 'principal', it must also be shown that the negligence was the 'proximate cause' of the damage sustained by the third party[13]. But if the third party did not believe that the 'agent' had authority, despite the appearance of authority, he cannot hold the 'principal' liable for such acts[14]. Likewise, the principal will not be liable if the third party knew that the agent had no authority to bind the principal. The case of *Overbrooke Estates Ltd v Glencombe Properties Ltd*[15] clearly shows this. The principal gave property to A, an auctioneer, to sell. The catalogue set out the conditions of sale which included a term that the principal gave no authority to the agent to make or give representations or warranties in respect of the property. The third party asked the agent about the intentions of the GLC with respect to the piece of property in question. He obtained what was in fact an incorrect reply. The third party bid for and bought the property. Then, he discovered the truth about the GLC's slum clearance programme which was going to affect the property. The question was whether the third party was bound by the contract. This depended upon the effect of the statement or warranty alleged to have been given by the agent with respect to the future intentions of the GLC. The court held that the third party was bound. The principal had informed the third party of the agent's lack of authority to give representations or warranties and the third party knew that

---

12 [1902] AC 325 at 341; see Extract 17, p 239. For cases where the representation did *not* induce the third party to deal with the agent see: *Bedford Insurance Co Ltd v Instituto de Resseguros do Brasil* [1985] QB 966, [1984] 3 All ER 766; *The Ocean Frost* [1986] AC 717.

13 *Swan v North British Australasian Co* (1863) 2 H & C 175. In this section we are not concerned with the principal's possible liability under the law of misrepresentation.

14 *Bloomenthal v Ford* [1897] AC 156, HL.

15 [1974] 3 All ER 511, [1974] 1 WLR 1335; see Extract 18, p 240.

the principal would not be bound by anything that the agent said. No estoppel could possibly arise in such a situation.

The position can become more complicated when the third party does not *actually* know, although he *ought* to have known, of such restrictions on the agent's authority. Put in a different way, the question is: 'Is there a duty on the third party to make inquiries as to the agent's authority?' The answer may vary according to the circumstances. If the agent is acting within the ambit of the usual authority which agents of his kind possess, there will normally be no duty to inquire unless the circumstances are suspicious. A duty, on the other hand, will exist if the agent is performing acts which lie outside the scope of his usual authority[16].

Before concluding this section, note should be taken of the simplification of the law that took place in the late 1980s in the context of third party dealings with agents of companies, incorporated under the Companies Acts, who without authority entered into transactions on behalf of their companies. The doctrine of constructive notice, which formerly operated in favour of but not against such companies, meant that third parties were deemed to know of limitations imposed on the company's agents by the company's memorandum or articles of association. This doctrine, which caused much hardship to third parties, was abolished by s 711A(1) of the Companies Act 1985 (as inserted by the Companies Act 1989, s 142). The position of third parties nowadays is therefore considerably improved, especially since s 35B of the Companies Act 1985 (as inserted by s 108(1) of the Companies Act 1989) expressly provides that 'a party to a transaction with a company is not bound to enquire as to whether it is permitted by the company's memorandum or as to any limitation on the powers of the board of directors to bind the company or to authorise others to do so'. Further, s 35A(1) of the Companies Act 1985 states that: 'in favour of a person dealing with a company in good faith[17], the power of the board of directors to bind the company, or to authorise others to do so, shall be deemed to be free of any limitation under the company's constitution'. The wording of this section makes it clear that it operates in favour of third parties though, of course, there is

16   Eg *Midland Bank Ltd v Reckitt* [1933] AC 1; cf *British Bank of the Middle East v Sun Life Assurance Co of Canada (UK) Ltd* [1983] 2 Lloyd's Rep 9, HL.

17   Unless the contrary is proved, good faith is presumed: s 35A(2)(c); and according to s 35A(2)(b) the third party is not to be deemed to be in bad faith 'by reason only of his knowing that an act is beyond the powers of the directors under the company's constitution'. Further details on this complicated area of company/ agency law should be sought in the standard works on company law. The changes are also summarised in Poole 'Abolition of the Ultra Vires Doctrine and Agency Problems' (1991) 12 Co Law 43.

no legal reason why the company cannot also claim rights under transactions thus concluded with third parties provided it ratifies the acts of its agents.

(iii) Alteration of third party's position

Finally, there must be 'an alteration' in the position of the third party resulting from reliance on the representation. This is all that is required according to dicta in some cases[18]. Other cases, however, speak of the need to show a 'detriment suffered by the third party — a more stringent requirement which, however, would appear to be more consistent with the conventional application of the principle of estoppel[19]. In the absence of any alteration of position, the third party may not rely on the apparent authority of the agent. Hence, in *Norfolk County Council v Secretary of State for the Environment*[20] the court held that a factory which had mistakenly been informed by a county planning officer that it had been granted permission by the planning committee to extend its plant was not entitled to rely upon the planning officer's apparent authority because the factory had successfully cancelled its contracts with suppliers for equipment for the factory extension without penalty and therefore had incurred no liabilities as a result of relying upon the council's representation that the planning officer was authorised to pass on this incorrect notice. In short, in the absence of a detriment there could be no binding representation.

(iv) Subsequent conduct of the principal

Even in the absence of requirements of apparent authority, one person may bind another by contract if the latter is precluded by his own subsequent conduct from denying that the contract was made on his behalf. In *Spiro v Lintern*[1] the wife of the defendant purported to enter into a sale contract concerning her husband's house. Although he had asked her to find an estate agent to dispose of the house, he had never given her authority to sell. Despite this, the wife entered into a written agreement of sale which was signed by the

---

18 Eg *Rama Corpn v Proved Tin and General Investments* [1952] 2 QB 147; *Freeman and Lockyer v Buckhurst Park (Mangal) Properties Ltd* [1964] 2 QB 480. 'The only detriment that has to be shown ... is the entering into the contract': *The Tatra* [1990] 2 Lloyd's Rep 51 at 59.
19 See eg *Farquharson Bros v King* [1902] AC 325; *Norfolk County Council v Secretary of State for the Environment* [1973] 3 All ER 673.
20 [1973] 3 All ER 673.
1 [1973] 3 All ER 319; followed in *Worboys v Carter* [1987] 2 EGLR 1.

plaintiff and the estate agents acting 'for the vendor'. Until this stage, the husband had done nothing to lead the plaintiff to believe that his wife was his agent; indeed, the vendor's estate agents seemed to have supposed that Mrs Lintern (and not Mr Lintern) was the owner of the house. Subsequently, however, Mr Lintern met the purchaser and in various ways encouraged the impression that his wife had been acting as his agent. Then, before leaving for abroad, he executed a formal power of attorney authorising his wife to complete the transaction. She chose instead to sell the house to a third party for a higher price and the plaintiff brought an action claiming specific performance. Since at the time of the signing of the sale agreement the wife had been acting for an undisclosed principal, her husband's subsequent conduct could not be treated as ratification. (We shall see below that an undisclosed principal cannot ratify a contract made without his authority). The court, however, held in favour of the plaintiff on the ground that Mr Lintern's behaviour, subsequent to the completion of the sale agreement, had induced the plaintiff to act to his detriment and, as a result, Mr Lintern was estopped from claiming that the contract had been entered into without his authority. The decision is interesting in that it has seemingly modified the traditional view that estoppel normally depends on a positive misrepresentation. The court expressed its view on this last point in the following manner:

'If A sees B acting in the mistaken belief that A is under some binding obligation to him and in a manner consistent only with the existence of such an obligation, which would be to B's disadvantage if A were thereafter to deny the obligation, A is under a duty to B to disclose the nonexistence of the supposed obligation'[2].

In short, there exists here almost an estoppel by inertia, bred of A's duty to disabuse B of the misapprehension under which A knows B labours.

4   AUTHORITY BY OPERATION OF LAW

Until now, we have been considering cases of agency which result from either a consensual agreement between the principal and the agent or a representation (by words or by conduct) made by the principal to a third party which, under certain circumstances, leads to what has been called agency by estoppel and which binds the principal to the acts of his 'agent'. We must now turn to consider a

2   Ibid, at 326.

further category of agency where the relationship arises by operation of law. Once again, one has to beware of the confused terminology employed. In a sense, most, if not all, cases of agency result from the operation of the law. The parties create certain factual situations to which the law ascribes legal consequences. But in the cases we are about to examine the parties have neither agreed to create an agency relationship nor have they represented to third persons dealing with them that one of them is acting as an agent for the other. It is true that in some cases one could argue that there is an implied consent on the part of the principal. As we shall see, a wife, or indeed a mistress who is cohabiting with her lover, can be taken to have the man's implied (or presumed, as it is sometimes called) authority to pledge his credit in certain matters. And one could also, for example, argue that someone who saves a vessel in distress does in a sense have the consent of its owner and can claim reasonable remuneration from him. Yet, there are other cases which fall into this category but cannot be satisfactorily explained in terms of consent. For instance, until fairly recently, a deserted wife could pledge her husband's credit for necessaries. It was difficult to explain such a result by implying consent — the very opposite was very likely to have been the case. It is better, therefore, to say that in the variety of cases which come under this general heading, the agency relationship arises because the law, for a number of reasons of policy, wishes this to happen. Under this general heading of agency by operation of law, we shall examine two different kinds of cases: namely, (i) agency of necessity and (ii) agency arising from cohabition.

(i) Agency of necessity[3]

This is by far the most important case of authority being conferred on a party by operation of law. As its name would suggest, *the law imposes an agency of necessity in a limited number of situations where a party (the 'agent'), confronted with an emergency which poses such an imminent threat to the property or other interests of another person that there is no opportunity to seek the latter's prior authority or instructions, acts for that person without his authority in order to preserve or protect that property or those interests.*

The term 'agency of necessity' covers a variety of cases which have one thing in common: that similar principles regarding emergencies

---

3 Interesting discussions can be found in: Birks '*Negotiorum Gestio* and the Common Law' (1971) 24 CLP 110; Treitel 'Agency of Necessity' (1953) 3 Univ W Aust LR 2; Aitken '*Negotiorum Gestio* and the Common Law: A Jurisdictional Approach' (1988) 11 Syd L R 567; Brown 'Authority and Necessity in the Law of Agency' (1992) 55 MLR 414.

seem to apply to all of them. One must remember, however, that agency is a triangular relationship and also bear in mind that in most cases the crucial relationship is that of principal and third party since, as we have emphasised, the *essential* characteristic of agency is the agent's power to affect the legal position of the principal as regards third parties. Using this as a criterion one could, with profit, separate the cases which are commonly examined under this heading into two broad groups. Such an analysis conforms to the view expressed by Lord Diplock in *China-Pacific SA v Food Corpn of India. The Winson*[4]:

'Whether one person is entitled to act as agent of necessity for another person is relevant to the question whether circumstances exist which in law have the effect of conferring on him authority to create contractual rights and obligations between that other person and a third party that are directly enforceable by each against the other. It would, I think, be an aid to clarity of legal thinking if the use of the expression "agent of necessity" were confined to contexts in which this was the question to be determined and not extended, as it often is, to cases where the only relevant question is whether a person who without obtaining instructions from the owner of the goods incurs expense in taking steps that are reasonably necessary for their preservation is in law entitled to recover from the owner of the goods the reasonable expenses incurred by him in taking those steps'.

The reason for this 'terminological suggestion' is, presumably, the belief that different circumstances may determine which of these two consequences is appropriate. Treitel[5] finds this proposed distinction unconvincing since 'the fact that both consequences depend on necessity makes it at least likely that similar factors will often be relevant to each of them'. Be that as it may, the significant fact remains that in the first group of cases discussed below all the effects normally incidental to agency based on agreement are present, whereas in the second group of cases the sole question is the compensation of the 'agent'. We therefore feel fully justified in dividing discussion of this subject into two parts.

First group: true cases of agency of necessity

As indicated, the first group includes cases of true agency, ie cases where the so-called agent can affect the legal position of the so-called principal *vis-à-vis* another person, usually by concluding a contract

4   [1982] AC 939 at 958, HL.
5   *The Law of Contract* (9th Edn, 1995), p 639.

which binds the so-called principal. This, therefore, is in every sense a true agency relationship, save that the agent's power neither derives from the will of the principal nor does it emerge from any kind of representation addressed by the principal to the third party. Rather, it arises directly as a result of the operation of law, and the consequence is that: (a) the agent can bind the principal; (b) he will have a defence if sued by the principal; and (c) he will, in appropriate circumstances, be entitled to claim reimbursement from the principal.

The cases included in this category could, in theory, be further divided into two sub-categories, namely: (i) cases where an agent, not hitherto an agent, is, by necessity, constituted agent for another; and (ii) cases where a person who is already an agent is, in view of the particular circumstances and the emergency in question, given by law a further or extended authority[6]. In practice, however, the distinction is often difficult to draw and it has not been widely adopted, even though at times it can help reconcile some of the contradictory dicta in the cases.

The origin of the doctrine of necessity and the leading cases that support it are to be found in mercantile law, and in shipping law in particular. In turn, many of the maritime rules can themselves be traced back to Roman law doctrines and, more especially, that of *negotiorum gestio* (administration of affairs). The association with mercantile and maritime law is crucial for there are only three main exceptions to English law's general rule that work done for another or services performed, if unrequested, will give rise to no legally enforceable right to remuneration: namely, agency of necessity, salvage, and the acceptance of a bill of exchange for honour *supra protest*; and all three of these topics were, originally, within the jurisdiction of the Admiralty Court — a court staffed by lawyers imbued in the civilian tradition and truly cosmopolitan in their outlook. Thus, it has long been the law that in an emergency the master of a vessel has power to deal with the vessel and her cargo outside the ordinary scope of his authority. Hence, in order to preserve the ship or the remainder of the cargo the master may jettison the goods to lighten the ship[7]. He may also sell[8] or hypothecate[9] a part or the whole of the vessel in order to raise money to pay for such repairs as are necessary to enable the vessel to continue her voyage. He may also incur expenses for cargo owners

---

6   See Scrutton LJ's judgment in *Jebara v Ottoman Bank* [1927] 2 KB 254; see Extract 19, p 242.
7   *The Gratitudine* (1801) 3 Ch Rob 240 at 256 per Lord Stowell.
8   *Gunn v Roberts* (1874) LR 9 CP 331 at 337 per Brett J.
9   *The Gratitudine*, ante.

in order to preserve the cargo, for example by unloading and drying it or employing men to save it from wreck, etc[10].

Attempts to expand the doctrine of necessity beyond cases of carriage of goods by sea have produced mixed but, on the whole, unfavourable results. On the one hand, the courts have been reluctant to create a terrene counterpart to maritime salvage. So, for example, as early as 1793 Eyre CJ refused to accord the rescuer of a quantity of timber the rights of a maritime salvor on the ground that such 'voluntary acts of benevolence … are charities … but not legal duties, [and] should depend altogether for their reward upon the moral duty of gratitude'[11]. In the nineteenth century Bowen LJ was still as categorical that 'no similar doctrine [to maritime salvage] applies to things lost upon land, nor to anything except ships or goods in peril at sea'[12]. The refusal to make such an extension may not be entirely logical since 'an agent may be faced with the same necessity to act whether he finds himself on foreign waters or on land'[13]. But not only has the common law traditionally been slow to adopt a position simply because logic seemed to require it; in the instant case, the different treatment of analogous situations may be explicable, as already indicated, by reference to the fact that the maritime cases were decided by courts that possessed a much less cloistered outlook and a stronger partiality for foreign (mainly Roman, civilian or law merchant) sources of authority[14].

10   See *Notara v Henderson* (1872) LR 7 QB 225; *Brown v Gaudet* (1873) LR 5 PC 134; *Hingston v Wendt* (1876) 1 QBD 367. Absent a case of necessity, however, it used to be that the master of a vessel had no implied authority to enter into salvage agreements binding upon cargo owners: *The Choko Star* [1990] 1 Lloyd's Rep 516, discussed by Munday 'Salvaging the Law of Agency' [1991] LMCLQ 1. But see now the Merchant Shipping Act 1995, s 224(1), implementing art 6(2) of the 1989 International Convention on Salvage. In *China-Pacific SA v Food Corpn of India, The Winson* [1982] AC 939 a salvage agreement was entered into on behalf of the owners of the *Winson* and its cargo. The salvors, not having a warehouse of their own, arranged with warehousemen for the proper storage of the salvaged goods. It was held by the court that in such circumstances no direct contract arose between the warehousemen and the cargo owners. Nevertheless, the salvors' storage expenses were claimable from the cargo owners. For criticism of this result, see Samuels (1982) 98 LQR 362.
11   *Nicholson v Chapman* (1793) 2 Hy Bl 254.
12   (1886) 34 Ch D 234, 248.
13   Stoljar *Law of Agency* (1961), p 154.
14   Similar reasons have been invoked to deny an agent power to borrow money in order to defray an urgent expense of his principal: see *Hawtayne v Bourne* (1841) 7 M & W 595 at 599, a case that Lord Lindley was to describe as authority for the proposition that an agent's 'power to do what is usual does not include a power to do what is unusual, however urgent' (*Lindley & Banks on Partnership* (17th Edn, 1995), para 12–16).

On the other hand, cases do exist in which judges have either uttered *obiter dicta* favouring the extension of the maritime principles to analogous terrene situations or invoked the terminology of implied authority to cope with unexpected emergencies confronting agents. An example of the first approach can be found in *Prager v Blatspiel, Stamp and Heacock Ltd*[15], where McCardie J pointed out that the doctrine of necessitous intervention could no longer be restricted to cases of carriage of goods by sea and acceptance of bills of exchange for honour, but should also apply to cases where an agent, who is unable to communicate with his principal, intervenes in an emergency *bona fide* in the interests of the parties concerned. McCardie J's views may only have been expressed *obiter*, but were repudiated less than three years later by Scrutton LJ in *Jebara v Ottoman Bank*[16], who observed:

'The expansion (advocated by McCardie J) becomes less difficult when the agent of necessity develops from an original and subsisting agency, and only applies itself to unforeseen events not provided for in the original contract. But the position seems quite difficult when there is no pre-existing agency … and still more difficult when there is a pre-existing agency, but it has become illegal and void by reason of war, and the same reason will apply to invalidate an implied agency of necessity'.

It was this last point that was in issue in *Jebara v Ottoman Bank* and, in view of what we have said above, Scrutton LJ not unreasonably decided that no agency of necessity arose.

In other instances, use has been made of the concept of implied authority, possibly in order to avoid the difficulties that arise whenever the notion of agency of necessity is mentioned. In *Poland v John Parr & Sons*[17], for instance, the Court of Appeal held that a servant had *implied* authority in an emergency to endeavour to protect his master's property when he saw it endangered. Academic writers, however, are not agreed upon whether this is rightfully described as a case of implied authority or whether it should be treated as an instance of necessitous intervention[18].

Whilst the bulk of authorities would undoubtedly reject the extension of agency of necessity to non-maritime situations, one further series of cases (dealing mainly with perishable goods) contributes to the uncertainty that pervades this area of the law. In

15   [1924] 1 KB 566 at 571–3; see Extract 20 at p 244.
16   [1927] 2 KB 254 at 271; see Extract 19 at p 242.
17   [1927] 1 KB 236 at 240 per Bankes LJ and at 244 per Scrutton LJ.
18   Goff and Jones *The Law of Restitution* (4th Edn, 1993), Chap 15.

Sims & Co v Midland Ry Co[19], for instance, a railway carrier sold tomatoes it had agreed to carry because they were deteriorating during a transport strike. Scrutton LJ opined obiter that the sale would have been lawful if the same conditions had obtained as are 'laid down in the case of a carrier by sea'[20] Similarly, in *Sachs v Miklos*[1] the defendant invoked the doctrine when sued for conversion of goods which he had sold but which belonged to the plaintiff. The defendant in this case had agreed, out of kindness of heart, to store some of the plaintiff's furniture. When, after a considerable time, he needed the space, he tried to get in touch with the plaintiff, but in vain. He then proceeded to sell the goods, purporting to act as the plaintiff's agent. The Court of Appeal refused to accept that there existed an emergency sufficient to justify the invocation of the doctrine of necessity. However, Lord Goddard CJ did say that the doctrine of necessity had always been invoked in cases of perishable goods or livestock. This is understandable since there is great urgency to dispose of perishables. But, in principle, other emergencies might conceivably arise, justifying the invocation of the doctrine even where no perishable goods are involved.[2]

Having outlined the types of case which are usually covered by the doctrine of agency of necessity, let us now turn our attention to the conditions which are necessary to create an agency of necessity.

Firstly, it is necessary to show that the agent was unable to obtain instructions from his principal. This will be the case even when the agent has communicated with his principal, but has failed to receive instructions[3]. It does not mean that it must be impossible to communicate, but it does mean that 'it must be practically impossible to get the owner's instructions in time'[4]. With today's improved communications, it may be difficult for the agent to establish that communication was a practical impossibility.

---

19   [1913] 1 KB 103.

20   Ibid at 112, See, also, *Great Northern Rly Co v Swaffield* (1874) LR 9 Exch 132.

1   [1948] 2 KB 23, [1948] 1 All ER 67. See also *Munro v Wilmott* [1949] 1 KB 295, [1948] 2 All ER 983.

2   It might be noted that ss 12, 13 of and Sch I to the Torts (Interference with Goods) Act 1977, which confer a power of sale on bailees of goods under prescribed circumstances — including when the bailee is unable to trace or communicate with the bailor (s 12(1)(b) and (c)), might now entitle the defendant in *Sachs v Miklos* to sell the goods without rendering himself liable in conversion. If, however, the requirements of the statute are not fulfilled, the defendant would still have to fall back upon the restricted protection afforded by the common law doctrine of agency of necessity.

3   *Gokal Chand-Jagan Nath v Nand Ram Das-Atma Ram* [1939] AC 106, [1938] 4 All ER 407. See also Lord Diplock's remarks in *The Winson* [1982] AC 939 at 961.

4   *Sims & Co v Midland Rly Co* [1913] 1 KB 103 at 112 per Scrutton J.

Secondly, the agent must satisfy the court that he acted in the interests of his so-called principal and in a *bona fide* manner[5]. For example, a salvor who stores the salvaged cargo may do so in order to preserve his lien on it rather than to safeguard the interests of the cargo owners. 'The law does not seem to have determined in this context what ensues where interests are manifold or motives mixed: it may well be that the court will look *to the interest mainly served or to the dominant motive*'[6].

Thirdly, the action taken by the agent must have been reasonable and prudent in the circumstances.

Fourthly, there must be some necessity — which, as a concept, includes some form of emergency — to compel the agent to act in the way in which he did. In *Australasian Steam Navigation Co v Morse*[7] Sir Montague Smith defined 'necessity' as follows:

'... the word "necessity" when applied to mercantile affairs where the judgment must, in the nature of things, be exercised cannot, of course, mean an irresistible compelling power — what is meant by it in such cases is, the force of circumstances which determines the course a man ought to take. Thus, when by the force of circumstances a man has a duty cast on him of taking some action for another and, under that obligation, adopts the course which, to the judgment of a wise and prudent man, is apparently the best for the interests of the person for whom he acts in a given emergency, it may properly be said of the course so taken that it was, in a mercantile sense, necessary to take it'.

---

5   *Prager v Blatspiel, Stamp & Heacock Ltd,* ante at 572 per McCardie J.
6   *China-Pacific SA v Food Corpn of India, The Winson* [1982] AC 939 at 966 (per Lord Simon of Glaisdale). The italicised part of the quotation raises an interesting point: if the two suggested tests (interest served; dominant motive) point to different solutions, must they somehow be combined or will one of them prevail? In some contexts it makes sense to adopt a test of dominant purpose (see, eg, *R v Crown Court at Southwark, ex p Bowles* [1998] 2 All ER 193, HL, where this concept, borrowed from administrative law, was applied to the issue of court orders in the criminal context for the disclosure of material in the hands of third parties). In the case of agency of necessity, however, it is submitted that 'the *interest* mainly served' should be the relevant consideration. If the interests of the 'principal' have been safeguarded by the actions of the 'agent', it is only fair that the latter should also be indemnified for his expenses. The question, however, has yet to receive an authoritative answer.
7   (1872) LR 4 PC 222 at 230. 'The relevant time, for the purpose of considering whether there was a necessity, or an emergency ... is ... the time when the existence of the supposed emergency became apparent': *The Winson* [1981] QB 403, 424, approved by Lord Simon of Glaisdale [1982] AC 939 at 965.

Second group: necessitous interventions that do not invoke all the incidents of agency

This group includes cases which are explained in terms of the doctrine of necessity or necessitous intervention. They are not, however, strictly speaking, agency cases because, the so-called 'agent' does not affect the legal position of his principal at all. All the agent wishes to prove is that his intervention was justified and, as a result, he either wishes to establish a defence (if he is being sued by the principal) or to claim remuneration from the principal. These cases are thus analogous to those which fall within the Roman law doctrine of *negotiorum gestio* and they wear a quasi-contractual character.

The leading example is that of a person who accepts a bill of exchange on which he is not otherwise liable in order to safeguard the honour of the drawer. In such a case the acceptor of the bill takes over the rights of the holder, from whom he has accepted it, against the drawer, for whose honour he has acted[8]. But the category can be extended and includes, amongst other things, salvage of ships and cargo, and cases where one person pays another's funeral expenses. However, it should be emphasised that there seems to be no general principle entitling a person acting to preserve or benefit the property of another to reimbursement or a lien[9]. Indeed, as Bowen LJ declared in *Falcke v Scottish Imperial Insurance Co*, a case that is said to 'cast a difficult shadow over this area'[10],

'The general principle is, beyond all question, that work or labour done or money expended by one man to preserve or benefit the property of another do not according to English law create any lien upon the property saved or benefited, nor even, if standing alone, create any obligation to repay the expenditure. Liabilities are not to be forced on people behind their backs any more than you can confer a benefit upon a man against his will'[11].

Thus, in *Hawtayne v Bourne*[12] miners, who had not been paid, obtained a warrant enabling them to seize their employer's machinery. The manager of the mine, on his own initiative, managed to borrow money to pay the wages and thereby averted the distress.

8   See now Bills of Exchange Act 1882, ss 65–8.
9   *Falcke v Scottish Imperial Insurance Co* (1886) 34 Ch D 234; *Nicholson v Chapman* (1793) 2 Hy Bl 254.
10 Birks *An Introduction to the Law of Restitution* (1993 reprint, Oxford) p 194.
11 (1886) 34 ChD 234, 248. The punctuation has been lightly amended along the lines advocated by Goff & Jones *The Law of Restitution* (4th Edn, 1993) p 369, note 58.
12 (1841) 7 M & W 595.

It was held that his action could not be justified on the grounds of either implied authority or necessity. Hence, he was not entitled to be indemnified by his company.

Whilst it remains the case that English law currently recognises no general principle entitling a party who intervenes in case of necessity to be compensated for his trouble[13], this situation is qualified by two further developments. First, ss 3(7) and 6(1) of the Torts (Interference with Goods) Act 1977 allow the person who has improved 'goods' an allowance in respect of the improvements where he is sued by the owner of the goods for wrongful interference with them. The statute does not however confer upon the improver an independent claim for the cost or the value of the improvements. Secondly, and more significantly, recent developments in the law of restitution suggest that the plaintiff may have a good claim if (*a*) there was an emergency so pressing as to compel intervention without the property owner's authority; (*b*) the intervener acted reasonably and in the best interests of the property owner; (*c*) the intervener was unable to obtain the 'principal's' instructions; and (*d*) perhaps more tentatively, the intervener is a professional performing a professional service[14]. Whilst there may once have been a widespread belief that this species of necessitous intervention was confined to the maritime context, support for the thesis that a more generalised restitutionary claim should be allowed in English law is forthcoming from *obiter dicta* of the Court of Appeal in the recent case of *Knight v Surrey Breakdown Ltd*[15]. The appellant's car was stolen by thieves and eventually abandoned in a pond, where the police found it. The police arranged for the car to be towed away by the respondents. As they did not enjoy a right to payment under the Road Traffic Regulation Act 1984, the respondents claimed their recovery and storage fees from the appellant under an agency of necessity (in the sense of a necessitous intervention). Whilst acknowledging that any attempt to develop this area of the law would have to contend in particular with those strong contrary *dicta* in *Falcke v Scottish Imperial Insurance Co*, and statements to like effect in *Bowstead*[16], Sir Christopher Staughton declared that the relevant law is now to be found in *Goff & Jones*. These authors question Bowen LJ's statement that necessitous intervention has no place outside the maritime

---

13 For an intriguing comparative survey, which illustrates how different the common-law outlook is in this context, see Dawson '*Negotiorum Gestio*: The Altruistic Intermeddler' 74 Harv L Rev 817 and 1073 (1961). See also Zimmermann *The Law of Obligations* (1996, Oxford), Ch 14.

14 *Goff & Jones*, pp 373–4.

15 27 April 1998, unreported (Transcript no CCRTF 96/1798 CMSZ).

16 *Bowstead and Reynolds* para 4-006, *sed quaere*.

context, contending that 'there is much to be said for the view that in English law an intervener should ... , in appropriate cases, be granted a restitutionary claim,' provided that the limits of any such claim are carefully defined and that it does not impose excessive burdens on landowners who will not have requested any intervention in the first place[17]. The facts of the *Surrey Breakdown* case did not fulfil the *Goff & Jones* criteria in as much there was no evidence of an emergency so pressing as to have compelled the respondents' intervention in the absence of the appellant's authority. Nevertheless, the case rekindles the question to the extent to which English law ought to allow recovery to a party who has been variously described as a 'necessitous intervener' or an 'officious intermeddler', according to one's view of the desirability of recognising a right to compensation in such cases, and also gives a fillip to those who would argue that English law move closer to traditional civilian thinking on this issue and allow recovery for necessitous intervention.

Salvage

Strictly speaking, this does not raise questions of agency, though to the extent that it is related to the salvor's rights to remuneration it bears some resemblance to the cases of the second group. The issue really is whether those who rescue property from the perils of the sea should be rewarded for their efforts. By all accounts, the law on this subject can be seen as a maritime permutation of *negotiorum gestio*[18], traceable to Roman law[19], and again an exception to the general rule that unrequested services performed for another cannot be rewarded. A glance at this topic may not therefore be out of place.

The rights of the maritime salvor have been granted because of the great perils traditionally encountered in sea transportation. The idea of fairness towards those who take great risks to preserve property was obviously a lesser consideration, at least as far as the common law was concerned, since it has steadfastly refused to extend the doctrine to cases of terrene dangers — indeed, even to services rendered to a vessel in non-tidal waters[20]. As the authors of the standard American treatise on the law of admiralty have observed: 'on land the person who rushes in to save another's property from

---

17 *Goff & Jones*, pp 372–3.
18 Aitken, *cit supra* note 3, pp 53, 581.
19 Digest lib 3, tit 5. See *The Calypso* (1828) 2 Hag Adm 209.
20 *The Goring* [1987] QB 687, [1987] 2 All ER 246, CA; affd by House of Lords at [1988] AC 831, [1988] 1 All ER 641.

danger is an officious intermeddler, the volunteer whom even equity will not aid'[1]. Why this distinction should be made is not entirely clear. A dictum of Bowen LJ in *Falcke v Scottish Imperial Insurance Co*[2] suggests that 'liabilities are not to be forced on people behind their backs any more than you can confer a benefit upon a man against his will'. Contemporary commentators have inclined to the view that 'the general principle of maritime salvage, embodying a derivation of *negotiorum gestio*, is fundamentally inimical to the common law's methods for regulating the contractual relations between citizens'[3]. According to this thesis, the only limited instances of *negotiorum gestio* in English law are to be found in those areas that come under the jurisdiction of the Admiralty Court. The decisions of the Court of Appeal and House of Lords in *The Goring*[4], refusing payment to salvors of a vessel rescued outside non-tidal waters, typifies this reasoning. For the majority's view in the Court of Appeal was that the jurisdiction of the Admiralty Court has 'broadly remained fixed where it had been fixed in 1391'[5] and that, therefore, if it originally excluded services performed in non-tidal waters, the payment of salvage could not, in such circumstances, be decreed.

(ii) Agency arising from cohabitation

This variety of agency presents us with some initial terminological difficulties. Treitel[6], for example, chooses to classify this category of agency under the heading of implied authority. Thus, he says that the very existence of this form of agency may be implied, either from conduct on a particular occasion or from some other relationship. Although this does represent one aspect of agency arising out of cohabitation, it is equally important to appreciate that there do exist some *theoretical* differences between implied authority and authority arising by operation of law. Notably, authority which is presumed to exist by operation of law is confined to 'necessaries'[7]. Nevertheless, leaving this issue to one side, it must first be emphasised that authority in these cases does not derive from legal wedlock but from the fact that the parties are cohabiting. Hence, this form of agency extends to wives who have been held to have authority to pledge their

1   Gilmore and Black *Law of Admiralty* (2nd Edn, 1915), p 532.
2   (1886) 34 Ch D 234 at 248–91.
3   Aitken, *cit supra* p 582 and references in note 164.
4   [1987] QB 687, [1987] 2 All ER 246; affd [1988] AC 831, [1988] 1 All ER 641.
5   Per Bingham LJ at p 718.
6   *The Law of Contract* (9th Edn, 1995), p 628.
7   *Miss Gray Ltd v Earl of Cathcart* (1922) 38 TLR 562 at 565.

husband's credit for household expenses[8], to mistresses[9], housekeepers and, indeed, it can be added that there is no reason why it should be confined to cases involving women. However, there must be cohabitation. Thus, there is no presumed agency from cohabitation in the case of a deserted mistress, nor in the case of a wife who is living in an hotel with her husband (since in this latter case there is no 'household')[10].

The following points may be noted:

(i) This form of agency arises in cases of *cohabitation* irrespective of the existence of a lawful marriage.

(ii) The husband's credit can only be pledged for 'necessaries'. In *Phillipson v Hayter*[11] Willes J defined necessaries as:

'things that are really necessary and suitable to the style in which the husband chooses to live, in so far as the articles fall fairly within the domestic department which is ordinarily confined to the management of the wife'.

Such items as food, clothing, medicine and the hiring of staff would normally qualify as necessaries, but things which are purely luxuries would not. In this connection, it can be said that it is the husband who sets the tone. If his ostensible mode of living is higher than his actual means would normally permit, it is appearances which count and his liability may be correspondingly greater than that of someone who does live according to his means[12].

(iii) Whether the things supplied are capable of being regarded as necessaries is a question for the judge to decide[13]. The burden of proving that the goods supplied actually *are* necessaries rests with the tradesman. It will be noticed that whereas the first question is one of law, the second is purely one of fact. Students of the law of contract will recall that a similar approach is adopted in the case of contracts for necessaries made by infants.

---

8   *Phillipson v Hayter* (1870) LR 6 CP 38 at 42; *Jewsbury v Newbold* (1857) 26 LJ Ex 247.
9   *Blades v Free* (1829) 9 B & C 167.
10   *Debenham v Mellon* (1880) 6 App Cas 24.
11   (1870) LR 6 CP 38 at 42.
12   See *Waithman v Wakefield* (1807) 1 Camp 120.
13   See *Phillipson v Hayter*, ante. The cases, however, reflect the philosophy of a bygone era and it is doubtful whether this can be accepted today in the rigid form expressed in the judgment quoted above.

(iv) Even if the goods are necessaries, the presumption that the woman has her husband's (or paramour's) authority to pledge his credit may be rebutted by him. In *Debenham v Mellon*[14] the Court of Appeal described the agency arising out of cohabitation as:

'a mere presumption of fact founded upon the supposition that wives cohabiting with their husbands ordinarily have authority to manage in their own way certain departments of the household expenditure, and to pledge their husband's credit in respect of matters coming within those departments'.

The presumption can thus be rebutted by contrary evidence showing, for example, that the tradesman had been warned not to sell goods on credit to the man's wife (or mistress) or that the woman was already well supplied with that particular variety of goods[15]. Alternatively, the husband or paramour may show that he had expressly forbidden the woman to do what she did[16] or, it would seem, he may prove that she was herself able to purchase the necessaries in question and thus did not need to rely on his credit[17].

14 (1880) 5 QBD 394 at 402.
15 *Seaton v Benedict* (1828) 5 Bing 28.
16 *Jolly v Rees* (1864) 15 CBNS 628.
17 *Morel Bros & Co Ltd v Earl of Westmorland* [1904] AC 11.

2 Want of authority and ratification

Up to this point we have been concerned with cases in which the agent has power to bind his principal. We have seen that this power may derive from a variety of sources. It may stem from express actual authority conferred under a contractual or consensual agreement reached between the agent and his principal; it may be the result of implied, usual or customary authority, if this is justified in the circumstances of the case; the agent may have ostensible or apparent authority; finally, he may be treated as if he had authority because the law, for reasons of policy, wishes to bind the so-called principal to acts done by his 'agent'. In all these cases the agent, for one reason or another, is given the *power* to affect the legal relations of his principal. Subject to what will be said later on, he can in all these circumstances create a contractual relationship between his principal and a third party. Now, we shall turn to cases involving lack or want of authority — in other words, cases in which the agent has no *a priori* authority of any kind to bind the principal. Such cases can be discussed from two angles. Firstly, the relationship between the principal and the third party can be explored, and then the relationship between the agent and the third party examined. This second aspect of want of authority on the part of the agent is usually treated under the general heading of relations between agent and third party. However, it may help to preserve the unity of the topic if we discuss it here rather than in a later chapter.

I PRINCIPAL AND THIRD PARTY. THE DOCTRINE OF RATIFICATION

A person can either act without authority or can exceed his existing authority. In such cases there is clearly no agency relationship. If nothing is done, the person on whose behalf the act was purported to be performed can neither sue nor be sued by the third party. The person on whose behalf the acts were purportedly done, however, may ex post facto decide to ratify them. If he does so, he adopts the agent's acts as if he had actually authorised them in the first place and an agency relationship springs into existence. In the words of Lord Sterndale MR in *Koenigsblatt v Sweet*: 'Ratification ... is equivalent to an antecedent authority ... and when there has been ratification the act that is done is put in the same position as if it had been antecedently authorised'[1]. Ratification has been defined in the American Restatement as,

'the affirmance by a person of a prior act which did not bind him *but which was done or professedly done on his account* whereby the act, as to some or all persons, is given effect as if originally authorised by him'[2].

English judges, too, have defined the doctrine in a similar manner. thus, Tindal CJ in *Wilson v Tumman*[3] declared:

'That an act done for another, *by a person not assuming to act for himself but for such other person*, though without any precedent authority whatever, becomes the act of the principal if subsequently ratified by him, is the known and well established principle of law. In that case the principal is bound by the act, whether it be for his detriment or his advantage and whether it be founded on a tort or a contract, to the same effect as by, and in all the consequences which follow from the same act done by his previous authority'.

The facts in *Wilson v Tumman* were simple. A sheriff, acting under a writ of execution in respect of a debt owed to the first defendant, wrongfully seized goods which did not belong to the debtor. The court held that the defendant could not become liable for the trespass by ratifying the seizure since the sheriff had not acted as his agent but as an officer of the court.

Although doubts have been expressed about the doctrine of ratification, there is nothing anomalous about it. It is perfectly logical that the principal may sue or be sued by the third party *after* he has ratified the agent's acts. After all, this is what both parties actually intended in the first place: the third party by contracting with the agent as representing someone else and the principal by ratifying the contract made by his purported agent. What the doctrine of

1   [1923] 2 Ch 314 at 325.
2   *Restatement of the Law of Agency* (2nd Edn, 1958), para 82 (emphasis added).
3   (1843) 6 Man & G 236 at 242 (emphasis added).

ratification does is to give effect to the 'real intentions of the parties'[4]. In this respect ratification differs from the 'anomalous' doctrine of the undisclosed principal, which we shall discuss in a later chapter. In the case of the undisclosed principal the third party contracts with the agent *as principal* and is not aware of the existence of the real principal. Therefore, he cannot be said to have intended to contract with the latter. In the case of ratification, however, since the third party is contracting with a person *who is purportedly acting for and on behalf of another*, he can be taken to wish to contract with that other person. Although this difference will become even clearer when we discuss the doctrine of the undisclosed principal, it is worth mentioning at this early stage.

Before discussing the detailed rules which govern ratification, let us first look at two cases which illustrate the wide scope of the doctrine. In the first — *Williams v North China Insurance Co*[5] — it was held that an insurance, which was effected without authority by one person purporting to act on behalf of another, could be ratified by the professed principal even after the loss had become known. This same doctrine has also been applied to unauthorised acts of Crown agents, enabling them to plead the defence of act of state and thus avoid incurring liability to third parties. Hence, in *Buron v Denman*[6] the defendant, a naval commander entrusted with the task of suppressing the slave trade, in the course of his duty liberated some slaves and destroyed a vessel belonging to the plaintiff which was used to transport them. The defendant's acts were communicated to the Lords of the Admiralty and were subsequently adopted and ratified by them. In an action for trespass it was held that although the plaintiff did have property in his slaves and was therefore entitled to bring an action in trespass, the minister of state's ratification of the defendant's act of freeing the slaves 'was equivalent to prior command and rendered it an act of state'. Therefore, the court concluded that the defendant acquired an immunity from suit in respect of his unlawful acts.

---

4   Fridman *The Law of Agency* (7th Edn, 1996), p 85. Although the relevant literature is in the main quite elderly, Seavey's 'The Rationale of Agency' 29 Yale LJ 859 (1920) remains a classical demonstration of the fact that the rules of agency need not be over-dependent upon any general theory of contract or tort. For a more recent discussion see Rochvarg 'Ratification and Undisclosed Principals' (1989) 34 McGill LJ 286.

5   (1876) 1 CPD 757.

6   (1848) 2 Exch 167. This, of course, is not a true agency case in the sense that the agent was entering into a contract for and on behalf of his principal.

(i) Who may ratify

The editors of *Bowstead* state that:

'The only person who has power to ratify an act is *the person in whose name or on whose behalf the act purported to be done,* and it is necessary that he should have *been in existence* at the *time* when the act was done, and *competent at that time and at the time of ratification* to be the principal of the person doing the act; but it is not necessary that at the time the act was done he was known, either personally or by name, to the third party'[7].

It will be noticed from this definition that there are certain requirements which relate to the principal's position and others which refer to the agent's intentions. For expositive purposes it is convenient to consider these two species of requirement separately.

(a) *The principal must be in existence at the time of the act.* The first requirement is that the principal is a person actually in existence. This rule used to give rise to many difficulties, especially in cases where promoters contracted on behalf of projected companies. The difficulties were compounded by the fact that a fine distinction used to be made between a contract signed by an agent purporting to act on *behalf* of a company[8] and a contract purporting to be that of the company itself whose agent merely affixed its seal to the contract[9]. In the former case, the agent's personal liability was more easily inferred; in the latter the transaction was treated as a complete nullity, with the agent (occasionally) acquiring no rights and incurring no liability under such contracts. It probably never actually was the case that 'every time an alleged company purports to contract — when there is no company in existence — everybody who is signing the contract is making himself personally liable.'[10] The liability of the agent was better viewed as a question of contractual construction in each case, with the court asking itself 'whether the agent intended himself to be a party to the contract.'[11] Nevertheless, such distinctions were perceived potentially to be too technical and, increasingly, incompatible with EC-inspired Directives[12]. The law was thus changed

---

7   *Bowstead and Reynolds on Agency* (16th Edn, 1996), para 2-058 (emphasis added).
8   *Kelner v Baxter* (1866) LR 2 CP 174.
9   *Newborne v Sensolid (GB) Ltd* [1954] 1 QB 45, [1953] 1 All ER 708.
10   Ibid, at 50 per Lord Goddard CJ.
11   *Phonogram Ltd v Lane* [1982] QB 938, 945 per Oliver, LJ. See also *Cotronic (UK) Ltd v Dezonie* [1991] BCLC 721, 724 per Dillon LJ and *Badgerhill Properties Ltd v Cottrell* [1991] BCLC 805, 809–12 per Woolf LJ.
12   *Phonogram Ltd v Lane* [1982] QB 938, [1981] 3 All ER 182; McMullen [1982] CLJ 47. On the EC Directives see Markesinis [1976] CLJ 112; Prentice (1973) 89 LQR 518; Collier and Sealy [1973] CLJ 1.

by s 36C(1) of the Companies Act 1985 (as substituted by s 130(4) of the Companies Act 1989), which section reads as follows:

'A contract which purports to be made *by or on behalf of* a company at a time when the company has not been formed has effect, subject to any agreement to the contrary, as one made with the person purporting to act for the company or as agent for it, and he is personally liable on the contract accordingly'.

The effect of this section is that the agent can no longer escape liability merely because he contracted 'as agent', but must also prove that there was a contrary exonerating agreement with the third party. Moreover, despite the concluding words of this section ('... agent ... personally liable'), it is likely that this provision also confers entitlements on such an agent[13]. The statute, however, has not given a company power to ratify pre-incorporation contracts. Moreover, as Treitel has noted: '[this] subsection does not apply where the contract purports to have been made by a company which had once existed and later been dissolved before the time of the putative contract'[14] for in such a case the agent is acting on behalf of the old company and not on behalf of a new one prior to incorporation[15].

Similarly, the non-existent company must be distinguished from the existing but mis-named corporation. In *Coral (UK) Ltd v Rechtman and Altro Mozart Food Handels Gmbh*[16] the director of a German trading subsidiary, following company re-organisation, innocently referred to the subsidiary by the German company group's old name when contracting for the sale of 12,000 tonnes of sugar on the subsidiary's behalf. Potter J absolved the director of personal liability on the contract, which the subsidiary had failed to perform, and held as a matter of fact that, even though mis-named there was ample evidence that the contract for the sale of sugar was intended exclusively to bind the plaintiff and the subsidiary trading company, which was declared liable as principal upon the contract.

(b) The second requirement referring to the position of the principal is not only that he is in existence but that he must be '*capable of being ascertained at the time when the act was done*'. In *Watson v Swann*[17] Willes J explained the requirement in the following manner:

'To entitle a person to sue upon a contract, it must clearly be shown

13 Treitel *The Law of Contract* (9th Edn, 1995), p 652.
14 Ibid.
15 *Cotronic (UK) Ltd v Dezonie* [1991] BCLC 721, CA.
16 [1996] 1 Lloyd's Rep 235. See also *Oshkosh B'Gosh Inc v Dan Marbel Inc Ltd* [1989] BCLC 507.
17 (1862) 11 CBNS 756. See also, *Southern Water Authority v Carey* [1985] 2 All ER 1077 at 1085.

that he himself made it, or that it was made on his behalf by an agent authorised to act for him at the time, or whose act has been subsequently ratified and adopted by him. The law obviously requires that the person for whom the agent professes to act must be a person capable of being ascertained at the time. It is not necessary that he should be named; but there must be such a description of him as shall amount to a reasonable designation of the person intended to be bound by the contract'.

In *Watson v Swann* an insurance broker was instructed to effect an open policy for the plaintiff against the danger of jettison, but was unable to do so since underwriters were not prepared to insure on account of bad weather. Instead, he declared certain deck cargo on the back of a general policy which he had previously effected for himself 'upon any kind of goods and merchandise, as interest might appear'. This document was duly initialled by the underwriters. A loss having been sustained, it was held, for the reasons stated above, that the plaintiff could not sue the underwriters upon this policy since the contract was not made by him. Nor was it made on his behalf, since at the time when the policy was effected by the agent the principal was not even known to him. A valid ratification is therefore dependent upon the principal having been capable of ascertainment at the time when the act of the 'agent' was performed.

However, some cases, especially in the area of marine insurance, suggest that Willes J's statement may be too narrowly expressed. Marine insurance policies are regularly taken out 'for the benefit of all those to whom they may appertain'. In *Hagedorn v Oliverson*[18] the agent took out insurance policies on goods generally on behalf of every person interested in them. It was held that any such person could subsequently ratify the insurance policy and sue the underwriters. In such cases it is commonly recognised that if the agent effects a policy subject to ratification, since loss may easily occur before ratification, this possibility can be taken to have been envisaged by the parties when they entered into the contract. Indeed, the selfsame reasoning has even been applied outside the realm of marine insurance. The guiding principle was expressed by Colman J in the following way:

'Where at the time when the contract of insurance was made the principal assured or other contracting party had no actual authority to bind the other party to the contract of insurance, but the policy is expressed to insure not only the principal assured but also a class of others who are not identified in that policy, a party who at the time when the policy was effected could have been ascertained to

18   (1814) 2 M & S 485.

qualify as a member of that class can ratify and sue on the policy as co-assured if at that time it was intended by the principal assured or other contracting party to create privity of contract with the insurers on behalf of that particular party'.[19]

Logically, it is difficult to see why ratification should be excluded in cases where the agent has acted in this manner or even where he has merely stated that he is acting 'for a principal'. If third parties (eg underwriters) are willing to contract under such terms and if principals are prepared to ratify such contracts, there seems no reason why the law should refuse to give effect to the parties' collective wishes, not least because it serves an obvious commercial convenience.

(c) The third requirement which should be noted is that *the principal must be competent at the time when the act was done by the agent.* This requirement overlaps to a certain extent with the notion, already examined, that the principal must be in existence at the time when the agent acts. The typical case, of course, concerns infants. Clearly, acts which can be done by infants can also be done by agents and if the agent has no authority the infant may, if he chooses, later ratify the unauthorised act. Thus, contracts for necessaries which can be made by an infant can also be made by agents acting for and on behalf of the infant. But where an act falls foul of the Infants Relief Act 1874 (as amended), then, since it cannot be done by the infant, it cannot perhaps be done through an agent. Section 1 of the 1874 Act states that:

'All contracts whether by specialty or simple contract, henceforth entered into by infants for the repayment of money lent or to be lent, or for goods supplied or to be supplied (other than necessaries) and all accounts stated with infants shall be absolutely void'.

Although an attentive reading of s 2 of the Infants Relief Act 1874 appeared to exclude such an interpretation[20], repeal of that provision by s 1 of the Minors' Contracts Act 1987 has possibly opened the way to an infant ratifying acts purportedly done on his behalf during infancy by an agent. Whether such a view recommends itself to the courts remains to be seen. Whilst it would be consistent with the general policy pursued in relation to ratification of infants' bargains, that has now resuscitated the traditional common law rule that a promise to perform an obligation, made during infancy, can in all

---

19 *National Oilwells (UK) Ltd v Davy Offshore Ltd* [1993] 2 Lloyd's Rep 582, 596–7. See also Reynolds 'Some Agency Problems in Insurance Law' in Rose (ed) *Consensus ad idem* (1996, London), esp at pp 82–3.

20 See 2nd Edn of this book, p 55.

cases be revived by a fresh promise without consideration after attaining the age of majority, the analogous cases of alien enemies and bankruptcy would postulate a different view.

Take the case where an alien enemy acts through an agent. In *Boston Deep Sea Fishing and Ice Co Ltd v Farnham (Inspector of Taxes)*[1] the appellants, who were a company of trawler owners, took control of a trawler belonging to a French company (in which they had a share) which happened to be in an English port when France fell to the Germans. The French company later purported to ratify all of the appellants' acts. Harman J held that at the time when the acts were done the French company was an alien enemy at common law. It was not a competent principal because it could not have done the acts itself and, therefore, its ratification of them was neither valid nor operative.

It is not enough that the principal simply has the capacity to ratify an act. The principal must in addition have possessed this capacity *at the time of the purported ratification.* In *Bird v Brown*[2] the defendants, acting undoubtedly in the interests of the consignor of goods but without his authority, ordered their stoppage in transitu. Transit had, in fact, ended and the goods would have been in the hands of the consignee (or his trustee in bankruptcy) but for the wrongful refusal of the captain of the vessel to deliver them up to him. Subsequently, the consignor ratified the agent's stoppage in transit. The court held that the ratification could not divest the trustee in bankruptcy of his right to possession, for at the time of ratification of the consignor no longer had the right to ratify the acts of the 'agent'.[3] Similarly, in *Dibbins v Dibbins*[4] the principal's ratification was held to be inoperative. Articles of partnership provided that, on the death of either partner, the survivor should have the option of purchasing the deceased's shares provided that he gave notice within three months of the death. The surviving partner was of unsound mind and his solicitor gave notice on his behalf. At that time the agent had no authority since his principal was insane. Later, however, an order was made under the Lunacy Acts authorising that notice be given on his behalf and this was duly done. By this time, however,

1   [1957] 3 All ER 204. See *Firth v Staines* [1897] 2 QB 70 at 75 per Wright J; Extract 21, p 246.
2   (1850) 4 Exch 786.
3   *Bird v Brown* (1850) 4 Exch 786 is also authority for the view that the retroactive effect of ratification will not be permitted to deprive a stranger to the contract of any property rights which had vested in him before ratification. See also the statement of Cotton LJ in *Bolton Partners v Lambert* (1889) 41 Ch D 295, 307 that 'an estate once vested cannot be divested ... by the application of the doctrine of ratification.'
4   [1896] 2 Ch 348.

the three-month period had elapsed. Not surprisingly, the court held that it was too late to ratify the original notice because at the time of ratification the principal had lost his option to purchase the shares.

Situations in cases like *Bird v Brown* and in *Dibbins v Dibbins*, where property rights are involved or where the validity of an act is contingent upon its being performed within a stipulated time limit, are to be distinguished from cases where the principal simply ratifies after the expiry of a time limit. In the most recent case of this latter type, *Presentaciones Musicales SA v Secunda*,[5] solicitors, who mistakenly believed that they enjoyed authority, issued a writ on behalf of a Panamanian company in April 1988 for breach of agency agreements and breach of copyright in respect of recordings of Jimi Hendrix concerts. In March 1991, the defendant learned that the company was in liquidation and sought to have the action struck out. In May 1991 the company liquidators purported to ratify the act of the solicitors. The question for the Court of Appeal was whether the unauthorised act could be ratified after expiry of the three-year limitation period applicable to the cause of action. The court held that it could. As is the case whenever there is a defect in a writ, the issue of this particular writ without authority was not a nullity merely because the solicitor acted without the sanction of the nominal plaintiff. Consequently, the latter was entitled to ratify after the limitation period, provided that the effect was not to extend the period for doing any relevant thing. Such was not the case here, as time was held to run from the date of the writ's issue. This case, along with others, suggests that, at least where the vesting of property rights is not in issue, if a time limit has been imposed for the accomplishment of a particular act or, say, for the acceptance of a contractual offer, the court will examine the purpose of the time limit and will only forbid ratification by the principal if expiry of the time limit is intended to affect the validity of the transaction.

The rule that the principal must have capacity to do the acts in question is also relevant in the context of company law. At common law, acts which were purportedly done on behalf of a company but which were *ultra vires* its statutes were totally without effect and could not be ratified, even by a unanimous vote of its shareholders[6]. This is no longer true for companies incorporated under the Companies Acts. Thus s 35(1) of the Companies Act 1985 (as inserted by s 108(1) of the Companies Act 1989) states that: 'The validity of an act done by a company *shall not be called into question* on the ground of lack of

5   [1994] Ch 271.
6   *Rolled Steel Products (Holdings) Ltd v British Steel Corpn* [1982] Ch 478, [1982] 3 All ER 1057.

capacity by reason of anything in the company's memorandum.' It will be noted that the italicised words suggest both that the company cannot rely on its own incapacity and, equally, that persons who have contracted with the company will not be allowed to invoke such lack of capacity in order to extricate themselves from any negotiated deals.[7] Finally, s 35(3) of the Companies Act 1985 has altered the common law in yet another way by providing for ratification (by special resolution) of acts of directors which, but for s 35(1) noted above, would be beyond the company's capacity.

(d) Finally, as stressed at the beginning of this chapter, *the principal can ratify only if it is shown that the agent was acting on his behalf.* In *Jones v Hope*[8] Thesiger LJ said,

'If there is one legal principle better established than another it is this, that nobody can ratify a contract purporting to be made by an agent except the party on whose behalf the agent purported to act'.

Thus, if A purports to act on behalf of P, P and no one else can ratify his act. What is important, however, is not what is in the agent's mind but what was reasonably understood by the third party. It is therefore incumbent upon the agent to make his intention to contract on behalf of another person obvious to the third party if the so-called principal is to be allowed to ratify the transaction. If the agent's *secret* intention was to contract for himself but he conveyed the impression to the third party that he was acting for another person, that other person may ratify the contract.

In *Re Tiedemann and Ledermann Frères*[9] an agent who had sold wheat for the principal noticed that the price was rising. He bought it back and re-sold it on the same day for a profit, purporting to act for the principal but in reality acting for himself. Third parties became suspicious and, when wheat prices began to fall, repudiated the contracts. The principal, then, having learned of his agent's speculations, sought to ratify these contracts and Channell J held that he was entitled to adopt them. Third parties were not disadvantaged in so far as they had purportedly contracted with the principal from the outset. True, the principal had gained a windfall, but in the absence of fraud on his part there was no reason to deprive him of the benefit of these transactions.

---

7   Members of the company are protected by s 35(2) which allows them to bring proceedings to restrain the company from doing an act which, but for the said s 35(1), would be beyond its capacity.
8   (1880) 3 TLR 247n at 251.
9   [1899] 2 QB 66.

Conversely, if an agent intends to act for his principal but fails to communicate this to the third party, then the principal cannot ratify. In *Keighley, Maxsted & Co v Durant*[10] R was authorised by the appellants to purchase a quantity of wheat at a certain price on joint account for himself and the appellants. He concluded a contract with the respondents at a slightly higher price without revealing that he was also acting for the appellants. The following day the appellants ratified the agreement and were subsequently sued by the sellers for not taking delivery. The House of Lords held that a contract made only by a person intending to contract on behalf of a third party, but without his authority, cannot be ratified by him so as to enable him to sue or be sued on the contract if the person who made the contract did not make it clear at the time of its making that he was acting for another party. Lord Macnaghten, after citing Tindal CJ's judgment in *Wilson v Tumman*[11], added:

'... a person ratifying the act of another, who, without authority, had made a contract openly and avowedly on his behalf, is deemed to be, though in fact he was not, a party to the contract. Does this fiction cover the case of a person who makes no avowal at all, but assumes to act for himself and for no-one else? If Tindal CJ's statement of the law is accurate, it would seem to exclude the case of a person who may intend to act for another, but at the same time keeps his intention locked up in his own breast; for it cannot be said that a person who so conducts himself does assume to act for anybody but himself'[12].

In this respect, English law treats disclosed and undisclosed principals differently since it only allows the former to ratify unauthorised acts. This duality of approach has been recently criticised by one American writer[13], but even he accepts that the present position is so well entrenched that it is unlikely to be altered by the courts. Indeed, in *Welsh Development Agency v Export Finance Co Ltd* Dillon LJ recently recognised this as 'clear law'.[14]

---

10 [1901] AC 240; see Extract 22, p 246. *Spiro v Lintern*, discussed above at pp 49–50, may, however, have provided a new way of binding the undisclosed principal where the conditions laid down in that case are satisfied.
11 (1843) 6 Man & G 236, 242.
12 [1901] AC 240 at 247.
13 Rochvarg 'Ratification and Undisclosed principals' (1989) 34 McGill LJ 286.
14 [1992] BCLC 148.

(ii) What acts may be ratified

Every act which can be done through an agent can be ratified by the person in whose name it was done, irrespective of whether it is lawful or unlawful. But acts which are void *ab initio* cannot be ratified. It is convenient to draw this distinction between unlawful and void acts.

(a) *Void acts.* Taking first the case of void acts, we have already seen that a company may not exceed its statutory powers and that every act done in excess of those powers is *ultra vires* the company and without effect. Thus, in *Ashbury Railway Carriage and Iron Co v Riche*[15] the directors of a company concluded an *ultra vires* contract. The contract could not be made binding on the company even though it subsequently received the approval of all its shareholders. The House of Lords held that, since the contract was void in its inception in that it clearly fell outside the provisions of the company's memorandum of association, it could not be ratified even by the assent of the whole body of shareholders. (As indicated above, this particular decision has now to be read in the light of s 35 of the Companies Act 1985). The position is different, of course, if the act done is *intra vires* the company but beyond the powers of the directors. As has already been stated, such acts may properly be ratified by the company.

Although the majority of cases in this area of the law of agency are concerned with companies, there is authority to support the view that the same principles apply to other species of void act. In *Brook v Hook*[16] for example, the court relied on the distinction between void and voidable acts. It is well-known that void acts are (in most cases) complete nullities whereas voidable acts are valid until they have been avoided. In *Brook v Hook* the defendant's name was forged by his brother-in-law in a promissory note given to the plaintiff. Before the note matured, the plaintiff saw the defendant and told him about the note. When the plaintiff discovered that the defendant had never signed the note, he threatened to bring legal proceedings. The defendant, anxious to avoid this, signed a memorandum purporting to ratify the act done on his behalf. It was held that the act itself was illegal, void and, therefore, incapable of ratification. In the words of Kelly CB:

'... the paper in question is no ratification, inasmuch as the act done — that is, the signature to the note — is illegal and void; and ...

---

15 (1875) LR 7 HL 653. See also, *Rolled Steel Products (Holdings) Ltd v British Steel Corpn* [1982] Ch 478, [1982] 3 All ER 1057.
16 (1871) LR 6 Exch 89.

although a *voidable* act may be ratified by matter subsequent, it is otherwise when an act is *originally and in its inception void*[17].

It would seem to follow from this pronouncement that a voidable act may be ratified whereas a void act cannot. However, one of the problems which accompanies this distinction is that there are cases where it is most difficult for the courts to decide whether the act in question should properly be regarded as void ab initio or voidable. For example, in *Danish Mercantile Co Ltd v Beaumont*[18] it was held that commencement of proceedings without the plaintiff's authority would result in an action being stayed. But it was open to the purported plaintiff to ratify his solicitor's act and to adopt the proceedings with the result that the original defect in the proceedings would be treated as cured[19]. The judgments in *Danish Mercantile Co Ltd v Beaumont* can only be reconciled with Kelly CB's dicta in *Brook v Hook* if one treats the unauthorised acts of the solicitor as voidable rather than void ab initio.

(b) *Unlawful acts.* Even unlawful acts may be ratified. The significance of this principle is two-fold. Firstly, a principal may, by ratifying an unauthorised act, retrospectively transform what was at the outset unlawful into something lawful. Thus, in *Whitehead v Taylor*[20] A distrained some goods in the name of B's landlord but without actually having the landlord's authority or consent. The landlord later approved the distraint and it was therefore deemed by the court to have been levied with his authority. Secondly, this rule may render the principal liable for the unlawful acts and, more particularly, for the torts committed by his agent. The extent of this liability is the subject of some dispute. The majority of cases dealing with this question are concerned with the torts of conversion and trespass. Without examining them in detail, the general position is stated by *Bowstead* in the following fashion:

'the doctrine of ratification, in so far as it makes one liable for the torts of another (as opposed to providing a defence to an action in tort), normally applies only to conversion, and possibly also to trespass to goods, where the fields of contract, tort and property overlap and liability is strict; and that in torts requiring personal fault it should not be regarded as significant'[1].

---

17 Ibid, at 99 (emphasis added).
18 [1951] Ch 680.
19 Ibid, at 687 per Jenkins LJ.
20 (1839) 10 Ad & El 210.
1   *Bowstead and Reynolds* para 2-052A.

(iii) Effects of ratification

In *Boston Deep Sea Fishing and Ice Co Ltd v Farnham (Inspector of Taxes)*[2] Harman J said: 'Ratification as we all know has a retroactive effect'. Ratification, therefore, produces ex post facto a situation which is analogous to the normal agency relationship. Firstly, it has the effect of vesting the person in whose name the acts were done with all the rights and duties which a principal would normally have vis-à-vis the third party with whom his agent has contracted. In *Risbourg v Bruckner*[3] an agent had purportedly acted on behalf of another person. This person subsequently ratified the agent's contract. In consequence of this ratification of the agent's acts, only the third party could be sued for breach of contract because the agent had dropped out of the transaction as soon as the contract had been ratified. Similarly, in *Buron v Denman*[4] we have already seen that the naval commander who freed the slaves could no longer be sued by their Spanish owner since the Crown, by ratifying his acts, had rendered them acts of state. Secondly, ratification may give the agent rights against his so-called principal, which he would not otherwise have enjoyed. In *Keay v Fenwick*[5] an agent, acting on the instructions of the managing owner of a ship, sold the vessel to a third party. The other co-owners of the vessel later approved the sale and the court held that they, too, along with the managing owner, were liable to the agent for his commission.

To summarise the position after ratification, one can say: (a) that the principal may sue or be sued by the third party after ratification; (b) that, as against the third party, the agent is discharged of all liability, especially for breach of warranty of authority (see below), unless he himself is a party to the contract in which case he, too, can sue or be sued; (c) that the agent cannot be held liable for exceeding his authority; and (d) that the principal will become liable to pay the agent reasonable remuneration or any indemnity for loss sustained by him.

It is important to note that ratification relates only to *past* acts and does not confer authority upon the agent to perform further acts. In *Irvine v Union Bank of Australia*[6] the directors of a company borrowed money in excess of their powers. Their unauthorised act was subsequently ratified by a majority of the shareholders. Ratification, however, was held not to be tantamount to authority

2   [1957] 3 All ER 204, [1957] 1 WLR 1051.
3   (1858) 3 CBNS 812.
4   (1848) 2 Exch 167.
5   (1876) 1 CPD 745.
6   (1877) 2 App Cas 366.

for the directors to continue borrowing in excess of their powers. This could be achieved only by the directors' complying with the company's articles of association and increasing their powers to borrow[7].

The retroactive effects of ratification can pose some difficult problems to which we must now turn our attention. Let us take the following situation: A purports to act as P's agent. T makes A an offer to sell him ten tons of wheat which A accepts. P, however, has not ratified the contract yet. Can T revoke his offer? The general principles of the law of contract tell us that an offer may be revoked before it has been accepted by the offeree. But who is the offeree in this case? Is it A or P? It is not A because T knew that A was not acting for himself but for P. On the other hand, P is not liable until he ratifies the contract. Nevertheless, once he has ratified, his ratification is held to have retrospective effects. Therefore, the contract in a sense will already have been concluded. For these reasons the usual rules of contract do not apply in this situation and we can say that T is bound and cannot revoke his offer even though P is not bound until he decides to ratify. If he does, then there is a contract between him and T, and P can sue or be sued by T. If he does not, T can do nothing more than sue A for breach of warranty of authority.

The above were the facts in the difficult case of *Bolton Partners v Lambert*[8] where the principal ratified his agent's act (an acceptance of an offer) after the third party had attempted to revoke his offer. The court here held that the third party was bound by his contract with the principal. The case could be explained by regarding the agent's acceptance as 'an act which can be repudiated or adopted by the principal at will, and so can give rise to a binding contract, which may be taken as having come into existence before the offeror attempted to revoke'. But the decision in *Bolton Partners v Lambert* potentially has some unsatisfactory implications for, if an offer is made to a person who professes to be the agent of a principal but who in fact has no authority to accept it on behalf of the so-called principal, the person making the offer will be in a worse position as regards withdrawing it than if it had been made directly to the principal. The acceptance of the unauthorised agent will bind the purchaser to the 'principal', but will not in any way bind the 'principal' to the purchaser. As Fry LJ pointed out:

'It seems to follow from (the above) that the intervention of a mere stranger may prevent a person who has made an offer from

7   Cf *Restatement of the Law of Agency* (2nd Edn, 1958), para 43(2).
8   (1889) 41 Ch D 295; see Extract 23, p 247.

withdrawing that offer until it be seen whether the person to whom it is made will ratify it or not, and consequently places that person in the difficult position of neither having a contract nor a right to withdraw an offer'[9].

At first sight, therefore, the retroactivity of ratification and the decision in *Bolton v Lambert* may create the impression that the position of the third party in such cases is unduly prejudiced. However, limitations to the rule in *Bolton v Lambert* have been worked out in practice and several in particular should be noted.

Firstly, ratification of a contract must take place within a reasonable time after its conclusion in order that the period of uncertainty should last as short a time as possible. This qualification of the doctrine in *Bolton v Lambert* was introduced in the case of *Metropolitan Asylums Board Managers v Kingham & Sons*[10] which involved an action for breach of contract to supply eggs. At the beginning of September 1888 the plaintiff, who was the manager of the Asylum, advertised for the supply of various foods. On 18 September the defendants put in a tender for eggs at a certain price for a period of six months commencing on 30 September 1888. On 22 September the Board of the Asylum met and passed a resolution accepting the defendants' offer, but it forgot to affix the corporation's seal on the acceptance. On the same day the plaintiff's clerk wrote to the defendants' clerk and informed him that the offer had been accepted. On 24 September the defendants withdrew their tender on the ground that they had made a mistake in the price when drawing up the tender. On 6 October at a meeting of the plaintiff company the acceptance was ratified and the seal affixed. Fry LJ held that the plaintiff could not rely on *Bolton v Lambert* for 'if the ratification is to bind, it must be made within a reasonable time after acceptance by an unauthorised person'[11]. Although in the *Metropolitan Asylums* case a

---

9   *Specific Performance* (6th Edn, 1921), p 733. Similarly critical is Wambaugh 9 Harv LR 60 (1895).

10   (1890) 6 TLR 217; see Extract 24, p 249.

11   In the same case Fry LJ, a known opponent of the rule in *Bolton v Lambert*, qualified the statement reproduced in the text above by adding the following rider: '… reasonable time can never extend after the time at which the contract is to commence'. This statement, however, was found to be too wide and was therefore not followed in *Bedford Insurance Co Ltd v Instituto de Resseguros do Brasil* [1985] QB 966, [1984] 3 All ER 766. The latter case suggests instead that ratification after the commencement of the contract could be valid if it was in favour of rather than against the interests of the third party. (Ratification of an unauthorised contract of insurance by the insurer after it had come into force should be valid against him since this would benefit the insured.)

delay of ten days was held to be unreasonable, too much should not be read into this. In the case of *Re Portuguese Consolidated Copper Mines Ltd*[12] Bowen LJ observed that 'mere time is nothing except with reference to the circumstances'. The criterion which is to be applied in such cases is the sensible one — what is reasonable in the circumstances of each case. 'Prima facie', said Bowen LJ, 'an offer made is a continuing offer until such time as indicated either by the parties, or by some good reason, for closing with it or refusing it. It is a question of fact in each case what the reasonable time is'[13]. If, on the other hand, for some reason ratification has to take place within a fixed time and this has expired, ratification will not be permitted to prejudice other parties. In the case of *Dibbins v Dibbins*[14], mentioned above, it will be remembered that the solicitor of the insane partner was not allowed to purchase on his behalf the shares of the dead partner as ratification took place after expiry of the three months allowed for exercise of the option to purchase the shares.

Secondly, the doctrine of *Bolton v Lambert* can be avoided if it can be shown that the third party's offer was *expressly* made subject to ratification. In such cases the offer is conditional and can be withdrawn since there is no binding contract until the agent's acceptance has been ratified. In *Watson v Davies*[15] the defendant made an offer to sell some property to some members of the board of a charity (the principal) which they accepted. The secretary of the board, however, stated that the deputation which had been shown the property in question and to whom the offer was made did not represent a quorum of the board and, therefore, could not act as a properly constituted board. Some days later the defendant revoked his offer. The entire board of the charity nevertheless proceeded to ratify the acceptance of the defendant's offer given by some of its members a few days earlier. It was held that the defendant was entitled to withdraw his offer since the members of the deputation had not warranted their authority to bind the board and it was clear that their acceptance of the defendant's offer was subject to ratification by the board properly constituted. *Watson v Davies* was followed in *Warehousing and Forwarding Co of East Africa Ltd v Jafferali & Sons Ltd*[16] (a case not without ambiguities) in which, inter alia, it

---

12 (1890) 45 Ch D 16 at 35.
13 Ibid. The time within which ratification must take place will, therefore, be abridged whenever the third party informs the 'principal' of his wish to withdraw from the contract.
14 [1896] 2 Ch 348.
15 [1931] 1 Ch 455; see Extract 25, p 250.
16 [1964] AC 1 at 9–10.

was said by Lord Guest that when the '(third) party to the contract has intimation of the limitation of the agent's authority neither party can be bound until ratification has been duly intimated to the other (third) party to the contract'. It would therefore appear from these authorities that the rule in *Bolton v Lambert* will only apply in cases where the third party is *not expressly warned* that the contract is subject to the principal's ratification. But, if, on the contrary, it has been indicated to the third party that the contract is subject to ratification by the principal, then either party can withdraw prior to communication to the third party of the fact that the principal has ratified.

The potential harshness of the retroactive effect of ratification is also avoided in two further instances. Firstly, it would appear that it is open to the third party and the agent to cancel their transaction by mutual consent before the principal ratifies it[17]. Secondly, as already mentioned, it is said that the doctrine of relation back will not be allowed to deprive a stranger to the contract of any proprietary rights vested in him before the moment of ratification[18].

Finally, it could be argued that the rule in *Bolton v Lambert* is further mitigated by the rule that if the third party commits what amounts to a breach of contract after the time of the agent's acceptance but prior to the principal ratifying the contract, he will not subsequently be held liable to the principal[19]. Thus, if T offers to work for X, and A purportedly accepts on X's behalf, X can subsequently ratify T's employment. But if T changes his mind and decides to work for Y after A's acceptance but before X's ratification of A's acceptance, T will not be liable to X, even if X eventually ratifies A's act.

From the above it should be clear that the harshness of *Bolton v Lambert* has probably been exaggerated. Its critics not only seem to ignore the considerable number of exceptions but also overlook the fact that if the principal ratifies, the third party will have obtained what he expected, and that if the principal does not ratify, the third party will then have an action against the agent for breach of warranty of authority (which will be discussed in section 2 of this chapter). Therefore, in the final analysis, the main hardship suffered by the third party is the possibility of uncertainty that may endure until the principal decides whether he wishes to ratify the contract or not. But

17 *Walter v James* (1871) LR 6 Exch 124.
18 *Bird v Brown* (1850) 4 Exch 786.
19 *Kidderminster Corpn v Hardwick* (1873) LR 9 Exch 13. In this sense *Fridman*, p 102. It should be noted, however, that *Kidderminster* was not referred to in *Bolton Partners v Lambert* and the two approaches are not easily reconcilable.

even this period of uncertainty can be curtailed if the third party informs the principal of his wish to withdraw from the contract.

(iv)   Method of ratification

Ratification may be either express or implied. Express ratification causes no difficulties and is self-explanatory. Implied ratification, however, must be deduced from the conduct of the 'principal' and the surrounding circumstances. In *The Bonita, The Charlotte*[20] Lushington J expressed the view obiter that if the shipmaster of a vessel sold it without the authority of its owner, and the latter subsequently received the money in full knowledge of the circumstances in which the vessel was sold, such a receipt could amount to ratification of the transaction. To similar effect, in *Waithman v Wakefield*[1] a wife purchased goods which were not necessaries and the husband kept them, refusing to return them to the vendor. It was held that the husband's conduct was tantamount to ratification of his wife's acts and he should, therefore, pay for the goods.

Whether silence can amount to ratification is a different matter. In one Commonwealth case, *Crampsey v Deveney*,[2] it was suggested that silence could not amount to ratification. As Wilson J pointed out in a subsequent Canadian decision in which she applied this reasoning, an intention to ratify can by no means be automatically read into someone's inertia. Indeed, in this particular case, she concluded that,

'silence and inactivity are not evidence of approval and adoption of the contract but rather of disquiet, disapproval and ignorance of rights, and, in the case of o .e of (the three children involved in the case), lack of knowledge that a contract had been made.'[3]

Some doubt still surrounds the question as to the effect produced by implied ratification by the 'principal' of only some of the acts performed by the agent[4]. Generally speaking, the better view appears to be that the principal cannot 'blow hot and cold', at the same time affirming the part of the contract which suits him and disaffirming the part which he dislikes. To allow him to do so would in effect mean that a *new* contract would come into existence into which the third party had never intended to enter. The adoption of part of a transaction should, therefore, be treated as ratification of the whole.

20   (1861) 1 Lush 252.
1   (1807) 1 Camp 120.
2   (1969) 2 DLR (3d) 161 at 164 per Judson J.
3   *713860 Ontario Ltd v Royal Trust Corpn of Canada* 22 January 1996, unreported (Ontario).
4   For a range of views, see Powell *The Law of Agency* (2nd Edn, 1960), p 138; and *Bowstead and Reynolds* para 2-077.

Finally, it should be noted that authority to conclude a contract which has to be evidenced in writing does not itself have to be in writing and, consequently, neither does the ratification of such a contract. Ratification of an act done by deed, however, is required to be in the form of a deed.

2 LIABILITY FOR WARRANTY OF AUTHORITY BY THE AGENT

Throughout this chapter we have been dealing with cases where the agent lacked authority. In the preceding paragraphs we have examined the consequences of ratification. In those cases the principal decides to adopt his 'agent's' acts and a posteriori an agency relationship arises. However, it may happen that the person in whose name and on whose behalf the agent purported to act never ratifies the acts. In such cases the 'principal' clearly incurs no liability and the question arises, what remedy can the third party pursue against the would-be agent? The answer is that, 'when the agent has no actual or ostensible authority' and the principal refuses to ratify, the third party must 'look for his remedy to the agent and rely, if he can, on breach by that agent of his implied warranty of authority'[5]. Therefore, the simple but not necessarily effective remedy available to the third party is to sue the agent. We now turn to examine this right of action.

If the agent has contracted personally, no problem arises as the third party can sue him on the contract. Whether the agent has contracted personally is entirely a question of construction of the relevant documents and the surrounding circumstances and this question will be examined in a later chapter. But if the agent is not a party to the contract, he will still incur liability since the third party has relied on his representation of authority. The nature of his liability, however, will depend on his state of mind. If the agent is fraudulent, the third party may either sue him in tort for deceit or he may choose to sue him for breach of warranty of authority. Liability in tort can also be based on the agent's negligence if the circumstances of the case fall within the ambit of the rule in *Hedley Byrne & Co Ltd v Heller & Partners Ltd*[6]. But it is more probable that the negligent agent will be sued for breach of his warranty of authority, unless the different measure of damages between actions

5   See Mocatta J in *Rasnoimport V/O v Guthrie & Co Ltd* [1966] 1 Lloyd's Rep 1 at 10. The decision is critically discussed by Reynolds in (1967) 83 LQR 189. See also *Grace Shipping Inc and Hai Nguan v CF Sharp & Co (Malaya) Pte Ltd* [1987] 1 Lloyd's Rep 207.
6   [1964] AC 465, [1963] 2 All ER 575. Liability in deceit will be incurred even if the agent believed that the principal would ratify: *Polhill v Walter* (1832) 3 B & Ad 114.

based on negligence or breach of warranty of authority (discussed briefly at the end of this section) makes it preferable for the plaintiff to try and base his action on negligence.

Actions for breach of warranty of authority will be justified whenever a person, *however innocently*, represents to a third party that he has authority to act for another person and the third party is thereby induced to act in a manner in which he would not have acted had the representation not been made. In such circumstances the so-called agent is deemed to have warranted the truth of his representation and will be liable for loss caused to the third party for breach of this warranty. This will be the case even if he acted in complete good faith, or mistakenly believing that he had such authority. Moreover, it should be noted that the mere fact that the agent has no ostensible or actual authority is not sufficient to exclude the implication of a warranty of such authority. In this manner, a master or an agent for the shipowner used to be held impliedly to warrant his authority even though it was clearly asserted in the nineteenth century case of *Grant v Norway*[7] that neither had ostensible authority to sign for goods which were not actually shipped.[8] This decision, which ran contrary to principle, did receive some House of Lords' support in the company law context.[9] However, the rule in *Grant v Norway* was the subject of persistent criticism[10] and has now been reversed by s 4 of the Carriage of Goods by Sea Act 1992, which provides that where a bill of lading has been signed by the master of a vessel, that shall be taken as 'conclusive evidence against the carrier of the shipment of the goods or ... of their receipt for shipment.'

The nature of the agent's liability for breach of warranty of authority has been widely discussed amongst academics. His liability has at times been described as 'contractual', 'quasi-contractual' or arising from a 'collateral contract'. Indeed, since *Hedley Byrne* there may even be instances where the liability can be described as tortious. Historically, the agent's liability for breach of his warranty of authority was regarded as contractual, especially since tortious liability was excluded in most cases and could only arise where there was evidence of fraud. Its contractual origins may serve to explain the absolute liability which is imposed on 'agents' of this kind,

7   (1851) 10 CB 665.
8   *Rasnoimport V/O v Guthrie & Co Ltd* [1966] 1 Lloyd's Rep 1.
9   *George Whitechurch Ltd v Cavanagh* [1902] AC 117.
10 See, eg, Munday 'The Curious Case of the Master's Ostensible Authority: Reflections on *The Saudi Crown*' (1986) 136 NLJ 508. The courts also tended to restrict the influence of the case: *The Nea Tyhi* [1982] 1 Lloyd's Rep 606; *The Saudi Crown* [1986] 1 Lloyd's Rep 261; *Blue Nile Co Ltd v Emery Customs Brokers (S) Pte Ltd* (1991) 320 LMLN 2.

virtually making them guarantors of their authority. In principle, the rule is severe and it would be more equitable to hold agents liable only if they had fraudulently or negligently represented that they possessed authority. But in fact there are some cases where statute has intervened to mitigate the rigours of the rule[11].

In spite of various attempts to confine the agent's liability to cases where he has acted negligently[12], the position generally is that the agent will be liable for breach of his warranty of authority no matter how innocently he may have acted. Thus, in *Yonge v Toynbee*[13] solicitors were instructed by a client to conduct his defence in an action which was then threatened and was later commenced against him. Before commencement of the action the client became insane and was certified as being of unsound mind. In ignorance of this fact the solicitors entered an appearance for him in the action and delivered a defence, to which the plaintiff replied. Further interlocutory proceedings then took place. Subsequently, when the plaintiffs discovered that their client was insane, they applied for the appearance and all subsequent proceedings to be struck out and for the defendant's solicitors to pay personally all their costs. The court held that the solicitors who had taken it upon themselves to act for the defendant in the action had thereby impliedly warranted that they had authority to do so and, therefore, were personally liable to pay the plaintiffs' costs in the action. The Court of Appeal in *Yonge v Toynbee* affirmed without reservation the earlier decision of *Collen v Wright*[14]. In that case Wright had acted as land agent for a man called Gardner and leased to the plaintiff for a period of twelve and a half years land belonging to Gardner. Gardner alleged and proved that he had conferred no authority upon Wright to agree a lease for so long a time. On discovering this, the plaintiff's solicitors wrote to Wright and said that if their action against Gardner was dismissed for lack of authority they would hold Wright liable for all costs and damages. Their action against Gardner was duly dismissed and the question for the court was whether Wright's estate could in fact be held liable. Willes J, delivering the judgment of the Court of Appeal, stated the law in the following manner:

'I am of opinion that a person, who induces another to contract with him as the agent of a third party by an unqualified assertion of his being authorised to act as such agent, is answerable to the person who so contracts for any damages which he may sustain by reason of

11   See eg Trustee Act 1925, s 29; Law of Property Act 1925, s 124.
12   *Smout v Ilbery* (1842) 10 M & W 1.
13   [1910] 1 KB 215; see Extract 27, p 254.
14   (1857) 8 E & B 647.

the assertion of authority being untrue ... The fact that the professed agent honestly thinks that he has the authority affects the moral character of his act; but his moral innocence, so far as the person whom he has induced to contract is concerned, in no way aids such person or alleviates the inconvenience and damage which he sustains. The obligation arising in such a case is well expressed by saying that a person, professing to contract as agent for another, impliedly if not expressly, undertakes to or promises the person who enters into such contract upon the faith of the professed agent being duly authorised, that the authority which he professes to have does in point of fact exist. *The fact of entering into the transaction with the professed agent, as such, is good consideration for the promise*[15].

The final sentence quoted from Willes J's judgment has been italicised because it supports the view taken both by Cheshire, Fifoot and Furmston[16] as well as by Wedderburn[17] that the agent's liability in such cases is based on a collateral contract made with the third party. It is true that one can argue that Willes J's judgment constructs a *new* and *independent* contract between the so-called principal and the third party based upon the exchange of promises: on the one side, the promise that the authority exists and on the other, the promise to perform the contractual obligations. The consequences of *Collen v Wright, Yonge v Toynbee*, and many other similar cases were conveniently summarised by Buckley LJ in *Yonge v Toynbee* where he stated:

'... the liability of the person who professes to act as agent arises (*a*) if he has been fraudulent, (*b*) if he has without fraud untruly represented that he had authority when he had not, and (*c*) also where he innocently misrepresents that he has authority where the fact is either (1) that he has never had authority or (2) that his original authority has ceased by reasons of fact or knowledge. Such last-mentioned liability arises from the fact that by professing to act as agent he impliedly contracts that he has authority, and it is immaterial whether he knew of the defect of his authority or not'[18].

Buckley LJ, however, went on to qualify these remarks, saying:

'This implied contract may ... be excluded by the facts of the particular case. If, for instance, the agent proved that at the relevant time he told the party with whom he was contracting that he did not know whether the warrant of attorney under which he was acting

15   Ibid, at 657–8 (emphasis added).
16   *The Law of Contract* (13th Edn, 1996), p 509.
17   [1959] CLJ 58 at 68.
18   [1910] 1 KB 215 at 227.

was genuine or not, and would not warrant its validity, or that his principal was abroad and did not know whether he was still living, there will have been no representation upon which the implied contract will arise ...'

Thus in *Halbot v Lens*[19], where the agent informed the third party that he had no authority to sign a contract, the court held that he could not be made liable for breach of warranty of authority. Similar considerations have been held to apply where the third party *ought* to have known that the agent was not warranting his authority[20].

The doctrine of warranty of authority has a wide application and may be invoked even in cases where the representation arises only impliedly or by conduct. Thus, in *Stuart v Haigh*[1] A, a shipbroker, signed a charterparty on behalf of P adding the words 'by telegraphic authority of P'. A was P's agent but had no power to authorise the charterparty. The shipbroker was held liable for breach of an implied warranty that he had authority to make the charterparty on behalf of P, even though he acted in good faith believing that the telegram from P gave him such authority.

Furthermore, the application of the doctrine of warranty of authority is not confined to contracts between the principal and third party but covers any transaction between them. In *Firbank's Executors v Humphreys*[2] the directors of a company issued a certificate for debenture stock which A agreed to accept in lieu of cash due to him from the company, even though all the debenture stock that the company had power to issue had already been issued. In this case it was held that the directors were liable to A under an implied warranty that they had authority to issue valid debenture stock in spite of the fact that they had acted in good faith, not knowing that all the stock had been issued. Lord Esher MR said:

'... Where a person by asserting that he has the authority of the principal induces another person to enter into *any transaction* which he would not have entered into but for the assertion, and the assertion turns out to be untrue, to the injury of the person to whom it is made, it must be taken that the person making it undertook that it was true and he is liable personally for the damage that has occurred'[3].

---

19 [1901] 1 Ch 344.
20 See *Lilly, Wilson & Co v Smales, Eeles & Co* [1892] 1 QB 456; *Fridman*, pp 247ff.
1   (1893) 9 TLR 488.
2   (1886) 18 QBD 54.
3   Ibid, at 60 (emphasis added).

The doctrine of warranty of authority also applies to cases where A represents to a third party that X has authority to bind B. If X has no such authority or acts in excess of his authority, then A will be liable for breach of warranty of authority to the third party. This was the case in *Chapleo v Brunswick Permanent Benefit Building Society*[4] where the directors of the company represented to a third party that the company's secretary had power to borrow money. In fact the secretary was borrowing in excess of the amount prescribed by the rules of the company. The court in *Chapleo* held the directors liable for breach of their warranty of authority to the third party even though they had acted innocently.

Not every representation made by a party regarding his supposed authority to act for another will give rise to liability. A party will only incur liability for breach of warranty of authority where the representation made is one of fact. If the representation is one of law, as opposed to one of fact — and the distinction is not always an easy one to draw, then the person making it will not be held liable to the party who relies upon it. In *Rashdall v Ford*[5] the directors of a company which had no borrowing powers persuaded a third person to advance them money on the security of a Lloyd's bond. The third party was aware of the fact that the company had no borrowing powers but believed, along with the directors, that the bond represented a valid security. This was a mistaken belief, but the directors were nevertheless held not to be liable since the question of the validity of the bond was one of law not of fact.

It is clear from what has been said already that an agent will not be liable for breach of his warranty of authority if the principal ratifies his acts. However, the fact that a principal may be bound by his agent's acts as a result of the operation of the doctrine of apparent or ostensible authority will not absolve the agent from this form of liability since he has not *actual* authority. Nevertheless, it should be observed that in the majority of cases where the agent has apparent or ostensible authority the third party will be unable to prove loss, since it is always open to him to sue the principal who originally held the agent out as having authority. To summarise the position, in order to render an agent liable for breach of warranty of authority a third party must be able to establish the following things:

(a) *The agent was purporting to act as agent.* If the principal's existence has never been disclosed, the agent is in any case personally liable on the contract he has made and there is no need for the third party

4   (1881) 6 QBD 696.
5   (1866) LR 2 Eq 750.

to sue him for breach of warranty of authority. Also, where a person holds himself out as an agent for a named person but is in fact acting as agent for an unnamed person, then the agent may be personally liable[6].

(b) *The agent must lack authority.* This may be either because he never possessed the authority in the first place or because his authority has been revoked or terminated. In this context an important protection was introduced by statute in favour of one type of innocent agent in cases where his authority was revoked. Section 5(1) of the Powers of Attorney Act 1971 provides:

'A donee of a power of attorney who acts in pursuance of the power at a time when it has been revoked shall not, by reason of the revocation, incur any liability (either to the donor or to any other person) if at the time he did not know that the power had been revoked'.

Thus, unlike other agents, the donee of a power of attorney, if unaware that his agency has been terminated, will not be liable to third parties to whom he continues to represent his authority under the implied warranty of authority.

(c) *The agent must not have expressed doubts about his authority or warned the third party of them.*

(d) *The third party must rely on this representation.* This requirement predicates the question, to whom should the agent's warranty have been given? Although some of the authorities could be read to say that any express or implied warranty must have been given by the agent to the third party and that, further, the transaction into which the third party was induced to enter must have been some form of dealing with the supposed principal, the relevant law is not so restricted. It was held in *Rasnoimport V/O v Guthrie & Co Ltd* that the third party need not have been the person to whom the warranty was actually addressed. As Mocatta J noted in this case, where agents had innocently signed false bills of lading that ultimately came into the hands of the plaintiff indorsees, to whom the warranty had not been directly made,

'I can see nothing extravagant or heterodox in holding that the implied warranty of authority ... was given by the (agents) to all whom they could reasonably foresee would become ... indorsees (of a bill of lading) and became actionable by such persons on proof of

6   *Savills v Scott* [1988] 1 EGLR 20.

their having acted in reliance upon the warranty and having suffered damage thereby. Common sense and principle alike seem to require this conclusion.'[7]

More recently, in *Penn v Bristol and West Building Society*[8] the Court of Appeal amplified this proposition by holding that the consideration for the agent's warranty need not be a transaction with the principal but could be supplied by the plaintiff entering into a transaction with a third party. Thus, when a solicitor, mistakenly believing that he had authority to act for both joint owners of a house, purported to negotiate on behalf of the vendors with another solicitor whom, he was aware, was acting for both the prospective purchaser and a building society which was lending money to finance the purchase, the solicitor's warranty that he was authorised to act for both vendors was given not only to the purchaser but also to the building society that lent money on the strength of that assurance to the purchaser.

(e) *The third party must have suffered damage.*

In conclusion, we should point out that the damages for breach of warranty of authority will be assessed by the courts according to the usual rules applicable to the law of contract. Thus, *Hadley v Baxendale*[9] will apply and the loss which was the 'natural and probable consequence or that which was reasonably contemplated by the parties to ensue' will be recoverable. It must be remembered, however, that liability is for the agent's breach of his warranty of authority and not for the breach of the contract which the third party purportedly made with the principal. Therefore, the damages will be limited to the loss which flowed from the agent's lack of authority. By way of illustration, in *Simons v Patchett*[10] an agent, purporting to act on behalf of P, bought a vessel from T. P refused to ratify the agent's act and the seller of the vessel (T) re-sold it to another party at a lower price (which was the best he could actually do in the circumstances). It was held by the court that T was entitled to recover from the agent by way of damages the difference between the original contract price and the actual sale price. This loss suffered by the seller of the ship quite clearly flowed from the agent's breach of his

7   [1966] 1 Lloyd's Rep 1, 13.
8   [1997] 3 All ER 470; see Extract 26, p 251.
9   (1854) 9 Exch 341. But the measure of damages will be different if the agent is sued in negligence under the common law or under the Misrepresentation Act 1967 (which also adopts a tort measure of damages see *Treitel*, p 334, n 57).
10 (1857) 7 E & B 568. For further examples, see *Bowstead*, pp 465–8.

warranty of authority. By the same token, if the principal happens to be insolvent, the third party can recover from the agent the amount he could have claimed from the principal — which might be little or nothing, depending on the degree of the principal's insolvency. In such cases, therefore, it may be advantageous to the third party to try to found his action in tort[11].

---

11 On the other hand, the picture may not be quite so clear-cut because costs thrown away by the third party/plaintiff as a result of claiming (unsuccessfully) against the principal can be recovered from the agent for warranting his authority: *Farley Health Products Ltd v Babylon Trading Co* (1987) Times, 29 July.

3 The relations between principal and agent

For most people the agency relationship is essentially contractual and it is in fact true that both the law of contract and the law of agency share much in common. Moreover, until the Common Law Procedure Act came into force the normal rights and duties of principal and agent were enforced by the action of assumpsit which, although of tortious origin, was employed in the law of contract. But this historical and logical relationship with the law of contract — and, indeed, with the law merchant (especially during the eighteenth and early nineteenth centuries) — should not overshadow the contribution equity has also made to this branch of the law. Equity's contribution is strongly felt in the relationship that exists between principal and agent, especially when the agent acts gratuitously. The agent is in many instances burdened by fiduciary duties which were developed by a Court of Chancery ever eager to lend its assistance whenever a person abused the confidence of another for whom he was acting. As McCardie J pointed out in *Armstrong v Jackson*:

'The position of principal and agent gives rise to particular and onerous duties on the part of the agent, and the high standard of conduct required from him springs from the *fiduciary relationship* between his employer and himself. His position is confidential. It readily lends itself to abuse. A strict and salutary rule is required to meet the special situation. *The rules of English Law as they now exist spring from the strictness originally required by Courts of Equity in cases where the fiduciary relationship exists*'[1].

---

1   [1917] 2 KB 822 at 826 (emphasis added). *Boardman v Phipps* [1967] 2 AC 46, [1966] 3 All ER 721, HL, is an example of how strict the law can be towards trustees and other fiduciaries.

A number of strict duties are imposed upon an agent. Notably, he is under a duty not to put himself in a situation where his interests will conflict with those of his principal; he is under a duty to make full disclosure of his interests in the transaction he has to perform; he is under a general duty not to delegate his office. It is quite clear from the early cases on the subject that the courts freely imposed these duties upon agents. As Dowrick observed, they 'did not pretend to be giving effect to what they might presume to have been the common intention of the parties in the particular case, nor did they seek for the elements of a valid contract between the parties before enforcing these rules. On the contrary, the judges *imposed* these duties and disabilities on agents generally ... Only if it happens in a particular case of agency that the parties expressly or tacitly agree on these very duties, and there exists a contract between them, do these incidents acquire the character of contractual terms'[2]. It should be clear from the above that the rights and duties of principal and agent may derive either from an agreement into which they have entered or simply from the fiduciary nature of their relationship. We shall therefore discuss the duties of the agent towards his principal as well as his rights against the principal with this distinction in mind.

I THE AGENT'S DUTIES TOWARDS HIS PRINCIPAL

(i) Duties arising from an agreement with the principal

An agent who has contracted with a principal to perform certain acts is under a contractual duty to perform them and must personally fulfil his obligations with reasonable care and diligence in accordance with the terms of his contract and the instructions of his principal. Where such a contractual arrangement exists, many of the usual incidents of agency may be expressly or implicitly incorporated

---

2   Dowrick 'The Relationship of Principal and Agent' (1954) 17 MLR 24, 31. Interestingly, in some other jurisdictions courts are coming to question whether equity's strict doctrines are wholly beneficial in the commercial domain. Thus, in *Chan v Zacharia* (1983) 154 CLR 178 Deane J observed, 'one cannot but be conscious of the danger that the over-enthusiastic and unnecessary statement of broad general principles of equity in terms of inflexibility may destroy the vigour which it is intended to promote in that it will exclude the ordinary interplay of the doctrines of equity and the adjustment of general principle to particular facts and changing circumstances and convert equity into an instrument of hardship and injustice in individual cases'. See generally Finn (ed) *Equity and Commercial Relationships* (1987), ch 7; *O'Sullivan v Management Agency and Music Ltd* [1985] QB 428. Such views may have repercussions for the law of agency one day.

into the contract or alternatively may be excluded from it. Analysing the above, one sees that:

Firstly, the agent is obliged to act in accordance with the terms of his contract and must perform his contractual undertakings. Thus, in *Turpin v Bilton*[3] an agent was instructed to insure his principal's vessel but failed to do so. In consequence, when the vessel was lost the owner was uninsured. It was held that the agent was in breach of his contractual duty to act and therefore was liable in damages to the principal. It would have been otherwise, however, if the defendant had endeavoured but failed to find persons ready and willing to underwrite the particular risk, provided that he had done all that was within his powers to perform his duties[4].

Similarly, the agent must not exceed his authority. A solicitor, for example, who compromises a case *against* the instructions of his client exceeds his authority and will be liable for breach of contract, even if he acted in the best interests of his client[5]. But as Lord Campbell CJ noted more generally:

'An attorney retained to conduct a case is entitled, in the exercise of his discretion, to enter into a compromise, if he does so reasonably skilfully and bona fide ... provided always that his client has given him no express directions to the contrary'[6].

Therefore, in the absence of such express directions a solicitor may compromise the action, provided always he is acting bona fide and in the best interests of his client[7]. Furthermore, subject to what will be said in the next paragraph, the agent should comply with his principal's instructions even if he regards them as foolish. But if the principal's instructions are ambiguous and can be interpreted in different ways, unless an obligation arises to seek further clarification of the principal the agent will be excused for opting to act bona fide in one way if it is not the way intended by the principal. It will be remembered that in *Ireland v Livingston*[8] it was held that the principal should suffer the consequences of his own imprecision.

Although the agent must generally follow his principal's instructions, he is not obliged to do so if he has been asked to

---

3   (1843) 5 Man & G 455.
4   Ibid, at 470.
5   *Fray v Voules* (1859) 1 E & E 839.
6   Ibid, at 847. For a solicitor's implied authority to enter into a compromise on behalf of his client see *Waugh v H B Clifford & Sons* [1982] Ch 374, [1982] 1 All ER 1095, CA (Extract 10, p 229). For a barrister's 'virtually unlimited authority in the conduct of his client's case' see *Re Debtors (No 78 of 1980)* (1985) Times, 11 May.
7   See discussion in chapter 1, 2(i).
8   (1872) LR 5 HL 395. See p 21, ante.

perform an illegal act or an act which at common law or by statute is null and void. In *Cohen v Kittell*[9] an agent, who was a turf commissioner, was sued by his principal for failing to place a bet. Since he was being asked to perform a wagering contract, it was held that the agent was not obliged to comply with his principal's instructions.

It will be clear from the above that the agent's duty to perform will only arise in cases where he has bound himself to act by contract. A gratuitous agent, in contrast, will not be liable for non-feasance. The normal rules of negligence will nevertheless apply and the gratuitous agent will be liable in tort if he undertakes to act (even though he is not obliged to do so) and starts to perform his duties negligently. However, it is doubtful if in such cases the gratuitous agent is under any *legal* duty to inform the principal that he does not intend to act, although as a matter of courtesy it may be appropriate for him to do so. Finally, it should be noted that in performing his duties the agent will normally be allowed to act in accordance with the prevailing custom of the trade unless this has been expressly or impliedly excluded. Where a business custom has not been excluded, it is 'to be considered as part of the agreement: and if the agreement be in writing, though the custom is not written it is to be treated exactly as if that unwritten customary clause had been written out at length'[10].

Secondly, it is not enough for the agent simply to follow his principal's instructions and perform his contractual duties; he must in addition act with due care and skill. It is sometimes said that the standard of care and skill which is expected of the agent depends upon whether he is contractually rewarded for his services or whether he is a gratuitous agent. In cases where there is a contract providing for his remuneration the agent must perform his duty exercising the care, skill, and diligence which is usual or necessary or proper in the type of work or business in which he is employed and which an agent in his position would be required to employ. Whether an agent in any particular case has been negligent is a question of fact[11].

9   (1889) 22 QBD 680. Cf *Fraser v B N Furman (Productions) Ltd* [1967] 3 All ER 57.
10   *Tucker v Linger* (1883) 8 App Cas 508 at 511 per Lord Blackburn. See also, *Cunliffe-Owen v Teather and Greenwood* [1967] 3 All ER 561 (broker acting in accordance with the prevailing practice of the Stock Exchange).
11   See, eg *Marston Excelsior Ltd v Arbuckle Smith & Co Ltd* [1971] 2 Lloyd's Rep 306; *Club Speciality (Overseas) Inc v United Marine (1939) Ltd* [1971] 1 Lloyd's Rep 482; *Everett v Hogg, Robinson and Gardner Mountain (Insurance) Ltd* [1973] 2 Lloyd's Rep 217. For extensive references, especially to Canadian cases, see Fridman *The Law of Agency* (7th Edn, 1996), p 158, n 2.

The nature of the agent's liability in cases where he has failed to exercise the requisite degree of care is not easy to identify. It is really one aspect of the well-known and troublesome topic of the relationship between contractual and tortious liability. In other words, how should liability which arises from a given set of facts which constitute both breach of contract and a tort be characterised? Is it contractual or tortious in character? The solution to this problem, which has exercised the minds of civilian and common lawyers alike[12], is far from easy and not devoid of practical significance, since different rules as to the extent of damages, periods of limitation and so on may apply[13]. This is not an appropriate place to discuss this issue at great length, not least because of the recent tendency of the courts to allow plaintiffs the option of suing their professional advisers either in contract or in tort[14]. Nevertheless, the degree of care and skill which the law of contract demands of an agent is similar to the normal duty of care in negligence: in the case of professional agents, this will mean the degree of care that is expected of the reasonable, average member of the profession in question.

What about gratuitous agents? Since their liability can only arise in tort it will not, according to traditional tort doctrine, be engaged in cases of pure inaction — a type of case unlikely to appear before the courts. More likely to raise legal issues will be cases involving the incompetent or negligent activities of a gratuitous agent. Common sense would suggest that the gratuitous agent — the person who is performing a 'favour' for his 'principal' — should not be held accountable in the same way as an agent who is rewarded for his efforts. Not all authors on agency, however, have espoused this view. Powell, for example, boldly asserted that 'the distinction between paid and gratuitous agents is unsound in principle'[15]. In his opinion, this is because the only difference (in law) between these two types of agency is that in the first we find consideration whereas in the second we do not. Since the doctrine of consideration is technically satisfied by the payment of a mere penny, creating a universal distinction between these two categories of case is in practical terms

---

12 For a comparative examination of this thorny problem see Weir 'Complex Liabilities' in vol XI of *International Encyclopaedia of Comparative Law* and the literature mentioned therein.

13 But see *H Parsons (Livestock) Ltd v Uttley Ingham & Co Ltd* [1978] QB 791, [1978] 1 All ER 525, CA and cf *Satef-Huttenes, Albertus SpA v Paloma Tercera Shipping Co SA, The Pegase* [1981] 1 Lloyd's Rep 175.

14 *Esso Petroleum Co Ltd v Mardon* [1976] QB 801; *Batty v Metropolitan Realisations Ltd* [1978] QB 554, [1978] 2 All ER 445; *Midland Bank Trust Co Ltd v Hett, Stubbs and Kemp* [1979] Ch 384, [1978] 3 All ER 571; *Ross v Caunters* [1980] Ch 297, [1979] 3 All ER 580.

15 *The Law of Agency* (2nd Edn, 1960), p 304.

pretty meaningless. The recent case of *Chaudhry v Prabhakar*[16] could be argued to uphold Powell's view. Regretfully, however, it also has some unfortunate features which leave the result (equating the position of gratuitous and paid agents), as well as the reasoning, open to some doubt.

In *Chaudhry* the plaintiff, after passing her driving test, asked the first defendant, a friend who knew more about cars than she did but was not a qualified mechanic, to help her purchase a secondhand car which had not been involved in any previous traffic accident. The first defendant found a car that was offered for sale by the second defendant, a car sprayer and panel beater. Though the first defendant noticed that the bonnet of the car had been repaired, he made no specific enquiries and advised the plaintiff to purchase the car. This she did. It transpired that the car had been involved in a serious accident, had been badly repaired, and was totally unroadworthy. The plaintiff successfully sued both defendants. In the Court of Appeal the sole question concerned the nature and scope of a gratuitous agent's liability. Whilst the court took the view that the agent owed a duty of care to the plaintiff, and that his skill was to be measured objectively, doubts were expressed as to whether counsel should have conceded the existence of a duty of care in the first place[17]. This and other dicta would suggest that where the 'principal' and 'agent' are friends, the totality of the circumstances may well indicate that the advice or representation made by the agent was made in a purely social context and without a voluntary assumption of responsibility[18]. Where this is true, the legal answer must be that there is no duty and thus the enquiry as to what the standard of care should have been and whether or not it was breached should become superfluous[19]. In practical terms, such an approach comes close to achieving the result suggested by common sense in the previous paragraph: namely, that gratuitous agents should be treated less severely than remunerated agents by downward adjustment of the standard of care they owe. *Chaudhry* may thus have produced the right result on its facts; but it should in no circumstances be seen as equating the position of gratuitous and remunerated agents.

---

16 [1988] 3 All ER 718.
17 Ibid, at 725.
18 Ibid, at 721–2.
19 See Brinkworth 'Gratuitous Agency: Liable or Not?' (1990) Bus LR 111.

(ii)   Fiduciary duties

It must be noted that, if the agency is contractual, every one of the
fiduciary duties which will be examined in this section may either
be expressly incorporated into or expressly excluded from the
contract entered into by the principal and the agent. Normally,
however, these duties will be implied into all agency relationships
and, for this reason, they are often referred to as the 'normal
incidents of agency'. The most important fiduciary duties of the
agent towards his principal are as follows: (a) the duty not to delegate
his office; (b) the duty not to put himself in a situation where his
duties as agent conflict with his own interests; (c) the duty not to
accept bribes; (d) the duty not to take advantage of his position in
order to gain benefits for himself; (e) the duty to hand over to the
principal money which he holds to his use, and to account to the
principal. We shall examine each of these duties in turn.

(a) *The duty not to delegate.* The Latin rubric, *delegatus non potest delegare*,
applies to the duty of both trustees and agents not to delegate their
office — a plain indication of the equitable origin of this duty. Since,
at least in the typical case, the agency relationship is created by and
based upon the confidence one person reposes in another, the agent
is in principle prohibited from delegating his authority to another
person or even appointing a sub-agent to do some of the acts which
he himself has to do. The maxim, according to Thesiger LJ in *De
Bussche v Alt*[20], 'imports that an agent cannot, without authority from
his principal, devolve upon another obligations to the principal
which he has himself undertaken to personally fulfil; and that
inasmuch as confidence in the particular person employed is at the
root of the contract of agency, such authority cannot be implied as
an ordinary incident in the contract.'

Deviation from the general rule is only permitted where strict
adherence of the duty not to delegate would prove unreasonable or
unjust. Thus, delegation is allowed in the following cases.

(1) Where delegation of authority or the employment of a sub-agent
is a usual practice in the trade in which the agent is engaged and
it is not unreasonable or inconsistent with the express terms of
the agency agreement[1].

(2) Where the principal is aware *at the time of the creation of the agency
relationship* that the agent intends to delegate his authority *and*
the principal does not object to this[2].

---

20   (1878) 8 Ch D 286 at 310; see Extract 28, p 257. See also, *Balsamo v Medici* [1984]
  2 All ER 304, and note by Whittaker in (1985) 48 MLR 86.
1   *Solley v Wood* (1852) 16 Beav 370 (country solicitor appointing town agent).
2   *Quebec and Richmond Railroad Co v Quinn* (1858) 12 Moo PCC 232.

(3) Where from the circumstances of the case and the conduct of the parties it can be presumed that the agent was intended to have power to delegate his authority[3].

(4) Wherever the agent's authority is such as to necessitate its execution, wholly or in part, with the assistance of another person or other persons[4].

(5) Wherever the act delegated is purely ministerial and one which does not require or involve confidence or discretion[5].

(6) Finally, where such delegation becomes necessary because of unforeseen circumstances[6].

Allam & Co v Europa Poster Services Ltd[7] provides a good illustration of a permissible sub-delegation. In that case the defendants carried on the business of outdoor advertising contractors. They obtained licences or agreements from owners of sites enabling them to display advertisements on those sites. They persuaded some owners to allow them to use sites currently used by the plaintiffs, who were competitors in the same business. The defendants also obtained from the site-owners authority, contained in a separate document, authorising them on behalf of the site-owners to give notice terminating any existing licences (including those with the plaintiffs) 'so soon as may be legally possible'. The defendants' solicitors sent such notices to the plaintiffs and one of the issues involved in the case was whether the maxim *delegatus non potest delegare* had been violated. The court held that what had been delegated to the solicitors was a *purely ministerial* act involving no confidence or discretion and therefore no complaint of unauthorised delegation could be brought. In contrast, estate agents, employed by a vendor of premises, normally cannot delegate their function to another firm of estate agents. Selling the vendor's property is not a purely ministerial act and estate agents who delegate their function will not be entitled to claim commission on any sale effected by sub-agents to whom they have improperly delegated their duties[8].

---

3   *De Bussche v Alt* (1878) 8 Ch D 286.

4   *Quebec and Richmond Railroad Co v Quinn* (1858) 12 Moo PCC 232.

5   *Allam & Co Ltd v Europa Poster Services Ltd* [1968] 1 All ER 826 (discussed below); *The Berkshire* [1974] 1 Lloyd's Rep 185 at 188.

6   For the power of trustees to delegate see Powers of Attorney Act 1971, s 9. As *Fridman*, p 167, correctly observes, 'the question of delegation is bound up with the problem of the agent's authority, and is to be settled by reference to that authority'.

7   [1968] 1 All ER 826.

8   *John McCann & Co v Pow* [1975] 1 All ER 129. In the same way, other classes of agent such as factors (*Solly v Rathbone* (1814) 2 M & S 298), brokers (*Cockran v Irlam* (1814) 2 M & S 301), and solicitors (*Re Becket, Purnell v Paine* [1918] 2 Ch 72) will not normally have implied authority to sub-delegate. As regards country solicitors, however, see *Solley v Wood* (1852) 16 Beav 370, fn 1 ante.

De Bussche v Alt[9] offers another good illustration of an authorised delegation of authority relieving the agent of all liability. In that case the agent, who was authorised to sell his principal's vessel in any port in India, Japan or China at a specific price, found that he was unable to do so. He therefore obtained his principal's permission to appoint a sub-agent in Japan to sell the vessel at the specified price. It was held that this was clearly a permissible delegation of authority by the agent. However, the Court of Appeal went further and held that since the sub-agent had an office only in Japan (and the principal was aware of this), this was 'pre-eminently' a case 'in which the appointment of substitutes at ports other than those where the agent himself carries on business ... must reasonably be presumed to be in the contemplation of the parties'[10]. Although in *De Bussche v Alt* the court would have been willing to presume from the circumstances an intention that the agent had the power to delegate his authority, the case is different, for example, where a shipmaster, authorised to sell goods, sends them to another person for sale without the permission of his principal merely because he himself is unable to find a purchaser. In such a case the shipmaster may be liable for breach of his duty not to delegate[11].

The consequences of *unauthorised* delegation are clear. The agent will be liable to the principal for breach of his duty not to delegate and the acts of the deputy agent or sub-agent may be held invalid. Moreover, in such cases no legal relationship whatsoever arises between principal and sub-agent. However, where the delegation is *authorised* the position may be more complicated. Thus, the mere fact that the agent has express or implied authority to delegate his functions does not necessarily mean that privity of contract will be created between principal and sub-agent.[12] In *Calico Printers' Association Ltd v Barclays Bank*[13] the plaintiffs had appointed Barclays Bank as their agent to collect the price of goods sold to a tradesman abroad. Barclays in turn appointed sub-agents operating locally to do the job for them and instructed the sub-agents to warehouse the goods and insure them against fire if the purchaser refused to take delivery. The sub-agents failed to insure the goods which were later destroyed by a fire. One of the questions that arose was whether the

9   (1878) 8 Ch D 286.
10   Ibid, at 311 per Thesiger LJ.
11   *Catlin v Bell* (1815) 4 Camp 183.
12   If privity of contract is created, the person appointed becomes agent of the principal and acquires the usual rights and duties of an agent. If no privity is established, the sub-agent *may* still have some rights or duties.
13   (1931) 145 LT 51.

sub-agents were liable to the principals. Wright J, at first instance, stated the position as follows:

'... English law ... has in general applied the rule that even where the sub-agent is properly employed there is still no privity between him and the principal; the latter is entitled to hold the agent liable for breach of the mandate which he has accepted and cannot, in general, claim against the sub-agent for negligence or breach of duty ... The agent does not as a rule escape liability to the principal merely because employment of the sub-agent is contemplated. To create privity it must be established not only that the principal contemplated that a sub-agent would perform part of the contract, but also that the principal authorised the agent to create privity of contract between the principal and the sub-agent, which is a very different matter requiring precise proof. In general, where a principal employs an agent to carry out a particular employment, the agent undertakes responsibility for the whole transaction, and is responsible for any negligence in carrying it out, even if the negligence be that of the sub-agent properly or necessarily engaged to perform some part, because there is no privity between the principal and the sub-agent'[14].

If, therefore, there is no privity between principal and sub-agent — and this is the attitude the courts are likely to adopt in the absence of 'precise proof' to the contrary — the sub-agent will be an agent *of the agent* and will have *no* contractual relationship with the principal. As a result, the sub-agent will be liable to account to the agent — not to the principal — who in turn will be accountable to the principal. Thus, in *Stephens v Badcock*[15], where an agent authorised to receive rents disappeared and was later adjudicated bankrupt, it was held that his clerk, who had received some of the rents, was not liable to account for them to the principal. Since the principal cannot sue the sub-agent in contract it would appear that the agent remains liable for the defaults of the sub-agent. This proposition finds support in the case of *Mackersy v Ramsays, Bonars & Co*[16], although in *Thomas Cheshire & Co v Vaughan Bros & Co*[17] Atkin LJ did suggest *obiter* that an agent's liability in such cases should be restricted to his exercising reasonable care in his selection of a sub-agent. In *Calico Printers' Association v Barclays Bank*[18] it was the absence of a contract which barred the principal's claim against sub-agents who had negligently failed to insure his goods. However, the *Calico* case was decided prior

14   Ibid, at 55.
15   (1832) 3 B & Ad 354.
16   (1843) 9 Cl & Fin 818.
17   [1920] 3 KB 240.
18   (1931) 145 LT 51.

to *Donoghue v Stevenson*[19] and *Hedley Byrne & Co Ltd v Heller & Partners Ltd*[20] and the question of the sub-agent's liability in tort awaits an authoritative solution by the higher courts. Anticipating the manner in which the question might be resolved, two competing considerations might be mentioned. On the one hand, it is the case that in recent years persons to whom goods have been bailed by agents have been held to owe both a duty of care to the bailors' principals and a contractual duty to the bailors themselves. This may afford some clue as to future trends[1]. On the other hand, in *Balsamo v Medici*[2] the High Court avoided granting an action in tort to the principal in such circumstances on the grounds that the money received by the sub-agent never became his property.

(b) *The agent's duty not to put himself in a situation where his duties to the principal conflict with his own interests.* This duty of 'fidelity', as it has sometimes been described, is nothing more than a special application of the equitable maxim that 'no person in a position of trust can be allowed to put himself in a situation in which his interest and his duty would be in conflict'. This has been affirmed by the courts in a number of cases. Thus, in *Parker v McKenna*[3] Lord Cairns LC said of this rule:

'Now the rule of this court ... as to agents is not a technical or arbitrary rule. It is a rule founded on the highest and truest principles of morality. No man can in this court, acting as an agent, be allowed to put himself in a position in which his interest and his duty will be in conflict'.

As will be seen presently, this is probably the most important of the agent's fiduciary duties and a number of other specific duties derive from it. The rule is clearly both sound and necessary. The agent

---

19   [1932] AC 562.

20   [1964] AC 465, [1963] 2 All ER 575.

1   See, *Lee Cooper Ltd v C H Jeakins & Son Ltd* [1967] 2 QB 1, [1965] 1 All ER 280; *Morris v C W Martin & Sons Ltd* [1966] 1 QB 716, [1965] 2 All ER 725. Similar vagueness surrounds many of the other rights and duties of the sub-agent *vis-à-vis* the principal. The reader is referred to the more detailed textbooks for discussion of these matters.

2   [1984] 2 All ER 304. Since the principal's loss in such cases is purely financial and the House of Lords, in its present mood, seems implacably opposed to the idea of compensation of pure economic loss through the law of torts, the principal's only claim would, in future cases, appear to be in contract against the agent. In *Balsamo v Medici* the contractual action against the sub-agent, based on the ground that the money had been received for the principal, also failed. The validity of this last point is doubted by Reynolds in 'Tort Actions in Contractual Situations' (1985) 11 NZULR 215.

3   (1874) 10 Ch App 96 at 118; see Extract 29, p 258.

should not be led into temptation and have to balance his own interests against those of his principal. This would happen, for example, if he were to purchase his principal's property since, in theory, he would be trying to achieve the impossible: namely, seeking the highest price for his principal's property whilst attempting to pay the lowest possible price for it himself. For similar reasons, agents — estate agents, for example — are not allowed to receive commission from both parties to the transaction, although from a comparative law point of view it could be noted that some systems consider that justice can be satisfactorily achieved when the commission rate is fixed by law — eg, at 4 per cent — and it is laid down that it shall be borne equally by vendor and purchaser, unless otherwise agreed between them. Equally, the agent should not be allowed to exploit his position in order to make personal profits.

All these situations are but instances where the agent's duties to his principal come into conflict with his own interests. The law, in fact, is even stricter and appears to assume that such conflict exists even where it can be proved that there was no actual conflict of interests. In the words of Lord Cranworth LC in *Aberdeen Rly Co v Blaikie Bros*:

'It is a rule of universal application, that no-one, having such duties to discharge, shall be allowed to enter into engagements in which he has, *or can have*, personal interest conflicting, or *which possibly may conflict*, with the interests of those whom he is bound to protect'[4].

Boardman v Phipps[5] illustrates the severity of this principle. The complicated facts of the case may, for our purposes, be summarised by saying that agents acting for trustees in connection with a certain company in which the trust had a major shareholding, acquired extra shares in the company, thus benefiting both the trust and themselves. The House of Lords held that the agents had to account for the profit they made because, inter alia, there was a possibility of conflict of duty and interest in that the agents would be unable to give unprejudiced advice since they were negotiating to buy the shares for themselves. As Lord Hodson said, 'even if the possibility of conflict is present between personal interest and the fiduciary position, the rule of equity must be applied'[6]. It is immaterial whether the contract is actually fair or not. Moreover, an agent cannot exonerate himself by adducing evidence to show that a particular

---

4   (1854) 1 Macq 461 at 471 (emphasis added).
5   [1967] 2 AC 46, [1966] 3 All ER 721.
6   Ibid, at 111.

trade custom allows agents to buy from and sell to their principals on their own behalf[7]. In Lord Hodson's words, in *Boardman v Phipps*:

'No person trading in a fiduciary position, when a demand is made upon him by the person to whom he stands in the fiduciary relationship to account for profits acquired by him by reason of his fiduciary position and by reason of the opportunity and knowledge, or either, resulting from it, is entitled to defeat the claim upon any ground save that he made profits with the knowledge and assent of the other person'[8].

Similar duties are imposed upon agents who enter into contracts or other such transactions with their principals — for example, by purchasing property belonging to the principal or selling other property to him which they themselves own. As Romilly MR observed in *Bentley v Craven*:

' ... Two principles with relation to the doctrine of principal and agent have been recognised from the earliest times. One is, that an agent employed to purchase cannot legally buy his own goods for his principal; neither can an agent employed to sell, himself purchase the goods of his principal. If he should do so, and thereby make a profit, the principal may either repudiate the transaction altogether or adopt it and claim for himself the benefit made by his agent. The same principle is applicable to a great many other relations, as to that of trustee and cestui que trust ...'[9].

In *McPherson v Watt*[10] two ladies appointed an agent to sell their property. Desirous of acquiring it himself, but unwilling to do so openly, he bought it in the name of his brother. When this was discovered, specific performance of the contract was refused. Similarly, it has been held that where the director of a company (being its agent) sells goods to it, the sale will not be binding on the principal — ie the company[11].

In both sets of circumstances referred to in *Bentley v Craven* the agent is obliged to make full disclosure to his principal and the onus rests with him to show that the sale or purchase price is a fair and adequate one, that it was as good as the principal could get in the market and that the principal gave his consent to the transaction in full knowledge of all the relevant facts. If the agent fails to satisfy any of these conditions, then the principal may elect either to rescind

7   *Robinson v Mollett* (1875) LR 7 HL 802.
8   [1967] 2 AC 46 at 105.
9   (1853) 18 Beav 75 at 76.
10   (1877) 3 App Cas 254.
11   Eg *Salomons v Pender* (1865) 3 H & C 639.

the contract made by the agent or to affirm it and claim any profit the agent has made. The usual rules governing rescission will apply. Rescission will not therefore be permitted, if the principal has failed to exercise his right within a reasonable time after discovering the truth, or if he may be taken expressly or impliedly to have consented to the transaction. Provided the right to rescind is exercised within reasonable time from discovery of the truth, it does not necessarily matter that considerable time has elapsed since the contract was made. For example, in *Oliver v Court*[12] an auctioneer purchased some land which he had been employed to sell. Although this fact only came to light 13 years later, the transaction was set aside. If, on the other hand, the principal decides to affirm his agent's contract, then he will be entitled to recover either the profit made by the agent or damages for breach of contract. Thus, in one case where an agent bought his principal's property without making the necessary disclosures and then resold it to a third party, it was held that the principal could claim from the agent the profit or the resale price[13].

Three further points need finally to be made in this context. Firstly, difficulties may arise when agents who have *ceased* acting as agents enter into contracts with their former principals. Does the duty to disclose continue to apply in such cases with equal vigour? The answer depends upon the circumstances of the particular case. Parker J in *Allison v Clayhills*[14] stated the law as follows:

'It appears to me to be quite clear that a solicitor is not wholly incapacitated from purchasing or taking a lease from his client, but where the relationship of solicitor and client exists, the onus of upholding the vitality of such a transaction will rest upon the solicitor. It is, I think, equally clear that, although the relationship of solicitor and client in its strict sense has been discontinued, the same principle applies so long as the confidence naturally arising from such a relationship is proved or may be presumed to continue ... In considering whether this onus lies on him (the solicitor), the *test* appears to me to be the proper answer to the question *whether in the particular transaction, he owes his client any duty in the contemplation of a court of equity*'.

Parker J then proceeded to give two illuminating examples of how this test works in practice, which deserve to be quoted at length:

'... If a solicitor is actually engaged to conduct or is conducting for his client an action, say, for slander and, while that action is pending,

---

12   (1820) 8 Price 127.
13   *Barker v Harrison* (1846) 2 Coll 546.
14   (1907) 97 LT 709 at 711, 712 (emphasis added).

meets his client in the hunting field and bargains and buys from him a horse, each party relying upon his own knowledge of horseflesh, that transaction will stand on the same footing as a transaction between strangers, because the matter is entirely outside any confidential relationship between the parties, and the solicitor owes his client no duty whatever in the particular matter. On the other hand, if a solicitor has once been employed, say, to manage his client's real estates, then although the employment may have entirely ceased, yet there may still be a duty on the solicitor's part towards his client — for example, that of possibly advising or possibly communicating information which he has obtained while acting as a solicitor ...'.

Parker J concluded:

'In considering whether in any particular transaction any duty exists such as to bring the ordinary rule into operation, all the circumstances of the individual case must be weighed and examined. Thus, a solicitor may by virtue of his employment acquire a personal ascendancy over a client and this ascendancy may last long after the employment has ceased'[15].

Secondly, not every potential conflict of interest will be treated as a breach of the agent's fiduciary duties. By way of variant on the theme, in *Kelly v Cooper*[16] an estate agent acted for adjacent beachside property owners in Bermuda. He omitted to inform the vendors that Ross Perot wished to buy both properties, converting them into a single estate. Given that it might have allowed each seller to demand more for his land, ought the agent to have told the principals of a potential buyer's interest in acquiring the adjoining sites? Despite the potential conflict of interests between the agent's duties to his two principals, Lord Browne-Wilkinson held not. He concluded that, since it was well known that estate agents often work for multiple vendors, 'there must be an implied term of the contract with such agent that he is entitled to act for other principals selling competing properties and to keep confidential the information obtained from each of his principals.'[17]

Finally, the question of gifts to agents should be mentioned. In principle, there is no objection to such gifts provided that the agent can prove that there was no undue influence on his part. But it must be remembered that:

---

15 See also *Demarara Bauxite Co v Hubbard* [1923] AC 673.
16 [1993] AC 205.
17 Ibid, p 214.

'The court, in dealing with such a transaction, starts with the presumption that undue influence exists on the part of the donee, and throws upon him the burden of satisfying the court that the gift was uninfluenced by the position of the solicitor ... This presumption is not a presumption which is entirely irrebuttable, though it is one which is extremely difficult to be rebutted'[18].

(c) *The duty not to accept bribes.* It is a self-evident rule that agents should not accept bribes or secret commissions from third parties with whom they deal on behalf of their principals and that they should pay over to their principals any moneys so received. In *Boston Deep Sea Fishing and Ice Co v Ansell*[19] a director of a company held shares in two other companies. He accepted bonuses from these companies in consideration for his placing orders from his own company with them. He also took a commission for a building contract he placed with one of the companies. It was held by the court that he should account to his own company for the bonuses and secret commission he had received, together with interest.

What amounts to a bribe was defined by Slade J in *Industries and General Mortgage Co Ltd v Lewis*[20] as follows:

'... A bribe means a payment of a secret commission, which only means (i) that the person making the payment makes it to the agent of the other person with whom he is dealing; (ii) that he makes it to that person knowing that that person is acting as the agent of the other person with whom he is dealing; and (iii) that he fails to disclose to the other person with whom he is dealing that he has made that payment to the person whom he knows to be the other person's agent'.

If these three conditions are satisfied and the agent has conducted himself in the manner requested by the briber, it will be presumed that the agent has been influenced by the bribe and has breached his duty to his principal. The presumption is irrebuttable and the principal's loss is considered to be at least equal to the amount of

18 *Wright v Carter* [1903] 1 Ch 27 at 57 per Stirling LJ.
19 (1888) 39 Ch D 339; see Extract 30, p 258.
20 [1949] 2 All ER 573 at 575. In *Anangel Atlas Compania Naviera SA v Ishikawajima-Harima Heavy Industries Co Ltd* [1990] 1 Lloyd's Rep 167 at 171 Leggatt J proposed the following more succinct definition: '... a bribe consists in a commission or other inducement which is given by a third party [or, one might add, his agent acting within the scope of his authority: *The Ocean Frost* [1986] AC 717 at 743] to an agent as such, and which is secret from his principal'.

the bribe. But the principal must not be aware of the bribe and, naturally, must not have consented to it[1].

An agent who, without his principal's consent, receives secret commissions will be criminally liable, as will the person offering the bribe[2]. The agent will *also* be liable to forfeit any commission or remuneration to which he would otherwise have been entitled from his principal[3]. The latter will in addition be entitled to dismiss the agent without notice[4], and the principal will be able to sue the agent for the amount of the bribe plus interest from the date upon which the bribe was received. A further action for deceit, both against the agent and the third party who dealt with him, may also be available to the principal.

Much more interesting, from both a theoretical and a practical point of view, is another question: must the principal choose between claiming the amount of the bribe (as money had and received) or damages for loss actually sustained? Alternatively, can the principal cumulate these two remedies and claim both sums from the bribed agent? The question was raised in *Mahesan v Malaysia Government Officers' Co-operative Housing Society Ltd*[5] and the House of Lords decided that the first answer was correct (ie remedies are alternative, not cumulative). This decision was reached, essentially, on two grounds: the first was technical and is linked to the precedent (or apparent precedent) of *United Australia Ltd v Barclays Bank Ltd*;[6] the second was policy-orientated: any contrary decision would give the principal a 'windfall' since it would enable him to claim both the amount of the bribe and damages. Both grounds of decision have been subjected to criticism, the latter because 'the interests in discouraging secret profits override the interests in preventing people from getting undeserved profit'. According to this reasoning (which, it is repeated, was rejected by the House of Lords) the deceived principal should be allowed to claim both amounts. Both

1   If the principal knows of the payment to his agent there is no bribe: *Anangel Atlas Compania Naviera SA v Ishikawajima-Harima Heavy Industries Co* [1990] 1 Lloyd's Rep 167.
2   Prevention of Corruption Act 1916, s 1. For the purposes of a *criminal* prosecution, proof of the corrupt motive of the third party is needed. The *civil* consequences, however, described in the text above, do not appear to depend on the presence of a corrupt motive in the third party: *Industries and General Mortgage Co Ltd v Lewis* [1949] 2 All ER 573.
3   *Andrews (or Andrew) v Ramsay & Co* [1903] 2 KB 635. Commission from *other* transactions can be claimed, but only if these transactions are severable from the tainted deal: *Nitedals Taendstickfabrik v Bruster* [1906] 2 Ch 671.
4   *Bulfield v Fournier* (1895) 11 TLR 282.
5   [1979] AC 374, [1978] 2 All ER 405, criticised by Tettenborn (1979) 95 LQR 68.
6   [1941] AC 1, [1940] 4 All ER 20, HL.

views have much to commend them but, it is submitted, the one taken by the House of Lords is preferable, at least on pure grounds of policy. For giving the deceived principal the choice between these two types of remedy in effect gives him the opportunity to claim whichever of the two sums is the larger. Thus, if the bribe is £10 and the loss £100, the second sum is claimable. In both cases the principal is fully compensated for his actual loss; and in the second situation the agent is 'punished' in so far as he is made to pay much more than his anticipated profit from the suspicious transaction. If further 'punishment' is needed, it should be left to the criminal courts to mete it out.

As if this area of law were not already sufficiently complex, in *A-G for Hong Kong v Reid*[7] Lord Templeman suggested that if a fiduciary receives a bribe or, as occurred in *Reid's* case where a corrupt prosecutor acquired properties with the proceeds of bribes in New Zealand, has converted it into other property, he holds it on trust for the beneficiary (ie, the principal). Given that ever since *Lister & Co v Stubbs*,[8] a case which has been treated as authoritative for over a century, the relationship between a principal and his agent who receives a bribe has been treated as one of debtor and creditor, the new view has caused some academic consternation. In particular, by conferring this equitable interest upon him, *Reid*, for no especially good reason, reinforces the position of the principal at the expense of other third parties in the event of the agent's insolvency.[9] It is not appropriate to import the unyielding doctrines of equity into every commercial context and it is conceivable that Lord Templeman's unexpected introduction of the equitable maxim that 'equity regards that as done which ought to be done'[10] will not win general legal support.

The cases discussed above have considered the principal's right to claim the bribe or damages, typically where the bribe has not been paid over to him by the agent. But what if such payment has been made? And does the retention of the bribe depend upon the principal's decision to affirm or set aside the tainted transaction? In *Logicrose Ltd v Southend United Football Club Ltd*[11] the court held that the bribe, being a secret profit, could be retained by the principal even if he chose to set aside the tainted transaction.

---

7 [1994] 1 AC 324.
8 (1890) 45 Ch D 1.
9 See generally Uff 'The Remedies of the Defrauded Principal after *Att-Gen for Hong Kong v Reid*' in Feldman & Meisel (eds) *Corporate Law: Modern Developments* (1996, London), pp 239–45.
10 [1994] 1 AC 324 at 336.
11 [1988] 1 WLR 1256; see Extract 31, p 259; Jones [1989] CLJ 22.

(d) *The agent's duty not to take advantage of his position or his principal's property in order to acquire a benefit for himself.* There are two duties contained within this rule and both overlap considerably with duties of the agent which we discussed earlier on. Indeed, these duties are analogous to the duty under which all agents have to eschew any personal interest in the transactions they are asked to carry out. But, clearly, in the former case, the agent's liability is not based on any profit he may have made but springs from his undisclosed participation in the transaction he was asked to carry out. In the latter case, however, the position is reversed and the agent's liability depends upon his obtaining some personal gain from his agency over and above his agreed remuneration. Let us now analyse these duties more closely.

The first one which we shall consider is the agent's duty not to use his position as agent in order to acquire a benefit — which is not necessarily the same thing as a bribe. The affinity between the duties of trustees and fiduciaries in this respect is striking and further illustrates the common equitable origin of these rules of agency. The leading case on this subject is *Keech v Sandford*[12]. Property had been leased to a trust and, when the lease terminated, the trustee renewed it in his own name. It was held by the court that the trustee must hold the lease for the benefit of the cestui que trust. The severity of this rule is demonstrated by the fact that in *Keech v Sandford* not only had the lease expired but the landlord had refused to renew it to him as trustee and only agreed to renew it when it became obvious that the trustee was *personally* acquiring the lease. *Keech v Sandford* concerned the lease of a market which had been devised to the trustee for the benefit of an infant. Before its expiration, the lessor made it known that he would not renew the lease to the infant, so the trustee took the lease personally. But as the Lord Chancellor said:

'I must consider this as a trust for the infant; for I very well see, if a trustee, on the refusal to renew, might have a lease to himself, few trust estates would be renewed to cestui que use'[13].

The rationale of the decision is, therefore, one of public policy. It reflects a desire to dissuade parties from unscrupulously using their fiduciary position to their own personal advantage.

As a corollary to this duty and, often, as a specific application of it, there is the second duty included under this heading, according to which an agent cannot, without his principal's consent, use to his own benefit property or confidential information which he has

12   (1726) Sel Cas Ch 61; see Extract 32, p 260.
13   Ibid, at 62.

acquired in his capacity as agent. A simple illustration would be the case of an agent who has been given money to purchase property and who, while the contracts are being drawn up, invests that money in his own deposit account and thus earns interest on his principal's money. In such cases it is clear that he must account for such moneys to his principal. As Lord Denning MR stated in *Phipps v Boardman*:

'It is quite clear that if an agent uses *property*, with which he has been entrusted by his principal, so as to make a profit for himself out of it, without his principal's consent, then he is accountable for it to his principal ... Likewise, with *information* or *knowledge* which he has been employed by his principal to collect or discover, *or which he has otherwise acquired* for use of his principal, then again if he turns it to his own use, so as to make a profit by means of it for himself, he is accountable ...'[14].

In *Ritchie v Couper*[15] the defendant was one of two co-owners of a vessel as well as being a provisions merchant. He supplied the vessel with provisions from his own business at market prices. The plaintiff — the other owner — alleged that the defendant should have done this at cost price. It was held that the defendant was only entitled to charge profit prices if it could be shown that the other partner, being aware of all the circumstances, had consented to pay market prices. In *Reid-Newfoundland Co v Anglo-American Telegraph Co Ltd*[16] the respondents were a cable company which had rights to construct and maintain telegraph lines under special statutory powers. They agreed with the appellants, who operated as lessees of the Newfoundland Railways, to erect for them a 'special wire' which was to be used only in connection with 'the operation of the said railway' and which was 'not to pass or transmit any commercial messages over the said special wire except for the benefit and account of the telegraph company'. A special clause in the agreement provided that these terms would also be binding upon the railway company's successors and assignees. The Newfoundland Railway Company, which had originally made the contract with the respondents, was eventually taken over by the Government which proceeded to lease the railway to the appellant company. The appellant company thus stepped into the shoes of the Newfoundland Railway Company but, in contravention of the above-mentioned clause, used the telegraph for its own business purposes. The Privy Council declared that,

---

14   [1965] Ch 992 at 1013–9 (emphasis added).
15   (1860) 28 Beav 344.
16   [1912] AC 555.

'... When ... the appellants used the special wire for the transmission of unprivileged messages an obligation in the nature of a trust arose on their part, and it became their duty to keep an account of the profits accruing from such use of the wire and to set their profits aside as moneys belonging to the respondents'.

Furthermore, it held that,

'Where the duty of persons is to receive property and to hold it for another and to keep it until it is called for, they cannot discharge themselves from that trust by appealing to the lapse of time. They can only discharge themselves by handing over that property to somebody entitled to it'[17].

In *Burdick v Garrick*[18] an agent was asked to sell his principal's property and invest the proceeds in the name of his principal. The agent sold the property and put the money into his own account. When he was later asked to account for these moneys, he pleaded the Statute of Limitations; but his plea was rejected on the grounds given above. There are innumerable cases illustrating the operation of this duty of the agent. Thus, in *Turnbull v Garden*[19], a gratuitous agent, who was asked to purchase a cavalry outfit for his principal's son, did so at a discount. It was held that he could not charge the principal the full price. Similarly, in *Thompson v Meade*[20] a stockbroker, who, having been instructed to purchase shares at a certain price, managed to obtain them at a lower price, was held not to be entitled to retain the difference.

The agent is also liable to account to his principal for any profits he has made using confidential information acquired in the course of his agency. *Peter Pan Manufacturing Corpn v Corsets Silhouette Ltd*[1] offers an instructive illustration of this general duty. The plaintiffs, an American company, designed and manufactured ladies' garments. Immediately before 1951 they developed a revolutionary new type of brassiere which without delay they patented and sold with success under various imaginative names. The defendants, who were English manufacturers, became interested in the new product and, after some negotiation, obtained a licence from the plaintiffs to manufacture and sell the goods in this country. In consequence, they were handed over 'a layout plan, specification and operation schedules, books of samples, patterns and the like, a complete set

17   Ibid, at 559–60.
18   (1870) 5 Ch App 233.
19   (1869) 20 LT 218.
20   (1891) 7 TLR 698.
1   [1963] 3 All ER 402.

of Peter Pan brassieres ...' etc. Some eight years later the plaintiffs' inventiveness produced a new improved brassiere, code-named U15 and U25, which they showed to the defendants' designer in confidence whilst he was visiting their factory in the USA. The defendants subsequently used the confidential information and manufactured similar products. It was held that the confidential nature of the information given to the defendants disentitled them from using it in competition with the plaintiffs. Therefore, an injunction was issued forbidding the defendants to make any further use of the information and they were ordered to account to the plaintiffs for all profits made from the sale of these goods. The agent's fiduciary duty thus continued to operate even after the termination of the agency and rendered the defendants' behaviour unlawful.

The above-mentioned duty is common to all fiduciary relationships and applies also to agency. To take a case more directly to the point, in *Lamb v Evans*[2] there was a trades directory consisting of advertisements furnished by tradesmen classified under headings denoting the different trades, the headings being composed by the plaintiff who was the registered proprietor of the directory. The plaintiff obtained this information through 'canvassers' whom he employed to work in specified districts to attract advertisements from local traders which would be inserted in the directory. The plaintiff discovered that some of his 'canvassers' proposed, upon the expiration of their agreements, to assist a rival publication by procuring similar advertisements. The court held that they were 'not entitled to use for the purposes of any other publication the materials which, while in the plaintiff's employment, they had obtained for the purpose of his publication'. As Lindley LJ said, succinctly summarising the law on this topic:

'What right has any agent to use materials obtained by him in the course of his employment and for his employer against the interests of that employer? I am not aware that he has any such right. Such a use is contrary to the relation which exists between principal and agent. It is contrary to the good faith of the employment and good faith underlies the whole of the agent's obligations to his principal. No case can, I believe, be found which is contrary to the general principle upon which this injunction is framed, viz, that an agent has no right to employ as against his principal materials which the agent has obtained only for his principal and in the course of his agency. They are the property of the principal. The principal has, in my judgment, such an interest in them as entitles him to restrain

2   [1893] 1 Ch 218.

the agent from the use of them except for the purpose for which they were got'[3].

This liability will arise irrespective of whether there is a contract between principal and agent, although, where such a contract exists, a breach of the above duty will also constitute a breach of the contract. It must be remembered, however, that this duty exists only so long as the information in question can be regarded as confidential. Hence, if it becomes available to the public at large, from that moment the agent is also free to make use of it without incurring liability to the principal.

It should be clear from the above that the aggrieved principal has a variety of remedies at his disposal. He can either seek an injunction to prevent the agent from making use of the confidential information, or he may sue him for damages for breach of contract, or alternatively bring an action against the agent to make him account for his profits.

(e) *The agent's general duty to account.* All agents who receive goods or money for their principals or from their principals are bound to keep the property separate from their own and in equity they are treated as if they were trustees of that property. Agents are equally obliged to keep proper accounts and to render account to their principals. As Lord Cottenham LC said in *Foley v Hill*:

'So it is with regard to an agent dealing with any property; he obtains no interest himself in the subject-matter beyond his remuneration; he is dealing throughout for another, and though he is not a trustee according to the strict technical meaning of the word, he is *quasi* a trustee for that particular transaction for which he is engaged; and therefore in these cases the courts of equity have assumed jurisdiction'[4].

Thus, if the agent fails to keep his own property separate from that of this principal, the latter may be entitled to a charge on the entire mixed property unless the agent is able to show which of it is his own[5]. And if the agent converts his principal's property into money or goods and then mixes it with his own, the principal may trace his property in the hands of the agent in its new form so long as it is identifiable[6]. But although in these cases the agent is treated as though he were a trustee, there is one case in which the agent literally does become a trustee for the principal: namely, whenever he is

3   Ibid, at 226.
4   (1848) 2 HL Cas 28 at 35–6.
5   See *Lupton v White* (1808) 15 Ves 432.
6   *Re Hallett's Estate, Knatchbull v Hallett* (1880) 13 Ch D 696.

instructed to purchase property for his principal and he does so in his own name[7]. In addition to the above, the agent is obliged to keep accurate accounts which he should be able to produce on request. If he fails to do so or if he keeps the accounts improperly, everything will be presumed against him.[8]

Finally, when an agency terminates the fiduciary duty to account may persist even after the contractual relationship between principal and agent has ceased. In *Yasuda Fire and Marine Insurance Co of Europe Ltd v Orion Marine Insurance Underwriting Agency Ltd*[9] a principal became suspicious of the way in which its two agents were transacting marine and aviation insurance business on its behalf. The principal terminated their contract, which had contained a clause expressly authorising the principal to inspect the agents' books. The agents subsequently refused the principal access to their books. The principal, however, obtained a declaration granting it access to over 100,000 computer and hard copy files held by the agents respecting re-insurance of the principal's interests partly on the strength of the latter's fiduciary duty to account. Although this duty could have been excluded by contract, had the parties so wished, it subsisted independently of the contract and of the contractual term which happened also to guarantee access to the agents' records in this particular case. More generally, the agent is obliged to return to his principal all documents originally handed over to him or prepared by him for the purpose of the agency relationship. A typical example would be architects who, on completion of their work, are obliged to hand over to their principals designs made for them[10].

2   RIGHTS OF THE AGENT AGAINST HIS PRINCIPAL

(i)   Remuneration

The most important right which an agent possesses against his principal is the right to be remunerated for his services. This right stems from contract. Therefore, with the exception of the 'commercial agent' whose position is now regulated by the Commercial Agents (Council Directive) Regulations 1993,[11] the agent will only be entitled to receive a commission for his services if

---

7   *Lees v Nuttall* (1829) 1 Russ & M 53. This same rule applies where the agent takes a lease in his own name on the principal's behalf.
8   *Gray v Haig* (1854) 20 Beav 219 at 226 per Romilly MR.
9   [1995] QB 174.
10   *Gibbon v Pease* [1905] 1 KB 810.
11   See post, pp 124-125.

there is an express or implied term in the contract of agency providing for his remuneration. The fact that this right is contractual means that it is not enjoyed by all classes of agent. For instance, agents of necessity, whose agency arises by operation of law, have no entitlement to commission. Similarly, agents who have bound their principals whilst acting outside the scope of their actual authority but within their apparent authority will be unable to claim remuneration for their services — unless their acts are ratified by their principals. In these cases the accent is placed, understandably, on the obligations created as between the principal and the third party, and the agent's relationship with the principal is either of little moment or even non-existent. However, in the majority of cases where the agent has acted on behalf of the principal in accordance with his contractual instructions, his right to remuneration will be determined by construction of the agency agreement concluded with the principal.

The terms of the contract

Where the parties in their contract have expressly provided for the remuneration of the agent, the terms they have agreed will govern their relationship and the courts will not override the will of the parties. Thus, in *Kofi Sunkersette Obu v Strauss & Co Ltd*[12] it was an express term of the agent's contract with a company that he would receive £50 per month by way of expenses but that the scale of his commission would be left entirely at the company's discretion. The Privy Council declined to determine the rate and basis of the commission which the agent claimed that he had earned. The parties had expressly left this at the complete discretion of the company. Sir John Beaumont spelt out the implications of a court here agreeing to fix the agent's rate of commission: 'to do so would involve not only making a new agreement for the parties but varying the existing agreement by transferring to the court the exercise of a discretion vested in the (company)'[13]. In other words, where the parties can be construed to have made express provision for remuneration, the courts will not interfere to vary the terms of the contract. This rule is further illustrated by a passage from the judgment of Plowman J in *Re Richmond Gate Property Co Ltd*:

'In the present case there was an express contract which relates to payment of remuneration, and the only question with which I am concerned is: according to the terms of that express contract, is any

12   [1951] AC 243.
13   Ibid, at 250.

sum payable for remuneration? When one finds that the express contract is that the remuneration payable is such sum as the directors may determine that the managing director shall have, and that the directors have not determined that any sum is to be payable to the managing director, it seems to me to follow as a necessary consequence that no remuneration can be claimed'[14].

Even if the commission agreed by the parties is derisory, the courts will not override the express terms of the contract.

If the parties have not incorporated an express term into their contract providing for remuneration of the agent, such a term may be implied by the courts. The implication of such a term will depend upon the circumstances of the case and will follow the normal rules governing implied terms in contracts. The courts will only be prepared to imply such a term into a contract of agency if it is clear that the parties must have intended the agent to have a right to remuneration; the rate of commission will then be determined by whatever appears reasonable to the court in all the circumstances of the case[15]. In many cases it will be apparent from the nature of the agent's employment that the parties could not be taken to have contemplated his acting gratuitously. In *Way v Latilla*[16] an agent undertook to furnish his principal with information on West African gold mines and concessions, but his contract did not provide for any right of remuneration. The court here held that there was a contract of employment and the surrounding circumstances obviously indicated that the services of the agent were not intended to be gratuitous. A term was therefore implied into the contract that the agent would receive a reasonable remuneration which the court fixed at £5,000, having regard to what the parties during their negotiations might be inferred to have considered reasonable in the circumstances. In fixing what amounts to reasonable remuneration in such cases, the courts may have regard to customs of the trade or profession carried on by the agent. But merely because the agent happens to be a member of a given profession, it does not follow

---

14   [1965] 1 WLR 335 at 338.
15   On implied contractual terms generally, see *Liverpool City Council v Irwin* [1977] AC 239, [1976] 2 All ER 39. Two principal tests have been propounded by the courts to determine if a term should be implied; the 'officious bystander' test (eg, *Reigate v Union Manufacturing Co (Ramsbottom) Ltd* [1918] 1 KB 592 at 605 per Scrutton LJ) and the business efficacy test (eg, *The Moorcock* (1889) 14 PD 64 at 68 per Bowen LJ). On the confusing relationship between these two approaches, see Burrows 'Contractual Co-operation and the Implied Term' (1968) 31 MLR 390 and Phang 'Implied Terms, Business Efficacy and the Officious Bystander — A Modern History' [1998] JBL 1.
16   [1937] 3 All ER 759.

that the courts are bound to accept what that particular profession claims to be its customary tariff for commission. As a Scots judge remarked in *Wilkie v Scottish Aviation Ltd*, 'merely because surveyors have agreed among themselves what they would like to be paid does not give them a legal right so to be paid'[17]. An agent wishing to prove a customary rate of commission charged by members of his profession has to show that the custom is valid in the normal manner: namely, it must be reasonable, certain, and notorious. He does not have to show that the principal actually knew of the custom, simply that it was generally recognised[18]. However, even if the custom is certain and notorious, it must still be reasonable in its results. In *Wilkie's* case a party employed a surveyor inter alia to value an airport and buildings for him. Their agreement made no reference to the surveyor's fees. When the work was completed, the surveyor submitted a bill for over £3,000 which, he insisted, complied with the Scale of Professional Charges of the Royal Institution of Chartered Surveyors. The employer paid £1,000 and the surveyor claimed to be entitled to the difference. The Court of Session held that the surveyor would only be entitled to the £3,000 if he could prove that it was customary for surveyors to charge according to this particular scale and, furthermore, the custom would only be admitted if the resulting fee was a reasonable one. Otherwise, the court would fix a fee which could be considered reasonable on some more equitable basis[19].

As will already be apparent, whether or not an agent becomes entitled to remuneration depends entirely upon the true construction of the terms contained in the parties' contract. Consequently, if the contract provides that the agent is only to receive his commission if he performs certain acts or brings about a specified result, his failure to do so will mean that he acquires no right to be remunerated. For example, in *Giddy and Giddy v Russell*[20] the plaintiffs were estate agents employed by Lord Russell on the terms that they would receive double commission if they found a purchaser for his leasehold interest before the end of May. They entered into negotiations with a certain Mrs Atherton who made an offer in March which was rejected by Lord Russell. Mrs Atherton then went to another firm of estate agents who proposed the same property to her. Without revealing her identity, she made another offer to Lord

17 1956 SC 198 at 205 per Lord President (Clyde).
18 *Lord Forres v Scottish Flax Co Ltd* [1943] 2 All ER 366 at 368 per Scott LJ.
19 A similar approach was adopted in the English case of *Miller v Beal* (1879) 27 WR 403.
20 (1904) 48 Sol Jo 415.

Russell which he accepted in June. The plaintiffs then sued Lord Russell, claiming that they were entitled to double commission, as originally agreed. The Court of Appeal accepted that the plaintiffs were entitled to their ordinary commission in that they had introduced the party who ultimately purchased the defendant's leasehold interest. But they had not earned their double commission since they had not fulfilled the special term of their agency which required them to find a purchaser by the end of May.

Similarly, where the agent has been instructed to perform his duties in a specified manner, if he acts outside the scope of that authority, no right to commission will arise. In *Mason v Clifton*[1] an agent was employed to obtain a loan for his principal 'on the usual terms'. It was alleged that the agent delegated this authority to a sub-agent who obtained a loan on altogether different terms, which the principal rejected. In this case Cockburn CJ declared that where an agent performs his duties in a manner different from that prescribed by the principal — namely, by obtaining a loan on different terms or by delegating his authority without the assent of his principal — he will not be entitled to any remuneration unless, of course, the principal later ratifies the agent's unauthorised acts. Hence, in *Marsh v Jelf*[2] an auctioneer, employed to sell property by auction, was not entitled to commission when he sold the property by private contract. Similar considerations apply if the agent, in the course of his agency, has breached one of his duties to the principal, entitling the latter to repudiate the contract. Once again, the agent will acquire no right to be paid commission.

Effective cause

In order to become entitled to commission, not only must the agent have successfully accomplished what he was employed to do; in addition, *he must be able to show that his services were the effective cause in bringing about that particular result*. In other words, he must have been directly instrumental in producing the desired event; his intervention must not have been merely incidental. This question of causation is one of fact in every individual case. Nevertheless, the notion of 'effective cause' can be clarified by examining decided cases, many of which involve estate agents[3].

---

1   (1863) 3 F & F 899. See also *Beable v Dickerson* (1885) 1 TLR 654.
2   (1862) 3 F & F 234.
3   See generally, Murdoch 'The Principle of Effective Cause' (1985) 276 EG 742 and 877.

The principle of 'effective cause' may require the agent to show more than just a simple causative link between his intervention and the happening of a desired event. Thus, in *Millar, Son & Co v Radford*[4] an agent was instructed to find a purchaser or a tenant for the principal's property. A tenant was found and the agent was paid his commission. Fifteen months later the tenant purchased the property and the agent, who in the meantime had not been concerned with the property, claimed further commission for having found the party who ultimately became the purchaser. The Court of Appeal rejected his claim. Collins MR declared that it was not sufficient for the agent to show that his intervention was the *causa sine qua non* in the transaction. He had in addition to show that he was the effective cause in bringing about the sale. In this case, as his active interest in the property had ceased as soon as the tenant entered into a lease with the principal, the agent was unable to show that he was directly instrumental in effecting a sale of property. Similar considerations applied in *Toulmin v Millar*[5] where an agent was employed to find a tenant for his principal's estate. He found a tenant who subsequently, without further intervention by the agent, purchased the principal's reversionary interest. The House of Lords held that the agent could not claim commission on this transaction as he had not been directly instrumental in bringing about the sale of the estate.

In *Barnett v Isaacson*[6] the concept of 'effective cause' is illustrated in somewhat different circumstances. The defendant wished to sell his business and agreed to pay £5,000 to the plaintiff if he introduced a purchaser. The plaintiff introduced the defendant to a certain Chatteris who, he said, would look for a buyer. In due course Chatteris became interested in the business and ultimately bought it himself. Six years later the plaintiff sued the defendant for his commission. The Court of Appeal pointed out that there was a stipulation in the agreement that commission was only to be paid if the plaintiff introduced a purchaser. Admittedly, he did introduce Chatteris to the defendant, but did so simply because he was himself unable to find a purchaser. Whereas the agreement required the plaintiff to introduce a person in the capacity of a purchaser, it was clear that Chatteris was introduced as an agent to find a purchaser. In short, the plaintiff's introduction was not the effective cause of Chatteris' purchasing the defendant's business and he was not therefore entitled to commission. In contrast, in *Cobbs Property Services Ltd v Liddell-Taylor*[7], even though the purchaser's initial curiosity had

---

4   (1903) 19 TLR 575.
5   (1887) 3 TLR 836. Cf *Rimmer v Knowles* (1874) 30 LT 496.
6   (1888) 4 TLR 645. See also *Mote v Gould* (1935) 152 LT 347.
7   [1990] 1 EGLR 49 at 50.

been stimulated by a conversation with the vendor's accountant, all approaches were made through the vendor's retained estate agent — whom the Court of Appeal determined therefore to have been the effective cause of the sale. As Ralph Gibson LJ mused, the vendor was 'not the first person to kick himself when he thinks he could have sold the property without the assistance of agents'.

The question whether a particular agent has been the effective cause in promoting a transaction can assume an acute form in cases where agents are acting in competition with one another. In *John D Wood & Co v Dantata*[8] the court had to determine which of two rival estate agents had been operative in the sale of a substantial property. Both had contributed to the ultimate sale in different ways but, as Nourse LJ concluded, the question for the court in such cases was to determine objectively whether either had, by his introduction, proven *the* effective cause of the sale. On the particular facts of the case, the first agents had effected the original introduction and, later in the negotiations, persuaded the purchaser to raise his offer to a level acceptable to the vendor.

In many of these cases, the advantage will lie with the first agent. As two recent decisions demonstrate, the second agent will only defeat the first's claim to commission if it can be shown that there has been a true break in negotiations, and hence in causation. In *Anscombe & Ringland Ltd v Watson*[9] agents were instructed to find a purchaser for a flat. A potential purchaser was found but the vendor rejected his offer, terminated the agents' retainer and temporarily withdrew the property from the market. Despite the agents continuing to maintain contact with this prospective purchaser and endeavouring to resuscitate the interest of the vendor, the latter adamantly refused to renew the agents' retainer and, in due course, employed second agents. The latter successfully negotiated a sale of the property to the same purchaser, who had in turn approached them. On these facts, the court found that there was a true break in the chain of causation, the first phase of negotiations having proven abortive, and therefore commission was only payable to the second agents. This case is not dissimilar from *Chesterfield & Co v Zahid*[10] where Garland J found on the facts that a second agent had reawoken a Saudi princess's interest in a noble town house after her initial approach through a first firm of estate agents had fizzled out. The second agent had made contact with her independently of the first. Therefore, there was evidence from which to conclude that the

8   [1987] 2 EGLR 23 at 25, CA.
9   [1991] 2 EGLR 28.
10   [1989] 2 EGLR 24.

original introduction had become spent, marking a definite break in the chain of causation.

Of course, as Garland J admitted, 'cases of this nature must vary infinitely on the facts, and questions of causation can give rise to endless argument'[11]. Not surprisingly, therefore, it is possible for more than one agent to become entitled to commission on the same transaction. Such an eventuality was contemplated by Drake J in *Lordsgate Properties Ltd v Balcombe*[12]. He suggested that it might come about either when a court found that both agents were actually instrumental in the sale or where two agents were simultaneously employed by the principal on different terms, both of which came to be fulfilled. The former circumstance is quite hard to imagine. As we have seen, the courts are anxious to identify the single effective cause underlying a transaction. Such an approach is not designed to produce two agents, each separately entitled to commission[13]. The latter circumstance is easier to conceive and was actually found to be present in *Lordsgate Properties Ltd v Balcombe*[14]. The principal had employed two estate agents on different terms, one to 'introduce an applicant who purchases' the property and the other who was to be paid commission should he be 'instrumental in negotiating a sale by private contract'. The first agent introduced the purchaser and the second persuaded the purchaser to increase his offer. In the circumstances, Drake J felt constrained to hold that both agents had earned their commission within the terms of their respective agreements with the vendor.

The agent's right to earn commission

Having considered what the agent must do in order to earn remuneration, a question which has frequently come before the courts is whether the principal, in turn, is under any obligation not to prevent the agent from earning his commission. The problem has tended to manifest itself in cases involving estate agents, whom we shall consider separately in a subsequent section. The general rule which the courts have developed, however, is that the agent may only sue his principal for damages to compensate him for having been deprived of an opportunity to earn commission if an express term of the contract imposes such a duty on the principal or if such a term must be implied in order to give the contract business efficacy.

---

11   Ibid, at 26.
12   [1985] 1 EGLR 20.
13   See, eg, *Barnett v Brown & Co* (1890) 6 TLR 463.
14   See also *Peter Yates & Co v Bullock* [1990] 2 EGLR 24, CA.

If the parties have expressly incorporated such a term into their contract, the agent will recover damages from his principal if the latter breaches his duty. But in the absence of any express provision, the courts have shown themselves generally unwilling to imply such a term. Indeed, in *Luxor (Eastbourne) Ltd v Cooper*[15] the House of Lords determined that in the case of estate agency contracts the courts would not be prepared to introduce an implied term that deprived the vendor of his power to prevent the agent from earning his commission. However, in all other forms of agency agreement the courts may imply such a term if it is essential to do so in order to give the contract business efficacy. *L French & Co Ltd v Leeston Shipping Co Ltd*[16] illustrates the operation of this rule. A firm of shipbrokers effected a time charterparty for eighteen months between charterers and shipowners. A clause provided that the brokers would be paid a commission of $2^1/_2$ per cent on hire paid and earned under the charterparty. After four months the owners sold the vessel to the charterers and the brokers sued the shipowners for damages equivalent to their loss of commission over the remaining 14 months which the charterparty still had to run. The House of Lords rejected the brokers' claim. No express provision in the agreement stated that the shipowners were not to deprive the brokers of an opportunity to earn their commission, and their Lordships felt it quite unnecessary to imply such a term as the charterparty already possessed full business efficacy. As Lord Buckmaster said:

'There is no need whatever in the present case for the introduction of any such term. The contract works perfectly well without any such words being implied, and, if it were intended on the part of the shipbroker to provide for the cessation of the commission which he earned owing to the avoidance of the charterparty, he ought to have arranged for that in express terms between himself and the shipowners'[17].

A similar view was taken by the Court of Appeal in *Marcan Shipping (London) Ltd v Polish SS Co, The Manifest Lipkowy*[18] where a shipbroker unsuccessfully claimed that a term be implied into his contract with the buyer of a vessel that commission would be paid once a contract was concluded, even if it was never executed. The court properly attached importance to both the fact that the express terms of the broking contract only provided for payment of commission by way

15   [1941] AC 108, [1941] 1 All ER 33; Extracts 35, p 262.
16   [1922] 1 AC 451.
17   Ibid, at 454–5. This question is further considered in the context of termination of agency in Chapter 6, post.
18   [1989] 2 Lloyd's Rep 138; see Extract 33, p 260.

of deduction from the purchase price once that price had been paid on completion and the first-instance judge's finding that shipbrokers were not customarily remunerated in such circumstances. Although Bingham LJ acknowledged that 'every case turns on its own facts and [that] this is not a field in which hard and fast rules can be laid down'[19], it is clear that in the absence of plain indications to that effect the courts will prove reluctant to imply such terms. In *Alpha Trading Ltd v Dunnshaw-Patten Ltd*[20] such a term was implied. Agents introduced a purchaser to the principal who, in breach of contract, failed to deliver to that purchaser. It was decided that the principal was liable to the agents for depriving them of their commission. The Court of Appeal was strongly influenced by the fact that the principal was actually in breach of the enforceable contract he had concluded with the third party, a circumstance that enabled it to distinguish those more numerous authorities where agents had been denied a similar right of recovery[1]. The court's anxieties at the harm that could be done were principals free to resile from their obligations to agents once the latter had performed their agencies, were neatly summarised in Lawton LJ's brief judgment, where he said:

'The life of an agent in commerce is a precarious one. He is like the groom who takes a horse to the water-trough. He may get his principal to the negotiating table but when he gets him there he can do nothing to make him sign, any more than the groom can make a horse drink ... Once the signing has been done, the agent is in a different position altogether, because by that time the principal has accepted the benefit of the agent's work. In these circumstances, he ought not to be allowed to resile from his obligations to the agent'[2].

Remuneration of 'commercial agents' under the Commercial Agents (Council Directive) Regulations 1993

The 'commercial agent', defined in Reg 2(1) as 'a self-employed intermediary who has continuing authority to negotiate the sale or purchase of goods on behalf of ... the principal, or to negotiate and conclude the sale or purchase of goods on behalf of and in the name of the principal', enjoys a right to remuneration under Reg 6(1), which lays down that

---

19 Ibid, at p 144.
20 [1981] QB 290.
1   As Bingham LJ pointed out in the *Marcan Shipping* case, fn 18, above, such an interpretation is unlikely to be necessitated where the breach of contract that prevents the agent from earning his commission is committed by the third party, and not by the principal.
2   [1981] QB 290 at 308.

'In the absence of any agreement as to remuneration between the parties, a commercial agent shall be entitled to the remuneration that commercial agents appointed for the goods forming the subject of his agency contract are customarily allowed in the place where he carries on his activities and, if there is no such customary practice, a commercial agent shall be entitled to reasonable remuneration taking into account all the aspects of the transaction.'

While Lawton LJ was correct to suggest that the life of an agent in commerce is normally precarious,[3] agents covered by the 1993 Regulations now enjoy greater security. The law will presume that it was intended that a reasonable rate of commission would be paid by the principal throughout the duration of the commercial agency, and Reg 7 spells out the transactions upon which a commercial agent will become entitled to commission. In the first instance, he is to receive commission on any transaction 'concluded as a result of his action' (Reg 7(1)(a)). It is questionable whether this requirement is identical to the common law concept of 'effective cause'[4]; the language does seem to indicate a laxer test. Indeed, this impression is confirmed by Reg 7(1)(b), which allows commission to be claimed 'where the transaction is concluded with a third party whom (the agent) has previously acquired as a customer for transactions of the same kind,' and by Reg 8 which deals with the problem of the agent whose agency is terminated but who is entitled to commission on any transaction 'mainly attributable to his efforts during the period covered by the agency contract' which has been entered into within a reasonable period after termination of the contract. The Regulations are plainly intended to give to the commercial agent a quite extensive right to earn commission.

Remuneration of estate agents[5]

One cannot overlook the fact that a high proportion of the cases dealing with the agent's right to remuneration concerns estate

3   *Alpha Trading Ltd v Dunnshaw-Patten Ltd* [1981] QB 290.
4   This view is corroborated in some sort by *Moore v Piretta PTA Ltd* (1998) Times, 11 May where, in calculating the agent's right to an indemnity under Reg 17(3), the court held that it was sufficient that the agent was 'instrumental' in winning business for the principal and that, in conformity with the Commission's intention to harmonise European law on the point along German lines, this meant that 'a small level of involvement is sufficient and it is enough that the agent has merely contributed to bringing the new customer ... the agent must have played an active role ...'.
5   See generally, Murdoch 'The Nature of Estate Agency' (1975) 91 LQR 857; *The Law of Estate Agency and Auctions* (3rd Edn, 1994). The sui generis nature of the estate agent's agency has been explored by Robinson in 'Estate Agents — Agents?' [1988] 15 Univ of Queensland LJ 46.

agents. Apart from being of considerable practical significance, estate agency provides an interesting illustration of both the way in which the agent earns his commission and the way in which the principal may legitimately prevent him from earning it. Although the Estate Agents Act 1979 now closely regulates many aspects of the conduct of the profession,[6] and the Property Misdescriptions Act 1991 imposes further controls, the activities of estate agents are governed in general by the same legal principles as those of other varieties of agent. Nevertheless, the application of these principles can pose special problems owing to the peculiar nature of the contract entered into by vendors and purchasers of real property. For these reasons, it is appropriate to examine — albeit briefly — the operation of the rules governing the remuneration of agents in the context of this class of contract.

The contract which a vendor enters into with an estate agent is, in virtually every case, a unilateral contract. The agent is not contractually bound to do anything. There is merely an agreement whereby the vendor promises to pay him a commission on the happening of a stipulated event — normally the sale of the property. Unless an agent supplies his client with information concerning his entitlement to commission before entering into the 'contract ... under which the agent will engage in estate agency work on behalf of the client', the Estate Agents Act 1979 provides that he will not be allowed to enforce it without special leave of the court[7]. Given that under the conventional form of unilateral contract the estate agent does not enter into a *contract* with the client until he has actually introduced a party who purchases the property, it is open to grave doubt just how effective this provision will prove[8].

Broadly speaking, contracts for the sale of land involve three separate stages. The first stage occurs when a purchaser makes an offer to the vendor 'subject to contract'. If accepted, this agreement does not constitute a binding contract in law. Both parties are free to withdraw from the transaction at any time prior to the second stage, which is when formal contracts are drawn up and exchanged

6   There are strong indications, particularly in Beldam LJ's judgment in *Antonelli v Secretary of State for Trade and Industry* [1998] 1 All ER 997, that the Act will be given a generous interpretation by the courts. In *Antonelli* the provision providing for the disqualification of estate agents who have committed various classes of criminal offence was construed by implication to apply retrospectively, to include convictions before foreign courts, to involve no double criminality requirement, and even to encompass property arson within the expression 'an offence involving ... violence'.

7   Section 18. It is tempting to compare the thrust of this provision with Lord Denning MR's judgment in *Jaques v Lloyd D George & Partners Ltd* [1968] 1 WLR 625 at 630.

8   See Reynolds [1980] JBL at 41.

by the parties. Only when contracts have been exchanged does there exist a binding executory contract for the sale of the property. The third and final stage in the process is when completion takes place: that is, when the title deeds to the property are formally handed over to the purchaser in exchange for the purchase price. Generally, it is only after the exchange of contracts that an estate agent becomes entitled to commission under his contract with the vendor. However, given that the vendor is free to withdraw from a sale entirely according to his caprice prior to the exchange of contracts, estate agents sometimes have claimed to have earned their commission at an earlier stage in the proceedings. A considerable body of case law has developed on the subject of the estate agent's right to remuneration and the vendor's power to prevent him earning it.

It used at one time to be held that the vendor owed a duty to his estate agent not to deprive him unreasonably of the opportunity to earn commission. For example, the majority of members of the Court of Appeal in *G Trollope & Sons v Martyn Bros*[9] held that when an estate agent introduced a purchaser to his principal and the latter *unreasonably* withdrew from negotiations with that particular party, the principal was liable in damages to the agent for preventing him from earning his commission. In the words of Maugham LJ, a term was to be implied into the contract that

'... where a person is employed to do work on behalf of another, payment to be made on completion of the work, there is a necessary implication that the employer will not do anything to prevent the earning of the remuneration, unless at any rate he has *some just excuse* for his interference with the course of events ...'[10].

Scrutton LJ delivered a powerful dissenting judgment in *Trollope's* case[11] and his views ultimately prevailed in the House of Lords in what has become the leading case on estate agents' commission, *Luxor (Eastbourne) Ltd v Cooper.*[12]

In *Luxor's* case vendors employed an estate agent to find a purchaser for their four cinemas, undertaking that the agent would receive a £10,000 fee on completion of the sale if he introduced a person who purchased the property for not less than £185,000. The agent introduced a potential buyer who offered £185,000 for the cinemas 'subject to contract'. The vendors, however, withdrew from negotiations and were sued for damages by the agent, who claimed that they had deprived him of the opportunity to earn commission.

---

9   [1934] 2 KB 436.
10   Ibid, at 456 (emphasis added).
11   See Extract 34, p 262.
12   [1941] AC 108, [1941] 1 All ER 33; see Extract 35, p 262.

The House of Lords seized this opportunity to review the question of estate agents' commission and unanimously held that, in order to give the contract business efficacy, there was no need to imply a term that the principal would not deprive the agent of an opportunity to earn commission. Given that a vendor is completely at liberty to withdraw from negotiations with the purchaser at any time prior to exchange of contracts, it would be totally unreasonable to imply a term into the contract of agency imposing fetters on that freedom. Furthermore, as the contract in *Luxor* shows, estate agents, in fixing their fees, allow for the possibility that for some reason a sale will not materialise. As Lord Russell of Killowen pointed out: 'A sum of £10,000, the equivalent of the remuneration of a year's work by a Lord Chancellor, for work done within a period of eight or nine days is no mean reward, and is one well worth a risk'[13]. The effect of the *Luxor* decision is that, in estate agency contracts where commission is payable on completion of the sale, without incurring any liability to his agent the vendor is entirely free to withdraw from the sale at any time prior to a binding executory contract coming into existence.

This is not to say that an estate agent will never under any circumstances be entitled to damages when his principal prevents him from earning commission. As in all cases of agency, this question turns entirely on construction of the precise terms of the contract — although as is already apparent, the scales are weighted heavily against the estate agent. For example, vendor and agent may have entered into what is known as a 'sole agency' agreement whereby the vendor undertakes not to sell his property through any other agent. Although in the absence of express prohibition, this will not render the principal liable if he sells the property privately[14], the agent will be entitled to damages if the vendor breaches his contract with the agent by selling his property through the offices of another agent[15]. It is nevertheless possible, as *Brodie Marshall & Co (Hotel Division) Ltd v Sharer*[16] shows, to draft a sole agency clause that entitles the agent to commission even if the vendor sells his property through his own sole initiative.

Estate agency agreements vary widely in their wording and the profession as a whole employs no single standard form contract. Whereas the agent's right to remuneration in the *Luxor* case was conditional upon completion of the sale, many estate agency

13   Ibid, at 44. See also *Bentall, Horsley & Baldry v Vicary* [1931] 1 KB 253 at 262 per McCardie J. As Phillips J once remarked, estate agents 'get paid for results and not for efforts': *Bentleys Estate Agents Ltd v Granix Ltd* [1989] 2 EGLR 21 at 23.
14   *Bentall, Horsley & Baldry v Vicary*, ante. Cf *Chamberlain and Williams v Rose* (3 December 1924, unreported) (noted by McCardie J in [1931] 1 KB at 261).
15   *Hampton & Sons Ltd v George* [1939] 3 All ER 627.
16   [1988] 1 EGLR 21.

contracts contain a term variously requiring the agent 'to find a purchaser' or 'to find a willing purchaser'. The courts have often been called upon to decide what is meant by such expressions as 'find a purchaser'. Two propositions emerge clearly from the cases.

Firstly, the agent only earns his commission if the purchaser he has introduced enters into a binding contract with the vendor. As Slade J explained in *Murdoch Lownie Ltd v Newman*[17], this means:

'a contract which binds both parties, ie which is a contract and is clothed with the necessary form required to make it an enforceable contract in law. But whether that be so or not, I am satisfied that the expression envisages a contract which, as against the party introduced by the agent, the vendor is entitled to have specifically performed or for whose breach he is at least entitled to recover damages'.

Hence, in *Peter Long & Partners v Burns*[18], where vendor and purchaser concluded a contract which was voidable owing to an innocent misrepresentation having been made by the agent, it was held that the contract could not be considered binding and the agent was not entitled to commission.

Secondly, the purchaser introduced by the agent must be willing and able to complete the purchase. This second proposition has emerged as a consequence of estate agents in their contracts attempting to devise formulae which ensure that their principals cannot escape liability by refusing to accept offers by persons willing to purchase. The courts have tended to interpret such terms strictly and have held that a third party who makes an offer 'subject to contract' or 'subject to survey' cannot be described as someone 'willing to purchase'. In other words, to be considered willing to purchase, a party must have made an unconditional offer[19].

In a sense, the only way in which an agent can prove the willingness of the purchaser is if he actually enters into a binding contract with the vendor. Indeed, some judgments hold that the agent is only allowed to prove that the third party was willing to purchase by showing that he did in fact enter into a binding contract[20]. The effect of this view is that an agent who undertakes to find someone 'willing to purchase' is, for most practical purposes, in the same position as an agent who contracts with the vendor on the usual terms. Judicial

---

17 [1949] 2 All ER 783 at 789.
18 [1956] 3 All ER 207.
19 *Graham and Scott (Southgate) Ltd v Oxlade* [1950] 2 KB 257, [1950] 1 All ER 856.
20 Eg *Dennis Reed Ltd v Goody* [1950] 2 KB 277 at 288 per Denning LJ.

pronouncements on this subject are not in complete accord and there is significant authority for the alternative view that the agent can demonstrate the purchaser's willingness, for example, simply by proving that he made an unconditional offer to the vendor[1]. Thus, in *Christie Owen and Davies v Rapacioli*[2] agents were employed to introduce 'a person ready, able and willing to purchase' the defendants' restaurant for a certain sum. The agent introduced a purchaser who agreed a price with the vendors, signed his part of the contract and paid a deposit to the estate agents. The defendants at this stage withdrew from the transaction and the Court of Appeal held that the agents had established that the purchaser was 'ready able and willing to purchase' and they were thus entitled to their commission. This interpretation, however, is open to objection on the grounds that, until the parties conclude a binding contract, the vendor is free to withdraw from negotiations or alter the terms of sale at will. Therefore, until the actual terms of the parties' agreement have been enshrined in a contract binding on both of them, it is impossible to fix the terms upon which the property is being purchased and pure speculation to speak of the purchaser's willingness to purchase on terms which, until then, may be freely varied by the vendor[3]. The better view, it is suggested, is that the estate agent can only establish the purchaser's willingness by showing that the parties did in fact conclude a binding contract of sale.

To summarise the position, as in the case of other classes of agent, the estate agent's right to remuneration is entirely dependent upon construction of the terms of the agency agreement. In general, the courts have taken the view that, unless its terms unequivocally exhibit a contrary intention, there is a strong presumption that the parties intended commission to be payable only in the event of an actual sale taking place[4].

(ii)   Indemnity

In addition to being able to claim remuneration from the principal for the services he performs, every agent has a right to be reimbursed all expenses and indemnified against all losses and liabilities incurred by him while acting within the scope of his authority. These are really two separate rights. But since they are governed by the same rules, it is convenient to discuss them together.

1   Ibid, at 283 per Bucknill LJ.
2   [1974] QB 781, [1974] 2 All ER 311.
3   See *Bowstead and Reynolds* para 7-019.
4   *Midgley Estates Ltd v Hand* [1952] 2 QB 432, [1952] 1 All ER 1394; see Extract 36 p 266.

In the majority of cases the principal's duty to indemnify his agent will derive from the contract of agency originally concluded between the parties. There may be an express term of the contract providing for this indemnity or such a term may be implied by the courts in order to give the contract business efficacy. The parties, of course, are free to exclude the agent's right to be indemnified: for example, the fundamental characteristic of *del credere* agency agreements is that the principal will be under no obligation to reimburse the agent if third parties fail to pay sums due under their contracts[5]. In the majority of contractual agencies, however, such a term will be present and the principal will be under a duty to indemnify his agent not only for all liabilities which the latter incurs as a result of a legal duty but also for those disbursements which the agent is under a strong moral obligation to meet[6]. But even if the agency is not contractual, the agent will still be entitled to an indemnity from his principal. Unless the agent is acting as a trustee (in which case equity will afford him remedies against the principal), his right to an indemnity will be founded upon quasi-contract and he can claim for all the expenses and losses which he has been compelled to incur by acting for the benefit of the principal, provided that the principal himself would otherwise have incurred those selfsame liabilities.

(a) *Expenses incurred by the agent acting within the scope of his authority.* The principal is under a general duty to indemnify his agent for all liabilities incurred whilst acting within the scope of his actual, implied or customary authority. For example, in *Chappell v Bray*[7] the plaintiff was empowered by his co-owners to employ a shipbuilder to effect some repairs to their vessel. After the shipbuilder had begun work, the defendant, who was one of the co-owners, sought to revoke the plaintiff's authority and gave notice that he would not pay his contribution towards any work done. The court held that as the mandate was already executed, it was impossible for the defendant to revoke the agent's authority. Therefore, since the plaintiff had incurred liabilities whilst acting within the scope of his actual authority, his claims for an indemnity against the defendant succeeded.

Similarly, an agent will be entitled to an indemnity for expenses he incurs whilst acting within the scope of his implied authority.

---

5   It should be mentioned that in certain professions it is customary to include the indemnity as part of the agent's remuneration. For example, unless their contracts expressly provide for the contrary, estate agents are not entitled to a separate indemnity over and above their commission: *Morris v Cleasby* (1816) 4 M & S 566.
6   Eg *Rhodes v Fielder, Jones and Harrison* (1919) 89 LJKB 15 (discussed below).
7   (1860) 6 H & N 145.

Thus, provided that the custom is reasonable, the courts will hold the principal bound to indemnify the agent against liabilities which arise out of the operation of a custom of trade. For example, it was a proven custom of the London freight market that, where a forwarding agent books space on board a ship for his principal's goods and that space for some reason is not taken up, he will stand personally liable to the shipowner for damages in respect of dead freight. In *Anglo Overseas Transport Ltd v Titan Industrial Corpn (UK) Ltd*[8] space reserved by the agents was left unfilled as a consequence of late delivery of the goods. The agents claimed an indemnity from the principal to cover the damages which they were under an obligation to pay to the shipowners. Barry J, having satisfied himself of the existence and the reasonableness of the custom, held that the agents' personal liability fell within the scope of their implied authority and, therefore, that they were entitled to be indemnified by the principal. If, on the other hand, a custom is held by the courts to be unreasonable, the principal will only be under a duty to indemnify his agent if he knew of the existence of the custom when he originally conferred authority upon the agent. Hence, in *Bayliffe v Butterworth*[9] a principal was adjudged liable to indemnify his broker on the grounds that at the material time he had known of a custom of the Liverpool Stock Exchange which rendered brokers personally liable in their dealings with one another.

It should be emphasised that the agent's right to an indemnity is not confined solely to payments made by the agent which discharge the principal of some legal liability. As mentioned already, it extends to all expenses which the agent has to meet whilst acting within the scope of his authority. Thus, in *Adams v Morgan & Co Ltd*[10] the agent, in the course of acting as manager of a business, became liable to pay supertax. As the limited company for whose benefit he was carrying on the business was a corporation, it could not have been assessed for supertax itself. Nevertheless, it was held that the clause in the agent's contract providing for an indemnity covered the agent's liability for supertax. But just as the indemnity extends beyond the legal liabilities of the principal, so too it may extend beyond the strict legal liabilities of the agent. In *Rhodes v Fielder, Jones and Harrison*[11] the defendant solicitors, who were London agents,

8   [1959] 2 Lloyd's Rep 152. For a case concerned with the reasonableness of a custom, see *Cropper v Cook* (1868) LR 3 CP 194.
9   (1847) 1 Exch 425.
10 [1924] 1 KB 751. Bankes LJ considered that this case was 'too clear for serious argument' (at 752).
11 (1919) 89 LJKB 15.

were employed by the plaintiff, a country solicitor, to act for him in respect of an appeal which was to be heard in the House of Lords. The defendant briefed counsel, who proceeded to win the case. The plaintiff then instructed his agents not to pay counsel's fees; but the agents disregarded this injunction and paid counsel out of moneys of the plaintiff in their possession. Lush J held that, although counsel would have been unable to sue the defendants for his fees, it would have been a serious case of professional misconduct if the London agents had not paid him. Consequently, they would have been entitled to an indemnity from their principal and, in the circumstances, were completely justified in applying his moneys to the payment of counsel's fees.

(b) *Expenses incurred by the agent acting in an unauthorised manner.* An agent is not entitled to claim an indemnity for liabilities he incurs whilst acting outside the scope of his authority[12]. In *Barron v Fitzgerald*[13] a principal empowered two agents to insure his life in their names. Contrary to instructions, they later insured his life in their own names and in the name of a third individual. It was held that, as they had acted outside the scope of their authority, the agents were not entitled to an indemnity in respect of premiums they had paid on the insurance policy. Similar reasoning applies in cases where the principal has successfully revoked his agent's authority before the latter enters into a binding contract with a third party.[14]

Expenses and liabilities which the agent incurs through his own fault equally will give rise to no indemnity. Thus, where a solicitor acted as agent in a prosecution for perjury and the prosecution failed as a result of the negligent way in which the agent drafted the indictment, it was held that he could not recover his expenses from the principal[15]. By the same token, in *Lage v Siemens Bros & Co Ltd*[16] agents, who incurred a fine in Brazil for failing to pay customs duty on a quantity of cable, failed to obtain an indemnity from their principal simply because the fine had been imposed as a consequence of the agents' breach of duty and, furthermore, could easily have been remitted if the agents had exercised reasonable diligence and offered the Brazilian Customs a satisfactory explanation for their actions.

---

12 That is, unless the principal subsequently ratifies the agent's unauthorised acts: *Hartas v Ribbons* (1889) 22 QBD 254.
13 (1840) 6 Bing NC 201.
14 *Warwick v Slade* (1811) 3 Camp 127.
15 *Lewis v Samuel* (1846) 8 QB 685.
16 (1932) 42 Ll L Rep 252.

Finally, an agent will not be entitled to claim reimbursement of expenses which he incurs in performing acts that he knows or must be taken to know, are illegal[17]. *Re Parker*[18] affords a good illustration of this principle. A candidate in an election employed an election agent to campaign on his behalf. The election agent's sub-agent made a number of illegal payments to canvassers contrary to the legislation then in force. The courts held that the sub-agent, in consequence, could not claim an indemnity from the candidate for these out-of-pocket expenses. It should be stressed that an agent's right to an indemnity is only forfeited when he performs acts which he knows or must be taken to know are unlawful. If he is unaware of the unlawful character of his actions, he may still claim an indemnity from his principal. For instance, in *Adamson v Jarvis*[19] an auctioneer was instructed to sell goods on behalf of a principal. Only after the auctioneer had effected a sale and handed the proceeds over to the principal was it discovered that the principal had no title in the goods. The true owner compelled the auctioneer to pay him the full value of the goods. The court, in turn, held the auctioneer entitled to an indemnity from the principal, for the transaction was not ex facie illegal and the auctioneer had no notice of the principal's want of title.

(iii)   The agent's lien

As we have now seen, during the course of his agency an agent may come to have a number of claims against his principal in respect of commission he has earned or expenses he has incurred. In order to facilitate recovery of these sums, the law accords to the agent a lien on the goods and chattels of his principal in respect of all claims arising out of his employment as agent. In essence, a lien entitles the agent to retain possession of his principal's goods until the latter has satisfied all the legitimate claims of the agent. It does not entitle the agent to sell or dispose of the goods, nor does property in them pass to the agent if the principal fails to meet his obligations. It merely entitles him to keep them in his possession[20].

---

17 Save to the extent that the agent may be entitled to a contribution from his principal under the Civil Liability (Contribution) Act 1978. See *Yeung Kai Yung v Hong Kong and Shanghai Banking Corpn* [1981] AC 787, 799–800 per Lord Scarman.

18 (1882) 21 Ch D 408.

19 (1827) 4 Bing 66.

20 'What is the nature of a solicitor's lien? It is merely a passive right, a right to hold the piece of paper or the piece of parchment, as the case may be, until he is paid. In this case it gives the solicitor no right against the fund, but merely a right to embarrass the person who claims the fund by the non-production of the piece

The law has for long drawn a distinction between two different varieties of lien: particular liens and general liens. A particular lien means that the agent's right to retain possession of his principal's goods can only be exercised in order to assist in recovery of moneys owed to him in respect of those particular goods. A general lien, in contrast, confers upon the agent a right to retain the principal's goods until the general balance of account between the principal and the agent is settled. By and large, the law has viewed general liens with suspicion and the position today is that an agent will be taken to have only a particular lien save in cases where the parties have expressly agreed that the agent should have a general lien or alternatively where custom prescribes that certain specified classes of agent — notably, factors, solicitors, bankers and stockbrokers — may exercise a general lien on their principal's goods.

(a) *Acquisition of the agent's lien.* A number of conditions must be satisfied before an agent can acquire a lien on his principal's goods and chattels. Provided that the parties have not expressly or impliedly agreed to exclude his right to a lien, the law requires that the agent must have lawfully come into possession of the principal's goods in his capacity as agent. Each of these conditions will be considered separately.

By definition, an agent can only exercise a lien if he has possession of his principal's goods. Normally, they will be in his actual possession. But the courts recognise the agent's right even when his possession is only constructive. For example, in *Bryans v Nix*[1] a principal employed a carrier to convey a cargo of oats to his agent in Dublin. He supplied the carrier with documents which clearly indicated that he was to hold the goods for the agent. In this case the court had no hesitation in holding that the agent had constructive possession of the goods — and, hence, a lien on them — from the moment that the principal handed them over to the carrier. Similarly, where an agent has acquired possession of the principal's goods but has handed them over to one of his own employees for safekeeping, they will be considered to be in his constructive possession and he will continue to be entitled to a lien over them[2].

---

of paper': *West of England Bank v Batchelor* (1882) 51 LJ Ch 199 at 200 per Fry J. Mustill J in *The Borag* [1980] 1 Lloyd's Rep 111 at 122 described it as a 'remedy of self-help'. Its exercise, however, will not be permitted to interfere with the course of justice and a court may grant relief in equity against the exercise of a solicitor's lien in such circumstances: *Ismail v Richards Butler (a firm)* [1996] 2 All ER 506.

1   (1839) 4 M & W 775.
2   Eg *M'Combie v Davies* (1805) 7 East 5 at 7–8 per Lord Ellenborough CJ.

The agent's lien is further circumscribed by the rule that the agent must have acquired possession of the goods by lawful means. If he gains possession of them unlawfully, no right of lien will arise. Thus, in *Taylor v Robinson*[3] a factor was instructed by his principal to purchase a large quantity of staves. It was agreed that they would continue to be stored on the seller's premises, rent being paid to the seller by the principal. The seller subsequently asked the factor to remove the goods from his yard, which the factor proceeded to do without the authority of his principal. It was held that under the original agreement the principal had retained possession of the goods and, having removed them unlawfully, the factor could not acquire a lien over them.

The third requirement is that the agent must have acquired possession of the goods in his capacity as agent. Therefore, if the principal simply deposits goods or chattels with the agent for safekeeping, the latter will not have gained possession of them as agent and will have no lien on them[4]. Furthermore, the agent's lien over the principal's goods and chattels only extends to claims against the principal arising out of the contract of agency under which the agent came to acquire the goods in question. For example, in *Dixon v Stansfield*[5] a factor, who regularly sold goods on behalf of his principal, on one isolated occasion acted as his insurance broker in effecting the insurance of a ship's cargo. He was held not to be entitled to a lien on the insurance policy in respect of moneys the principal owed him in his general capacity as factor. The agent's lien only allows him to retain goods and chattels in order to secure payment of sums due under the agency agreement to which those particular goods relate. As Jervis CJ pointed out, 'a man is not entitled to a lien simply because he happens to fill the character which gives him such a right, unless he has received the goods ... in the particular character to which the right attaches'[6]. This same principle is further illustrated by the case of *Houghton v Matthews*[7]. A factor had sold two parcels of goods to a third party on behalf of his principal. Neither of these parcels had been paid for when the third party decided to employ the factor himself and duly sent him some indigo to sell. When, shortly afterwards, the third party became bankrupt, the factor claimed a lien on the parcel of indigo for moneys still owed to him by the third party in respect of the two original sales. The court held that the factor had no lien on the third party's goods as

---

3   (1818) 8 Taunt 648.
4   *Muir v Fleming* (1822) Dow & Ry NP 29.
5   (1850) 10 CB 398.
6   Ibid, at 418.
7   (1803) 3 Bos & P 485.

the factor's claims against him had arisen prior to his being employed as the latter's agent.

Even though an agent may have satisfied all the conditions enumerated above and lawfully obtained possession of his principal's goods in his capacity as agent, he will only acquire a lien provided that the agency agreement does not expressly *or impliedly* exclude this right. The courts generally are reluctant to deprive the agent of his lien. But where the terms of the agreement are clearly inconsistent with its existence, the agent will be held to have no right to retain the principal's goods. By way of illustration, in *Re Bowes*[8] a party deposited a life insurance policy with his banker together with a memorandum explicitly stating that it was not to be charged with overdrafts exceeding £4,000. The court held that the effect of the memorandum was to exclude the banker's right to a general lien as the terms of this particular agreement were entirely inconsistent with the banker's common law right to retain the insurance policy as security for the settlement of the party's general balance of account.

Once a lien does attach to the principal's goods or chattels, it affords the agent a broad measure of protection. It is valid not only against the principal himself but also against third parties who subsequently acquire title or rights in the goods. Thus, in one case where an agent had a lien on an insurance policy, the agent's right in the security was not defeated when the principal afterwards assigned the policy to a third party[9]. Equally, the agent continues to enjoy the protection of his lien even if his principal subsequently becomes insolvent or commits an act of bankruptcy[10]. However, the agent normally cannot acquire more extensive rights in the goods than those which the principal possessed when the lien first attached. In other words, the agent takes his lien subject to any existing rights and equities of third parties. For example, in *Peat v Clayton*[11] a debtor assigned certain shares to the plaintiffs as trustees for his creditors, but refused to hand over the share certificates. Notwithstanding this assignment, he then employed a firm of stockbrokers who sold the shares on the Stock Exchange, executed a transfer and received the

---

8   *Re Bowes, Earl of Strathmore v Vane* (1886) 33 Ch D 586. See also *Walker v Birch* (1795) 6 Term Rep 258; *Brandao v Barnett* (1846) 12 Cl & Fin 787.
9   *West of England Bank v Batchelor* (1882) 51 LJ Ch 199.
10 *Re Capital Fire Insurance Association* (1883) 24 Ch D 408 at 420 per Cotton LJ (insolvency); *Robson v Kemp* (1802) 4 Esp 233 at 236 per Lord Ellenborough CJ (bankruptcy).
11 [1906] 1 Ch 659. Only in those cases where statute has intervened (eg the Factors Act 1889) or where the agent has retained negotiable instruments without notice of any defect in his principal's title will he acquire his lien free of existing third party equities.

purchase-money. A dispute arose as to who was entitled to the shares. The brokers claimed a lien on them, but Joyce J held that the brokers could only have acquired a lien on the debtor's interest in the shares and, therefore, their lien was subject to the prior right of the plaintiffs under the deed of assignment.

(b) *Loss of the agent's lien.* In the normal course of events the agent's lien will automatically be extinguished when the principal tenders payment of all sums due to the agent. There are, however, two further ways in which the agent may come to lose his lien on the principal's goods or chattels.

Firstly, the agent may choose to waive his rights. If the agent acts in a way that suggests an intention to abandon his lien or if his conduct is inconsistent with its continued existence, the courts will consider that he has waived his rights. In *Weeks v Goode*[12] an agent had a lien on a lease belonging to his principal. The principal demanded the return of the lease, but the agent refused to hand it over on grounds quite unconnected with the fact that he possessed a lien on the document. In this case the court construed the agent's behaviour to have amounted to a waiver of his rights to retain possession of the lease as his acts were quite inconsistent with the continuing existence of the lien. Similarly, in *Forth v Simpson*[13] a court construed that where a party stabled racehorses but freely allowed their owners to take them out and race them at will, his conduct was not consistent with continuing possession of the horses and that he had thereby lost his lien.

Secondly, since the lien is by definition a possessory right, it will be lost if the agent voluntarily chooses to part with possession of the goods or chattels to which the lien adheres. Hence, in *Sweet v Pym*[14], where a factor shipped some bales of cloth to this principal on account and at the expense and risk of the latter, it was held that the factor had thereby surrendered his lien on the goods. As Best CJ pointed out in *Jacobs v Latour*, 'a lien is destroyed if the party entitled to it gives up his right to the possession of the goods'[15]. Nevertheless, it should be stressed that the agent must have voluntarily parted with possession. If the agent loses his possession as a result of fraud or deception, for example, he will not be deprived of his rights in the goods. Hence, in one case where one of the partners in a firm of

12 (1859) 6 CBNS 367.
13 (1849) 13 QB 680. Although this was not an agency case, it is still illustrative of the principle under discussion.
14 (1800) 1 East 4.
15 (1828) 5 Bing 130 at 132.

solicitors, unbeknown to the others, took away a number of documents on which the firm possessed a lien, Kay J held that the firm had not lost its rights in consequence of the wrongful removal of the paper[16].

(c) *The lien of the sub-agent.* Although the general rules governing the agent's lien are set out above, the position of the sub-agent requires separate treatment as it involves slightly more intricate relationships. When an agent delegates his authority to a sub-agent, the latter may be entitled to exercise a lien on the principal's goods even though his claims for remuneration and indemnity will only lie against the agent[17]. Whether or not the sub-agent acquires a lien will depend upon the scope of the *agent's* authority.

Provided that his appointment was authorised by the principal, the sub-agent will be entitled to a lien in respect of all claims which arise in the authorised course of his sub-agency. But if the principal did not authorise his appointment, he will acquire no lien. Thus, in *Solly v Rathbone*[18] a factor employed to deal in timber became financially embarrassed and delegated his authority to a sub-agent without the assent of his principal. The sub-agent was aware that the timber did not belong to the factor and Lord Ellenborough CJ held that he was not entitled to a lien on the principal's goods.

However, even though the principal may have authorised his appointment, the sub-agent may not be aware that the agent is acting on behalf of a principal. Where the principal chooses to remain undisclosed, the courts hold that the sub-agent may exercise against the principal the lien which he would have possessed against the agent, had the latter in fact been the owner of the goods. This lien extends to all claims which arise prior to the sub-agent's discovering the existence of the principal. This rule is exemplified by the case of *Mann v Forrester*[19]. An agent employed a broker to effect a policy of insurance. The broker did not know that the agent was acting on behalf of another party and when, in due course, he was paid £200 by the underwriters he claimed a lien on the moneys recovered and applied £167 to settling his general balance of account with the agent. Although he knew by this time that he was acting as a sub-agent, Lord Ellenborough CJ held that since the insurance broker's claims

---

16   *Re Carter, Carter v Carter* (1885) 55 LJ Ch 230. See also *Wallace v Woodgate* (1824) Ry & M 193.

17   Unless, of course, privity exists between principal and sub-agent, in which case the sub-agent will be in a similar position and will possess the normal remedies of an agent against his principal.

18   (1814) 2 M & S 298.

19   (1814) 4 Camp 60. See also *Westwood v Bell* (1815) 4 Camp 349.

against the agent had accrued before he knew of the principal's existence, the sub-agent possessed a lien and was entitled to apply the principal's moneys to settling the balance of his account with the agent.

4 The effects of agency-relations between principal and third party

Having discussed the legal relations which exist between principal and agent, we must now turn to examine what is generally considered to be the most important aspect of the agency relationship: namely, the legal relations which are created between the principal and the third party. From the outset it is necessary to draw a distinction between two separate categories of principal. As we have repeatedly seen in the examples discussed thus far, in the majority of cases the fact that the agent is acting on behalf of a principal will have been made known to the third party. The agent may have actually named his principal, in which case he will be acting for a *named*, disclosed principal. Alternatively, the third party may merely have been informed or made aware that the agent was acting for a principal whose name was not given, in which case the agent is said to be acting for an *unnamed*, but disclosed principal. The *unnamed principal* can be considered a product of what Lord Lloyd has called the 'beneficial assumption'[1] that in the commercial domain a third party is presumed willing to contract with anyone whom the other party may happen to represent unless the third party manifests a plain contrary intent. This principle was laid down in emphatic form by Diplock LJ in *Teheran-Europe Co Ltd v S T Belton (Tractors) Ltd* who stated:

'Where an agent has ... actual authority and enters into a contract with another party, intending to do so on behalf of his principal, it matters not whether he discloses to the other party the identity of his principal, or even that he is contracting on behalf of a principal at all, if the other party is willing or leads the agent to believe that he is willing to treat as a party to the contract anyone on whose behalf

---

1   *Siu Yin Kwan v Eastern Insurance Co Ltd, The Osprey* [1994] 2 AC 199, 209.

the agent may have been authorised to contract. In the case of an ordinary commercial contract such willingness of the other party may be assumed by the agent unless either the other party manifests his unwillingness or there are other circumstances which should lead the agent to realise the other party was not so willing.'[2]

In both situations the important feature of the agency is that the existence of a principal has been made known to the third party. However, when considering the legal relations which spring up between the principal and the third party, these cases of *disclosed* agency must be clearly distinguished from another class of case where the agent contracts without disclosing the fact that he is acting as an agent — in other words, where the agent acts on behalf of an *undisclosed* principal[3]. In cases of undisclosed agency, the third party will be entirely ignorant of the fact that the agent is acting on behalf of another person and will be under the impression that the agent himself is the principal in the transaction. It is only after he has contracted with the agent that the third party may come to discover the existence of the principal.

There are a number of reasons for differentiating between cases of disclosed and undisclosed agency, which will become clearer in due course. In the first place, the rules governing the personal liability of the agent on contracts he enters into with third parties will vary according to whether or not the principal was disclosed at the time of contracting[4]. Equally, as was mentioned in an earlier chapter[5], the scope of the agent's power to bind his principal will differ according to whether or not the latter's existence was disclosed. We have seen that, provided he discloses his intention to act on behalf of the principal, an unauthorised contract made by an agent may subsequently be ratified by the principal[6]. Ratification is retroactive in its effects and ex post facto produces a situation similar to that which arises in the normal course of events when an agent contracts with the full authority of his principal. However, since, by definition, the agent who acts for an undisclosed principal will not have informed the third party that he intends to contract on behalf

2   [1968] 2 QB 545, 555.
3   Although this is the orthodox view, it should be noted that the courts sometimes blur the distinction between the categories of unnamed and undisclosed principals. For instance, Lord Denning MR in *Teheran-Europe Co Ltd v S T Belton (Tractors) Ltd* [1968] 2 All ER 886 at 889, spoke of 'an undisclosed principal ... even though his name and even his existence is undisclosed'. This blurring of the distinction between unnamed and undisclosed agency is to be deprecated.
4   See further, Chapter 5, post.
5   See Chapter 2, ante.
6   *Keighley Maxsted & Co v Durant* [1901] AC 240; see Extract 22, p 246.

of another, the undisclosed principal cannot ratify the unauthorised acts of his agent. Therefore, the agent of an undisclosed principal has no power to bind the principal beyond the scope of his actual authority[7]. The agent who acts for a disclosed principal, in contrast, may act outside the scope of this authority and still bring the principal into direct contractual relations with the third party, provided always that the principal actually ratifies his acts. But quite apart from these considerations, the main reason for discussing undisclosed agency separately from disclosed agency resides in the anomalous character of the rules governing the undisclosed principal in English law.

I DISCLOSED AGENCY

Where an agent, acting within the scope of his authority, contracts with a third party on behalf of a disclosed principal, direct contractual relations are established between the principal and the third party. The principal can therefore sue and be sued by the third party on the contract which the agent has made on his behalf. This principle is fundamental to the law of agency and, indeed, the basic purpose of agency always was to bring the principal and the third party into direct contractual relations with one another.

In cases of disclosed agency, the crucial element is the scope of the agent's authority. In our first chapter we discussed at length the various ways in which this authority may arise. Clearly, if the agent has actual, express or implied authority to make a particular contract, the principal will be bound by his agent's acts and will also be entitled to sue on the contract. The precise scope of the agent's actual authority may give rise to questions of construction and these were briefly discussed in our first chapter. However, if the contract falls within that authority, the principal cannot escape liability. Thus, in *Camillo Tank SS Co Ltd v Alexandria Engineering Works*[8], where a principal's ship was compelled to undergo repairs at Alexandria, the principal authorised an agent to verify the repairs at Alexandria, the principal authorised an agent to verify the repairs effected and 'approve' the bill submitted by the repairers. The agent approved the repairers' bill which the principal later sought to contest. The courts were called upon to decide whether the agent's authority to

---

7 *Watteau v Fenwick* [1893] 1 QB 346, it should be said, may afford a solitary exception to this general principle. However, as was argued earlier, although this case can perhaps in some measure be explained in terms of other doctrines, in reality the case is something of a maverick defying fully reasoned exposition: see ante, pp 34–36.

8 (1921) 38 TLR 134.

'approve' the bill meant that the agent actually had the power to 'agree' the debt on behalf of the principal. The House of Lords determined that this was what was meant by the term 'approve'. Therefore, since the agent was expressly empowered to agree the debt on behalf of the principal, the effect of his signature on the bill was said to be the same as if the principal himself had been on the spot in Alexandria and signed the document personally[9]. Consequently, the principal could not escape liability to the repairers.

The agent's authority, however, will not always be actual, express or implied authority. For example, we have seen that direct contractual relations can be established retroactively between principal and third party in cases where the agent enjoys no authority, provided that the principal subsequently ratifies the agent's unauthorised acts. Where ratification has taken place, the principal may sue and be sued on the contract concluded with the third party in the normal manner. Similarly, we have already seen that an agent may have only apparent authority to bind his principal or that in certain circumstances an agency of necessity may arise. In both these latter cases the principal will be bound by the acts of his agent and will incur contractual liability to the third party, although the principal is almost certainly not entitled to take the initiative and sue the third party on contracts made by these species of agent. Therefore, the general position is that where the agent acts within the scope of his authority on behalf of a disclosed principal, direct contractual relations are established between the principal and the third party. The principal may in all cases be sued by the third party on the contract and, where the agent has actual, express or implied authority or where his unauthorised acts have been ratified, the principal also may himself sue the third party.

In contrast, if the agent has acted outside the scope of his authority and ratification has not taken place, the principal will incur no liability to the third party. In *Comerford v Britannic Assurance Co*[10] the plaintiff had effected a policy of insurance with the defendant company on the life of her husband. The policy recited that the insured sum after premiums had been paid for two years was to be £75. Before the first premium had been paid a superintendent employed by the company promised the plaintiff that if her husband died as a result of accident rather than disease within the first three years of the policy, she would be paid £150. During the course of the second year of the insurance, the husband was accidentally

9   Ibid. at 144 per Lord Shaw of Dunfermline.
10   (1908) 24 TLR 593.

drowned and the plaintiff sued the defendant for the full £150. Although Bray J was prepared to hold that the superintendent in fact made the promise to the plaintiff, he had no actual authority from his principal to do so and there was nothing to show that the defendant had acted in such a way as to clothe the superintendent with apparent authority to give this promise. Therefore, as the agent had acted entirely without authority, the principal was not bound by the promise and was not liable to pay the plaintiff the full £150. Similarly, in *Wiltshire v Sims*[11], where a stockbroker sold his principal's stock on credit, it was held that the principal was not bound by the broker's acts since he had no actual authority to sell on credit and such authority could not be implied as it was neither usual nor customary for brokers to sell stock on these terms. As Lord Ellenborough CJ observed: 'The broker here sold the stock in an unusual manner; and unless he was expressly authorised to do so, his principal is not bound by his acts'[12].

But even though the agent may appear to have authority to bind his principal, the latter will escape liability if it can be shown that the third party had notice of the agent's actual lack of authority. Apparent authority only arises where the third party is induced by a representation of the principal reasonably to believe that the agent has authority to bind the principal. Thus, where it can be proven that the third party was aware of the agent's lack of authority, the principal naturally will incur no liability. In *Jordan v Norton*[13] a father expressly informed the owner of a mare that his son only had authority to take delivery of the horse provided that a certain warranty was given. The owner failed to give the warranty, but delivered the mare to the son. As the owner had express notice of the limitations imposed upon the son's authority, the father was not bound by his son's acts.

The third party, however, need not have express notice of the agent's lack of authority. Constructive notice will suffice. In *Jacobs v Morris*[14] a tobacco merchant appointed an agent under a power of attorney to carry on his business in London. By misrepresenting that his power of attorney authorised him to borrow money, the agent obtained from the defendant a loan of £4,000 on the security of bills drawn on his principal. The agent then appropriated this money to his own use. The defendant had been shown the document conferring the power of attorney but had declined to read it, preferring to trust to the word of the agent. In fact, the power of

11 (1808) 1 Camp 258.
12 Ibid, at 259.
13 (1838) 4 M & W 155.
14 [1902] 1 Ch 816.

attorney did not authorise the agent to borrow money. The Court of Appeal held that the defendant in these circumstances had constructive notice of the agent's lack of authority. The defendant had had the opportunity to verify the terms of the agent's power but, by negligently failing to examine the document, had permitted the agent to commit this fraud on the principal. Since the defendant could be fixed with constructive notice, the principal was not bound by the loan. Alternatively, the third party may be fixed with notice of a limitation on an agent's authority if, by a usage of trade, a given species of agent is generally recognised not to have authority to bind his principal by certain acts[15].

Many of the cases involving third party notice of the agent's lack of authority will turn on their particular facts. In *Dilusso Kitchens Ltd v Crawford*[16], for instance, Neill LJ, with some reluctance, held that the appellants, specialist designers and suppliers of fitted kitchens, had not represented to the respondent that a former salesman, who had pursued a contract with the respondent after changing employer, was acting on their behalf. Although conceding that there was some injustice in applying the same standards of observation to a housewife purchasing a fitted kitchen as to a banker, the Court of Appeal on the facts concluded that the respondent was not relying on any representation that the agent was still employed by the appellants: she had ordered units not to be found in the Dilusso catalogue, the order form was clearly headed 'Discount Kitchens Ltd' (albeit a somewhat similar company name), and she had made her cheque payable to 'Discount', not to 'Dilusso'.

(i) Some special cases

The above rules, which generally govern the legal relations between the disclosed principal and the third party, are subject to a number of special exceptions. These principally concern negotiable instruments and contracts concluded by deed.

(a) *Negotiable instruments.* Owing to the fact that negotiable instruments circulate freely in commerce and are liable to come into the hands of persons who know nothing of the circumstances under which they were issued, the Bills of Exchange Act 1882 includes a number of provisions which apply to agents who sign bills of

15 See, eg, *Grant v Norway* (1851) 10 CB 665, a case criticised by Reynolds (1967) 83 LQR 189, 193–6 and Munday 'The Curious Case of the Master's Ostensible Authority' (1986) 136 NLJ 508. For further discussion, see ante p 84.
16 (1988) Times, 5 December; sub nom *Discount Kitchens Ltd v Crawford* [1989] CLY 51, CA.

exchange, promissory notes or cheques on behalf of their principals. The basic rule, laid down in s 23 of the Act, is that the principal cannot be made liable on any negotiable instrument unless his signature appears on it. However, s 91(1) further provides that it is not necessary that the principal actually sign the instrument with his own hand; it will be sufficient if his signature is written on the document by some other person by or under his authority. Thus, the principal will be bound if the agent, acting within the scope of his authority, signs the instrument with the principal's name. The agent, in signing for his principal, must make it quite clear that he is signing the document only in his capacity as agent[17]. But where the agent does append his principal's signature by procuration, the third party is put upon notice that the agent's authority to sign is limited and the principal will only be liable if the agent was in fact acting within the scope of that authority[18].

(b) *Contracts by deed.* Contracts entered into under seal are also subject to special rules. A principal may neither sue nor be sued on such a contract unless he is named as a party to it and it is executed in his name[19]. This is the case even if the contract purports to be made on his behalf. Hence, in *Schack v Anthony*[20], where the master of a ship entered into a charterparty by deed in his own name 'as agent for the owners', it was held that, as they were not named as parties in the deed, the principals could not sue on the contract. But although the general rule is that, in order to sue and be sued the principal must be named as a party to the deed, this is subject to some exceptions. In particular, if the agent who contracts by deed contracts as *trustee* for the principal, equity will allow the principal to sue on the contract. In *Harmer v Armstrong*[1] an agent was appointed to purchase from a third party the copyright in a number of periodicals. The agent entered into an agreement with the third party under seal as agent and trustee for the principal. The third party subsequently breached the agreement and the principal sought to obtain a decree of specific performance compelling him to fulfil his contractual obligations. The Court of Appeal held that, as the deed had been executed by the agent as trustee for the principal, the latter was

---

17 Bills of Exchange Act 1882, s 26(1). See further, Chapter 5, post.
18 See *Reckitt v Barnett, Pembroke and Slater Ltd* [1929] AC 176; *Morison v Kemp* (1912) 29 TLR 70 (cases where the third party accepted cheques from the agent for the agent's private purposes which the third party must have known were not authorised by the principal).
19 *Re International Contract Co, Pickering's Claim* (1871) 6 Ch App 525.
20 (1813) 1 M & S 573.
1   [1934] Ch 65.

entitled to sue the third party on the contract and specific performance was granted.

Statute, too, has to some extent modified the position of the principal whose agent contracts under seal. Although the drafting of the provision is obscure, s 7(1) of the Powers of Attorney Act 1971 provides that:

'The donee of a power of attorney may, if he thinks fit—

(*a*) execute any instrument with his own signature and, where sealing is required, with his own seal, and
(*b*) do any other thing in his own name,

by the authority of the donor of the power; and any document executed or thing done in that manner shall be as effective as if executed or done by the donee with the signature and seal, or, as the case may be, in the name, of the donor of the power'.

This provision, which replaced s 123 of the Law of Property Act 1925, might at first sight appear to have abrogated the common law rule that a principal may only sue and be sued on contracts under seal if he is named as a party in the deed and it is executed in his name. However, the decision in *Harmer v Armstrong*[2] makes it clear that the common law rule still survives. The effect of s 7, therefore, is confined to cases where the agent is appointed under a power of attorney. In such cases, provided that the agent is acting within the scope of his authority, he may execute a deed in his own name and the principal may sue and be sued on the deed[3].

A further statutory provision which permits the principal to sue on deeds to which he is not a party is s 56(1) of the Law of Property Act 1925. This section provides that a person may take an immediate interest in land or other property, or the benefit of any condition, right of entry, covenant or agreement over or respecting land or other property, even though he has not been named as a party to the conveyance or other instrument. The effect of this provision is that, even though it was his agent who was a party to the deed, the principal may acquire an interest in land under the instrument and may sue on the deed.

---

2   Ibid.
3   For fuller discussion of the possible interpretations of the Powers of Attorney Act 1971, s 7(1), see *Bowstead and Reynolds* para 8-088; Fridman *The Law of Agency* (7th Edn, 1996), pp 220–1.

(ii) Cases where the agent has undertaken contractual liability

Although the agent who contracts on behalf of a named or unnamed, disclosed principal does not normally become a party to the contract, we shall see in the next chapter that there are a number of ways in which such an agent can contract personal liability to the third party[4]. If the agent does contract personally, the third party may be entitled to enforce his rights against either the agent or the principal. However, a doctrine has grown up that, in these circumstances, if the third party, for example, obtains judgment against the agent or elects to give him exclusive credit, the third party may not subsequently sue the principal. As Scrutton LJ pointed out in *Debenham's Ltd v Perkins*[5]:

'When an agent acts for a disclosed principal, it may be that the agent makes himself ... personally liable as well as the principal. But in such a case the person with whom the contract is made may not get judgment against both. He may get judgment against the principal or he may get judgment against the agent who is liable as principal, but once he has got judgment against either the principal or the agent who has the liability of the principal, he cannot then proceed against the other party, who might be liable on the contract if proceedings had been taken against him ... first'.

The assumption underlying Scrutton LJ's judgment is that where the agent has undertaken contractual liability, the intention of the parties is that liability should be alternative and that the third party should be put to his election as to whether to pursue his remedy against the agent or the principal. This outlook has been subjected to vigorous criticism; but it is clear that the notion of election is well engrained in this context, at least in the traditional rhetoric of the courts.

The crucial problem, of course, must be to determine what constitutes an election on the part of the third party. This is a question of fact in every case. However, it is tolerably clear that where the third party sues the agent to final judgment, he will be held conclusively to have chosen to hold the agent rather than the principal liable. In *Priestly v Fernie*[6] it was decided that a third party could not sue the principal after having obtained judgment against

---

4   These circumstances are enumerated in Wright J's judgment in *Montgomerie v United Kingdom Mutual SS Association* [1891] 1 QB 370, 371–2; see Extract 4, p 223.
5   (1925) 133 LT 252 at 254. See also *Benton v Campbell, Parker & Co* [1925] 2 KB 410, 414 per Salter J.
6   (1865) 3 H & C 977.

the agent, even though that judgment remained unsatisfied. Although sometimes treated as an example of election by the third party, strictly speaking this case probably did not turn upon election at all. Rather it may have illustrated the doctrine of merger of actions. This doctrine would hold that since there exists only a single obligation, once judgment is given against the agent, the third party is precluded from suing the principal to judgment for there cannot be two judgments arising out of a single obligation. In short, the two causes of action merged when the third party obtained judgment against either the agent or the principal. This rule concerning joint debtors, it should be noted, has now been altered by s 3 of the Civil Liability (Contribution) Act 1978.

Priestly v Fernie may be contrasted with the case of *Calder v Dobell*[7] where the court did purport to apply the doctrine of election. A broker was employed to purchase cotton for a principal whose identity was divulged to the seller. Bought and sold notes were exchanged with the broker and the cotton was invoiced to the broker, who refused to take delivery. Although the seller had dealt exclusively with the broker, he later brought an action against the principal. The court determined that the seller's dealing solely with the broker did not amount to an election to give exclusive credit to the agent and the seller was therefore entitled to sue the principal. The law, then, requires a clear and unequivocal act on the part of the third party before it will hold that election has taken place[8].

As has been indicated, it is open to question whether election can claim a legitimate role in the context of disclosed agency[9]. Many of the relevant decisions can be viewed as cases involving the formation of the contract rather than as cases where a third party is making a subsequent election. Moreover, even if one is endeavouring to read the intentions of the third party at the time when he concludes his contract with the agent acting for a named or unnamed principal, there is no strong reason to presume that he will always opt for the alternative liability of the agent and the principal rather than for their joint and several liability. After all, joint liability is both more advantageous to the third party and, legally, might appear more conventional. In short, Scrutton LJ's basic assumption in *Debenham's Ltd v Perkins* may be unrealistic and, arguably, contradicts the most probable intentions of the parties to the contract. Although, as we shall see, there may be stronger grounds for recognising a doctrine of election in the context of undisclosed principals, the notion looks

7   (1871) LR 6 CP 486.
8   See further, pp 166–168.
9   See notably, Reynolds 'Election Distributed' (1970) 86 LQR 318; *Bowstead and Reynolds* para 8-117.

distinctly unconvincing in cases of disclosed agency[10]. It has been suggested that the majority of disclosed agency cases are explicable on other grounds and even that it is still technically possible for the courts to jettison the doctrine. However, it should not be lost from sight that there is a wealth of judicial dicta to support its application in the context of disclosed agency. It is thought likely, therefore, that no matter how irrational it may appear, the courts will persist in appealing to the notion of election and imposing alternative rather than joint and several liability.

(iii) Settlement with the agent

In general, once direct contractual relations have been established between the disclosed principal and the third party, the agent drops out of the transaction and ceases to exert any influence over their legal relationship. Thus, the third party cannot discharge his obligations to the principal by making payment to the agent. Nor can the principal resist the claims of the third party by showing that he has already settled with his agent. But although payments made to the agent by either party do not normally operate to discharge them from contractual liability, this rule is subject to certain qualifications.

(a) *Where the principal settles with his agent.* Payments made by the principal to his agent will operate to discharge him from liability to the third party if the latter's conduct induces the principal to believe that his liability to the third party has already been discharged for him by the agent. To take a simple illustration, in *Wyatt v Marquis of Hertford*[11] the third party, who was owed money by the principal, chose to take a security from the agent to whom he gave a receipt as though he had received payment. Unaware of what the agent had done, the receipt induced the principal to believe that the agent had paid the third party and, in consequence, the principal settled with his agent. It was held that in these circumstances the third party was not entitled to sue the principal. As Parke B declared in *Heald v Kenworthy*[12].

'If the conduct of the seller would make it unjust for him to call upon the buyer for the money; as for example, where the principal is

---

10   For recent judicial consideration of this passage, see *Lang Transport Ltd v Plus Factor International Trucking Ltd* (1997) 143 DLR (4th) 672, 689–90 per Catzman, JA.

11   (1802) 3 East 147.

12   (1855) 10 Exch 739 at 746.

induced by the conduct of the seller to pay his agent the money on the faith that the agent and seller have come to a settlement on the matter, or if any representation to that effect is made by the seller either by words or conduct, the seller cannot afterwards throw off the mask and sue the principal'.

The older cases sought to justify this rule on the grounds that it would be unjust to hold the principal liable to pay his debt to the third party twice over[13]. However, subsequent decisions — notably, *Irvine & Co v Watson & Sons*[14] — have rejected this rationale, preferring to regard the rule as a case of estoppel. The courts now confine themselves to asking whether the conduct of the third party was such as to induce the principal to pay the agent under the mistaken belief that the agent had settled with the third party.

Such conduct may take a variety of forms and it will be a question of fact in every individual case whether the conduct of the third party has given rise to an estoppel. For example, although the third party's delay in seeking payment from the principal will not always raise an estoppel[15], it may do so 'if a delay has intervened which may reasonably lead the principal to infer that the (third party) no longer requires to look to the principal's credit, such a delay for example as leads to the inference that the debt is paid by the agent, or to the inference that though the debt is not paid the (third party) elects to abandon his recourse to the principal and to look to the agent alone'[16].

(b) *Where the third party pays the agent.* Although the third party generally can only discharge his contractual liability by paying the principal, there are certain circumstances in which payment made to the agent will bind the principal. Notably, this is the case where the principal has authorised the agent to receive payment on his behalf. The authority of the agent may either be express, implied or apparent. Alternatively, it may result from the principal ratifying the unauthorised acts of the agent: for example, if the agent is paid by the third party and the principal in turn accepts payment from the agent, the principal will be considered to have ratified the third party's payment to the agent. But in the absence of any such authority, payments to the agent will not discharge the third party

---

13 Eg *Thomson v Davenport* (1829) 9 B & C 78; Extract 40, p 271; *Smyth v Anderson* (1849) 7 CB 21.
14 (1880) 5 QBD 414.
15 Eg *Davison v Donaldson* (1882) 9 QBD 623.
16 *Irvine & Co v Watson & Sons* (1879) 5 QBD 102 at 107–8 per Bowen J (affd at (1880) 5 QBD 414).

of liability. In *Butwick v Grant*[17] a traveller, acting for a supplier, obtained an order for some coats from a tradesman. The tradesman was aware that the traveller was probably acting as an agent. The coats were sent by the supplier together with an invoice bearing his name, but the tradesman paid the traveller. It was held that, as the agent had no authority to receive payment, the third party still remained liable to pay the principal.

The principal may expressly confer upon the agent a general authority to receive payment. Alternatively, he may give his agent authority to receive payment in a particular manner — for example, in cash. In the latter case, payment made to the agent in a different manner only affords the third party a good discharge if it can be shown that the principal held the agent out as having apparent authority or if trade usage endows him with implied authority to receive payment in that particular way. For example, in *The Netherholme, Glen Holme and Rydal Holme*[18] the principals had authorised their brokers to receive payments under certain insurance policies in cash according to the recognised custom of the trade. The brokers instead took a bill of exchange and subsequently became insolvent. The Court of Appeal held that, since the taking of the bill was outside the scope of the brokers' authority and also contrary to recognised business custom, the insurers had not obtained a good discharge and were still liable to pay the principal. For similar reasons, in *Williams v Evans*[19], where an auctioneer was authorised to sell goods on the condition that they were paid for before delivery, Blackburn J held that payment by bill of exchange did not discharge the purchaser.

2 UNDISCLOSED AGENCY

Thus far we have been exclusively concerned with cases of agency where the third party has been aware that the agent is acting on behalf of a principal. We must now turn to consider the legal relationships which arise in a different category of case, where the third party contracts with the agent unaware that the latter is contracting as agent.

---

17 [1924] 2 KB 483.
18 (1895) 72 LT 79.
19 (1866) LR 1 QB 352.

(i)   The doctrine of the undisclosed principal

When an agent concludes a contract on behalf of an undisclosed principal, the general rule is that, provided the agent acted within the scope of his authority, evidence may subsequently be adduced to show that the undisclosed principal was the real principal in the transaction and he may sue and be sued on the contract concluded by his agent.

This doctrine is widely regarded as anomalous. English law has always displayed reluctance to recognise the validity of contracts entered into for the benefit of third parties and tenaciously adhered to a rigid doctrine of privity of contract. Since the third party will be ignorant of the existence of an undisclosed principal, privity of contract logically is only established between the third party and the agent[20]. However, irrespective of the wishes of the third party, the undisclosed principal is permitted to intervene on his agent's contract. The effect of this rule is that the principal comes to acquire rights and liabilities under a contract to which originally he was not a party.

Since the late nineteenth century a distinguished chorus of writers has despaired of offering any principled explanation for this highly peculiar doctrine. Sir Frederick Pollock, for instance, characterised it as 'inconsistent with the elementary doctrines of the law of contract'[1], whilst Oliver Wendell Holmes thought it was 'opposed to common sense'[2]. Ames argued that the doctrine of the undisclosed principal 'ignores fundamental legal principles' and, for that reason, it was 'highly important that it should be recognised as an anomaly'[3]. Judges, too, at the turn of the century, began to perceive that it was anomalous[4]. In fact, it was probably no coincidence that, at a time when a more objective approach was coming to be adopted in respect of all matters affecting the formation of contracts, the doctrine should suddenly have appeared to lawyers as utterly irregular[5].

---

20   Although we take the line that the contract is made between agent and third party and that the undisclosed principal intervenes upon it, there are *dicta* suggesting that the principal is a party to the contract. To the extent that there is a controversy — one in which Staughton, LJ in *Welsh Development Agency v Export Finance Co Ltd* [1992] BCLC 148 declined to become involved — the reader is referred to *Bowstead and Reynolds* para 8.070.

1   (1887) 3 LQR 359. See also (1898) 14 LQR 2, 5.

2   See 'The History of Agency' in *Select Essays in Anglo-American Legal History*, vol 6, p 404.

3   18 Yale LJ 443 (1909).

4   Eg, *Keighley, Maxsted & Co v Durant* [1901] AC 240 at 261 per Lord Lindley.

5   See Atiyah *The Rise and Fall of Freedom of Contract* (1979), p 499.

The curious doctrine of the undisclosed principal has provoked a considerable literature, but defies any entirely satisfactory explanation. Whilst academic writers have variously sought to explain the principal's right of intervention as a form of trust or as a primitive and highly restricted form of assignment[6], the courts have preferred to justify the doctrine simply on grounds of commercial convenience. As Lord Lindley observed in *Keighley, Maxsted & Co v Durant*:

'As a contract is constituted by the concurrence of two or more persons and by their agreement to the same terms, there is an anomaly in holding one person bound to another of whom he knows nothing and with whom he did not, in fact, intend to contract. But middlemen, through whom contracts are made, are common and useful in business transactions, and in the great mass of contracts it is a matter of indifference to either party whether there is an undisclosed principal or not. If he exists it is, to say the least, extremely convenient that he should be able to sue and be sued as a principal, and he is only allowed to do so upon terms which exclude injustice'[7].

It may be possible, however, to reconstruct the way in which the principal's right to intervene on his agent's contract developed historically[8]. In the eighteenth century, when trade was perhaps conducted at a gentler pace, the agent was often a factor entrusted with possession of the principal's goods who sold them under executed contracts of sale. The third party would solely be interested in the agent and it was of little moment whether the principal was disclosed or not. It suited both the principal and the third party individually to look only to the agent and there was no need to seek any direct contractual relationship between principal and third party. But as the tempo of trade quickened in the nineteenth century and trade on credit terms became the norm, so commercial agents were

---

6   See notably Goodhart & Hamson 'Undisclosed Principals in Contract' [1931] 4 CLJ 320, 336. On the possible relationship between the doctrine and the non-assignability of rights at common law, see Weir 'Contracts in Rome and England' 66 Tulane L Rev 1615, 1630–1 (1992) and 'Passing of Ownership under Contract of Sale' in *Vendita e' transferimento della proprieta della prospettiva storico-comparatistica* (1991), p 403. The various theories elaborated over the years are passed in review by Stoljar *The Law of Agency* (1961), pp 228–33.

7   [1901] AC 240 at 260–1. Cf *Freeman and Lockyer v Buckhurst Park Properties (Mangal) Ltd* [1964] 1 All ER 630 at 644 per Diplock LJ; Extract 14, p 233. For all its peculiarity, the vigour of the doctrine was exemplified in the House of Lords decision in *Boyter v Thomson* [1995] 3 All ER 135, esp p 138 per Lord Jauncey where the rules relating to undisclosed principals were held to be incorporated by implication into the Sale of Goods Act 1979, s 14.

8   This account owes much to the exhaustive researches of *Stoljar*, pp 204–11.

obliged to take greater risks and bankruptcies were not uncommon[9]. This is arguably reflected in the fact that the earliest cases where the principal is allowed to intervene involve bankrupt agents. The courts were willing to recognise that the principal retained a property both in the goods he entrusted to the agent and in their proceeds of sale as against the assignee in bankruptcy[10]. From these modest beginnings, despite an isolated hiccough provoked by an obstinate jury in *Scrimshire v Alderton*[11], the principal's right to sue the third party soon developed into a firmly entrenched body of doctrine[12]. Executory bargains, too, came to be encompassed by the rule practically without demur. With the rise of the broker, both undisclosed and unnamed principals became a commonplace of commercial life and it came about that in many transactions the identity of the principal was a matter of no particular importance or interest to the third party. As Holmes was later to observe, the principal's right to sue may have 'no profounder origin than the thought that the defendant, having acquired the plaintiff's goods by way of purchase, fairly might be held to pay for them in an action of contract and that the rule then laid down has been extended since to other contracts'[13].

The third party's converse right to sue the principal seems to have been accepted by the courts virtually without question since the eighteenth century, when the rule suddenly emerged'[14]. The rationale for this right enjoyed by the third party may lie in that 'common law equity', diagnosed by Pollock, which can be expressed as 'the feeling that a person who (has) got the advantage of a purchase ought to pay for it if the agent to whom the seller really trusted was not able to do so'[15].

Whatever its historical origin, it is important to emphasise that the doctrine of the undisclosed principal, which has since developed beyond the confined needs of eighteenth and nineteenth century factors and brokers, can still be justified today in terms of its

9   For a more detailed account of the rise of the commercial factor, see Munday 'A Legal History of the Factor' (1977) 6 Anglo-American LR 221.
10   See, eg, *Scott v Surman* (1742) Willes 400.
11   (1743) 2 Stra 1182.
12   Eg, *George v Clagett* (1797) 7 Term Rep 359; *Drinkwater v Goodwin* (1775) 1 Cowp 251.
13   'Agency' 5 Harv L Rev 1, 4 (1892). It may be possible to mount a similar argument in support of the social utility of a device by which the liability of the *apparent* principal can be substituted for that of the real, concealed principal: Cardozo *The Paradoxes of Legal Science* (1928), pp 70–71. See, eg, Chapter 5 1(iv), post.
14   Eg, *Snee v Prescott* (1743) 1 Atk 245; *Nelson v Powell* (1784) 3 Doug KB 410; *Thomson v Davenport* (1829) 9 B & C 78; See Extract 40, p 271.
15   (1887) 3 LQR, at 359.

acknowledged commercial convenience. It may even be justifiable on economic grounds in overcoming strategic bargaining behaviour in cases, say, where a seller would otherwise seek to reap advantage from a disclosed buyer's deep pocket[16]. But, in addition, there are grounds for saying that it is a just doctrine. As Goodhart and Hamson have argued:

'... Justice is often served by allowing the undisclosed principal to be paid directly by the third party, especially in cases where the agent was used as a factor and fails before payment by the third party. In such cases, the principal would recover only a dividend in the bankruptcy of the agent if he were not allowed to receive the price directly from the third party. The third party is, no doubt, willing to pay the principal directly; and there seems to be no reason in justice why the other creditors of the agent should take a benefit from the money which, in common sense, belongs to the principal alone on the price of his goods'[17].

(ii) Contracts upon which the undisclosed principal may not intervene

Although the doctrine may prove convenient from a commercial point of view, Lord Lindley's claim that the undisclosed principal's right to intervene on his agent's contract is never allowed to work injustice is more debatable. In certain circumstances the principal is in fact precluded from suing on the contract concluded by the agent. However, the restrictions on his right to sue are not extensive and, as we shall see, there still remain cases where the principal is entitled to intervene even though his identity is far from being a matter of indifference to the third party.

(a) *The terms of the contract.* The undisclosed principal is not permitted to intervene on a contract made by his agent if his intervention would contradict an express or implied term of that contract. As McNair J said in *Finzel, Berry & Co v Eastcheap Dried Fruit Co*:

'It is clear law today that a person who has concluded a contract in his own name may prove by parol evidence that he was acting for an undisclosed principal *unless he has contracted in such terms as to show that he was the real and only principal*, and ... it (is) really a question of the construction of the particular contract which determine(s)

---

16 Barnett 'Squaring Undisclosed Agency with Contract Theory', 75 Col L Rev 1969, 1976–1977 (1987).
17 'Undisclosed Principals in Contract' [1931] 4 CLJ at 321.

whether parol evidence (is) admissible to prove that some person other than the party named in the written contract (is), in fact, the true principal'[18].

The undisclosed principal's intervention may be expressly excluded by the terms of his agent's contract. For example, in *United Kingdom Mutual SS Assurance Association v Nevill*[19], Tully, the managing part-owner of a vessel, became a member of a mutual insurance association and insured the ship under the rules of the association. The insurance policy and the association's rules prescribed that only members could be made liable to pay contributions in the nature of premiums. However, since Tully had become bankrupt, the association sought to claim contributions from the defendant, who was also a part-owner of the vessel but not a member of the association. It was held that the defendant could not be made liable for these contributions because the terms of the contract explicitly stipulated that only members could incur this liability. Thus, the managing part-owner had expressly contracted as principal in the transaction. To have allowed the association to sue the defendant would have been to recognise the existence of 'an undisclosed member', and such a thing cannot exist[20]. Therefore, as this case illustrates, it is possible for the terms of the agent's contract *expressly* to exclude the intervention of an undisclosed principal.

More frequently, however, the courts have been called upon to determine whether the undisclosed principal's intervention has been *impliedly* excluded by the terms of his agent's contract. This question first arose in the case of *Humble v Hunter*[1] where the court laid emphasis upon the form of the contract as a means of excluding the intervention of an undisclosed principal. In this case the agent entered into a charterparty with the defendant purporting to contract as 'CJ Humble, Esq, *owner* of the good ship or vessel called the *Ann*'. The principal sought to sue on this contract. But it was held that, as the agent had described himself as the *owner* of the ship, he had contracted as the sole principal in the transaction and parol evidence was not admissible to show that in reality he had contracted on behalf of another. As one of the judges pointed out, it would have been different if the agent had merely described himself in the contract as 'the contracting party': since such a description would have been ambiguous, evidence would have been admitted to explain

---

18   [1962] 1 Lloyd's Rep 370 at 375 (emphasis added). See also, *Dunlop Pneumatic Tyre Co Ltd v Selfridge & Co Ltd* [1915] AC 847 at 864 per Lord Parmoor.
19   (1887) 19 QBD 110.
20   Ibid, at 117 per Lord Esher MR.
1   (1848) 12 QB 310.

the capacity in which he had contracted[2]. At all events, 'the assertion of title to the subject-matter of the contract'[3] rendered inadmissible parol evidence which contradicted the terms of the written contract.

In subsequent cases the courts have differed in their interpretations of *Humble v Hunter*. Whilst they have sometimes held that the case is authority for a rule that parol evidence is not admissible to vary or contradict the written contract, the better view is that the undisclosed principal is excluded from intervening on contracts where the agent may be shown impliedly to have contracted as the sole principal in the transaction[4]. Thus, where the agent contracts as 'owner' or 'proprietor'[5], he may be construed to be impliedly undertaking that there is no principal concealed behind him. In contrast, where an agent enters into a contract describing himself as a 'tenant', for example, it has been held that the description 'tenant' no more negatives agency than would the description 'contracting party', and parol evidence has been admitted to show that the agent was acting on behalf of an undisclosed principal[6].

In *F Drughorn Ltd v Rederiaktiebolaget Trans-Atlantic*[7], where an agent for an undisclosed principal had described himself as the 'charterer' of a vessel in his contract with the third party, Viscount Haldane sought to explain the distinction drawn between these two classes of case. On the one hand, there were cases like *Humble v Hunter* where the agent made an assertion of title to property and where it became a term of the contract that the agent should contract as owner of that property. In these cases it was not permissible to contradict the contractual terms by adducing evidence to show that another party was the real owner. But, on the other hand, there were cases where the description adopted by the agent was not inconsistent with the intervention of an undisclosed principal:

'... the term "charterer" is a very different term from the term "owner" or the term "proprietor". A charterer may be and prima facie is merely entering into a contract. A charterparty is not a lease — it is a chattel that is being dealt with, a chattel that is essentially a mere subject of contract; and although rights of ownership or rights akin to ownership may be given under it prima facie it is a contract for

---

2   See (1848) 17 LJ NS QB 350 at 352 per Patteson J.
3   (1848) 12 QB 310 at 316 per Wightman J.
4   See, eg, Goodhart & Hamson 'Undisclosed Principals in Contract' [1931] 4 CLJ 320, 327.
5   See, eg, *Formby Bros v Formby* (1910) 102 LT 116.
6   *Danziger v Thompson* [1944] KB 654 at 657 per Lawrence J; see Extract 37, p 267.
7   [1919] AC 203; see Extract 38, p 268.

the hiring or use of the vessel. Under these circumstances it is in accordance with ordinary business common-sense and custom that charterers should be able to contract as agents for undisclosed principals who may come in and take the benefit of the charterparty'[8].

The effect of the decision of the House of Lords in *Drughorn's* case has been considerably to limit the scope of the rule in *Humble v Hunter*[9]. It will now only be in exceptional cases that the undisclosed principal's intervention will be held inconsistent with the terms of the contract, and possibly only in cases where the agent can be construed to have contracted as the owner of property. Such a trend can be detected in Morris J's decision in *O/Y Wasa SS Co Ltd v Newspaper Pulp and Wood Export Ltd*[10]. In this case the agents had described themselves in a charterparty as 'the disponent owners'. Although this case came close to resembling *Humble v Hunter*, Morris J considered the phrase 'disponent owner' to be 'somewhat vague' and capable of covering someone who could dispose of a ship without being the actual owner[11]. Therefore, the terms of the contract were not inconsistent with the agents acting on behalf of an undisclosed principal. This decision may be contrasted with the later case of *The Astyanax*[12], where the Court of Appeal agreed that a party's use of the description 'disponent owner' was neutral, but held that the surrounding circumstances and the course of negotiations on this occasion were inconsistent with the relevant party's having contracted in the capacity of a mere agent on behalf of the registered owners of a vessel.

(b) *The personality of the parties.* The undisclosed principal's right to intervene on his agent's contract may also be affected by personal factors. Although parol evidence is generally admissible to prove that the agent was in fact acting on behalf of an undisclosed principal, the courts hold that the principal may not intervene in circumstances where the personality of either the agent or the principal is an especially relevant factor. Broadly speaking, this means that the principal is not entitled to sue on contracts where the third party clearly intended only to contract with the agent and with no one else.

8   Ibid, at 207 per Viscount Haldane.
9   Indeed, in *Epps v Rothnie* [1945] KB 562, [1946] 1 All ER 146, Scott LJ went so far as to suggest that *Humble v Hunter* had been overruled by the House of Lords in *Drughorn's* case.
10   (1949) 82 Ll L Rep 936.
11   Ibid, at 954.
12   *Asty Maritime Co Ltd and Panagiotis Stravelakis v Rocco Giuseppe and Figli SNC, The Astyanax* [1985] 2 Lloyd's Rep 109; see Extract 39, p 269.

Equally, it may signify that the principal can be excluded from intervening in cases where the third party would never have agreed to contract with him, had he been aware of his identity. Given that the existence of the principal by definition is concealed from the third party, there is of course a sense in which it could be said that in all cases of undisclosed agency the third party intended to contract solely with the agent. However, the very existence of the doctrine of the undisclosed principal puts paid to this line of argument and, as we shall see, the courts have imposed comparatively little restriction on the undisclosed principal's right to intervene on his agent's contracts.

The courts will not permit the undisclosed principal to sue the third party where the latter's contract with the agent is one which the third party entered into relying entirely upon the agent's personal skill or solvency. In *Greer v Downs Supply Co*[13] a third party contracted with an agent solely as a means of obtaining a set-off which would settle a debt owed to him by the agent. The undisclosed principal subsequently sought to bring an action against the third party on the agent's contract. But the Court of Appeal held that in these circumstances the principal was not entitled to sue. The third party had contracted with the agent solely for personal reasons and the principal was thereby debarred from intervening on the contract. Thus, where the third party has contracted with the agent for reasons personal to the agent and these reasons induced him to contract with the agent to the exclusion of the principal or anyone else, the undisclosed principal is not entitled to sue on his agent's contract[14].

Similar considerations will apply in the case of all personal contracts[15]. Thus, if the contract is one in respect of which the

---

13 [1927] 2 KB 28.
14 Ibid, at 35 per Scrutton LJ. It is permissible to wonder whether, in view of the rights of set-off enjoyed by the third party in cases where the undisclosed principal seeks to intervene on the agent's contract, the Court of Appeal was strictly obliged to come to this conclusion on the importance attaching to the agent's skill and solvency in *Greer v Downs Supply Co*.
15 See Goodhart & Hamson, ante, at 340–1. What counts as a personal contract in this context may not coincide with what so qualifies in other legal contexts. Thus, whereas in the case of the law governing assignment an insurance contract would normally be considered personal, in *Siu Yin Kwan v Eastern Insurance Co Ltd* [1994] 1 All ER 213 the Privy Council allowed an undisclosed principal to intervene on a policy of insurance because it found that the actual identity of the principal was a matter of indifference to the insurer and not material to the risk. A contract of indemnity insurance, Lord Lloyd stated, was not personal in the same sense as a contract to paint a portrait and there was no rule of law that a contract of insurance constituted an invariable exception to the general rule that an undisclosed principal could intervene on his agent's contract. For comment, see Tettenborn [1994] CLJ 223, and Halladay [1994] LMCLQ 174.

benefits cannot be assigned or where performance can only be made by the contracting party, the undisclosed principal may not be permitted to intervene. For example, if the third party employs an artist to paint his portrait, this is a personal contract which cannot be performed vicariously. The third party has contracted for the artist's individual skills and the latter is therefore precluded from revealing later that he was in reality acting for an undisclosed principal.

Just as the third party may have wished specifically to contract with the agent and no-one else, there is a further limited class of case where the undisclosed principal sometimes will not be permitted to intervene on the grounds that the third party expressly desired not to contract with the principal. Normally, an undisclosed principal cannot be prevented from intervening on his agent's contract merely because the third party would not have contracted, had he known that the principal was in fact being represented by the agent. In *Dyster v Randall & Sons*[16] the plaintiff knew that the defendant would not agree under any circumstances to sell certain land to him. He therefore employed an agent to negotiate the purchase of the property without revealing the fact that he was acting for a principal. Upon discovering that the agent had been acting for the plaintiff, the defendant sought to resist performance of the contract on the grounds that he had been deceived by the agent. The court held that the contract could be enforced by the undisclosed principal in this case. It was not a personal contract and the identity of the real purchaser consequently was not a material ingredient. The mere failure to disclose that the agent is acting for a particular principal, even if the latter is aware that the third party would not have contracted with him, will not deprive the principal of his right to intervene on the agent's contract.

However, the position is different if the agent has misrepresented the identity of his principal In *Archer v Stone*[17] the defendant specifically asked the agent, Archer, whether he was acting for Smith and the agent untruthfully replied that he was not. When Archer subsequently sought specific performance of the contract, North J held that since this misrepresentation — which he termed 'a lie appurtenant' — induced the third party to contract with him, specific performance would not be granted:

'If (the agent) tells a lie relating to any part of the contract or its subject matter, which induces another person to contract to deal with

---

16   [1926] Ch 932.
17   (1898) 78 LT 34.

his property in a way which he would not do if he knew the truth, the man who tells the lie cannot enforce his contract'[18].

These cases would suggest that, unless the contract is a personal contract, the principal can only be prevented from intervening if the agent has expressly denied that he is acting on his behalf. However, a judgment of McCardie J in *Said v Butt*[19] would further hold that sometimes a principal cannot intervene in cases where the third party can show that he would never have agreed to contract with the principal, though no positive representation has been made to the third party.

In *Said v Butt* the defendant, who was the managing director of a theatre, had for some time been involved in a dispute with Said arising out of allegations Said had made concerning the sale of tickets by the theatre. The theatre was presenting a new play, 'The Whirligig', and Said was anxious to attend the first night performance. Twice his personal application for a ticket had been refused. Therefore, he employed Pollock as his agent to acquire a ticket for him without disclosing his name. On his arrival at the performance, Said was refused admittance and in consequence he brought an action against Butt for breach of contract. McCardie J, evidently proceeding upon the assumption that the contract in cases of undisclosed agency is concluded between the principal and the third party, held that this contract was affected by mistake as to the identity of the contracting party and Said's action therefore failed. The correctness of this decision is open to question. It is axiomatic to the law of agency that in the first instance the third party contracts with the agent, not with the undisclosed principal. If McCardie J had proceeded upon this basis, the proper question would have been whether this particular contract with Pollock was of such a personal nature as to exclude the intervention of the principal. It was accepted that a first night performance at the theatre was a special event and that the management only disposed of first night tickets to those whom it selected. However, there was no evidence that in this case the defendant had placed positive reliance upon the character of the agent, Pollock. It was only later that he sought to place negative reliance upon the fact that Pollock was not acting for Said. Hence, strictly speaking, this was not a personal contract where the third party had placed particular reliance upon the skill, solvency or, indeed, character of the agent. Although the reasoning in *Said v Butt* cannot be supported, the decision has not been overruled and it still

18   Ibid, at 35 per North J.
19   [1920] 3 KB 497.

offers authority for the proposition that, where the personal element is 'strikingly present'[20] in the contract made with the agent, an undisclosed principal may not intervene[1].

It should be emphasised that the cases treated hitherto relate to *agents* who have acted on behalf of undisclosed principals with whom the third party was averse to entering into legal relations. If it can be established, however, that the person with whom the third party negotiated was not actually an agent, but was acting as a principal in his own right, then the above-mentioned restrictions on his ability to bind the third party may be circumvented. Thus, in *Nash v Dix*[2] the defendants sought to resist the plaintiff's claim for specific performance of a contract to sell a Congregational chapel on the grounds that the plaintiff was secretly acting as agent for a committee of Roman Catholics, who proposed using the building for Roman Catholic worship and whose earlier and more direct overtures had already been rejected by the defendant vendors. The plaintiff had contracted to purchase the chapel on the understanding that the Roman Catholic committee would in turn buy it from him at £100 profit. North J was prepared to find that, in the rather special circumstances obtaining in this case, the plaintiff was not an agent of the committee but was purchasing the property for himself with a view to re-sale at a profit:

'The fact that (the plaintiff) knew that the defendants would have been reluctant to sell to a person who was buying as agent for the Roman Catholics, did not touch the case if he were buying, not as agent for the Roman Catholics, but on his own account'[3].

20   Ibid, at 503 per McCardie J. It may be added that in *Dyster v Randall & Sons* ante, fn 16, Lawrence J did suggest that the only case where the principal would not be permitted to intervene would be where 'some personal consideration formed a material ingredient'. However, it will be recalled that in that case the mere fact that the party would not otherwise have sold land to the principal was not considered to afford sufficient grounds for refusing specific performance of the contract at the principal's behest.

1   Although *Said v Butt* is anathema to agency lawyers, some contract textbooks view it more indulgently. Thus, Beale, Bishop & Furmston, *Contract: Cases and Materials* (3rd Edn, 1995), p 976 accept it uncritically as authority for the proposition that an undisclosed principal cannot intervene on his agent's contract if it 'involves some personal element'. Treitel also appears to approve the case to the extent that it coincides with his contention that the appropriate rule would be that 'an undisclosed principal should not be allowed to intervene if he knows that the third party does not want to deal with him' (*The Law of Contract* (9th Edn, 1995), p 647.

2   (1898) 78 LT 445.

3   Ibid, at 448.

Had the plaintiff, however, expressly misrepresented his position and actually informed the defendants that the property was not destined to find its way into the hands of the Roman Catholic committee, North J would have considered the case altered[4].

Thus far we have only considered cases where the third party is seeking to resist the undisclosed principal's action on the grounds that he contracted personally with the agent. The question remains: does the principal also dispose of a similar defence against the third party who sues him on a contract made personally with the agent? This question has not yet fallen to be considered by the courts. It would certainly satisfy lawyers' instinctive desire for logical symmetry to hold that such a defence is open to the principal, and there is no absolutely overwhelming reason for not making it available to him. Nevertheless, as Lord Steyn once remarked, 'the pursuit of logical symmetry is not the ultimate goal of the law'.[5] It may be possible to perceive a moral distinction between cases where the undisclosed principal seeks to profit from a contract into which the third party has the strongest reasons for not entering and cases where that selfsame principal may afford an alternative source of liability for a third party who was induced to contract with an agent in circumstances where, had the third party been fully apprised of the facts, he would most probably not have contracted. In the latter case, say, if T has sold perishable goods to A, who secretly was acting for an unwelcome undisclosed principal, P, if A becomes insolvent or refuses to pay, there is some justice in holding that, should he so desire, T be permitted to turn to P for payment. After all, P set the train of events in motion. P, therefore, is not wholly blameless; and it is not self-evident that P can properly be allowed to resist T's claims on the ground that, had T not been deliberately kept in ignorance of the true facts, T would never have contracted with or delivered goods up to an agent, A, who was covertly acting in league with the unacceptable principal, P.

(iii)   The legal effects of undisclosed agency

The agent for an undisclosed principal contracts with the third party in his own name. Therefore, as long as the principal remains concealed, the agent may sue and be sued on the contract. However, his right to sue is lost if the principal decides to intervene — for example, if the principal sues or settles with the third party[6]. Similarly, the agent's liability under the contract may be affected by the third

---

4   Ibid, at 449. *Archer v Stone* (1898) 78 LT 34.
5   *Mills v R* [1995] 3 All ER 865, 874.
6   Eg *Atkinson v Cotesworth* (1825) 3 B & C 647.

party becoming aware of the existence of the principal, for, in such cases, the third party is said to dispose of a right of election, which enables him to bring his action against the principal rather than the agent. In either of these eventualities the undisclosed principal comes to acquire rights and liabilities under the contract resembling those possessed by a disclosed principal. Consequently, we must now turn to examine the extent to which the legal relations established between an undisclosed principal and a third party differ from those which arise in cases of disclosed agency.

(a) *The third party's right of election.* In cases of undisclosed agency the third party's right of action in the first instance will lie against the agent who contracted in his own name. But when the third party discovers the existence of the principal, the law affords him a right of election and he may choose whether to sue the principal or the agent on the contract[7]. It seems firmly established that, once he has exercised this right, the law will not then allow him to change his mind and sue the other party. As was indicated earlier[8], this restriction on the third party's freedom of action embodies the doctrine of merger and proceeds upon the idea that in both disclosed and undisclosed agency there exists only a single obligation, that liability under it is alternative and that a judgment obtained against either the agent or the principal operates to extinguish the obligation completely[9]. What is more contentious, however, is the extent to which English law holds that acts performed by the third party short of suit to final judgment may operate as an election, preventing him from subsequently pursuing his remedy against the other party[10].

Obviously, a right of election can only arise once the third party has learned of the existence and the identity of the principal. Indeed, in order to constitute a binding election it must be shown not only that the third party had full knowledge of all the relevant facts[11] but also that he performed some truly unequivocal act indicating a firm intention to look exclusively to one party rather than the other. What amounts to an unequivocal act is a question of fact. The reported decisions reveal the courts generally reluctant to hold that an irrevocable election has taken place. For example, in *Clarkson, Booker*

7   *Priestly v Fernie* (1865) 3 H & C 977; *Kendall v Hamilton* (1879) 4 App Cas 504 at 514–5 per Lord Cairns LC.
8   See ante, p 150.
9   *Priestly v Fernie* (1865) 3 H & C 977.
10   Notably, see Reynolds 'Election Distributed' (1970) 86 LQR 317, 320–8.
11   *Thomson v Davenport* (1829) 9 B & C 78; See Extract 40, p 271.

Ltd v Andjel[12] an agent failed to pay for some airline tickets which he had booked through the plaintiff company without disclosing that he was acting for a principal. Having learned of the existence of the principal, the company wrote to both principal and agent requesting payment before serving a writ on the principal. Having next discovered that the principal was insolvent, the company abandoned these proceedings and sought to sue the agent. The agent argued that the commencement of proceedings against the principal amounted to an election on the part of the company to hold the principal liable. Although it judged this case to fall very close to the borderline, the Court of Appeal held that the plaintiff's serving a writ on the principal did not constitute an unequivocal act showing a clear intention to look exclusively to the principal. Russell LJ considered that service of a writ against the agent or the principal, constituting as it does the first step in the legal enforcement of his rights, would 'point significantly towards a decision to exonerate the other' and that in appropriate circumstances something short of final judgment could suffice to demonstrate an unequivocal election. However, in view of the very obvious paucity of authority on the point, it may not be too rash to suggest that the only circumstance in which one can be confident that an election has taken place is where the third party has actually sued the principal or the agent to final judgment.

Whether in the context of disclosed or undisclosed agency, the doctrine of merger provokes confusion. Seizing upon the mutually inconsistent dicta on election, an adventurous New Zealand judge has sought to approach the subject 'on the basis of principle'[13]. Thomas J considered that 'waiver' more accurately describes the doctrine familiarly known as election; that cases holding that obtaining judgment against a party constituted an election should be 'read with caution'; and, most significantly, that the logic of holding that only one person can be held liable on one obligation in any single contract is 'not entirely persuasive'. In consequence, whether liability under a contract is joint or joint and several, 'election' only occurs when once, with full knowledge of the facts, judgment has been enforced, not merely sought against a party. As the judge boldly asserted, 'a party entering into a joint contract must intend to hold the two parties liable for the one debt or obligation

---

12 [1964] 2 QB 775, [1964] 3 All ER 260; see Extract 41, p 272. See also *Pyxis Special Shipping Co Ltd v Dritsas and Kaglis Bros Ltd, The Scaplake* [1978] 2 Lloyd's Rep 380.

13 *L C Fowler & Sons Ltd v St Stephens College Board of Governors* [1991] 3 NZLR 304 at 308; see Extract 42, p 273.

and the law should reflect that expectation'[14]; such an expectation may even be discernible in the case of undisclosed principals, depending upon construction of the contract effected between agent and third party. Although these comments are obiter and arguably cavalier of the accumulated learning in this sphere, they are nonetheless welcome for their clarity and pertinence.[15]

(b) *The third party's right of set-off.* Since in cases of undisclosed agency the contract in the first place is concluded between the agent and the third party, there is a general rule that the undisclosed principal intervenes on his agent's contract subject to all the equities and defences with which the third party could have met an action brought by the agent. As Sir Montague Smith declared in *Browning v Provincial Insurance Co of Canada*[16]:

'By the law of England, speaking generally, an undisclosed principal may sue and be sued upon mercantile contracts made by his agent in his own name, subject to any defences or equities which without notice may exist against the agent'.

Thus, it has for long been settled that where the third party is sued by the undisclosed principal, provided that his right against the agent accrued before he had actual notice of the principal's existence, he may avail himself of all defences — including set-offs — which he would have possessed against the agent, notwithstanding that those defences may be personal to the agent.

In the eighteenth-century case of *Rabone v Williams*[17] a factor, acting for an undisclosed principal, had sold some goods to the defendant. In upholding the defendant's right to set off a debt owed to him by the factor on another account, Lord Mansfield CJ declared:

'Where a factor, dealing for a principal but concealing that principal, delivers goods in his own name, the person contracting with him has a right to consider him to all intents and purposes as the principal; and though the real principal may appear and bring an action upon that contract against the purchaser of the goods, yet that purchaser may set off any claim he may have against the factor in answer to the demand of the principal. This has been long settled'[18].

This broad statement might suggest that whenever a right of set-off against the agent accrues to a third party before he actually knows

14   Ibid, at p 309.
15   For a similar view, see now Reynolds [1994] JBL at pp 151–2.
16   (1873) LR 5 PC 263 at 272.
17   (1785) 7 Term Rep 360n.
18   See also, *George v Clagett* (1797) 7 Term Rep 359.

of the principal's existence, he will automatically be allowed to set off these sums against any claim brought by the undisclosed principal. In other words, Lord Mansfield CJ would appear to be saying that the undisclosed principal's position is analogous to that of an assignee who takes an assignment of a chose in action subject to all those equities which have priority over the right of the assignor[19]. Although such a principle would find favour with a number of writers[20], the courts in fact have restricted the third party's rights of set-off to cases where the undisclosed principal's conduct has raised an estoppel. The leading authority for this proposition is the House of Lords' decision in *Cooke & Sons v Eshelby*[1]. A firm of brokers sold some cotton to a third party without disclosing that they were acting as agents. The third party knew that the brokers sometimes dealt on their own account and sometimes acted as agents. However, in this specific transaction he had no particular belief whether they made this contract on their own account or for a principal. When the undisclosed principal sued for the purchase price, the third party sought unsuccessfully to set off against this claim other moneys owed to him by the brokers. The House of Lords held that in the circumstances it was not sufficient for the third party merely to show their agent had acted in his own name:

'It must also be shown that the agent was enabled to appear as the real contracting party by the conduct, or by the authority, express or implied, of the principal. The rule thus explained is intelligible and just; ... it rests upon the doctrine of estoppel. It would be inconsistent with fair dealing that a latent principal should by his own act or omission lead a purchaser to rely upon a right of set-off against the agent as the real seller, and should nevertheless be permitted to intervene and deprive the purchaser of that right at the very time when it had become necessary for his protection'[2].

Since in this case the third party was unable to establish that the conduct of the principal had induced him to believe that the agent was selling on his own account, he was held to have no right of set-off.

The decision in *Cooke & Sons v Eshelby* is not open to serious objection, since the court took the view that the agent was aware of

19 See generally Bell *Modern Law of Personal Property in England and Ireland* (1989), pp 377–8; Marshall *The Assignment of Choses in Action* (1950), pp 181–91. The rule applies to both equitable assignments and legal assignments executed under the Law of Property Act 1925, s 136.
20 Eg *Bowstead and Reynolds* para 8-111.
1   (1887) 12 App Cas 271; see Extract 43, p 277.
2   Ibid, at 278–9 per Lord Watson.

the risk that a principal might intervene[3]. However, the introduction of the doctrine of estoppel into this area of the law has been roundly criticised[4]. Indeed, one member of the House of Lords admitted to hesitation in saying that the decision rested upon estoppel at all[5]. Estoppel places the emphasis squarely upon the conduct of the principal and it is not easy to perceive why the third party's right of set-off should depend upon a representation being made by a principal of whose existence he is completely ignorant[6]. In all cases of undisclosed agency the agent is, in a sense, held out to be the principal. As there will always be this representation by the principal inherent in the factual situation of any undisclosed agency, it is only confusing to suggest that there is need to have further recourse to representations and the doctrine of estoppel. It would seem preferable to adopt a rule that more obviously recognised that, in the case of undisclosed agency, the contract is in fact made between the agent and the third party and that would therefore allow the third party a right of set-off in all cases where he had no actual notice of the principal's existence[7].

(c) *Cases where the third party settles with the agent.* Just as the third party may be entitled to set off debts owed to him by the agent when sued by the undisclosed principal, so too he may have a complete defence to the principal's action if he can show that he has already settled with the agent. The undisclosed principal allows his agent to appear to the third party to contract as principal. Therefore, if the third party pays the agent before discovering that a principal exists, this payment also operates to discharge his liability to the principal. In *Coates v Lewes*[8] the plaintiffs employed an agent to sell some linseed oil, knowing that this agent always acted in his own name. The agent sold the oil to the defendant, who paid him. When the plaintiffs subsequently brought an action against the defendant to recover the purchase price Lord Ellenborough CJ held that, since they had authorised the agent to deal with the oil as though he were the principal in the transaction, the defendant's payment to the agent was binding upon the principal.

---

3   Eg Pollock (1887) 3 LQR 358.
4   Reynolds 'Practical Problems of the Undisclosed Principal Doctrine' (1983) 36 CLP 119, 124–5.
5   (1887) 12 App Cas at 282–3 per Lord FitzGerald.
6   Cf our earlier discussion of the decision in *Watteau v Fenwick* [1893] 1 QB 346; p 34, ante.
7   For detailed consideration of the question, see Derham 'Set-off and Agency' [1985] 44 CLJ 384, 386–402.
8   (1808) 1 Camp 444.

As in the case of set-off, this defence will only be available to the third party if he can show that the principal's conduct induced him to believe that the agent was in fact the principal in the transaction[9]. Our earlier observations on the subject of estoppel in the context of set-offs will therefore apply with equal force to cases of settlement with the agent.

(d) *Cases where the principal settles with the agent.* Earlier in this chapter we saw that a disclosed principal's obligations to the third party may be discharged by payment to the agent if it can be shown that the third party induced the principal to settle with his agent[10]. A judgment of Blackburn J in *Armstrong v Stokes*[11] would suggest that a similar rule obtains in cases of undisclosed agency. Agents had purchased goods from the plaintiff without disclosing that they were acting for a principal. Before the plaintiff had learned of his existence, the principal paid the purchase price to his agents who later found themselves unable to pay the plaintiff. Blackburn J held that this payment discharged the principal of his obligation to the plaintiff for, to have made him pay twice over, would have produced 'intolerable hardship'.

This decision, which appears to hold that the third party can no longer sue an undisclosed principal once the latter has chosen to settle with his agent, is logically indefensible and almost certainly would not be followed by the courts today. Indeed, in *Irvine & Co v Watson & Sons*[12] Bramwell LJ described *Armstrong v Stokes* as 'a very remarkable case' decided on its own particular facts. Certainly, if a disclosed principal's payment to his agent only discharges him of liability to the third party if the latter has induced him to settle with the agent, it is difficult to see how an *undisclosed principal* can be induced to settle with his agent by a third party who is not even aware of his existence. It therefore seems preferable to treat the state of accounts between the undisclosed principal and the agent as immaterial and to hold that settlement with the agent will not discharge the principal of his obligations to the third party[13].

9   Eg *Ramazotti v Bowring* (1859) 7 CBNS 851.
10   *Heald v Kenworthy* (1855) 10 Exch 739.
11   (1872) LR 7 QB 598.
12   (1880) 5 QBD 414.
13   For a different view of these cases, see Reynolds 'Practical Problems of the Undisclosed Principal Doctrine' (1983) 36 CLP 119, 133–5.

3 UNAUTHORISED DISPOSITIONS OF PROPERTY BY THE AGENT

Thus far we have been concerned almost exclusively with the contractual aspects of the law of agency. However, given that the object of the majority of contracts concluded by agents is the transfer of property between principal and third party, it is appropriate at this juncture to look briefly at some of the special rules governing the transfer of title to property in the context of the law of agency.

The agent's ability to pass a good title in his principal's property to third parties is, in the first instance, dictated by the scope of his authority. Provided that the disposition made by the agent falls within the scope of that authority, it will operate to transfer a good title to the third party. Complications only arise when the agent makes an unauthorised disposition of his principal's property. In such cases the maxim of property law, *nemo dat quod non habet*, normally applies, for the agent in general can only pass a good title to the third party if he was authorised to do so by the principal. However, where the agent has acted outside the scope of his authority, it must be remembered that not only the principal's interests may deserve protection. As Denning LJ pointed out in *Bishopsgate Motor Finance Corpn Ltd v Transport Brakes Ltd*:

'In the development of our law, two principles have striven for mastery. The first is the protection of property. No one can give a better title than he himself possesses. The second is the protection of commercial transactions. The person who takes in good faith and for value without notice should get a good title. The first principle has held sway for a long time, but it has been modified by common law itself and by statute so as to meet the needs of our times'[14].

We must therefore turn to examine these exceptions to the principle that no one can pass a better title than he himself possesses. At common law we shall see that the doctrine of apparent ownership, subsequently adopted in the Sale of Goods Act 1893 (now the Sale of Goods Act 1979), permits an innocent third party in certain circumstances to acquire a good title in property which the agent had no authority to transfer. Similarly, we shall discover that innocent third parties are protected in their dealings with 'mercantile agents'

---

14 [1949] 1 All ER 37 at 46. Lord Denning MR remarked *in arguendo* in *Reid v Metropolitan Police Comr* [1973] QB 551 at 556 that 'the tendency now is to protect the innocent purchaser'.

who, under the Factors Act 1889, have an implied authority to deal with the property of their principals.[15]

(a) *The doctrine of apparent ownership*. In an earlier chapter we discussed the way in which the principal is bound by the acts which his agent performs within the scope of his apparent authority. Since the conduct of the principal induces third parties to believe that the agent possesses authority, this holding out creates an estoppel and the acts of the agent bind the principal. As we emphasised in our discussion of *Watteau v Fenwick*[16], the doctrine of apparent authority can only properly apply in cases where the principal is disclosed. However, if the principal remains undisclosed, the agent may appear to third parties as the *owner* of property entrusted to him by the principal. In consequence, a parallel doctrine has grown up which holds that where the principal has clothed his agent with all the *indicia* of title and enabled him to appear to third parties to be the owner of property, dispositions of that property by the agent will be binding upon the principal and third parties will come to acquire a good title to it.

Although we are solely concerned with its specialised application to the law of agency, it should be noted that apparent ownership is a general common law doctrine which affects all manner of property transactions. Thus, in relation to the sale of goods, s 21(1) of the Sale of Goods Act 1979 now specifically provides:

'Subject to the provisions of this Act, where goods are sold by a person who is not the owner thereof, and who does not sell them under the authority or with the consent of the owner, the buyer acquires no better title to the goods than the seller had, *unless the owner of the goods is by his conduct precluded from denying the seller's authority to sell*'.

For our present purposes, the essential question is to determine when the principal will by his conduct be precluded from denying the agent's authority to dispose of his property. It should be said from the outset that the relevant case law is complex and conflicting and, indeed, the majority of authorities on apparent ownership do not directly concern the law of agency at all. However, they do have an important bearing on the question as to when the principal will be held to have clothed his agent with the *indicia* of ownership.

15 There was once a principle that bona fide purchasers could acquire good title to property, even if stolen, if they purchased it in market overt. This picturesque exception was however abolished by the Sale of Goods (Amendment) Act 1994.
16 [1893] 1 QB 346. See p 34, ante.

In *Central Newbury Car Auctions Ltd v Unity Finance Ltd*[17] the plaintiffs, who were motor dealers, agreed to sell a car on hire-purchase to a rogue called Cullis. They handed over both the car and the registration book to Cullis who, representing himself as the registered owner, in turn sold the car to an innocent third party. The Court of Appeal was called upon to decide whether the plaintiffs, by surrendering possession of both the car and the registration book, were precluded by the doctrine of apparent ownership from denying Cullis' authority to sell. By a majority, the court held that the plaintiffs were not estopped from asserting title to the car. The mere fact that they had handed over possession of the car to Cullis did not raise an estoppel. Something more was required in order to show that the plaintiffs had allowed Cullis to appear as the owner of the vehicle. Similarly, the fact that they had allowed Cullis to have possession of the registration book did not raise an estoppel because a registration book is not a document of title and, indeed, contains an express warning that its possessor may not be the legal owner of the vehicle. The *Central Newbury* case, therefore, establishes the proposition that an owner will not be estopped from asserting title to property merely because he has allowed another party to have possession of it. Possession alone is not sufficient.

It is impossible to lay down hard and fast rules as to what will be required by the courts beyond mere possession of the property by the agent. This will largely depend upon the circumstances of individual cases. However, before they will apply the doctrine of apparent ownership, the courts will require some clear evidence that the principal enabled his agent to appear to third parties to be the owner of the property. Thus, in *Rimmer v Webster*[18] the plaintiff handed a mortgage bond over to a broker with instructions to sell it. The broker persuaded the plaintiff to execute a transfer of the bond to him. The transfer was duly registered in the prescribed statutory form and included a false acknowledgment that the broker had paid the plaintiff £2,000 for the bond. The broker then sub-mortgaged the bond to the defendant. It was held in these circumstances that, since the plaintiff had clothed the broker with all the *indicia* of ownership by allowing him to become the registered owner, the plaintiff was precluded from denying the broker's right to mortgage the bond. Similarly, in *Eastern Distributors Ltd v Goldring*[19] the Court of Appeal held that an owner of a van had dealt with his vehicle in such a way as to enable a dealer to appear to third parties

17   [1957] 1 QB 371, [1956] 3 All ER 905; see Extract 44, p 279.
18   [1902] 2 Ch 163.
19   [1957] 2 QB 600, [1957] 2 All ER 525; see Extract 45, p 280.

to be its owner. The owner, who wished to raise sufficient money to put down a deposit on a new car, had signed a fraudulent agreement with the dealer which made it appear that the owner was purchasing the van from the dealer on hire-purchase. The planned fraud never took place, but the dealer purported to sell the van to the plaintiffs, as originally agreed. The owner had always retained possession of his van and when, in turn, he sought to sell it to the defendant, the courts were called upon to determine the validity of the original sale made by the dealer to the plaintiffs. Devlin J held that, although the dealer had not authority to sell the van, the owner had provided him with documents which clearly enabled him to represent himself to the plaintiffs as entitled to sell the van to them[20]. The owner had clothed him with the *indicia* of ownership and, under s 21(1) of the Sale of Goods Act 1893[1], was precluded from denying the dealer's authority to make the sale.

The courts tend to refer to the effect of apparent ownership in terms of estoppel. However, it should be noted that the doctrine creates a rather special kind of estoppel in that it operates to transfer a *real* title in property to the third party[2]. In this sense, apparent ownership constitutes a true exception to the maxim *nemo dat quod non habet.*

(b) *Authorised dispositions made by the agent in an unauthorised manner.* Cases where the principal is estopped from showing that his agent lacked authority to transfer property to a third party must be distinguished from another class of case where the agent has express authority to deal with his principal's property, but does so in an unauthorised manner. As we have already seen, where an agent has authority to deal with his principal's property, the principal will be bound by any disposition made by the agent within the scope of that authority and the third party will acquire a good title. However, the question whether a third party can acquire a good title to property which the agent, for example, has been authorised to sell, but which he proceeds to sell in an unauthorised manner, has inexplicably occasioned the courts difficulty.

In *Lloyds and Scottish Finance Ltd v Williamson*[3] the plaintiffs handed over a Jaguar motor car to Peerless, a firm of motor repairers and dealers, with instructions that they repair it and then try to obtain offers for it. Later, these instructions were modified and Peerless were

20 See *Mercantile Credit Co Ltd v Hamblin* [1964] 3 All ER 592 at 605 per Pearson LJ.
1   See now, s 21(1) of the Sale of Goods Act 1979.
2   *Eastern Distributors Ltd v Goldring* [1957] 2 QB 600, [1957] 2 All ER 525 at 532 per Devlin J; Extract 45, p 280.
3   [1965] 1 All ER 641; see Extract 46, p 283.

authorised to sell the car provided that they paid over £625 of the purchase price to the plaintiffs. The agents proceeded to enter into a complex financial arrangement with a purchaser called Lunt whereby they sold the car to Lunt, who in turn paid the purchase price over to another party to whom Peerless were indebted. As a result of these transactions the motor car came into the hands of a third party and the plaintiffs were not paid £625 out of the purchase price, as originally agreed. The plaintiffs sued for conversion and sought to argue that the sale of the car to Lunt by Peerless had not transferred a good title. The Court of Appeal rejected this contention. Salmon LJ held that, since the plaintiffs had allowed Peerless to appear as the principals in the transaction, clothing them with all the *indicia* of ownership, provided it could be shown that Lunt had bought the car in good faith believing Peerless to be the owners, the sale was binding upon the plaintiffs[4].

Although the Court of Appeal partially concealed the true ratio of the case by unduly emphasising that the plaintiffs had held out the agents as the owners of the motor car, it did not decide the case on the basis of estoppel. On the contrary, the crucial factor was that the principal had *expressly* authorised the agent to sell the vehicle. In other words, this case provides a clear example of the principal being held bound by a disposition of property made by his agent *within the scope of the agent's actual authority*. It is important not to confuse this kind of case with those we discussed earlier in the context of apparent ownership.

(c) *The Factors Act 1889*. The provisions of the Factors Act 1889 confer a wide authority upon certain classes of agent to transfer good title in their principals' goods to third parties, even though they have no express authority to do so. The main provision of the Act, s 2(1), lays down:

'Where a mercantile agent is, with the consent of the owner, in possession of goods or of the documents of title to goods, any sale, pledge, or other disposition of the goods, made by him when acting in the ordinary course of business of a mercantile agent, shall, subject to the provisions of this Act, be as valid as if he were expressly authorised by the owner of the goods to make the same; provided that the person taking under the disposition acts in good faith, and has not at the time of the disposition notice that the person making the disposition has not authority to make the same'.

---

4   Ibid, at 645.

Given its relative complexity, it seems desirable to analyse separately the various conditions which must be satisfied under this enactment before an agent can pass property in his principal's goods to a third party[5].

Firstly, the agent must be shown to be a 'mercantile agent' within the meaning of the Factors Act 1889. The title of the Act today is something of a misnomer. Traditionally, a 'factor' was defined as an agent into whose possession goods were entrusted by a principal and who customarily had power to sell them in his own name[6]. However, the body of the Act contains no reference to 'factors', but refers exclusively to 'mercantile agents', who are defined in s 1(1) in the following manner:

'The expression "mercantile agent" shall mean a mercantile agent having in the customary course of business as such agent authority either to sell goods, or to consign goods for the purpose of sale, or to buy goods, or to raise money on the security of goods'.

Ignoring its obvious tautology, this definition has come to encompass a very wide class of persons indeed. The mercantile agent, within the meaning of the Act, need not carry on the activities of a recognised class of agent, such as broker or factor. Although mere employees or servants fall outside this definition, it has been held that a person acting as agent in a single, isolated transaction may be a mercantile agent for the purposes of the Act provided that he was acting in the ordinary course of his business[7]. Similarly, the Act has been held to apply to agents operating under such arrangements as 'sale or return' agreements[8] or 'stocking plans'[9] and it would appear that even owners of goods may sometimes become mercantile agents for the purposes of the Act[10].

The second requirement imposed by the Act is that the agent must have possession of the goods or documents of title and he must have acquired possession of them in his capacity as a mercantile agent.

---

5 For detailed treatment of this enactment, see Benjamin *Sale of Goods* (5th Edn, 1997), paras 7-029–7-052.

6 *Baring v Corrie* (1818) 2 B & Ald 137 at 143 per Abbott CJ. The factor did not necessarily have to be vested with power to sell the goods in his own name: *Stevens v Biller* (1883) 25 Ch D 31 at 37 per Cotton LJ. See generally, Munday 'A Legal History of the Factor (1977) 6 Anglo-American LR 221, 246–50.

7 Eg *Lowther v Harris* [1927] 1 KB 393.

8 *Weiner v Harris* [1910] 1 KB 285.

9 *St Margaret's Trusts v Castle* [1964] CLY 1685.

10 See *Lloyds Bank Ltd v Bank of America National Trust and Savings Association* [1937] 2 KB 631, [1937] 3 All ER 312; on appeal, [1938] 2 KB 147, [1938] 2 All ER 63, CA. Cf *Belvoir Finance Co Ltd v Harold G Cole & Co Ltd* [1969] 2 All ER 904.

Thus, in *Staffs Motor Guarantee Ltd v British Wagon Co Ltd*[11] a car dealer sold a lorry to the defendant company. The company then let the lorry out to the car dealer on hire-purchase and the latter promptly sold it to the plaintiffs. The plaintiffs sought to argue that, as the car dealer was a mercantile agent within the meaning of the Factors Act, he had transferred good title in the lorry to them under s 2(1) even though he had no express authority to sell the vehicle. In rejecting this contention, MacKinnon J declared:

'Because one happens to entrust his goods to a man who is in other respects a mercantile agent, but with whom he is dealing not as a mercantile agent but in a different capacity, I do not think it is open to a third party who buys the goods from that man to say that they were in his possession as a mercantile agent and that therefore he had power to sell them to a purchaser and so give him a good title to them. The claimant must be able to assert not only that the goods were in the man's possession as a mercantile agent, *but also that they were entrusted by the owner to him as a mercantile agent*'[12].

In a subsequent case Chapman J ridiculed the suggestion that, if a man loans his car to the next-door neighbour whilst he is away on holiday and the neighbour happens to be a motor dealer, the man is thereby running the risk of losing title to the car merely because the neighbour is a mercantile agent who may decide to 'flog it to some fly-by-night'[13]. The agent must have been entrusted with the goods or documents of title in his capacity as a mercantile agent.

A third requirement is that the mercantile agent must have received possession of the goods or documents of title 'with the consent of the owner'. Clearly, this condition will have been satisfied if the owner has handed his goods over to the agent to sell on his behalf. However, difficulties arise in cases where the owner has voluntarily conferred possession of his goods upon a mercantile agent for some purpose other than sale, whereupon the agent fraudulently sells them to an innocent purchaser. In *Pearson v Rose and Young Ltd*[14] the plaintiff handed his car over to a mercantile agent solely in order to see what offers it might attract. The agent was instructed not to sell the car. But shortly after taking delivery, the agent fraudulently sold it to a third party. The plaintiff brought an action against the defendants for detinue and conversion, arguing that he had not *consented* to the agent's having possession of the car.

11 [1934] 2 KB 305; see Extract 47, p 285.
12 Ibid, at 313 (emphasis added).
13 *Astley Industrial Trust Ltd v Miller* [1968] 2 All ER 36 at 40.
14 [1951] 1 KB 275, [1950] 2 All ER 1027.

However, Denning LJ rejected this contention and held that the plaintiff had consented. His Lordship was of the view that it was sufficient that the owner should have consented to the agent's having possession of the goods for some purpose connected with his business as a mercantile agent. Since the statute was intended to afford a measure of protection to innocent third parties, the emphasis was to be placed on the conduct of the owner in conferring possession upon the agent rather than upon the owner's precise state of mind when he did so:

'That means that the owner must consent to the agent having (the goods) for a purpose which is in some way or other connected with his business as mercantile agent. It may not actually be for sale. It may be for display or to get offers, or merely to put in his showroom; but there must be a consent to something of that kind before the owner can be deprived of his goods'[15].

The fourth condition imposed by the Act is that the agent must have disposed of the goods 'when acting in the ordinary course of business of a mercantile agent'. The meaning of these words has fallen to be considered by the courts in a number of cases. In *Oppenheimer v Attenborough & Son*[16] the plaintiff, a diamond merchant, handed over some diamonds to an agent who was to show them to potential purchasers. The agent fraudulently pledged the stones with the defendant pawnbrokers who were unaware that it was not customary for brokers in the diamond trade to pledge diamonds entrusted to them. When sued by the plaintiff, the defendants claimed that the disposition made by the broker was valid under s 2(1) of the Factors Act. The question which the Court of Appeal was called upon to consider was whether the expression 'acting in the ordinary course of business of a mercantile agent' was sufficiently wide to include dispositions which were not customary within that particular mercantile agent's trade. The court held that it was. As Buckley LJ explained:

'The plaintiff's argument involved that we should read that (expression) as "of such mercantile agent", or, "of a mercantile agent in such trade as that in which he carries on business". I do not think it means that. I think it means "acting in such a way as a mercantile agent in the ordinary course of business of a mercantile agent would act", that is to say, within business hours, at a proper place of business, and in other respects in the ordinary way in which a mercantile agent would act, so that there is nothing to lead the pledgee to suppose

---

15   [1951] 1 KB 275 at 288.
16   [1908] 1 KB 221; see Extract 48, p 286.

that anything is being done wrong, or to give him notice that the disposition is one which the mercantile agent had not authority for'[17].

Thus, the Act protects third parties who have dealt with a mercantile agent who acted in the manner in which such an agent might generally be expected to act. The way in which a mercantile agent might be expected to act is a question of proof in every case. Hence, in *Newtons of Wembley Ltd v Williams*[18], where the defendant was able to establish that there was a recognised secondhand car market operating in Warren Street, a cash sale made by the mercantile agent on the street kerb was construed to have been made 'in the ordinary course of business of a mercantile agent'.

The fifth and final requirement of s 2(1) is that the third party must have acted in good faith and without notice that the agent had no authority to make the disposition in question. The onus of proving good faith rests with the third party. Although actual notice is normally required in commercial transactions, the courts may infer from the circumstances of the case that the third party must have had notice of the agent's want of authority[19]. For example, the fact that the agent has sold an automobile without its accompanying log book may be construed to have afforded the third party notice that the agent may have been acting without the owner's authority[20].

Provided that all these conditions have been satisfied, a mercantile agent's unauthorised dealings with a third party will be held valid and binding upon the principal. As will have been observed, the provisions of the Factors Act are quite technical and, in response to this, it is interesting to observe that in a vigorous dissenting judgment in *Beverley Acceptances Ltd v Oakley*[1] Lord Denning MR displayed some impatience with the Act and suggested that literal interpretation of it was a thing of the past. 'We can go by the spirit which lies behind (it). Modern law has made (it) a particular application of general principle'. His Lordship insisted, therefore, that the traditional notion of *nemo dat quod non habet* should no longer prevail and emphasis had now to be placed squarely on protecting anyone who takes in good faith and for value without notice. Donaldson and Slade LJJ did not associate themselves with this novel and expansive outlook and, for the time being, it can safely be assumed that the traditional approach to interpretation of the Factors Act will hold sway.

---

17   Ibid, at 230–1.
18   [1965] 1 QB 560, [1964] 3 All ER 532.
19   *Janesich v George Attenborough & Son* (1910) 102 LT 605 at 606 per Hamilton J.
20   *Pearson v Rose and Young Ltd* [1951] 1 KB 275 at 289 per Denning LJ.
1   [1982] RTR 417 at 426.

4 LIABILITY FOR THE TORTS OF THE AGENT

As was indicated in the first chapter of this book, the liabilities of principals and masters for the torts of their agents and servants overlap to a quite significant extent. Agents, after all, are not infrequently the employees of their principals. Whilst both agents and servants are, of course, personally liable for torts they commit, their principals' and masters' liabilities for such torts can prove more problematic. In the law of tort it is firmly established that a master is liable for torts committed by his servant in the course of the latter's employment. In the law of agency, in contrast, apart from the obvious case where a principal incurs primary liability by personally instigating or ratifying a particular tortious act by the agent, the principal is normally considered liable for any torts involving representations which the agent may have committed whilst acting within his actual or ostensible authority[2].

Since the agent's chief role is to bring the principal and the third party into direct contractual relations, torts committed by agents often involve the making of and third parties' reliance upon representations by the agent. The resulting liabilities are complex, deriving from either (i) tortious liability under the doctrine of *Hedley Byrne & Co Ltd v Heller & Partners Ltd*[3], (ii) perhaps more traditionally, the tort of deceit, and (iii) in the event of a concluded contract, an overlapping liability to the third party under the Misrepresentation Act 1967. Where torts involve an element of representation, we have already seen that the courts hold that the outer limits of an employee's course of employment are dictated by the scope of his ostensible authority[4]. Indeed, the three members of the Court of Appeal in *Armagas Ltd v Mundogas SA, The Ocean Frost*[5] went so far as to suggest that, as regards torts involving reliance by a plaintiff on representations made to him by an agent or servant, as opposed to other kinds of tort, the two tests of 'course of employment' and 'ostensible authority' are exactly coextensive.

Liability under the Misrepresentation Act 1967 will in most cases only concern the principal. Section 2(1), which imposes liability in damages on 'another party' who has made a negligent

---

2 *Uxbridge Permanent Benefit Building Society v Pickard* [1939] 2 KB 248, [1939] 2 All ER 344, CA.
3 [1964] AC 465, [1963] 2 All ER 575, HL.
4 *Lloyd v Grace Smith & Co* [1912] AC 716, HL. There is some suggestion that a principal can, by disclaimer, restrict the scope of his agent's ostensible authority to make representations on his behalf: see *Collins v Howell-Jones* (1980) 259 Estates Gazette 331, a decision criticised by Murdoch, (1981) 97 LQR 522.
5 [1985] 1 Lloyd's Rep 1 at 71; affd [1986] AC 717, CA.

misrepresentation to the third party inducing him to contract, has been held by Mustill J in *The Skopas*[6] to have no application to an agent who is not actually another party to the contract. Only if both principal and agent have assumed contractual liability to the third party will the latter acquire rights against the agent under the Act. In all cases, however, the agent may incur liability for negligent misstatement under the *Hedley Byrne* principle, and his principal may also be liable if the agent made the misstatement whilst acting within the scope of his authority. Broadly, *Hedley Byrne* liability will depend upon the third party demonstrating the existence of a duty of care owed to him by the agent personally and/or by the principal; this, in turn, will require the presence of a 'special relationship'. Such a relationship arises if it is plain that in the circumstances it would be reasonable for the third party to trust that the agent will exercise reasonable care and that the agent, who is providing information or advice to the third party, is aware or ought to know that the third party relies upon him to exercise such care[7]. Moreover, since *Caparo Industries plc v Dickman*[8], following the current philosophy on the question of duty of care, the existence of such a duty will depend upon the third party establishing not only the requisite degree of 'proximity' but also that it is 'fair, just and reasonable' that the law should impose a duty of care on that defendant. The impact of the House of Lords' decision in *Caparo* was, for instance, apparent in Sir Donald Nicholls V-C's decision in *Gran Gelato Ltd v Richcliff (Group) Ltd*[9].

In *Gran Gelato* the question arose whether a solicitor acting for a seller of an interest in property owes a duty of care to a purchaser when answering the latter's preliminary inquiries. The solicitor had wrongly told the purchaser that, to the lessor's knowledge, there were no rights affecting superior leasehold titles which might inhibit the tenant's enjoyment of the property. It was common ground that the principal owed a duty of care to the intending purchaser of the lease for his agent's misstatement. But the Vice-Chancellor held that, since the purchaser enjoys a remedy against the vendor for negligent misrepresentation and since the solicitor already owes a duty of care to the vendor employing him, unless the solicitor can be shown on the facts to have undertaken personal liability to the purchaser, he owes no similar duty of care to the latter even if that means that the purchaser finds himself bereft of any remedy in the event of the

6   [1983] 2 All ER 1.
7   See *Hedley Byrne & Co Ltd v Heller & Partners Ltd* [1964] AC 465, esp at 486 per Lord Reid.
8   [1990] 2 AC 605, [1990] 1 All ER 568, HL.
9   [1992] 1 All ER 865.

vendor's insolvency. A vendor's insolvency, characterised by the court as 'an ordinary risk of everyday life'[10], was an insufficiently weighty factor to overturn the judge's view that a right of action against an agent was not in general necessary to give third parties reasonable protection in the context of sales of interests in land. This does not necessarily mean that agents will invariably escape liability for negligent misstatement, but as in *Smith v Eric S Bush (a firm)*[11], where a mortgagor would have been without a remedy against the seller of property if denied the right to sue a negligent surveyor, 'good reason ... should exist before the law imposes a duty when the agent already owes to his principal a duty which covers the same ground and the principal is responsible to the third party for his agent's shortcomings'[12].

Torts of representation, however, do present one particularity in the context of agency. Since two separate parties are involved, the principal and the agent, their individual states of mind can differ and one may make a false representation without the knowledge of the other. Thus, an agent may innocently utter a misrepresentation which the principal knows to be untrue, or an agent, without the knowledge of the principal, may knowingly make a false representation to the third party. The courts have had to determine the extent to which, in these circumstances, the agent and the principal may be held liable to the third party. Clearly, if a false representation is made at the express behest of the principal, who knows it to be untrue, then the principal will be liable to the third party in deceit[13]. The principal, in this case, is personally liable and only if the agent is also aware of the falsity of the representation will the latter be held jointly and severally liable[14]. Conversely, where the agent is fraudulent and his representation is made within the scope of his authority, actual or ostensible, the principal will again incur liability. Thus, in *Briess v Woolley*[15] the managing director of a company, without the knowledge of his shareholders, in the course of selling shares in the company on their behalf made fraudulent representations concerning the company's production figures. Once

---

10 Ibid at 873.
11 [1990] 1 AC 831, [1989] 2 All ER 514, HL.
12 [1992] 1 All ER 865 at 873.
13 Alternatively, if the principal consciously acquiesces in a false representation — as, for example, by deliberately omitting to enlighten his agent as to the true state of affairs known to him — he will probably be held liable in deceit: *Cornfoot v Fowke* (1840) 6 M & W 358 at 370 per Rolfe B.
14 Wherever the principal and agent are joint tortfeasors, a right to contribution may arise under the Civil Liability (Contribution) Act 1978.
15 [1954] AC 333, [1954] 1 All ER 909, HL.

it was determined that the sale was expressly authorised by the shareholders, the House of Lords had no hesitation in holding that the shareholders were liable for their agent's fraud. But if an agent, in making a representation, has acted outside the scope of his authority or if the principal has innocently made a false representation[16], the principal will not be held liable to the third party in tort.

16 This appears to be the case even if the agent happens to be in possession of the true facts. As Devlin J observed in *Armstrong v Strain* [1951] 1 TLR 856 at 872: 'You may add knowledge to knowledge, or, as Slesser LJ put it, state of mind to state of mind. But you cannot add an innocent state of mind to an innocent state of mind and get as a result a dishonest state of mind.'

5 The effects of agency-relations between agent and third party

Having reviewed the effects produced by the contract of agency as between principal and third party, we shall now turn to examine the nature of the legal relationship between the agent and the third party. We shall first be considering under what circumstances an agent may become personally liable under contracts he makes with third parties before going on to discuss the contractual rights he may acquire against them.

I THE CONTRACTUAL LIABILITY OF THE AGENT

Normally, when an agent, acting in his capacity as agent, makes a contract with a third party, he neither becomes a party to the contract nor does he incur personal liability under it. As we shall see, there are in fact a number of important exceptions to this rule. However, in the absence of special circumstances rendering the agent a party to the contract, once contractual relations have been established between the principal and the third party, the agent drops out of the transaction. Thus, in *Wakefield v Duckworth & Co*[1] the defendants were solicitors acting on behalf of a client charged with manslaughter. The solicitors ordered from a photographer some photographs which were to be used at the trial. Although the photographer knew that the defendants were acting for a client, he sued them for his fees, maintaining that they were personally liable to him under the contract. The court rejected this claim, Lord Coleridge observing:

'There is no question that the plaintiff knew that the defendants were solicitors acting on behalf of a client, and that being so, apart from

1   [1915] 1 KB 218.

any other considerations, they were agents acting on behalf of a principal. Prima facie in such a contract the plaintiff would have to have recourse to the principal and not to the agent'[2].

This general rule is further illustrated by Lord Selborne LC's decision in *Royle v Busby & Son*[3]. A solicitor acting for a judgment creditor, in the course of his duty as solicitor, lodged a writ of fieri facias at the office of the sheriff with a request for execution. The sheriff employed one of his officers to execute the writ and the officer subsequently sought to recover his fees from the solicitor. It was held that unless the sheriff's officer could show an express or implied undertaking by the solicitor that he would be personally liable for the fees, no claim would lie against him since he was merely acting as the agent of the judgment creditor. As the court pointed out, 'there is no reasonable ground on which it can be implied that the solicitor, who, in the proper course of his duty to his client, simply delivers a writ to the sheriff for execution, thereby enters into a personal contract to pay such fees'[4]. Therefore, unless the agent has in some way undertaken personal liability, only the principal and the third party will acquire rights and liabilities under a contract made by the agent on behalf of his principal.

The strength of this general principle is perhaps indicated by the fact that, where an agent, purporting to act as agent, makes a contract with a third party without the authority of his principal, he will not be held personally liable on that contract. In *Lewis v Nicholson and Parker*[5] the defendants, purporting to act as agents for their principal, made an agreement with the plaintiff. In fact, they had no authority to act on the principal's behalf in this particular transaction. Consequently, when the principal failed to fulfil his obligations under the agreement, the plaintiff sought to make the defendants personally liable on the contract. His claim failed and Lord Campbell CJ declared:

'I think in no case where it appears that a man did not intend to bind himself, but only to make a contract for a principal, can he be sued as principal, merely because there was no authority. He is liable, if there was any fraud, in an action for deceit, and, in my opinion, as at present advised, on an implied contract that he had authority, whether there was fraud or not ... But I think that to say that he is liable as principal is to make a contract, not to construe it'[6].

2   Ibid, at 220.
3   (1880) 6 QBD 171.
4   Ibid, at 174.
5   (1852) 18 QB 503.
6   Ibid, at 511–2.

This decision clearly shows that, in determining whether an agent incurs personal liability under the contracts he makes, the courts will not construe contracts in such a way as to override the parties' intentions. In *Lewis'* case it was plain from the negotiations which took place that the plaintiff had no intention of contracting with the agent. Therefore, it was not open to him at a later date to change his mind and seek to hold the agent personally liable. This, however, does not mean that he is left without a remedy. He may sue the agent for damages for breach of his warranty of authority even though he may not sue him on the contract.

Contracts where the agent undertakes personal liability

Although, as a general rule, he does not become personally liable on contracts he makes on behalf of his principal, an agent may in fact incur personal liability in a wide variety of circumstances. A straightforward case is where the agent acts on behalf of an undisclosed principal. Since the third party will be ignorant of the existence of the principal, his contract is with the agent, who will be liable under it[7]. It is true that the third party, upon discovering the principal's existence, may elect to sue him instead of the agent. But if he elects to sue the agent, the latter cannot escape liability by showing that he was acting on the principal's behalf[8].

Similarly, it is possible for an agent expressly to undertake personal liability on the contract he makes with a third party. In such cases the courts will give effect to the terms of the contract and hold the agent liable to the third party. The only point of difficulty which arises in such cases is to determine whether the intention of the parties was to hold the agent solely liable on the contract or whether it was intended to hold either principal or agent liable to the third party. This is a problem which applies to many of the situations discussed in this chapter, and it has begun to attract the attention of both judges and academic lawyers. In the majority of cases in the past the courts have tended to prefer the former interpretation and hold that where the agent undertakes personal liability, he does so to the exclusion of the principal's liability. But, as Luxmoore LJ observed in *International Rly Co v Niagara Parks Commission*[9], 'there is nothing to prevent the agent from entering into a contract on the basis that he is himself to be liable to perform it as well as his

---

7   In *Muldoon v Wood* (1 April 1998, unreported) the Court of Appeal described as elementary law that the agent can be sued personally if he fails to disclose his principal.
8   Eg *Saxon v Blake* (1861) 29 Beav 438.
9   [1941] AC 328 at 342.

principal'. Indeed, in some of the more recent cases, the courts seem to have displayed greater willingness to entertain the possibility that it was intended that both principal and agent were to be liable under the contract[10]. However, it is still unclear when the courts will be prepared to hold both principal and agent liable under the contract; and in those cases where the agent undertakes liability, the tendency is still to hold him solely responsible to the third party.

As an agent may incur personal liability in a variety of ways, we shall now consider separately a number of categories of case where the courts will hold that the agent has contracted personally with the third party.

(i) Contracts made by the agent under seal

Where an agent executes a deed in his own name, he will be held personally liable on it, even if he describes himself on the document as acting on behalf of another named party. This is a special rule which applies to contracts made under seal and is exemplified by the case of *Hancock v Hodgson*[11]. The defendants were directors of a company which purchased a copper and tin mine in Cornwall for £4,500. They contracted under seal to pay the purchase price within 18 months 'out of ... payments ... to be made by subscribers or shareholders in the said company'. Even though the deed expressly recited that they were acting on behalf of the company, they were held personally liable to pay the plaintiff the purchase price when it fell due. As was said in another case, 'there (is) nothing unusual or inconsistent in the nature of the thing, that one should covenant to another that a third person should do a certain thing, as that he should go to Rome. The party to whom the covenant is made may prefer the security of the covenantor to that of the principal'[12].

(ii) Negotiable instruments

Special rules also apply in cases where an agent has signed a bill of exchange, a promissory note or a cheque. Of course, if his signature does not appear on the instrument, he will not incur any liability on it. However, if he has signed the instrument without indicating that he is acting solely as an agent and the bill is drawn on him, he will

---

10 Eg *The Swan* [1968] 1 Lloyd's Rep 5 (see Extract 49, p 288); *Teheran-Europe Co Ltd v S T Belton (Tractors) Ltd* [1968] 2 QB 545. [1968] 2 All ER 886 (see Extract 50, p 290). See Reynolds 'Personal Liability of an Agent' (1969) 85 LQR 92; 'Agency: Theory and Practice' (1978) 94 LQR 224.

11 (1827) 4 Bing 269.

12 *Appleton v Binks* (1804) 5 East 148 at 149.

be held liable as acceptor. Consecrating Lord Ellenborough CJ's crisp dictum in *Leadbitter v Farrow*, 'unless (a man who puts his name to a bill of exchange) says plainly, "I am the mere scribe", he becomes liable'[13], s 26(1) of the Bills of Exchange Act 1882 specifically provides that in order to escape liability on bills he has signed the agent must have added words to his signature indicating that he was acting on behalf of a principal, or in a representative capacity. Merely adding words describing himself as an agent, or as filling a representative character, will not exempt him from personal liability. He must make quite clear that he has signed the bill solely in a representative capacity[14].

(iii) Signatures of company officers under the Companies Act 1985

A special and very strict rule applies to signatures of officers of companies. Under s 349(4) of the Companies Act 1985, if an officer of a company or someone on its behalf signs or authorises to be signed on behalf of the company any bill of exchange, promissory note, endorsement, cheque or order for money or goods in which the company's name is not mentioned, the signatory is personally liable to the holder of such an instrument for the amount it represents, unless of course the holder is duly paid by the company. In applying this provision, and its predecessors, the courts have been exceptionally fussy. In *Durham Fancy Goods Ltd v Michael Jackson (Fancy Goods) Ltd*[15], a case which the judge aptly described as a 'cautionary tale', Donaldson J held that 'M Jackson (Fancy Goods) Ltd' was not an accurate representation of the drawee's company name; therefore, had it not been for the fact that the relevant words were entered on the bill of exchange by the drawer, thereby estopping the latter from relying on the inaccurate designation, the directors of the defendant company who had signed the bill would have been held personally liable on it under s 349(4). In *Lindholst & Co A/S v Fowler*[16] the omission of the word 'Limited' from bills accepted by the defendant on behalf of 'Corby Chicken Co Ltd' proved fatal and rendered the agent personally liable. So strict is this rule that a finical case law has grown up, for example, declaring 'Co' an acceptable substitute for the word 'Company'[17] or 'Ltd' a recognised surrogate

13 (1816) 5 M & S 345, 349.
14 See generally, *Byles on Bills of Exchange* (26th Edn, 1988), pp 65–8.
15 [1968] 2 QB 839, [1968] 2 All ER 987.
16 [1988] BCLC 166, CA.
17 Eg, *Barber and Nicholls Ltd v R & G Associates (London) Ltd* (1982) 132 NLJ 1076; *Banque de l'Indochine v Euroseas Group Finance Co Ltd* [1981] 3 All ER 198.

for 'Limited'[18]. Section 349(4) operates as a regular trap for unwary company officers who, even though mere victims of unintentional oversight, will still be denied the remedy of rectification of the document[19]. As Potter J observed in *Rafsanjan Pistachio Producers Co-operative v Reiss*, to allow rectification 'would ... be to negate the plain intention of the Act by depriving the recipient of the (instrument) of the benefit of a statutory liability imposed upon the signatory as a quasi-penalty'[20]. Some of the cases, confessedly, make grotesque reading; it is only cheering that the rule applies solely to agents signing on behalf of companies.

(iv)   Contracts in writing

In all other cases where the agent has made a contract in writing with the third party, the question whether he has incurred personal liability under that contract will depend upon the intention of the parties which, as Brandon J explained, 'is an objective intention of both parties, based on what two reasonable businessmen making a contract of that nature, in those terms and in those surrounding circumstances, must be taken to have intended'. Moreover 'where a contract is wholly in writing, the intention depends on the true construction, having regard to the nature of the contract, and the surrounding circumstances, of the document or documents in which the contract is contained'[1]. The cases on this subject are both numerous and conflicting. Nevertheless, this is a question of considerable importance and it is possible to lay down some general guidelines on the way in which the courts decide whether the agent has incurred personal liability under the contract.

The fundamental principle is that, unless a contrary intention appears elsewhere in the document, an agent who signs a contract in his own name without any qualification will be deemed to have contracted personally. Thus, in *Parker v Winlow*[2] an agent, acting for

---

18   *Durham Fancy Goods Ltd v Michael Jackson (Fancy Goods) Ltd* [1968] 2 QB 839, [1968] 2 All ER 987.

19   *Blum v OCP Repartition SA* [1988] BCLC 170.

20   [1990] BCLC 352 at 363. Cf *Jenice Ltd v Dan* [1993] BCLC 1349 where the judge, citing a passage from Hobbes' *Leviathan* to the effect that 'words are counters of wise men, they do but reckon by them, but they are the money of fools' and pointing to several misspelt names of cases in the skeleton argument and the published law reports (see pp 1352i and 1354f), declined to reach the 'nonsensical conclusion' (p 1356) that a misspelt company name ('Primkeen' instead of 'Primekeen') automatically triggered the agent's liability under the Companies Act 1985, s 349(4).

1   *The Swan* [1968] 1 Lloyd's Rep 5 at 12 per Brandon J; see Extract 49, p 288. See also *Foalquest Ltd v Roberts* [1990] 1 EGLR 50 at 53.

2   (1857) 7 E & B 942.

a named principal, signed a charterparty without qualifying his signature by any indication that he was making the contract solely as agent. As none of the terms of the contract were clearly inconsistent with such a construction, the court held that, by signing the document without qualification, the agent had made himself personally liable on the charterparty. This case may usefully be contrasted with *Gadd v Houghton*[3] where a firm of fruit brokers had signed a contract for the sale of some fruit. Although their signature was without qualification, in the body of the contract there appeared the words 'we have this day sold to you on account of James Morand & Co Valencia ...'. The court in this case held that the declaration that the defendants were acting 'on account of James Morand & Co' showed that there was no intention that the brokers should contract personally with the buyer. As James LJ said, 'when a man says that he is making a contract "on account of" someone else, it seems to me that he uses the very strongest terms the English language affords to shew that he is not binding himself, but is binding his principal'[4]. But although the courts will allow an agent who has signed the contract without qualification to rely on terms within the contract which plainly show that he was contracting solely as agent, it may be unwise to try to read too much into the authorities. As Staughton LJ remarked in a subsequent case involving insurance policies, where counsel had invoked *Gadd v Houghton* on account of the similar contractual wording, 'a decision on similar but different words used by a fruit broker is scarcely any authority for the meaning of words used in an insurance contract in 1983'[5]. 'Each contract', it must therefore be emphasised, 'has to be construed in its own context and having regard to its terms'[6].

In order to escape personal liability, it is not necessarily enough for the agent merely to have described himself in the contract as 'agent', 'broker' or whatever. In itself, such a designation may only indicate that the party was employed as an agent, not that he *contracted* solely as an agent. In other words, it may amount only to words of description, not to a qualification of the capacity in which he acted. As Brandon J said in *The Swan*:

'where ... the person is merely stated to be an agent, or the word "agent" is just added after his signature, the result is uncertain, because it is not clear whether the word is used as a qualification or

---

3   (1876) 1 Ex D 357; see Extract 6, p 225.
4   Ibid, at 359. Cf *Tudor Marine Ltd v Tradax Export SA, The Virgo* [1976] 2 Lloyd's Rep 135; *Jugoslavenska Linijska Plovidba v Hulsman (trading as Brusse and Stippel Import-Export), The Primorje* [1980] 2 Lloyd's Rep 74.
5   *Punjab National Bank v De Boinville* [1992] 1 Lloyd's Rep 7 at 31.
6   Ibid, at 12 per Hobhouse J.

merely as a description ... . In general it would seem that in such a case the person does not avoid personal liability, although there may be exceptions to this general rule depending on the other terms of the contract or the surrounding circumstances'[7].

Thus, in *Sika Contracts Ltd v B L Gill and Closeglen Properties Ltd*[8] the first defendant, a chartered civil engineer, entered into a contract with the plaintiff for the repair of some beams on premises owned by the second defendant. The first defendant signed the contract in his own name, merely appending the words 'chartered civil engineer'. While acknowledging that in practice it may be unusual for parties in such circumstances to add phrases like 'as agent only' to their signatures, Kerr J held that the first defendant's reference to his professional qualification was not sufficient to exclude his personal liability.

Therefore, in order not to be held personally liable, we may conclude that the agent must append to his signature words clearly indicating that he is making the contract solely as an agent. The leading authority for this proposition is the decision of the House of Lords in *Universal Steam Navigation Co Ltd v J McKelvie & Co*[9]. This case arose out of a charterparty which had been signed by agents in the following manner: 'For and on behalf of James McKelvie & Co (as Agents). J A McKelvie.' In the body of the agreement James McKelvie & Co were described as 'charterers'. As a result of delay, demurrage became payable to the owners of the vessel under the terms of the charterparty. The owners brought their action against the agents, James McKelvie & Co, claiming that they had made themselves parties to the contract by describing themselves as 'charterers' in the body of the agreement. The House rejected the owners' claim against the agents on the grounds that the words appended to their signature, 'as Agents', plainly showed that they did not intend to bind themselves to the contract. As Viscount Cave LC observed:

'If the respondents had signed the charterparty without qualification, they would of course have been personally liable to the shipowners; but by adding to their signature the words 'as agents' they indicated clearly that they were signing only as agents for others and had no intention of being personally bound as principals. I can imagine no other purpose for which these words could have been added; and

---

7   [1968] 1 Lloyd's Rep 5 at 13.
8   (1978) 9 BLR 11; see Extract 51, p 291.
9   [1923] AC 492; see Extract 52, p 292.

unless they had that meaning, they appear to me to have no sense or meaning at all'[10].

Although there might be 'highly improbable or conjectural' cases where the agent's signature, with the expression 'as agent' appended, could be contradicted by the contents of the agreement, Lord Shaw of Dunfermline went so far as to hold that, normally, appending the words 'as agents' to the signature would be a conclusive assertion of agency and a conclusive rejection of the responsibility of a principal[11].

It is manifest from these authorities that, where there is a contract in writing signed by the agent, there must be clear indications either contained in the body of the agreement or appended to the signature showing that it was not intended that the agent was to contract personally with the third party. In several cases, however, agents have sought to escape liability by showing that, although the written contract suggests that they were parties to the contract, other extrinsic or parol evidence contradicts the document and establishes that they were in fact contracting solely as agents, not as principals. For example, in *Higgins v Senior*[12] the defendants were commission agents who agreed to sell 1,000 tons of iron to the plaintiff iron merchants. The defendants signed the sold note 'John Senior & Co. William Senior'. No iron was ever delivered and the plaintiffs sued the agents for non-delivery. Although the sold note bore no mention of the fact that the defendants were contracting for the Varteg Iron Co, they sought to adduce other evidence showing that in reality they had contracted solely as agents and did not intend to be personally liable under the contract. Parke B refused to admit this evidence, for 'to allow evidence to be given that the party who appears on the face of the instrument to be personally a contracting party, is not such, would be to allow parol evidence to contradict the written agreement; which cannot be done'[13]. Thus, the courts hold that the terms of the written contract indicating that the agent contracted personally cannot be contradicted by parol evidence.

But although the agent will not be permitted to adduce parol evidence in order to escape liability, such evidence may be admitted by the courts in order to show the contrary. Thus, in a number of cases where, on the face of the written agreement, it appeared that the agent had not contracted personally, it has been held that parol

10   Ibid, at 495.
11   Ibid, at 499.
12   (1841) 8 M & W 834; see Extract 53, p 293. See also *Magee v Atkinson and Townley* (1837) 2 M & W 440.
13   (1841) 8 M & W 834 at 844. See also *Sika Contracts Ltd v BL Gill and Closeglen Properties Ltd* (1978) 9 BLR 11 at 18–19.

evidence could be given of the existence of a custom or usage of the trade rendering the agent liable in spite of the terms of the contract. For instance, in *Hutchinson v Tatham*[14] the defendants chartered a ship for the conveyance of a cargo of currants from the Ionian Islands. Although the defendants signed the charterparty 'as agents to merchants', thus suggesting that they were not contracting personally, evidence was admitted to show that it was a usage of trade that, if the name of the principal was not disclosed within a reasonable time, the agents thereby rendered themselves personally liable. Brett J made it clear that the custom would not have been admitted if it had been inconsistent with the terms of the written instrument[15]. For example, if the custom had shown that agents in such cases were always held personally liable from the outset, such evidence would flatly have contradicted the written agreement and would have been ruled inadmissible[16]. However, as the evidence of the custom merely qualified the terms of the contract by showing that, although prima facie not liable, agents in these circumstances could come to incur personal liability if they failed to disclose the identity of their principals within a reasonable time, it could be admitted.

While evidential limitations imposed by the parol evidence rule dominate the construction of contracts entered into by the agent in writing, the situation is quite different in the case of oral contracts. Difficulty has sometimes been experienced in this connection in the case of the agent who acts for an unnamed principal. Although there is some weak authority for suggesting that whenever an agent contracts on behalf of an unnamed principal there exists an initial presumption that he renders himself personally liable under the contract unless a contrary intention can be shown[17], the orthodox view is that in such cases there is no initial presumption of liability and it is simply for the courts to construe the objective intention of the parties as a question of fact. Hence in *The Santa Carina*[18], where it was known to the plaintiffs that the defendant brokers supplied bunkers to a ship at Penang as agents, the Court of Appeal unanimously held that to succeed in their action against the defendant brokers the onus lay with the plaintiffs to establish facts from which a court could infer that the defendants were to be personally liable on the contract, notwithstanding that they were

14   (1873) LR 8 CP 482; see Extract 54, p 293.
15   Ibid, at 487. See also *Pike v Ongley* (1887) 18 QBD 708.
16   Eg *Barrow & Bros v Dyster, Nalder & Co* (1884) 13 QBD 635.
17   *Benton v Campbell, Parker & Co Ltd* [1925] 2 KB 410 at 414 per Salter J.
18   *N & J Vlassopoulos Ltd v Ney Shipping Ltd, The Santa Carina* [1977] 1 Lloyd's Rep 478; see Extract 55, p 294.

known by the plaintiffs to be acting in the capacity of agents. This ruling is particularly important in the case of brokers, customarily acting as they do for principals whose identity they do not disclose, and is not without its critics[19].

(v) Agents for foreign principals[20]

An agent may incur personal liability on contracts he enters into on behalf of a foreign principal. Although the doctrine has declined in importance in recent times, there used to be a strong presumption that, when an agent acted for a foreign principal, the third party in this country contracted with the agent, who incurred personal liability under the contract, and no privity was created between the third party and the foreigner. One of the earliest cases on the subject held:

'But where a factor to one beyond the seas buys or sells goods for the person to whom he is factor, an action will lie against or for him in his own name; for the credit will be presumed to be given to him in the first case, and in the last the promise will be presumed to be made to him, and rather so, as it is so much for the benefit of trade'[1].

The presumption that it was not intended to create privity of contract between principal and third party held sway in the courts until this century. The doctrine developed in response to the conditions of trade which prevailed at the time: the long distances separating principal and third party, slow and unreliable communications and the fact that the English merchant would know the home agent but not necessarily the foreigner led to it being the common practice for the agent to incur personal liability on the contracts he made on behalf of a foreign principal[2]. This presumption, however, was only a presumption of fact, in the sense that it could be rebutted by showing that the parties had evinced a contrary intention. Therefore, where the terms of the contract or the surrounding circumstances clearly indicated that the intention was to create privity of contract between the foreign principal and

---

19 See Reynolds 'Practical Problems of the Undisclosed Principal' (1983) 36 CLP 119. Cf also *US Restatement of the Law of Agency* (3rd Edn), para 321.
20 See generally, Hudson 'Agents for Foreign Principals' (1966) 29 MLR 353; Munday 'A Legal History of the Factor' (1977) 6 Anglo-American LR 221, 235–42.
1 *Gonzales v Sladen* (1702) cited in *Bullen's Nisi Prius* (5th Edn) at 130.
2 Eg *Elbinger AG für Fabrication von Eisenbahn Material v Claye* (1873) LR 8 QB 313 at 317 per Blackburn J; *Hutton v Bullock* (1874) LR 9 QB 572 at 573 per Bramwell B.

the third party, the courts gave effect to that intention[3]. Conversely, where the terms of the contract showed that the parties did not intend such privity to arise, the courts, once again, respected the parties' intentions and held the agent personally liable on the contract concluded with the third party[4]. Thus, where the contractual terms made the parties' intentions clear, the doctrine had no application. However, where the terms of the contract were unclear or ambiguous, the courts had recourse to the presumption that the parties did not intend direct legal relations to arise between principal and third party and, consequently, held the agent personally liable.

In view of the way in which conditions of trade have changed in more recent times, rendering international transactions far less perilous from a commercial point of view than once they were, it is not surprising that the foreign principal doctrine has now lost some of its potency. Although a number of cases have held that there still exists a weak presumption in favour of the personal liability of the agent whenever he acts on behalf of a foreign principal[5], the preponderance of judicial opinion today favours the view that there is no longer a presumption, but that the foreign character of the principal is merely one of the facts which the court will take into account when construing the parties' agreement[6]. From a practical point of view, it probably makes little difference whether a weak presumption of fact still lingers on or whether the principal's foreign domicile is treated simply as a fact which the court will weigh in the balance when interpreting the intention of the parties. The essential point remains the same: unless a contrary intention can be detected, the fact that the agent has acted on behalf of a foreign principal may lead the court to hold that he has rendered himself personally liable on the contract he has made with the third party. However, the principal's foreign character will now often be considered only of minimal importance. For example, in *Teheran-Europe Co Ltd v S T Belton (Tractors) Ltd*[7], since the contract did not involve the extension

---

3   Eg *Green v Kopke* (1856) 18 CB 549; *Miller, Gibb & Co v Smith and Tyrer Ltd* [1917] 2 KB 141 at 162–3 per Bray J.

4   Eg *Ireland v Livingston* (1872) LR 5 HL 395; *Armstrong v Stokes* (1872) LR 7 QB 598.

5   Eg *HO Brandt & Co v Morris & Co Ltd* [1917] 2 KB 784; *Rusholme and Bolton and Roberts Hadfield Ltd v S G Read & Co (London) Ltd* [1955] 1 All ER 180; *Cox (trading as Port of Richborough) v Sorrell* [1960] 1 Lloyd's Rep 471. See Hudson 35 Can Bar Rev 336 (1957).

6   Eg *Maritime Stores Ltd v H P Marshall & Co Ltd* [1963] 1 Lloyd's Rep 602; Extract 56, p 296; *Teheran-Europe Co Ltd v S T Belton (Tractors) Ltd* [1968] 2 QB 545, [1968] 2 All ER 886; see Extract 50, p 290; *Anglo-African Shipping Co of New York Inc v J Mortner Ltd* [1962] 1 Lloyd's Rep 610.

7   [1968] 2 All ER 886.

of credit by the third party, the Court of Appeal, in determining whether it was intended to make the principal a party to the contract, attributed little weight to the fact that the unnamed principal was an Iranian company. But as Diplock LJ went on to say, the foreign character of the principal 'may have considerably more weight in determining whether the mutual intention of the other party and the agent was that the agent should be personally liable to be sued *as well as* the principal, particularly if credit has been extended by the other party'[8]. This statement has significant implications. For, whereas it used to be held that the agent acting for a foreign principal might be personally liable in place of the principal, Diplock LJ is here suggesting that the agent may be held liable in addition to the principal, thus affording the third party an option as to whether to sue the principal or the agent. Naturally, this alternative liability of the principal or the agent will only arise if it is possible to put this construction upon the parties' contract, and it remains unclear when the courts will be prepared to do this. However, in so far as it may afford the third party a wider measure of protection and more closely approximate to commercial realities, Diplock LJ's initiative in *Teheran-Europe* is to be welcomed[9].

(vi) Contracts made by an agent on behalf of a fictitious or non-existent principal

Where an agent, purporting to act in that capacity, makes a contract with a third party on behalf of a principal who does not exist, the agent may be held to have intended to bind himself personally to that contract. This problem has commonly arisen in the context of company law and on a number of occasions the courts have been called upon to consider the effect of contracts made by agents on behalf of companies which have not yet been registered. The reader will find a brief discussion of the topic in the second chapter of this book under the general heading of ratification. Here, it suffices to say that where an agent makes a contract with a third party on behalf of a principal who does not exist, the legal position may be stated as follows:

---

8   Ibid, 892–3 (emphasis added). More recently, in a case where an agent, claiming to act for a named principal, was found actually to be acting for another unnamed principal and held personally liable, the judge did remark that it was obvious that though persons 'may be willing to trade with an English registered company without further inquiry they might take a different view with a company registered in the Channel Islands': *Savills v Scott* [1988] 1 EGLR 20 at 21.

9   See fn 10, p 188 and accompanying text.

(a) If the purported principal is a company which has not yet been 'formed', under s 36(4) of the Companies Act 1985 (now incorporated as s 130(4) of the Companies Act 1989) the agent will be considered to have contracted personally unless a clear contrary intention has been expressed in the terms of the agreement with the third party.

(b) In all other cases which do not concern unformed companies, the courts will objectively construe the terms of the agreement in order to determine whether it was intended that the agent should incur personal liability. The third party's position in such circumstances has been notably improved by the Companies Acts of 1985 and 1989 that have abrogated the doctrine of constructive notice which used to deem third parties to know of any limitations on the agent's authority imposed by a company's memorandum or articles of association[10].

(c) However, in cases where it was not intended that the agent should be personally liable, the third party may still possess some remedy against the agent. He may be able to sue him for breach of his warranty of authority, for deceit or, conceivably, for negligent misstatement.

2   CONTRACTUAL RIGHTS OF THE AGENT

To a large extent, the agent's right to sue on contracts he makes with third parties follows similar rules to those we have outlined in the preceding section dealing with the agent's contractual liability.

The general rule is that, where an agent, acting solely in his capacity as agent, makes a contract on behalf of his principal, he acquires no rights under the contract and is unable to sue the third party on it. Thus, in *Fairlie v Fenton*[11] a cotton broker sold a quantity of goods to a third party stating in the contract note that he was acting on behalf of a named principal and appending the word 'broker' to his signature. He later sought personally to sue the buyer for failure to take delivery of the goods. However, the court held that, as the written agreement plainly indicated that it was not intended to make him a party to the contract, the broker was not entitled to sue the buyer thereon[12]. Similarly, in *Repetto v Millar's Karri and Jarrah Forests*

10   See ante, pp 72-73.
11   (1870) LR 5 Exch 169.
12   Cf *Gadd v Houghton* (1876) 1 Ex D 357; see Extract 6, p 225.

Ltd[13], where the master of a ship had signed bills of lading as agent for the owners, it was held that he could not sue the charterers for freight under the bills as he was not a party to the contract.

But where, according to the true construction of the contract, it was the intention of the parties that the agent should have rights as well as liabilities under it, he will be entitled to sue the third party. For example, in *Short v Spackman*[14] a broker entered into a contract in his own name with a third party to purchase whale oil on behalf of his unnamed principal. The broker later agreed to re-sell the oil to another merchant. Upon learning of this, the principal wrongfully renounced the contract and refused to have anything further to do with the goods. The seller declined to deliver the oil and the broker sought to sue him for non-delivery. The court held that as the agent had contracted personally with the third party, he was entitled to sue the seller and his right was in no way prejudiced by the fact that the principal had decided to repudiate his agent's contract.

In addition, there are a number of special circumstances where agents are entitled to sue on the contracts they make. Notable among these is the case of the agent who acts on behalf of an undisclosed principal. As has already been explained, when the principal is undisclosed, the contract in the first instance is between the agent and the third party and the agent is, of course, entitled to sue on it. However, there are also certain classes of agent whom the law has traditionally allowed to sue third parties on the grounds that they either have a 'special property' in the subject matter of the contract or possess a lien over it[15]. Auctioneers, for example, are considered to have a special interest in the sales they effect and may sue the highest bidder for the price. As Salter J said in *Benton v Campbell, Parker & Co Ltd*[16]:

'The auctioneer sues for the price by virtue of his special property and his lien, and also, in most cases, by virtue of his contract with the buyer, that the price shall be paid into his hands, and not by virtue of the contract of sale'.

Although the auctioneer's right in the past was often explained solely in terms of the special property he has in the goods which he is selling[17], it is now clear that his right to sue derives from a collateral

---

13   [1901] 2 KB 306. See also *Freight Systems Ltd v Korea Shipping Corpn. The Korea Wonis-Sun* (1990) 290 LMLN 3 (agent who contracted 'o/b' (on behalf of) shippers had contracted as agent and had no right to sue on the contract).
14   (1831) 2 B & Ad 962.
15   On liens generally, see Chapter 3.
16   [1925] 2 KB 410 at 416.
17   Eg *Williams v Millington* (1788) 1 Hy Bl 81 at 84 per Lord Loughborough LC.

contract into which he and the highest bidder have entered[18]. Factors, too, are held to be entitled to sue third parties on contracts they have concluded as agents[19]. Once again, the factor's right has tended to be explained in terms of the lien he enjoys over the principal's goods. However, since by definition the factor is entitled to deal with his principal's goods in his own name and has possession of them, it is likely that this right to sue would now be justified on the basis of the true construction of his contract with the third party[20].

One particularly interesting question which has arisen in the context of the agent's contractual rights is the following. Where the agent has purported to contract with a third party on behalf of a named principal but, in reality, is himself the principal, does he acquire rights against the third party under the contract? In *Bickerton v Burrell*[1] this question received a qualified negative answer. The plaintiff sued an auctioneer for the return of a deposit paid in respect of a ground rent he had acquired at auction 'for C Richardson'. Upon the auctioneer objecting that the principal, C Richardson, was the proper person to bring the action, the plaintiff sought to show that Mrs C Richardson, his housekeeper, was not in fact the principal in the transaction and that she had no interest in the purchase. Therefore, as the true principal, he claimed to be entitled to sue the auctioneer. The court denied his title to sue on the contract and Lord Ellenborough CJ declared:

'... where a man assigns to himself the character of agent to another whom he names, I am not aware that the law will permit him to shift his situation, and to declare himself the principal, and the other to be a mere creature of straw'[2].

However, some members of the court went on to suggest that the plaintiff would have been entitled to sue the auctioneer if he had undeceived him before bringing the action. This reasoning was taken up subsequently in *Rayner v Grote*[3]. The defendant had contracted to buy goods from the plaintiff, whom he believed to be acting for a named principal. Later, having learned that the plaintiff was in reality the principal, the defendant affirmed the contract by accepting

---

18   See *Chelmsford Auctions Ltd v Poole* [1973] QB 542 at 548–9 per Lord Denning MR. See generally, Murdoch *The Law of Estate Agency and Auctions* (3rd Edn, 1994), pp 350ff.

19   Eg *Drinkwater v Goodwin* (1775) 1 Cowp 251 at 255–6 per Lord Mansfield CJ.

20   See *Bowstead*, para 9–021.

1   (1816) 5 M & S 383; see Extract 57, p 296.

2   Ibid, at 386.

3   (1846) 15 M & W 359; see Extract 58, p 297. Cf *Newborne v Sensolid (GB) Ltd* [1954] 1 QB 45, [1953] 1 All ER 708.

delivery and paying for part of the goods. It was held that the plaintiff thereby became entitled to sue the defendant for non-acceptance of the remainder of the goods as his affirmation of the contract showed that he was not prejudiced by the agent's revealing that he was the true principal. Alderson B, however, was at pains to indicate that the 'agent' in such cases would not always be permitted to cast off his cloak and reveal the true character in which he acted.

'In many such cases, such as, for instance, the case of contracts in which the skill or solvency of the person who is named as the principal may reasonably be considered as a material ingredient in the contract, it is clear that the agent cannot then shew himself to be the real principal and sue in his own name'[4].

Thus, in *The Remco*[5] it was held that an agent could not enforce a contract for the charter of a ship against the defendant shipowners since the latter clearly considered the identity of the charterers important. The agent had represented to the shipowners who his principal was and it could be shown that the defendants were interested in who was responsible for payment of freight and that they would not have agreed to the terms of the contract had they known that, in reality, the agent was the principal in the transaction. Alderson B in *Rayner v Grote* also suggested that, whenever the contract remained entirely executory, the agent should not be allowed to sue in his own name. Nevertheless, it would seem that, provided he has become aware of the true position and is not prejudiced thereby, the third party may be sued by the 'agent'.

Although such a rule is unlikely to work grave injustice, it is difficult to justify in terms of standard principles of the law of agency. An agent who acts on behalf of a named principal normally drops out of the transaction and a contract only arises between the principal and the third party. The agent cannot intervene and claim the benefit of the contract, for the terms will make it clear that the third party's intention was to contract with the person named as principal, not with the agent. Furthermore, if the original contract in cases like *Rayner v Grote* is in writing, the admission of evidence that the 'agent' was really the principal will offend against the parol evidence rule which we encountered earlier in this chapter. In light of such considerations, it is not altogether surprising that no satisfactory explanation for this rule has been advanced[6].

---

4   (1846) 15 M & W 359 at 365.
5   *Gewa Chartering BV v Remco Shipping Lines Ltd, The Remco* [1984] 2 Lloyd's Rep 205.
6   See further, *Bowstead*, para 9–088. Even more difficult to justify is Hirst J's decision in *Fraser v Thames TV* [1984] QB 44, [1983] 2 All ER 101 that a party claiming to

But if, as sometimes happens, the third party contracts with an agent who informs him that he is acting for a principal whom he does not name, the courts on several occasions have held that the agent for the unnamed principal may subsequently reveal himself as the real principal and sue on the contract. One argument for allowing the agent for an unnamed principal to act in this way has been that, by agreeing to contract with an unspecified principal, the third party has signified his indifference to the identity of the other contracting party[7]. At the same time, it cannot be inferred that the third party was content to contract with anyone in the world other than the agent and, although one judge admitted that for someone to act as agent for himself is 'a somewhat curious position'[8], the shipping cases where the problem has typically arisen have not thrown up situations where the notion of agency is utterly inconsistent with the agent's acting in the capacity of principal. Hence, the rule seems to be that a contracting party may masquerade as an agent for an unnamed principal without forfeiting his right to sue on the contract.

---

contract as an agent may later reveal that he was in fact an additional principal whom the courts will allow to be joined as a co-plaintiff in any action brought by the original principal against the third party: see Tettenborn [1983] 42 CLJ at 211.

7   Eg *Schmaltz v Avery* (1851) 16 QB 655 at 662 per Patteson J. Cf *Sharman v Brandt* (1871) LR 6 QB 720 (a case whose ratio, it has to be said, is obscure).

8   *Harper & Co v Vigers Bros* [1909] 2 KB 549 at 561 per Pickford J.

6 Termination of agency

Having concluded our examination of the legal effects produced by the agency relationship, it remains to consider the rules which govern termination. Agency may be terminated in two principal ways. Termination may be brought about either through the conscious act of the parties or, alternatively, by operation of law. These two modes of termination will be discussed separately.

I TERMINATION BY ACT OF THE PARTIES

In the normal course of events, agency comes to an end when the agent has fulfilled his mandate or, if he was employed to act for a fixed term, when that period of time has expired[1]. However, in cases where the legal relations between principal and agent originally derive from an agreement, these relations can be terminated prematurely by the parties simply agreeing to the voluntary discharge of their relationship. Similarly, either party can bring the agency to an end merely by giving notice to the other of an intention to withdraw from the agreement. The principal is generally free to revoke and the agent free to renounce his agency in the case of ordinary agency agreements. Of course, if the agreement derives from contract, the principal may be liable in damages for prematurely terminating the agent's agency. However, an agent cannot compel the principal to continue with the contract, because a court will not order specific performance of a personal contract.

Although the general rule is that agencies can be freely terminated, in the case of commercial agencies regulated by the

---

1   Although it is normal for such fixed terms to be expressly agreed by the parties, they may come to be implied by custom: *Dickinson v Lilwal* (1815) 4 Camp 279.

Commercial Agents (Council Directive) Regulations 1993, Reg 15 specifies minimum periods of notice for termination. The parties are free to agree longer periods of notice, should they so wish, provided that the period to be observed by the principal is not shorter than that to be observed by the commercial agent (Reg 17(3)). Otherwise, however, the position is that for the first year of a commercial agency contract, the minimum period of notice is one month, for the second year commenced it is two months, and for the third year commenced and for subsequent years three months' notice at least must be given.

It should be noted that even at common law some agreements have been construed to constitute more than just 'pure agency agreements.' In *Martin-Baker Aircraft Co Ltd v Canadian Flight Equipment Ltd*[2], for example, an agent agreed not only to sell the principal's products throughout North America, but also to expend much time and money developing his principal's business and, in exchange for sole agency rights, to refrain from handling the products of any competitors. In view of the duties and restrictions imposed on the agent, McNair J decided that this agreement more closely resembled the relationship between master and servant than just that of simple principal and agent. Thus, he held that the agreement was not freely revocable by either party, but could only be revoked on reasonable notice being given. In the absence of such special circumstances, however, the general principle is that agency agreements may be freely revoked by the principal, subject to certain important exceptions.

(i)   Irrevocable agencies[3]

With a view to protecting the interests of the agent or third parties, the law holds certain classes of agency agreement to be irrevocable.

(a) *Authority coupled with an interest.* First, the courts have consistently held that where principal and agent have entered into a valid contract of agency whose underlying purpose is to secure or protect some interest of the agent, that agency is to be treated as irrevocable:

2   [1955] 2 QB 556, [1955] 2 All ER 722. See also *Smart v Sandars* (1848) 5 CB 895 where Wilde CJ stated that 'where an agreement is entered into on sufficient consideration, whereby an authority was given for the purpose of securing some benefit to the donee of the authority, such an authority is irrevocable. That is usually meant by an authority coupled with an interest, and which is commonly said to be irrevocable.'

3   See generally Reynolds 'When is an Agent's Authority Irrevocable?' in Cranston (ed) *Making Commercial Law* (1997, Oxford), pp 259ff.

that is, the agent's authority can only be revoked by the principal with the consent of the agent. The classical statement of this doctrine was delivered by Williams J in *Clerk v Laurie*[4]:

'What is meant by an authority coupled with an interest being irrevocable is this – that where an agreement is entered into on a sufficient consideration, whereby an authority is given for the purpose of securing some benefit to the donee of the authority, such as authority is irrevocable'.

The operation of the rule is neatly illustrated by the case of *Gaussen v Morton*[5]. A principal, who owed a large sum of money to William Forster, conferred upon the latter a power of attorney to sell certain lands and to discharge the debt out of the proceeds of the sale. But when the principal later sought to revoke his agent's authority, Lord Tenterden CJ held that the agency created was irrevocable as it constituted an authority coupled with an interest. It could here be said that the object of the agent's mandate was to secure the debt owed to him by the principal. It must therefore be emphasised that an agency will only be treated as irrevocable where its explicit object is to secure some particular interest or to confer some particular benefit upon the agent. The mere fact that revocation of the agent's mandate will prevent his earning commission, for example, is not regarded as a sufficient interest to render the agency irrevocable[6].

(b) *Executed authority.* A second cluster of cases is often gathered under the head of irrevocable agencies, although there is probably no need to justify these decisions on this ground. These cases arise where the agent has commenced performance of his mandate and during the currency of the agency incurred liabilities on behalf of the principal for which the latter is liable to indemnify him, but the agent proceeds to satisfy those liabilities only after the principal has terminated the agency. The courts are minded to treat such agencies also as irrevocable. Although the decision has been affected by subsequent legislation, *Read v Anderson*[7] illustrates this species of case. An agent was employed to lay bets on his principal's behalf and to settle them if they were lost. The agent incurred liabilities in performance of his duties and settled the claims after his agency terminated. The court held that the principal could not unilaterally revoke his agent's authority. As was unequivocally stated by Wilde B

4   (1857) 2 H & N 199 at 200 (*in arguendo*).
5   (1830) 10 B & C 731. See also *Smart v Sandars* (1848) 5 CB 895.
6   *Frith v Frith* (1906) 94 LT 383. See Chapter 3 for discussion of the agent's right to earn commission.
7   (1884) 13 QBD 779. See now Gaming Act 1892, s 1.

in *Chappell v Bray*[8], another case where the court had recourse to this reasoning, 'an authority cannot be revoked if it has passed an interest and has been executed'. The introduction of the concept of irrevocability complicates matters unnecessarily, even if it does capture in some sense the idea that obligations can endure even after termination of the agency agreement. The agent simply has a contractual (or even a restitutionary) claim for the sums owed by the principal, given that the obligations arose during the currency of the agreement[9].

(c) *Statutory authority.* Finally, it should be added that certain statutes afford protection to parties against the effects of revocation of an agent's authority[10]. Thus, after the manner of s 45 of the Bankruptcy Act 1914 (now repealed), the Insolvency Act 1986 provides that where, after the commencement of his bankruptcy, a bankrupt incurs a debt to a banker or other person by reason of making a payment which otherwise is void under the Act, for a variety of purposes the debt will be deemed to have been incurred prior to the commencement of bankruptcy provided that the banker or other party had no prior notice of the bankruptcy and that it is reasonably practicable for the amount to be recovered from the person to whom payment was made (s 284(5)). Such provision is applicable in cases where an agent is employed.

(ii)   Revocable agencies

Apart from the cases of irrevocable agency mentioned above, the general rule is that, in the absence of any contractual term to the contrary, the principal is free to revoke his agent's authority at any time, provided that the agent has not already fulfilled his obligations. Thus, in *Campanari v Woodburn*[11] an agent was employed to sell a picture on the understanding that he would be paid £100 solely on condition that he succeeded in selling it. Before effecting a sale, his authority was revoked. Jervis CJ held that on the construction of this agreement the agent was not entitled to commission given that he had sold the picture after revocation of his mandate. 'It must be taken to have been part of the original compact between the (agent) and the (principal), that, whereas, on the one hand, he would receive a large sum if he succeeded in selling the picture, so, on the other hand, he would take the chance of his authority to sell being

---

8   (1860) 6 H & N 145 at 152.
9   See *Reynolds*, pp 259–60.
10   See, eg, Powers of Attorney Act 1971, s 5, discussed below.
11   (1854) 15 CB 400. Cf the reasoning of the House of Lords in *Luxor (Eastbourne) Ltd v Cooper* [1941] AC 108, [1941] 1 All ER 33; see Extract 35, p 262.

revoked'. By the same token, in *Hampden v Walsh*[12] a principal was held entitled to revoke his agent's authority to lay a wager with a third party on the grounds that revocation had taken place before the agent had actually paid over any money to that third party.

The immediate effect of revocation is to terminate the legal relationship between the parties. Revocation is prospective in its effects. Therefore, both principal and agent will continue to be entitled to sue one another on claims which arose prior to termination. For example, the principal may still proceed against the agent if he performed his agency in a negligent manner, just as the agent will still be entitled to be indemnified by the principal in respect of expenses incurred or commission earned for services performed before revocation of the agreement.

One problematical question posed by revocation, however, is whether in any circumstances the agent is entitled to compensation not only for commission earned prior to revocation but also for commission which he might have earned had his authority not been revoked[13]. The cases indicate that this will depend upon construction of the particular agreement. In *Rhodes v Forwood*[14], an agent was employed for seven years to sell all coal which the owner of a colliery elected to send to Liverpool. After four years the owner sold the colliery and the agent sued for loss of future commission. The House of Lords rejected the agent's claim on the grounds that the agreement had been entered into subject to the risk that the colliery might not continue to make use of his services and, in this particular case, there was no express or implied term of the contract which provided that the agreement should absolutely continue for a period of seven years. Although the courts are averse to taking this course, 'in some cases it may be necessary to give effect to a transaction, that the law should imply a stipulation not wilfully to put an end to a business'[15]. Thus, in *Turner v Goldsmith*[16] the Court of Appeal construed another agreement to have bound the principal to employ the agent for the full term stipulated in the contract. Turner was employed for a period of five years to sell 'any shirts or other goods manufactured by Goldsmith'. After two years Goldsmith's factory was destroyed by fire and he went out of business. In this case, since the contract neither specifically referred to the factory nor required that the shirts actually be manufactured by Goldsmith nor even that the goods sold be shirts, the court held that it was not impossible for the defendant to carry on business in articles of the kind mentioned in

---

12 (1876) 1 QBD 189.
13 See further Chapter 3, ante.
14 (1876) 1 App Cas 256.
15 *Hamlyn & Co v Wood & Co* [1891] 2 QB 488 at 493 per Bowen LJ.
16 [1891] 1 QB 544.

the agreement and it refused to imply a term that the continuance of the contract was conditional upon the continued existence of the factory[17]. As these cases demonstrate, at common law the agent's right to compensation for loss of future commission turns entirely upon construction of the precise terms of the agency agreement[18].

'Commercial agents' regulated by the Commercial Agents (Council Directive) Regulations 1993, however, follow a different régime. Regulation 17 mysteriously provides that after termination of the agency contract, even if it has been terminated by the agent's death (Reg 17(8)), the commercial agent will be entitled either to compensation or to an indemnity from his former principal. Moreover, it is left to the parties to determine in their contract which form of reimbursement to adopt in the event of termination. Only if the contract fails to specify a preference does Reg 17(2) provide that 'the agent shall be entitled to be compensated rather than indemnified.' The concepts of compensation and indemnity owe their origins to French and German law respectively, and compensation in particular bears little resemblance to the English notion of contractual damages[19]. 'Indemnity', which does not preclude the agent from also seeking damages from his former principal (Reg 17(5)), is based upon the extent to which the agent

'(a) has brought the principal new customers or has significantly increased the volume of business with existing customers and the principal continues to derive substantial benefits from the business with such customers; and

(b) the payment of this indemnity is equitable having regard to all the circumstances and, in particular, the commission lost by the commercial agent on the business transacted with such customers.' (Reg 17(3)).

'Compensation', in contrast, is intended to cover the damage the agent suffers in consequence of termination of his relations with the principal (Reg 17(6)). To this end, damage is 'deemed to occur

---

17 Ibid, at 550 per Lindley LJ. For cases where courts have been prepared to imply such terms in order to endow contracts with business efficacy, see *Alpha Trading Ltd v Dunnshaw Patten Ltd* [1981] QB 290, [1981] 1 All ER 482; *Comet Group plc v British Sky Broadcasting Ltd* (1991) Times, 26 April.

18 For a general discussion of the question, see Paull J's judgment in *Shackleton Aviation Ltd v Maitland Drewery Aviation Ltd* [1964] 1 Lloyd's Rep 293.

19 For an informative analysis of these provisions, see Saintier 'New Developments in Agency Law' [1997] JBL 77. In *Moore v Piretta PTA Ltd* it was held that in construing the meaning of 'indemnity' under Reg 17 an English court was obliged to look at the relevant German law upon which this concept in the Directive was modelled in order to promote harmonisation of EU law in respect of commercial agents.

particularly' when termination takes place in the following circumstances: namely, when they

'(a) deprive the commercial agent of the commission which proper performance of the agency contract would have procured for him whilst providing his principal with substantial benefits linked to the activities of the commercial agent; or
(b) have not enabled the commercial agent to amortize the costs and expenses that he had incurred in the performance of the agency contract on the advice of his principal.' (Reg 17(7)).

The concept of 'proper performance of the agency contract' in Reg 17(7)(a) is novel to English law, and there are already indications that the Court of Appeal acknowledges that this Regulation introduces a method of assessing compensation distinct from traditional common law principles[20]. As Saintier explains, under French law the notion of agency has come to resemble a sort of 'quasi partnership' with both partners deemed to be striving towards a common goal, the development of a commercial clientèle. Moreover, unlike English agency law, the clientèle is not viewed as belonging to the principal but as a shared asset of their commercial collaboration. Compensation under French law therefore recognises a 'common interest mandate' in commercial agencies, and is designed to reimburse the agent 'the value of the lost share of the market' principal and agent jointly created[1]. Whether, via a reference to the European Court of Justice, this conception of compensation enters English law remains to be seen.

Although compensation and indemnity are payable in a wide range of circumstances, these rights will be lost if the principal terminates the agency following the agent's failure to carry out his obligations in such a way as to justify his dismissal under English law (Regs 18(1) and 16), or if the agent has assigned his rights and duties under the agency to a third party (Reg 18(b) and (c))[2]. Otherwise, as Reg 19 makes clear, the parties may not derogate from Regs 17

---

20 See *Page v Combined Shipping and Trading Co Ltd* [1997] 3 All ER 656. Subsequently, in *Duffen v FRA BO SpA* (1998) Times, 15 June the Court of Appeal has held that 'compensation' under the Regulations may be payable to the agent by way of augmentation of any common law damages due to him upon termination of the agency. It could be added that, by analogy with the right of 'indemnity' under Reg 17(5), English courts are likely to have regard to French law in interpreting the scope of 'compensation' under Reg 17(6): *Moore v Piretta PTA Ltd*. The latter case has, incidentally, already determined that 'the phrase "agency contract" [in Reg 17(6)] means simply "the agency"'.

1 *Saintier*, esp at p 80. As one author noted, 'the purpose of the Directive is to provide a form of no-fault package': Roberts 'Agents and Compensation' (1995) 145 NLJ 453.

2 Reg 18 was lightly amended by SI 1993/3173.

and 18 'to the detriment of the commercial agent before the agency contract expires'.

2 TERMINATION BY OPERATION OF LAW

Just as agency can be terminated by a deliberate act of the parties, so too it can be brought to an end by operation of law independently of the will of the parties. There are four principal ways in which this can come about.

(i) *Death.* Unless the agency is irrevocable, the death of either the principal or the agent brings the legal relationship to an immediate end. Since the contract of agency is considered to be a personal contract in which the identity of the parties is of central importance, when the agent dies his obligations do not pass to his executors. Similarly, when the principal dies the contract automatically terminates. As the principal's death terminates the agent's authority, the agent can no longer bind the principal by acts which he purports to perform in the latter's name. But rights against the principal which have already vested in the agent prior to death may still be exercised against the principal's estate.

The automatic effect of death on agency agreements is exemplified in *Campanari v Woodburn*[3] which was referred to earlier in this chapter. Before the agent in that case succeeded in selling the picture, his principal died. The agent, *knowing nothing of the death,* effected a sale and then sought to recover his commission from the principal's personal representative. Although the court granted the agent compensation on a quantum meruit for the services he had rendered, it held that he was not entitled to recover commission under the contract which had automatically terminated on the principal's death. It would seem that the only circumstances in which an agent may possibly recover commission when he performs his mandate after the principal's death are where the latter's executors subsequently ratify his acts[4].

(ii) *Insanity.* Unless the agency is irrevocable, the supervening insanity of either the agent or the principal automatically terminates the agreement. The insanity of the agent means that he is incapable of acting any longer, whilst the principal's insanity is held to bring the agency to an end because 'where such a change occurs to the principal that he can no longer act for himself, the agent whom he has appointed can no longer act for him'[5].

3   (1854) 15 CB 400. See also, *Blades v Free* (1829) 9 B & C 167.
4   *Foster v Bates* (1843) 12 M & W 226. Sed quaere.
5   *Drew v Nunn* (1879) 4 QBD 661 at 666 per Brett LJ.

As between principal and agent the automatic operation of this rule poses few problems. Difficulties, however, arise when agents acting for principals who have become insane contract with third parties who are unaware of the principal's infirmity. In *Drew v Nunn*[6] a husband, who had represented his wife as having authority to act for him, became insane but later recovered his sanity. Whilst he was insane his wife ordered goods from the plaintiff who knew nothing of the husband's complaint. Following his recovery, the husband refused to pay for the goods on the grounds that his wife's authority had automatically terminated when he became insane. Brett LJ rejected this contention chiefly on the grounds that 'when one of two persons both innocent must suffer by the wrongful act of a third person, that person making the representation which, as between the two, was the original cause of the mischief, must be the sufferer and must bear the loss'[7]. Although the characterisation of an insane principal's omission to warn third parties of his agent's loss of authority poses considerable conceptual difficulties, presumably this ruling means that, even though the principal's insanity puts an end to his agent's actual authority, the agent may still continue to have apparent authority to bind the principal until the third party learns that the agency has been terminated. But a subsequent decision of the Court of Appeal in *Yonge v Toynbee*[8] would seem to hold that the third party in such circumstances may alternatively hold the agent liable. A firm of solicitors had continued to act for a principal who, *unknown to them* had become insane. It was here decided that the solicitors were personally liable to third parties with whom they had subsequently dealt. By acting for the principal, the solicitors impliedly warranted that they had authority to act whereas their authority had in fact terminated upon the principal's being certified[9].

The notion that acts accomplished by the agent are to be treated as the acts of the principal can prove highly inconvenient in this context. In the specialised case of powers of attorney (formal agreements executed under seal whereby the attorney is granted

---

6   (1879) 4 QBD 661.
7   Ibid, at 667–8. See also, *Elliot v Ince* (1857) 7 De GM & G 475 at 487 per Lord Cranworth LC. Cf *Sorrell v Finch* [1977] AC 728, [1976] 2 All ER 371 where the House of Lords held that when an estate agent misappropriated a deposit paid to him by a prospective purchaser of property, the vendor was not liable for the acts of the agent, for an estate agent has neither implied nor apparent authority to accept a deposit on such terms as to make the vendor liable; see Extract 9, p 226.
8   [1910] 1 KB 215; see Extract 27, p 254.
9   The inflexibility and pragmatic incoherence of these rules have been criticised by Meiklejohn 'Incompetent Principals, Competent Third Parties, and the Law of Agency' 61 Ind LJ 115 (1986).

authority to act on behalf and in the name of the donor of the power) the Powers of Attorney Act 1971 intervened to absolve from personal liability any attorney whose powers, unbeknown to him, have been revoked under the doctrine formulated in *Yonge v Toynbee*. Furthermore, this Act lays down that innocent third parties may rely upon the apparent authority of such an agent and transactions into which they have entered will be binding upon the donor of the power[10]. More recently, the Enduring Powers of Attorney Act 1985 was passed to allow 'a person, while capable of managing his or her affairs, to select somebody who will be responsible for managing his or her affairs if there is a supervening incapacity'[11]. This reform, designed to cater for an ageing population where the mental incapacity of a growing number of donors will be attributable to the onset of senility, has proven popular and, according to a survey commissioned in 1989 by the Lord Chancellor's Department, largely successful[12]. It could be argued that in providing for the initial execution of enduring powers of attorney the 1985 Act did not sufficiently take into account the common law rules of agency[13]. But Hoffmann J perceived no problem in this regard in *Re K*[14], although significantly Commonwealth jurisdictions of late have been careful to spell out the legal capacity demanded of a donor at the moment of the instrument's execution[15].

(iii) *Bankruptcy*. Generally speaking, the bankruptcy of the principal automatically terminates agency since bankruptcy amounts to a legal incapacity. Equally, an agency agreement may come to an immediate end upon the bankruptcy of the agent. But this will depend upon the nature and terms of the agreement[16]. In general, the agent's legal incapacity can prove less disastrous than that of the principal. Both these rules, it should be said, are subject to important qualifications, but these fall outside the scope of an introductory work[17].

---

10   Powers of Attorney Act 1971, s 5.
11   *Re R* [1990] 2 All ER 893 at 895 per Vinelott J. See generally Cretney *Enduring Powers of Attorney. A Practitioner's Guide* (4th Edn, 1996).
12   The report's findings are summarised in Kerridge 'Enduring Powers of Attorney' (1991) 141 NLJ 983.
13   See Munday 'The Capacity to Execute an Enduring Power of Attorney in New Zealand and England' [1989] 13 NZULR 253.
14   [1988] Ch 310, [1988] 1 All ER 358.
15   See, eg, Creyke 'Enduring Powers of Attorney: Cinderella Story of the 80's' (1991) 21 UWALR 122, 130–1.
16   Eg *Elliott v Turquand* (1881) 7 App Cas 79 (an agent's right of set-off arising out of mutual dealings with the principal prior to notice of the principal's act of bankruptcy).
17   For more detailed treatment of this topic, See Fletcher *The Law of Insolvency* (2nd Edn, 1996).

(iv) *Frustration.* In cases where the agency agreement is embodied in a contract, the doctrine of frustration may apply. As in the case of any other contract, a supervening frustrating event rendering performance of the contract illegal, impossible or something radically different from what the parties originally contemplated will automatically put an end to the contract[18]. By way of illustration, in *Marshall v Glanvill*[19] a commercial traveller employed by the defendant became liable during the war to serve in the armed forces under the terms of the Military Service Act 1916. Upon enlisting, he sued the defendant for six months' commission by way of damages for dismissal without notice. McCardie J held that the Act rendered performance of the parties' contract impossible and, as frustration had therefore taken place, no commission was payable by the principal.

3 EFFECTS OF TERMINATION

As was mentioned earlier in this chapter, as between principal and agent, termination of agency brings the agent's actual authority to an immediate end. Only those rights against the principal which accrued to him prior to termination will survive – for example, his right to claim commission already earned. However, agency involves a tripartite relationship and, as far as third parties are concerned, the agent may in certain circumstances still be able to bind his principal to contracts entered into with them even after termination of his mandate. We have already seen in our discussion of the ways in which agency can be terminated by operation of law that in the case of the principal's insanity, for instance, the courts have evolved rules which safeguard the interests of third parties innocently dealing with agents who in fact have ceased to possess authority to act[20]. Similarly, it has been mentioned that the legislature has occasionally provided for an agent's authority to survive termination of his agency. But even in cases where the agent's authority has been terminated by the principal's *revoking* his mandate, the principal may continue to be bound by bargains which the agent purports to enter into with third parties on his behalf.

---

18 On the doctrine of frustration generally, see Treitel, *The Law of Contract* (9th Edn, 1995), pp 763 et seq.
19 [1917] 2 KB 87.
20 See *Drew v Nunn* (1879) 4 QBD 661. Writers have occasionally argued that a similar rule should apply in the case of death. Conceivably, *Smout v Ilbery* (1842) 10 M & W 1 affords weak authority for this proposition.

Revocation of agency by the principal immediately terminates the agent's actual authority to act for him. The agent, however, may still appear to third parties to be invested with authority to bind the principal. The fact that survival of *apparent* authority in the agent may mislead innocent third parties has led to the common law rule that if, after revocation, a principal continues to hold out his agent as having authority to act for him, then the principal will be held liable to third parties on contracts concluded by his agent, provided that third parties have not had notice that the agent's authority has been terminated[1]. Thus, in *Trueman v Loder*[2] the defendant had employed a certain agent for a number of years and it was common knowledge within the mercantile community that this agent acted on his behalf. The defendant revoked his authority. However, the agent then proceeded to enter into a contract for the sale of tallow to a third party. No tallow was delivered and Lord Denman CJ held that, since the purchaser had no notice that the agent's authority had been revoked, the principal was liable to him for the non-delivery of the merchandise. In other words, the principal was bound by the acts of the erstwhile agent because, to the third party, he still *appeared* to have authority to act. Similar reasoning was applied in the case of *Curlewis v Birkbeck*[3]. A plaintiff had sent some horses to an agent to be sold on his behalf. The agent proceeded to sell them to the defendant. However, the defendant did not know that the plaintiff had previously revoked his agent's authority to sell the horses or to receive the purchase price for them. The defendant paid the agent and Cockburn CJ decided that if the defendant had no notice of the agent's want of authority, his payment to the agent operated as a good discharge of the debt and was binding upon the principal.

---

1   The cases indicate that the principal need not personally furnish third parties with notice of revocation. Provided that they learn of termination of the agent's authority from a trustworthy source, they will be fixed with notice. It is tempting to draw a parallel between this rule and the analogous rule governing revocation of offers in the law of contract: see *Dickinson v Dodds* (1876) 2 Ch D 463.

2   (1840) 11 Ad & El 589. See also *Willis Faber & Co Ltd v Joyce* (1911) 104 LT 576.

3   (1863) 3 F & F 894.

Part two

Case extracts

1　Lloyd v Grace, Smith & Co [1912] AC 716

Lord Shaw of Dunfermline … The case is in one respect the not infrequent one of a situation in which each of two parties has been betrayed or injured by the fraudulent conduct of a third. I look upon it as a familiar doctrine as well as a safe general rule, and one making for security instead of uncertainty and insecurity in mercantile dealings, that the loss occasioned by the fault of a third person in such circumstances ought to fall upon the one of the two parties who clothed that third person as agent with the authority by which he was enabled to commit the fraud. Nor do I think it doubtful that it would be quite unsound in law if this result could be avoided by an investigation of the private motives – in the direction of his own, as distinguished from his master's, benefit – which animated an agent in entering into a particular transaction within the scope of his employment. The bulk of mercantile dealings are not direct, but are conducted through agents vested with an ostensible authority to act for their employers. When the authority is of a limited kind, the person transacting with such an agent is bound to assure himself that the limits are not exceeded, – a familiar instance of which is the case of bills signed per procuration. But when the authority does ostensibly include within its scope transactions of a particular character, then quoad a third party dealing in good faith with such an agent, the apparent authority is, as is well settled, equivalent to the real authority and binds the principal … In the present case, as I have stated, it has been clearly found that the fraud was committed in the course of, and within the scope of, the duties with which the defendants had entrusted Sandles as their managing clerk. In my opinion, they must in these circumstances stand answerable in law for their agent's misconduct.

2　United Bank of Kuwait Ltd v Hammoud; City Trust Ltd v Levy [1988] 3 All ER 418

Staughton LJ … For the court to enforce a solicitor's undertaking as such, it is an essential requirement that there be a promise made in his capacity as a solicitor: *United Mining and Finance Corpn Ltd v Becher* [1910] 2 KB 296 at 306, per Hamilton J. The promise of one partner binds the other members of the firm if it was an act for carrying on in the usual way business of the kind carried on by the firm: see Partnership Act 1890, s 5. A contract made by a servant or other agent binds the principal if it was made with the ostensible authority of the principal.

Those three propositions, or some or one of them, are the crucial rules of law for the determination of the two appeals before the court. Although they are to be found in different compartments of the law, they all provide the same test, at any rate so far as these cases are concerned. Was Mr Emmanuel's undertaking given in his capacity as a solicitor? Was it an act for carrying on in the usual way the business of the firm? Was it made with ostensible authority? All three questions in effect are the same.

It is agreed on all hands that Mr Emmanuel had neither express nor implied authority to give the promise that he made in these two cases. We were referred to some elderly decisions, and to *Halsbury's Laws of England*, 4th Edn, vol 44 (1983), pp 109–111, para 140 which is supported by elderly cases in the footnotes, as showing what types of transactions are and are not within the ordinary authority of a solicitor. That material should today be treated with caution, in my judgment; the work that solicitors do can be expected to have changed since 1888; it has changed in recent times and is changing now. So I prefer to have regard to the expert evidence of today in deciding what is the ordinary authority of a solicitor.

The evidence establishes that two requirements must be fulfilled before an undertaking is held to be within a solicitor's ordinary authority. First, in the case of an undertaking to pay money, a fund to draw on must be in the hands of, or under the control of, the firm; or at any rate there must be a reasonable expectation that it will come into the firm's hands. Solicitors are not in business to pledge their own credit on behalf of clients unless they are fairly confident that money will be available so that they can reimburse themselves. Secondly, the actual or expected fund must come into their hands in the course of some ulterior transaction which is itself the sort of work that solicitors undertake. It is not the ordinary business of solicitors to receive money or a promise from their client, in order that without more they can give an undertaking to a third party. Some other service must be involved.

It is for those reasons, I suppose, that the parties to these appeals agree that Mr Emmanuel had no actual or implied authority to give his undertakings. Neither requirement was in fact fulfilled in these cases. But the plaintiffs did not know that. They were led to believe, as Glidewell LJ has demonstrated, that both requirements were satisfied. Can they then say that Mr Emmanuel was acting in his capacity as a solicitor, or carrying on in the usual way business of the kind carried on by the firm, or acting with the ostensible authority of a principal?

I agree with the conclusion of French J that Mr Emmanuel had actual authority to represent himself as what in fact he was: a qualified solicitor in the employment of Ivor Levy & Co. So too in the United Bank of Kuwait case he had actual authority to represent himself as a partner in the firm of Donald, Darlington & Nice, whether or not a salaried partner is correctly described as a partner in law. One has next to consider whether Mr Bloch and Mr Darlington in that case, and Mr Levy in the other, are bound by what Mr Emmanuel himself said about the transactions in which he was engaged.

It is elementary law that an agent cannot hold himself out; the holding out must come from his principal, or from some agent duly authorised by the principal. So one might think that what Mr Emmanuel himself said about the two transactions in which he was engaged could not by itself demonstrate that they were part of the ordinary business of solicitors, and thus within the authority which he was held out as having. But the defendants in these appeals do not take that point; and in my judgment they are right not to take it. The decisions in *Lloyd v Grace Smith & Co* [1912] AC 716 and *Uxbridge Permanent Benefit Building Society v Pickard* [1939] 2 KB 248, [1939] 2 All ER

344 show that a third party is only concerned as to whether a transaction appears to be of a kind that is within the ordinary authority that the agent is held out as having, not whether it is in fact a transaction of that kind. To depart from that doctrine would gravely weaken the credit which is given to solicitors' undertakings; it would also do much to destroy the rule that any agent can be held out as having general ostensible authority to bind his principal. On the facts of these two cases I agree with Glidewell LJ that the transactions reasonably did appear to the plaintiffs to be of a kind that was within the ordinary authority of a solicitor. Hence I too would allow the first appeal and dismiss the second ...

Lord Donaldson MR ... I fully accept that the burden of proof lies on the banks to satisfy the court that Mr Emmanuel had ostensible authority to give the undertakings sued on. I also accept that no bank should accept the unsubstantiated assertion of a stranger that he is a solicitor. And of course neither bank did. They checked and received information that Mr Emmanuel was indeed a solicitor in practice with Donald, Darlington & Nice in the case of the United Bank of Kuwait transaction and with Ivor levy & Co in the case of the City Trust transaction.

It is at this point that the burden of proof, although still on the banks, changes dramatically. Practising solicitors are not to be regarded as potential fraudsters or accomplices to fraud. No person is admitted to the Roll of Solicitors unless the Law Society has been satisfied not only that he or she has complied with the training regulations, ie that they are competent lawyers, but also that, as individuals, they are of a suitable character to be members of a learned and respected profession: see s 3 of the Solicitors Act 1974. Indeed every solicitor on admission is given a certificate signed by the Master of the Rolls for the time being certifying that 'Upon examination and enquiry touching the fitness and capacity of [the named person] to act as a solicitor of the Supreme Court, I am satisfied that [he] [she] is a fit and proper person so to act ...'

I make this elementary point, because it is a factor of which banks can legitimately take account in their dealings with those who are known to be admitted solicitors. Prima facie they are to be taken to be men and women of good character whose word is their bond and whose statements do not require that degree of confirmation and cross-checking which might well be appropriate in the case of statements by others who are not members of so respected a profession. This is not to say that a dishonest solicitor is a contradiction in terms. Alas, they do exist, but they are an almost insignificant part of the profession and the possibility that any particular solicitor is dishonest can be disregarded in the absence of some factor putting a bank on inquiry.

In both cases it was submitted that the banks should have been alerted and made further inquiries because the nature of the underlying professional business between Mr Emmanuel and Mr Hammoud (in the United Bank of Kuwait case) and Mr Emmanuel and his anonymous client (in the City Trust case) was not apparent to the bank. In particular it was suggested that it was not apparent that he was rendering his client 'solicitorial' services, meaning thereby professional services of a nature such that they called for a trained lawyer.

Why is this so strange? Banks should know, and are entitled to rely on the fact, that solicitors are trained to preserve the confidentiality of their clients' business. This does not involve simply keeping secret that which they are asked not to divulge. It involves keeping to themselves everything about their clients and their clients' business which it is not necessary for others to know and neither bank had any need to know.

When it comes to the suggestion that it was not apparent that Mr Emmanuel was performing 'solicitorial' services for his clients, there are two answers. The first I have already given – confidentiality. The banks were never told exactly what services he was providing and there was no reason why they should have been. The second is that the ordinary course of the professional work of a solicitor extends far beyond giving legal advice and assistance. The argument seemed almost to be that no-one consults a lawyer other than on a legal problem, the members of the Bar being wholesalers, lawyers to the trade, and the members of the solicitors' profession retailers, lawyers to the public. Not so.

I say nothing about the position of members of the Bar as being immaterial for present purposes, but the solicitor's role is much wider than this. They are, to use an old-fashioned expression, 'men of affairs.' The public would be wise to consult them, and does consult them, when faced with unusual problems which may or may not have hidden legal aspects and which do not clearly raise issues within the special expertise of some other profession. The great, and perhaps unique, value of the professional advice of solicitors is to be found in a combination of factors which those who consult them are entitled to expect, and usually get: total independence, total integrity, total confidentiality, total dedication to the interests of the client, competent legal advice and competent other more general advice based on a wide experience of people and their problems, both in a personal and in a business context. The need to maintain this enviable situation is, of course, the reason and justification for the unforgiving attitude adopted by the profession towards those of their number, and there will inevitably be a few, who fall below the standards required of them.

3   Armagas Ltd v Mundogas SA, The Ocean Frost [1985] 1 Lloyd's Rep 1

Robert Goff LJ ... There is ample authority that a master may be vicariously liable for the fraud of his servant. This was so held by Chief Justice Holt in *Hern v Nichols* (1700) 1 Salk 289: in most recent years, the same conclusion was reached in the leading cases of *Barwick v English Joint Stock Bank* (1867) LR 2 Exch 259, and *Lloyd v Grace, Smith & Co* [1912] AC 716, in which the House of Lords held that a master may be so liable where the servant's fraud is committed solely for his own benefit. Furthermore there is authority that, where a servant is authorised to do a certain act and while doing that act he assaults the plaintiff, he may be held to have committed the assault in the course of his employment if it is an improper mode of carrying out that which he was employed to do (see *Dyer v Munday* [1895] 1 QB 742); and there is also authority that, where an agent bribes the clerk of the plaintiff in order to obtain information concerning the plaintiff which he was employed to obtain by legitimate means, the action of the agent in bribing the clerk may likewise be held to be committed within the course of his employment (see *Hamlyn v John Houston & Co* [1903] 1 KB 81). If a servant who is authorised by his master to conclude a certain contract with a third party, induces him to enter into the contract by a fraudulent misrepresentation, that may likewise be thought to be a wrongful mode of doing that which he is authorised to do so that the fraudulent misrepresentation is made in the course of his employment. It may also be thought to be immaterial whether the misrepresentation is itself within the actual or ostensible authority of the servant. The existence of such authority would be relevant to the question whether the representation could be imputed to the master, so that he is bound by it; for example, if it amounted to a collateral warranty, actual or ostensible authority would be essential before the master could be held liable for breach of the warranty. But, it may be said, actual or ostensible authority should not be decisive of the question whether the master is vicariously liable for the servant's tort, for which in any event the measure of damages is different.

In my judgment, however, the weight of authority is against this approach. In cases of fraud at least, involving as they do a representation by the servant in reliance upon which the third party has acted to his detriment, the master can only be vicariously liable for the servant's fraud where he has acted within his ostensible authority. If this were not the law, in many cases where the servant has warranted his authority, fraudulently or even negligently, the master would be vicariously liable for the tort; there is no trace in the authorities of this being so. Similarly, if this is not the law, it is difficult to understand how, in certain cases where there has been an unsuccessful attempt to establish that a servant or agent acted within his ostensible authority, there was no alternative claim for damages on the basis of vicarious liability for deceit; for a prominent example of such a case, see *Slingsby v District Bank Ltd* [1932] 1 KB 544. In other cases, the reasoning of the Court is consistent only with the proposition that the criterion for the master's vicarious liability is that the servant acted within his ostensible authority. I refer in particular to the judgments of the Court of Appeal in *Uxbridge Permanent Benefit Building Society v Pickard* [1939] 2 KB 248 at 253–254 per Sir Wilfrid Greene MR, and at p 258 per Lord Justice MacKinnon and to the leading case of *Lloyd v Grace, Smith & Co* in which Lord Macnaghten, in the context of a claim against the master for damages for his servant's deceit, treated (at p 736) the expressions 'acting within his authority' and 'acting in the course of his employment' as meaning one and the same thing. A similar approach was adopted in the House of Lords in *George Whitechurch Ltd v Cavanagh* [1902] AC 117; *Ruben v Great Fingall Consolidated* [1906] AC 439; and *Kleinwort, Sons & Co v Associated Automatic Machine Corpn* (1934) 50 TLR 244. Only in the third of these last cases, the *Kleinwort* case, was there in fact a claim for damages for fraudulent misrepresentation; but each case was concerned with a fraud of a secretary of a company, and in each case the analysis was the same, the liability of the company being held to depend on whether the secretary acted within his authority. Similarly, as I read it, the advice of the Privy Council delivered by Lord Wilberforce in *Kooragang Investments Pty Ltd v Richardson & Wrench Ltd* [1982] AC 462, is based on the assumption that the respondents were only vicariously liable for negligent valuations by their servant where those were within the actual or ostensible authority of the servant.

It is right that we should ask ourselves: why should ostensible authority, which prima facie appears to be relevant to the question whether the servant's unauthorised act should be imputed to the master, also provide the criterion for the master's vicarious liability for his servant's deceit? In considering this question, we must bear in mind the circumstances in which a servant's fraudulent act may fall within his ostensible authority. Generally speaking, his act will be within his ostensible authority when it is within that class of acts which a person in his position usually has authority to perform; it will not be within his ostensible authority, either when it does not fall within that class of acts, or where, in the case of the particular servant, his authority is limited, and the third party has notice of the limitation on his authority. Now, in cases of deceit, we are concerned with liability for a representation made by the servant to a third party. The dealings which that servant is employed to enter into with third parties, including the promises and representations which comprise those dealings, are to be identified with reference to his authority, either his actual authority or (by virtue of estoppel) his ostensible authority. In considering whether a master is vicariously liable for a particular fraudulent misrepresentation of his servant, it is in theory necessary to enquire – (1) what the servant was employed to do, and (2) whether the wrongdoing of the servant constituted a wrongful mode of doing that which he was authorised to do. However, since we are here concerned with liability for a misrepresentation, the second question does not arise, because it cannot be said that the making of an unauthorised misrepresentation, even one which induces an authorised transaction, is an improper mode of concluding that transaction; for, where some representations fall within the servant or agent's authority and some do not, only those which do so can be said to constitute modes of performance of that which he has been authorised to do.

This approach can moreover, in my judgment, be justified as a matter of policy. For where the servant's wrong consists of a misrepresentation upon which the plaintiff relies, if that misrepresentation is not within the ostensible authority of the servant, the plaintiff is placing reliance on a statement by the servant which, as I have already indicated, either does not fall within the class of acts which a person in his position is usually authorised to perform, or is a statement made in circumstances where the plaintiff has notice that his authority is limited. In either case, in my judgment, the plaintiff is placing his reliance exclusively upon the servant; and it is understandable that it should be the policy of the law in those circumstances, not merely that the unauthorised acts should not be imputed to the master, but also that the master should not be vicariously liable for the servant's wrong.

On this basis, those torts which involve reliance by the plaintiff upon a representation by the servant should be distinguished from other wrongs, for example those which involve intentional or negligent physical acts by the servant. In the latter class of case, the ostensible authority of the servant does not provide the criterion of the master's vicarious liability: see, in particular, *Bugge v Brown* (1919) 26 CLR 110 at 116 et seq, per Mr Justice Isaacs and at 132 per Mr Justice Higgins. So where a servant is authorised to carry on a certain dealing or transaction with the plaintiff, and reinforces his approach with an (unauthorised) physical assault upon him, his master may be vicariously liable for the assault (see *Dyer v Munday*); but where the servant induces the plaintiff to enter into an authorised transaction by means of a fraudulent misrepresentation which is not within his ostensible authority, the master will not be vicariously liable for the fraud. It also follows that there are acts of a servant for which a master may be vicariously liable, although they are not within the servant's ostensible authority; so that the conclusion which I have reached on the authorities is not inconsistent with the dictum of Lord Denning in *Navarro v Moregrand Ltd* upon which Mr Alexander relied.

For these reasons, in agreement with the conclusion reached by the Judge on this point, I am of the opinion that Mundogas is not vicariously liable to Armagas for the deceit of its servant, Mr Magelssen, such deceit consisting of a misrepresentation which was outside the ostensible authority of Mr Magelssen.

4 Montgomerie v United Kingdom Mutual SS Association Ltd [1891] 1 QB 370

Wright J ... There is no doubt whatever as to the general rule as regards an agent, that where a person contracts as agent for a principal the contract is the contract of the principal, and not that of the agent; and prima facie, at common law the only person who may sue is the principal, and the only person who can be sued is the principal. To that rule there are, of course, many exceptions. First, the agent may be added as the party to the contract if he has so contracted, and is appointed as the party to be sued. Secondly, the principal may be excluded in several other cases. He may be excluded if the contract is made by a deed inter partes, to which the principal is no party. In that case, by ancient rule of common law, it does not matter whether the person made a party is or is not an agent. This, however, does not apply here, as this instrument is a deed-poll. Another exception is as regards bills and notes. If a person who is an agent makes himself a party in writing to a bill or note, by the law merchant a principal cannot be added. Another exception is that by usage, which is treated as forming part of the contract or of the law merchant, where there is a foreign principal, generally speaking the agent in England is the party to the contract, and not the foreign principal; but this is subject to certain limitations. Then a principal's liability may be limited, though not excluded. If the other party elects to sue the agent he cannot afterwards sue the principal. Again, where the principal is an undisclosed principal, he must, if he sues, accept the facts as he finds them at the date of his disclosure, so far as those facts are consistent with reasonable and proper conduct on the part of the other party. Again, if the principal is sued, he is entitled to an allowance for payments which he may have made to his agent if the other party gave credit originally to that agent. Also, and this is very important, in all cases the parties can by their express contract provide that the agent shall be the person liable either concurrently with or to the exclusion of the principal, or that the agent shall be the party to sue either concurrently with or to the exclusion of the principal.

5   Fairlie v Fenton (1870) LR 5 Exch 169

Kelly CB ... The numerous cases cited to us shew that in certain contracts the agent may himself sue as principal; but in none does it appear that a broker has successfully maintained an action on a contract made by him as broker. He may, no doubt, frame a contract in such a way as to make himself a party to it and entitled to sue, but when he contracts in the ordinary form, describing and signing himself as a broker, and naming his principal, no action is maintainable by him. Though innumerable contracts of this nature daily take place, yet no instance has occurred within my own recollection, nor has any instance been cited to us, where an action has been brought by a broker describing himself as such in the contract, and not using words which expressly or by necessary implication make him the contracting party. Without further arguing the point, it is enough to refer to this unbroken rule as the settled law upon the subject.

Cleasby B ... There is no doubt a broker cannot sue; he has no authority to sell in his own name, or to receive the money, and has nothing to do with the goods. This is so laid down in *Story on Agency*, ss 28–34, 109: 'To use the brief but expressive language of an eminent judge, "a broker is one who makes a bargain for another, and receives a commission for so doing." Properly speaking, a broker is a mere negotiator between the other parties, and he never acts in his own name, but in the names of those who employ him. When he is employed to buy or sell goods, he is not intrusted with the custody or possession of them, and is not authorised to buy or to sell them in his own name' (s28). 'So, a broker has ordinarily no authority virtute officii, to receive payment for property sold by him' (s 109). The distinction between a broker and an auctioneer has been already pointed out in argument. My only doubt has been whether the use of the words 'I have', etc, ought to be held to import a personal participation in the contract, the usual course being departed from; but my opinion is, it ought not. The form is also in some other respects a little peculiar, as in its reference to the rules of the Cotton Brokers' Association; but it has not been shewn that those rules treat the broker as a principal in the transaction. The rule must, therefore, be made absolute.

6   Gadd v Houghton & Co (1876) I Ex D 357

Mellish LJ ... The question is whether, on the true construction of this contract, Houghton & Co sold the goods themselves or entered into a contract on behalf of Morand & Co. The language used must be interpreted according to its plain and natural meaning. As is said in the note to *Thomson v Davenport*[1], when a man signs a contract in his own name he is prima facie a contracting party and liable, and there must be something very strong on the face of the instrument to shew that the liability does not attach to him. But if there are plain words to shew that he is contracting on behalf of somebody else, why are we not to give effect to them? I can see no difference between a man writing '1, A B, as agent for C D, have sold to you', and signing 'A B;' and his writing, 'I have sold to you' and signing 'A B for C D the seller'. When the signature comes at the end you apply it to everything which occurs throughout the contract. If all that appears is that the agent has been making a contract on behalf of some other person, it seems to me to follow of necessity that that other person is the person liable. This is one of the simplest possible cases. How can the words 'on account of Morand & Co' be inserted merely as a description. The words mean that Morand & Co are the people who have sold. It follows that the persons who have signed are merely the brokers and are not liable.

1   2 Sm LC 6th Edn, 344.

7   Ireland v Livingston (1872) LR 5 HL 395

Lord Chelmsford ... Now it appears to me that if a principal gives an order to an agent in such uncertain terms as to be susceptible of two different meanings, and the agent *bona fide* adopts one of them and acts upon it, it is not competent to the principal to repudiate the act as unauthorised because he meant the order to be read in the other sense of which it is equally capable. It is a fair answer to such an attempt to disown the agent's authority to tell the principal that the departure from his intention was occasioned by his own fault, and that he should have given his order in clear and unambiguous terms. It would be most unjust, after the Plaintiffs have honestly acted upon what they conceived to be the wishes of the Defendant, as expressed in his order that he should be allowed to repudiate the whole transaction and throw the loss of it upon the Plaintiffs in order (as his correspondence shews) to escape from a speculation which had become a losing one in consequence of the market prices of sugars having fallen.

8   Hely-Hutchinson v Brayhead Ltd [1967] 3 All ER 98

Lord Denning MR ... I need not consider at length the law on the authority of an agent, actual, apparent or ostensible. That has been done in the judgments of this court in the case of *Freeman & Lockyer (a firm) v Buckhurst*

Park Properties (Mangal) Ltd[1]. It is there shown that actual authority may be express or implied. It is *express* when it is given by express words, such as when a board of directors pass a resolution which authorises two of their number to sign cheques. It is *implied* when it is inferred from the conduct of the parties and the circumstances of the case, such as when the board of directors appoint one of their number to be managing director. They thereby impliedly authorise him to do all such things as fall within the usual scope of that office. Actual authority, express or implied, is binding as between the company and the agent, and also as between the company and others, whether they are within the company or outside it.

Ostensible or apparent authority is the authority of an agent as it *appears* to others. It often coincides with actual authority. Thus, when the board appoint one of their number to be managing director, they invest him not only with implied authority, but also with ostensible authority to do all such things as fall within the usual scope of that office. Other people who see him acting as managing director are entitled to assume that he has the usual authority of a managing director. But sometimes ostensible authority exceeds actual authority. For instance, when the board appoint the managing director, they may expressly limit his authority by saying he is not to order goods worth more than £500 without the sanction of the board. In that case his *actual* authority is subject to the £500 limitation, but his *ostensible* authority includes all the usual authority of a managing director. The company is bound by his ostensible authority in his dealings with those who do not know of the limitation. He may himself do the 'holding-out'. Thus, if he orders goods worth £1,000 and signs himself 'Managing Director for and on behalf of the company', the company is bound to the other party who does not know of the £500 limitation (see *British Thomson Houston Co Ltd v Federal European Bank Ltd*[2] which was quoted for this purpose by Pearson LJ, in *Freeman & Lockyer v Buckhurst Park Properties (Mangal) Ltd*[3]). Even if the other party happens himself to be a director of the company, nevertheless the company may be bound by the ostensible authority. Suppose the managing director orders £1,000 worth of goods from a new director who has just joined the company and does not know of the £500 limitation, not having studied the minute book, the company may yet be bound.

1   [1964] 2 QB 480, [1964] 1 All ER 630.
2   [1932] 2 KB 176, [1932] All ER Rep 448.
3   [1964] 2 QB 480 at 499, [1964] 1 All ER 630 at 642.

9   Sorrell v Finch [1976] 2 All ER 371

Lord Edmund-Davies ... The primary basis of the vendor's liability seemingly is that, to engage an estate agent 'to find a purchaser' is to confer on him authority to receive money as agent for his principal (per Hodson LJ in *Ryan v Pilkington*); it seems, therefore, to be a case of actual, though implied, authority ... But the validity of such a conclusion depends on the extent to which the taking of a pre-contract deposit *on such terms as to make the prospective vendor liable therefor* can be regarded as reasonably incidental to the simple engaging of an estate agent to find a ready, willing and able purchaser. Some limits on his authority to commit the owner must be, and have been, imposed; for example, the estate agent cannot enter into a binding contract of sale (*Keen v Mear*[1]) nor one of letting (*Navarro v Moregrand Ltd*[2]). And, as I ventured to point out in *Barrington v Lee*[3]:

'… it is too simplistic to say that, because it was the would-be vendor who appointed the estate agent in the first place and so put him in a position to receive a deposit, the justice of the case demands that the vendor should be held liable to recompense the purchaser if loss results'.

The same could be said of many persons undoubtedly appointed as agents certain of whose activities nevertheless fall outside their authority: see the minority observations of Lord Halsbury LC in *Farquharson Brothers & Co v King & Co*[4]. In such circumstances, as in the instant case, where the issue raised is, which of two innocent parties is to suffer for the default of a third, the matter has to be determined in accordance with strict legal principle and with nothing else. As Dixon CJ said in *National Insurance Co of New Zealand v Espagne*[5]: 'Intuitive feelings for justice seem a poor substitute for a rule [of law] antecedently known, more particularly where all do not have the same intuitions.' For my part, I remain of the view I expressed in *Barrington v Lee*[3] that:

'… the just solution of the problem of which of two innocent parties should suffer should depend very largely (and possibly conclusively) on what rights could have been asserted by each of them in respect of the money in the agent's hands at all material times'.

It being common ground that, before a contract was concluded, neither vendor nor estate agent could gainsay the purchaser's demand for its return, I fail to see that the justice of the case demands that the vendor, however personally innocent, should be held liable to repay the depositor in the event of the agent defaulting. It is not open to the prospective purchaser to deny knowledge of his unfettered legal right to get his money back at that stage, and if, with that actual or imputed knowledge, he chooses to pay a deposit and leave it in the estate agent's hands, while one must naturally have sympathy with him, such intuitions of justice as I possess do not demand that he should be recouped by a vendor who shares his innocence and differs from him only in engaging someone to find a purchaser for his house. In this I am glad to find myself in the company of Sir John Pennycuick, who, in the present case, said: 'I do not myself find much force in the consideration of relative hardship'.

It has to be said respectfully that the hitherto prevailing majority view as to the authority of an estate agent in the pre-contract stage is an extremely odd one. It involves the *inference* that he possesses the authority of the vendor to receive it as his agent; but, although the deposit is received in that representative capacity, the recipient must nevertheless return it to the depositor at his request and the principal has *no* control over it, save that, in the words of Sachs J in *Goding v Frazer*[6]:

'There seems to be nothing in law to preclude the vendor from making such bargain as he would wish with the estate agent as to how and by whom any deposit should be held, and in particular (if he so preferred) from arranging that the deposit be paid into the hands of his solicitor or of himself'.

I know of no such right in the vendor nor of any support for it in the authorities, and in my judgment it is non-existent. It is right to add that the learned judge seemed later to have resiled from that view: see *Burt v Claude Cousins & Co*[7]. It is the fact that in this alleged relationship of agency the vendor has no control over property alleged to have been received on his behalf which makes it so unlikely and so wide a departure from the ordinary law (see *Edgell v Day*[8]) as to be unacceptable. Equally odd, with respect, is the view expressed by Sachs LJ[9] in *Burt v Claude Cousins & Co* that, 'A claim manifestly does lie against the estate agent whatever the answer to the question as to status of capacity', whereas it is a truism that where an agent makes a contract solely in his capacity as agent, he is not liable to the third party thereon, even if sums paid to him as agent by a third party still remain in his possession (*Ellis v Goulton*[10] and *Bowstead on Agency*[11]). For my part, the difficulty is not cleared up by adverting, as Megaw LJ did in *Burt v Claude Cousins & Co*[12], to the fact that an agent may undertake personal liability to the third party in the course of making a contract on behalf of his principal, and that it would not be foreign to the concept of agency for the estate agent to have authority from the prospective vendor to take the deposit as his agent and to take it subject to the obligation that he must repay it to the depositor on demand. In none of the reported cases did the estate agent expressly enter into any such arrangement with the vendor and I see no ground for employing one. On the contrary, the better view appears to me to be that his liability to account to the depositor rests solely on an implied term of the transaction between him and the depositor and springs in no way, direct or indirect, from the relationship between him and the vendor.

In my respectful judgment, these cases have unfortunately been 'off course' ever since the extempore judgments in *Ryan v Pilkington*[13] were delivered, despite the repeated efforts of Lord Denning MR to put matters right. It may well be that the prevailing error sprang originally from a two-fold source which was itself attributable to confusing terminology. First, the styling of the intermediary as an 'estate agent' may, however subconsciously, have induced the notion that whatever he did in relation to the vendor's property he did on his behalf; as my noble and learned friend, Lord Salmon, observed in the course of submissions, such confusion might never have arisen had the intermediary been styled a 'realtor' or some such other description. And, secondly, the consistent assertion right back to *Rayner v Paskell*[14] that he received a pre-contract deposit as a 'stakeholder' may well have led to blurring the difference between his position vis-à-vis the depositor according to whether the deposit was paid before or after the contract of sale had been concluded ... Hodson LJ[15] made clear that no expert evidence was called concerning the practice of estate agents and that 'the question of law whether the action of the agent here was within the scope of his authority is not directly covered by authority, and one has to apply first principles'. In my respectful judgment, it is not in accordance with first principles to hold the estate agent in such circumstances as the present as authorised to receive *on the vendor's behalf* a pre-contract deposit in the absence of express or implied authority so to do, and in neither way was such authority here given. Nor does the prospective vendor's knowledge that a deposit had been received of itself impose any liability on him to repay it.

1   [1920] 2 Ch 574 at 579, [1920] All ER Rep 147 at 151.
2   [1951] WN 335.
3   [1972] 1 QB 326 at 339, [1971] 3 All ER 1231 at 1239.
4   [1902] AC 325 at 331, 332, [1900–3] All ER Rep 120 at 123.
5   (1961) 105 CLR 569 at 572.
6   [1966] 3 All ER 234 at 239, [1967] 1 WLR 286 at 293.
7   [1971] 2 All ER 611 at 620, 621, [1971] 2 QB 426 at 447, 448.
8   (1865) LR 1 CP 80.
9   [1971] 2 All ER 611 at 622, [1971] 2 QB 426 at 449.
10 [1893] 1 QB 350.
11 13th Edn (1968), art 117, p 373.
12 [1971] 2 All ER 611 at 627, [1971] 2 QB 426 at 455.
13 [1959] 1 All ER 689, [1959] 1 WLR 403.
14 (1948) [1971] 2 All ER 628n, [1971] 2 QB 439n.
15 [1959] 1 All ER at 692, 693, [1959] 1 WLR at 408, 409.

10 Waugh v HB Clifford & Sons Ltd [1982] Ch 374, [1982] 1 All ER 1095

Brightman LJ ... The law thus became well established that the solicitor or counsel retained in an action has an *implied* authority as between himself and his client to compromise the suit without reference to the client, provided that the compromise does not involve matter 'collateral to the action'; and *ostensible* authority, as between himself and the opposing litigant, to compromise the suit without actual proof of authority, subject to the same limitation; and that a compromise does not involve 'collateral matter' merely because it contains terms which the court could not have ordered by way of judgment in the action ...

In none of the cases cited to us has there been any debate on the question whether the implied authority of the advocate or solicitor as between himself and his client is necessarily as extensive as the ostensible authority of the advocate or solicitor vis-à-vis the opposing litigant. The possibility of difference seems to have been adverted to by Byles J in the *Prestwich* case (1865) 18 CBNS 806, 809. In my judgment there is every reason to draw a distinction.

Suppose that a defamation action is on foot; that terms of compromise are discussed; and that the defendant's solicitor writes to the plaintiff's solicitor offering to compromise at a figure of £100,000, which the plaintiff desires to accept. It would in my view be officious on the part of the plaintiff's solicitor to demand to be satisfied as to the authority of the defendant's solicitor to make the offer. It is perfectly clear that the defendant's solicitor has ostensible authority to compromise on behalf of his client, notwithstanding the large sum involved. It is not incumbent on the plaintiff to seek the signature of the defendant, if an individual, or the seal of the defendant if a corporation, or the signature of a director.

But it does not follow that the defendant's solicitor would have *implied* authority to agree damages on that scale without the agreement of his client. In the light of the solicitor's knowledge of his client's cash position it might be quite unreasonable and indeed grossly negligent for the solicitor to commit his client to such a burden without first inquiring if it were acceptable. But that does not affect the *ostensible* authority of the solicitor to compromise, so as to place the plaintiff at risk if he fails to satisfy himself that the defendant's solicitor has sought the agreement of his client. Such a limitation on the ostensible authority of the solicitor would be unworkable. How is the opposing litigant to estimate on which side of the line a particular case falls?

It follows, in my view, that a solicitor (or counsel) may in a particular case have ostensible authority vis-à-vis the opposing litigant where he has no implied authority vis-à-vis his client. I see no objection to that. All that the opposing litigant need ask himself when testing the ostensible authority of the solicitor or counsel, is the question whether the compromise contains matter 'collateral to the suit'. The magnitude of the compromise, or the burden which its terms impose on the other party, is irrelevant. But much more than that question may need to be asked by a solicitor when deciding whether he can safely compromise without reference to his client ...

I think it would be regrettable if this court were to place too restrictive a limitation on the ostensible authority of solicitors to bind their clients to a compromise. I do not think we should decide that matter is 'collateral' to the action unless it really involves extraneous subject matter, as in *Aspin v Wilkinson* (1879) 23 Sol Jo 388, and *Re a Debtor* [1914] 2 KB 758. So many compromises are made in court, or in counsel's chambers, in the presence of the solicitor but not the client. This is almost inevitable where a corporation is involved. It is highly undesirable that the court should place any unnecessary impediments in the way of that convenient procedure. A party on one side of the record and his solicitor ought usually to be able to rely without question on the existence of the authority of the solicitor on the other side of the record, without demanding that the seal of the corporation be affixed; or that a director should sign who can show that the articles confer the requisite power upon him; or that the solicitor's correspondence with his client be produced to prove the authority of the solicitor. Only in the exceptional case, where the compromise introduces extraneous subject-matter, should the solicitor retained in the action be put to proof of his authority. Of course it is incumbent on the solicitor to make certain that he is in fact authorised by his corporate or individual client to bind his client to a compromise. In a proper case he can agree without specific reference to his client. But in the great majority of cases, and certainly in all cases of magnitude, he will in practice take great care to consult his client, and I think that his client would be much aggrieved if in an important case involving large sums of money he relied on his implied authority. But that does not affect his *ostensible* authority vis-à-vis the opposing litigant.

11 Watteau v Fenwick [1893] 1 QB 346

Wills J ... The plaintiff sues the defendants for the price of cigars supplied to the Victoria Hotel, Stockton-upon-Tees. The house was kept, not by the defendants, but by a person named Humble, whose name was over the door. The plaintiff gave credit to Humble, and to him alone, and had never heard of the defendants. The business, however, was really the defendants'; and they had put Humble into it to manage it for them, and had forbidden him to buy cigars on credit. The cigars, however, were such as would usually be supplied to and dealt in at such an establishment. The learned county court judge held that the defendants were liable. I am of opinion that he was right.

There seems to be less direct authority on the subject than one would expect. But I think that the Lord Chief Justice during the argument laid down the correct principle, viz, once it is established that the defendant was the real principal, the ordinary doctrine as to principal and agent applies – that the principal is liable for all the acts of the agent which are within the authority usually confided to an agent of that character, notwithstanding limitations, as between the principal and the agent, put upon that authority. It is said that it is only so where there has been a holding out of authority – which cannot be said of a case where the person supplying the goods knew nothing of the existence of a principal. But I do not think so. Otherwise, in every case of undisclosed principal, or at least in every case where the fact of there being a principal was undisclosed, the secret limitation of authority would prevail and defeat the action of the person dealing with the agent and then discovering that he was an agent and had a principal.

12 Rhodian River Shipping Co SA and Rhodian Sailor Shipping Co SA v Halla Maritime Corpn, The Rhodian River and Rhodian Sailor [1984] 1 Lloyd's Rep 373

Bingham LJ ... The true ratio of this decision [*Watteau v Fenwick*] is not altogether easy to perceive, and certainly the case does not appear to have sired a line of authority, but the case perhaps reflects an undeveloped doctrine that an undisclosed principal should be vicariously liable on contracts made by an agent where they are contracts which a person would ordinarily make in the position which the principal has allowed the agent to assume (see *Edmunds, PO v Bushell and Jones* (1865) LR 1 QB 97, relied upon by the Court in *Watteau v Fenwick* and *Bowstead on Agency*, 14th Edn, p 72). I would myself be extremely wary of applying this doctrine, if it exists ...

13 Sign-O-Lite Plastics Ltd v Metropolitan Life Insurance Co (1990) 73 DLR (4th) 541

Wood JA ... It is not clear from the reasons of the learned trial judge whether he concluded, as a matter of law, that an undisclosed principal could not be held liable for the unauthorised acts of its agents, or whether he accepted that such liability was possible providing such acts fell within the scope of authority generally implied or usually given to such agents, but concluded that the evidence fell short of establishing the scope of authority usually given or implied to shopping mall managers in connection with the sort of contract at issue. In any event he did refer to the decision in *Watteau v Fenwick* [1893] 1 QB 346, the authority generally relied upon in support of the conceptually difficult notion that usual or implied authority can be a basis for fixing an undisclosed principal with liability for the unauthorised acts of his agent. For the cross-appeal to succeed, it must be established that the law of British Columbia accepts such a doctrine ...

The learned editors of *Bowstead on Agency*, 15th Edn (1985), describe the decision in *Watteau v Fenwick* as 'dubious' ...

The only English case in which *Watteau v Fenwick* has apparently been followed was the decision of the Divisional Court in *Kinahan & Co v Parry* [1910] 2 KB 389 which was reversed on other grounds: see [1911] 1 KB 459, CA. I have not been able to find a reported case in which it has been followed in Canada. On the contrary, it was the subject of considerable doubt expressed by three out of four judges of the Ontario Supreme Court, Appellate Division, in *Becherer v Asher* (1896) 23 OAR 202, and was authoritatively rejected by the same court in *McLaughlin v Gentles* (1919) 46 OLR 477, 51 DLR 383.

In the latter case, one Chisholm acted as the on-site agent of the four appellants in the development of a mine in northern Ontario. The court found that his authority was limited, and that in violation of that limitation he contracted with the respondent for certain goods which were sold and delivered to the mine site. At the time of the transaction the respondent had no knowledge that anyone other than Chisholm had an interest in the mine. The trial judge gave judgment for the respondent without giving any reasons.

After much fact-finding, necessitated by the lack of reasons from the judge below, Hodgins JA, who gave the reasons for the court, considered *Watteau v Fenwick*, its antecedents and a number of subsequent cases, including *Kinahan & Co v Parry* and *Becherer v Asher*, and then concluded at pp 394–5 of the report:

'In view of the doubt expressed as to the case which is relied on as rendering the appellants liable because of the bare fact of agency, I think it is open to this Court to follow *Miles v McIlwraith*, untrammelled by the decisions I have mentioned. It seems to be straining the doctrine of ostensible agency or of holding out, to apply it in a case where the fact of agency and the holding out were unknown to the person dealing with the so-called agent at the time, and to permit that person, when he discovered that his purchaser was only an agent, to recover against the principal, on the theory that he is estopped from denying that he authorised the purchase. *It appears to me that the fact that there was a limitation of authority is at least as important as the fact that the purchaser was an agent.* The vendor did not know either of these facts, and so did not draw any conclusion involving the principal when he sold and delivered the goods. Should he be permitted, when he elects to look to the principal, to do so upon any other terms than in accordance with the actual authority given at that time? It is entirely different where there is a holding out as agent and the fact of agency is known, but where neither is an element in the bargain nor the reason why credit was given, and so not an additional security known to the vendor at the time, no equity should be raised in favour of the vendor as against the principal so as to make the latter liable'. (Emphasis added.)

This reasoning was adopted in its entirety in the case of *Massey-Harris Co Ltd v Bond* [1930] 2 DLR 57 at p 62, [1930] 1 WWR 72 (Alta SC). Since then the reports which I have had an opportunity to research are bereft of any hint that *Watteau v Fenwick* should be considered good law.

It is astonishing that, after all these years, an authority of such doubtful origin, and of such unanimously unfavourable reputation, should still be exhibiting signs of life and disturbing the peace of mind of trial judges. It is surely time to end any uncertainty which may linger as to its proper place in the law of agency. I have no difficulty concluding that it is not part of the law of this province.

14 Freeman and Lockyer v Buckhurst Park Properties (Mangal) Ltd [1964] 1 All ER 630

Diplock LJ ... We are concerned in the present case with the authority of an agent to create contractual rights and liabilities between his principal and a third party whom I will call 'the contractor'. This branch of the law has developed pragmatically rather than logically, owing to the early history of assumpsit and the consequent absence of a general jus quaesitum tertio in English law. But it is possible (and for the determination of this appeal I think it is desirable) to restate it on a rational basis. It is necessary at the outset to distinguish between an 'actual' authority of an agent on the one hand, and an 'apparent' or 'ostensible' authority on the other. Actual authority and apparent authority are quite independent of one another. Generally they co-exist and coincide, but either may exist without the other and their respective scopes may be different. As I shall endeavour to show, it is on the apparent authority of the agent that the contractor normally relies in the ordinary course of business when entering into contracts.

An 'actual' authority is a legal relationship between principal and agent created by a consensual agreement to which they alone are parties. Its scope is to be ascertained by applying ordinary principles of construction of contracts, including any proper implications from the express words used, the usages of the trade, or the course of business between the parties. To this agreement the contractor is a stranger; he may be totally ignorant of the existence of any authority on the part of the agent. Nevertheless, if the agent does enter into a contract pursuant to the 'actual' authority, it does create contractual rights and liabilities between the principal and the contractor. It may be that this rule relating to 'undisclosed principals', which is peculiar to English law, can be rationalised as avoiding circuity of action, for the principal could in equity compel the agent to lend his name in an action to enforce the contract against the contractor, and would at common law be liable to indemnify the agent in respect of the performance of the obligations assumed by the agent under the contract.

An 'apparent' or 'ostensible' authority, on the other hand, is a legal relationship between the principal and the contractor created by a representation, made by the principal to the contractor, intended to be and in fact acted on by the contractor, that the agent has authority to enter on behalf of the principal into a contract of a kind within the scope of the 'apparent' authority, so as to render the principal liable to perform any obligations imposed on him by such contract. To the relationship so created the agent is a stranger. He need not be (although he generally is) aware of the existence of the representation. The representation, when acted on by the contractor by entering into a contract with the agent, operates as an estoppel, preventing the principal from asserting that he is not bound by the contract. It is irrelevant whether the agent had actual authority to enter into the contract.

In ordinary business dealings the contractor at the time of entering into the contract can in the nature of things hardly ever rely on the 'actual' authority of the agent. His information as to the authority must be derived either from the principal or from the agent or from both, for they alone know what the agent's actual authority is. All that the contractor can know is what they tell him, which may or may not be true. In the ultimate analysis he relies either on the representation of the principal, ie apparent authority, or on the representation of the agent, ie warranty of authority. The representation which creates 'apparent' authority may take a variety of forms of which the commonest is representation by conduct, ie, by permitting the agent to act in some way in the conduct of the principal's business with other persons. By so doing the principal represents to anyone who becomes aware that the agent is so acting that the agent has authority to enter on behalf of the principal into contracts with other persons of the kind which an agent so acting in the conduct of his principal's business has normally 'actual' authority to enter into.

In applying the law, as I have endeavoured to summarise it, to the case where the principal is not a natural person, but a fictitious person, viz, a corporation, two further factors arising from the legal characteristics of a corporation have to be borne in mind. The first is that the capacity of a corporation is limited by its constitution, ie, in the case of a company incorporated under the Companies Act, by its memorandum and articles of association; the second is that a corporation cannot do any act, and that includes making a representation, except through its agent. Under the doctrine of ultra vires the limitation of the capacity of a corporation by its constitution to do any acts is absolute. This affects the rules as to the 'apparent' authority of an agent of a corporation in two ways. First, no representation can operate to estop the corporation from denying the authority of the agent to do on behalf of the corporation an act which the corporation is not permitted by its constitution to do itself. Secondly, since the conferring of actual authority on an agent is itself an act of the corporation, the capacity to do which is regulated by its constitution, the corporation cannot be estopped from denying that it has conferred on a particular agent authority to do acts which, by its constitution, it is incapable of delegating to that particular agent. To recognise that these are direct consequences of the doctrine of ultra vires is, I think, preferable to saying that a contractor who enters into a contract with a corporation has constructive notice of its constitution, for the expression 'constructive notice' tends to disguise that constructive notice is not a positive, but a negative doctrine, like that of estoppel of which it forms a part. It operates to prevent the contractor from saying that he did not know that the constitution of the corporation rendered a particular act or a particular delegation of authority ultra vires the corporation. It does not entitle him to say that he relied on some unusual provision in the constitution of the corporation, if he did not in fact so rely.

The second characteristic of a corporation, viz, that unlike a natural person it can only make a representation through an agent, has the consequence that, in order to create an estoppel between the corporation and the contractor, the representation as to the authority of the agent which creates his 'apparent' authority must be made by some person or persons who have 'actual' authority from the corporation to make the representation. Such 'actual' authority may be conferred by the constitution of the corporation itself, as, for example, in the case of a company, on the board of directors, or it may be conferred by those who under its constitution have the powers of management on some other person to whom the constitution permits them to delegate authority to make representations of this kind. It follows that, where the agent on whose 'apparent' authority the contractor relies has no 'actual' authority from the corporation to enter into a particular kind of contract with the contractor on behalf of the corporation, the contractor cannot rely on the agent's own representation as to his actual authority. He can rely only on a representation by a person or persons who have actual authority to manage or conduct that part of the business of the corporation to which the contract relates. The commonest form of representation by a principal creating an 'apparent' authority of an agent is by conduct, viz, by permitting the agent to act in the management or conduct of the principal's business. Thus, if in the case of a company the board of directors who have 'actual' authority under the memorandum and articles of association to manage the company's business permit the agent to act in the management or conduct of the company's business, they thereby represent to all persons dealing with such agent that he has authority to enter on behalf of the corporation into contracts of a kind which an agent authorised to do acts of the kind which he is in fact permitted to do normally enters into in the ordinary course of such business. The making of such a representation is itself an act of management of the company's business. Prima facie it falls within the 'actual' authority of the board of directors, and unless the memorandum or articles of the company either make such a contract ultra vires the company or prohibit the delegation of such authority to the agent, the company is estopped from denying to anyone who has entered into a contract with the agent in reliance on such 'apparent' authority that the agent had authority to contract on behalf of the company.

If the foregoing analysis of the relevant law is correct, it can be summarised by stating four conditions which must be fulfilled to entitle a contractor to enforce against a company a contract entered into on behalf of the company by an agent who had no actual authority to do so. It must be shown: (a) that a representation that the agent had authority to enter on behalf of the company into a contract of the kind sought to be enforced was made to the contractor; (b) that such representation was made by a person or persons who had 'actual' authority to manage the business of the company either generally or in respect of those matters to which the contract relates; (c) that he (the contractor) was induced by such representation to enter into the contract, ie that he in fact relied on it; and (d) that under its memorandum or articles of association the company was not deprived of the capacity either to enter into a contract of the kind sought to be enforced or to delegate authority to enter into a contract of that kind to the agent.

The confusion which, I venture to think, has sometimes crept into the cases, is, in my view, due to failure to distinguish between these four separate conditions, and in particular to keep steadfastly in mind (first) that the only 'actual' authority which is relevant is that of the persons making the representation relied on, and (second) that the memorandum and articles of association of the company are always relevant (whether they are in fact known to the contractor or not) to the questions (i) whether condition (b) is fulfilled, and (ii) whether condition (d) is fulfilled, and (but only if they are in fact known to the contractor) may be relevant to (c) as part of the representation on which the contractor relied.

15 Rama Corpn Ltd v Proved Tin and General Investments Ltd [1952] 2 QB 147

Slade J ... a person cannot set up an ostensible or apparent authority unless he relied on it in making the contract or supposed contract ... Ostensible or apparent authority which negatives the existence of actual authority is merely a form of estoppel, indeed, it has been termed agency by estoppel, and you cannot call in aid an estoppel unless you have three ingredients: (i) a representation, (ii) a reliance on the representation, and (iii) an alteration of your position resulting from such reliance.

16 Egyptian International Foreign Trade Co v Soplex Wholesale Supplies Ltd and PS Refson & Co Ltd, The Raffaella [1985] 2 Lloyd's Rep 36

Browne-Wilkinson LJ ... It is important to bear in mind that the doctrine of holding out is a form of estoppel. As such, the starting point is that the principal must be shown to have made a representation, which the third party could and did reasonably rely on, that the agent had the necessary authority. The relevant enquiry, therefore, in all cases is whether the acts of the principal constitute a representation that the agent had a particular authority and were reasonably so understood by the third party. This requires the Court to consider the principal's conduct *as a whole.* In many cases, the holding out or representation by the company consists solely of the fact that the company has invested the agent with a particular office, eg 'managing director' or 'secretary'. For example, in a case such as *British Bank of the Middle East v Sun Life Assurance of Canada (UK) Ltd* [1983] 2 Lloyd's Rep 9, the only holding out by the defendants to the third party was to invest someone with the title 'Branch Manager', which enabled him so to describe himself in correspondence relied upon by the third party: in such a case, the only representation which the third party can reasonably rely upon is the representation that that person has the powers normally or usually enjoyed by a branch manager. Therefore, in such a case, the only relevant enquiry is as to the powers normally enjoyed by branch managers in general. But where, as in the present case, the holding out is alleged to consist of a course of conduct wider than merely describing the agent as holding a particular office, although the authority normally found in the holder of such an office is very material, it must be looked at as part and parcel of the whole course of the principal's conduct in order to decide whether the totality of the principal's actions constitute a holding out of the agent as possessing the necessary authority.

I therefore cannot accept either of the ways in which Mr Stamler put his case. It is not right in this case simply to enquire what is the normal authority of documentary credit managers in general. Nor is it right to start by seeking to establish the normal authority of documentary credit managers in general and then looking to see whether there are any additional factors which alter the position. The only correct approach is the one adopted by the Judge, which is to consider the whole of Refson's conduct to determine whether it amounted to a holding out by Refson of Mr Booth as having the necessary authority.

The expert evidence accepted by the Judge shows that documentary credit managers are to be found in three different types of bank: clearing banks, merchant banks and trading banks. The working methods of clearing banks are different from those of the other two and as Mr Stamler accepted, can be ignored. Normal practice in merchant and trading banks is that they have two categories of authorised signatories, category A (who can bind on their sole signatures) and category B (who cannot). Lists of category A and B signatories are confidential and could not have been known to anyone in the position of the plaintiffs. In merchant and trading banks some (but not all) managers are category A signatories. In such banks, it is common for there to be a particularly close relationship between a particular senior manager and one particular customer. Mr Spiers (one of the plaintiff's experts) gave evidence that, in this type of bank, it is not unusual for a manager to concentrate on, and look after, one customer: in such a case, he said that the manager has 'complete authority, within the banking parameters to do what is required'. Mr Stamler suggested that the evidence of the other expert witness for the plaintiffs, Mr Stephens, did not justify the Judge's view that he supported Mr Spiers' evidence, since it did not indicate that documentary credit managers in general enjoyed this 'general authority'. Mr Stephens (who had been documentary credit manager at Kleinworts) said in his original report that, as such manager, he had not had authority to bind on his sole signature but, when made a 'full' or 'senior' manager, he was given such authority. In my judgment, when Mr Stephens' evidence is read as a whole, it is clear that he remained documentary credit manager throughout: in the earlier stages he did not have authority to commit on his sole signature, but in the later stages (when he was given wider functions in addition to that of documentary credit manager) he did. I do not find this in any way inconsistent with the evidence of Mr Spiers. The picture which emerges is that a documentary credit manager may or may not be a sole signatory: if he in fact looks after a client's affairs generally (as opposed to being limited to documentary credits alone) he would be expected by those who know the practices of such banks to have general authority to bind the bank and to be an A signatory (as Mr Stephens himself became in his later days as documentary credit manager) ...

... [It was] submitted that a principal cannot be held liable as a result of the agent holding himself out as possessing an authority he does not in fact possess: [counsel for the defendants] relied on remarks to that effect in the *Freeman & Lockyer* case at 505, *Attorney-General for Ceylon v Silva* [1953] 1 Lloyds Rep 563; [1953] AC 461 at 471 and 479, *The British Bank of the Middle East* case and *Armagas Ltd v Mundogas SA* [1985] 1 Lloyd's Rep 1. As at present advised, I am not satisfied that the principle to be derived from those cases is as wide as Mr Stamler suggests: they were all cases or dicta dealing with the position where the agent had neither authority to enter into the transaction nor authority to make representations on behalf of the principal. It is obviously correct that an agent who has no actual or apparent authority either (a) to enter into a transaction or (b) to make representations as to the transaction cannot hold himself out as having authority to enter into the transaction so as to effect the principal's position. But, suppose a company confers actual or apparent authority on X to make representations and X erroneously represents to a third party that Y has authority to enter into a transaction; why should not such a representation be relied upon as part of the holding out of Y by the company? By parity of reasoning, if a company confers actual or apparent authority on A to make representations on the company's behalf but no actual authority on A to enter into the specific transaction, why should a representation made by A as to his authority not be capable of being relied on as one of the acts of holding out: There is substantial authority that it can be: see *British Thomson-Houston Co Ltd v Federated European Bank Ltd* [1932] 2 KB 176, especially at 182 (where the only holding out was an erroneous representation by the agent that he was managing director); the *Freeman & Lockyer* case per Lord Justice Pearson at 499, and *Hely-Hutchinson v Brayhead Ltd* [1968] 1 QB 549 per Lord Denning MR at 593. If, as I am inclined to think, an agent with authority to make representations can make a representation that he has authority to enter into a transaction, then the Judge was entitled to hold, as he did, that Mr Booth, as the representative of Refson in charge of the transaction, had implied or apparent authority to make the representation that only one signature was required and that this representation was a relevant consideration in deciding whether Refson had held out Mr Booth as having authority to sign the undertaking.

17 Farquharson Brothers & Co v C King & Co [1902] AC 325

Lord Lindley ... Capon sold the plaintiffs' timber without their authority and sold it to the defendants. The defendants honestly bought the timber, and they had no notice that Capon had no right to sell it; but there was no sale in the market overt, and the Factors Acts do not apply. The mere fact, therefore, that the defendants acted honestly does not confer upon them a good title as against the plaintiffs, the real owners of the timber. The plaintiffs are entitled to recover the timber or its value, unless they are precluded by their conduct from denying Capon's authority to sell (Sale of Goods Act 1893, s 21, and see s 61). Capon sold under the name of Brown, representing himself to be an agent of some persons named Bayley, who were well known in the timber trade. The defendants bought on the faith of his being what he pretended to be. What have the plaintiffs done which precludes them from denying, as against the defendants, Capon's right to do what he pretended he was entitled to do. Putting the question in another form: What have the plaintiffs done to preclude them from denying, as against the defendants, Capon's right to sell to them? To answer those questions it is necessary to consider what the plaintiffs did.

Capon was the plaintiffs' confidential clerk; they gave him a limited power of sale to certain customers, and a general written authority to sign delivery orders on their behalf; and the plaintiffs sent that written authority to the dock company which stored the plaintiffs' timber. This authority would, of course, protect the dock company in delivering timber as ordered by Capon, however fraudulently he might be acting, if the dock company had no notice of anything wrong. By abusing his authority Capon made timber belonging to the plaintiffs deliverable by the dock company to himself under the name of Brown. In that name he sold it, and procured it to be delivered to the defendants. What is there here which precludes the plaintiffs from denying Capon's right to sell to the defendants?

What have the plaintiffs done to mislead the defendants and to induce them to trust Capon? Absolutely nothing. The question for decision ought to be narrowed in this way, for it is in my opinion clear that, when s 21 of the Sale of Goods Act has to be applied to a particular case, the inquiry which has to be made is not a general inquiry as to the authority to sell, apart from all reference to the particular case, but an inquiry into the real or apparent authority of the seller to do that which the defendants say induced them to buy.

It was pointed out by Parke J, afterwards Lord Wensleydale, in *Dickinson v Valpy*[1], that 'holding out to the world' is a loose expression; the 'holding out' must be to the particular individual who says he relied on it, or under such circumstances of publicity as to justify the inference that he knew of it and acted upon it. The same principle must be borne in mind in dealing with cases like the present. I do not myself see upon what ground a person can be precluded from denying as against another an authority which has never been given in fact, and which the other has never supposed to exist.

It was urged that the dock company was led by the plaintiffs to obey Capon's orders and to deliver to Brown, and that the defendants were induced by the dock company to deal with Brown, or at all events to pay him on the faith of his being entitled to the timber; so that in fact the plaintiffs, through the dock company, misled the defendants. This is ingenious but unsound. Except that delivery orders were sent in the name of Brown to the defendants, and were acted on by the dock company, there is no evidence connecting the dock company with the defendants in these transactions; and the answer to the contention is that the defendants were misled, not by what the plaintiffs did nor by what the plaintiffs authorised the dock company to do, but by Capon's frauds.

It is, of course, true that by employing Capon and trusting him as they did the plaintiffs enabled him to transfer the timber to any one; in other words, the plaintiffs in one sense enabled him to cheat both themselves and others. In that sense, everyone who has a servant enables him to steal whatever is within his reach. But if the word 'enable' is used in this wide sense, it is clearly untrue to say, as Ashhurst J said in *Lickbarrow v Mason*[2] 'that wherever one of two innocent persons must suffer by the acts of a third, he who has enabled such third person to occasion the loss must sustain it'. Such a doctrine is far too wide; and the cases referred to in the argument and commented on by Vaughan Williams LJ shew that it cannot be relied upon without considerable qualification.

Lamb v Attenborough[3], which is very like this, is a good illustration of the unsoundness of the doctrine in question if taken literally. *Johnson v Crédit Lyonnais Co*[4] is another illustration to the like effect. So far as I know, the doctrine has never been judicially applied where nothing has been done by one of the innocent parties which has in fact misled the other ... In the present case, in my view of it, Capon simply sold the plaintiff's goods and sold them to the defendants, and the defendants' title is not improved by the circumstance that the theft was the result of an ingenious fraud on the plaintiffs and on the defendants alike. The defendants were not in any way misled by any act of the plaintiffs on which they placed reliance; and the plaintiffs are not, therefore, precluded from denying Capon's authority to sell.

1   (1829) 10 B & C 128 at 140, 34 RR 355.
2   (1787) 2 Term Rep 63, 1 RR 425.
3   (1862) 1 B & S 831.
4   (1877) 3 CPD 32.

18 Overbrooke Estates Ltd v Glencombe Properties Ltd [1974] 3 All ER 511

Brightman J ... An agent, as between himself and a third party, has such authority as is actually conferred on him by his principal or such authority as has ostensibly been conferred on him because of the manner or circumstances in which he has been held out as an agent. The plaintiff company asserts – and this is not in dispute before me – that no actual authority has been conferred by the plaintiff company on Willmotts to make any representations or give any warranties relating to this property. Counsel for the plaintiff company also submits that no ostensible authority was conferred on Willmotts to make representations or give warranties having regard to the auction catalogue and condition R(b). This states, in terms, that no such authority was conferred. The defendant company, it was submitted, cannot rely on misrepresentations made by the agent of the plaintiff company, which the defendant company knew or ought to have known the agent had no authority to make on behalf of its principal.

Counsel for the defendant company seeks to escape from this reasoning in two ways. His first argument is based on the decision of the Court of Appeal in *Mendelssohn v Normand Ltd*[1]. In that case a motorist had parked his car in a garage on the terms endorsed on a ticket which was handed to him. These terms – which the Court of Appeal considered to form part of the contract – exempted the garage owners from any responsibility for the safety of the car's contents and also provided by condition 6: 'No variation of these conditions will bind the garage proprietors unless made in writing signed by the duly authorised manager'. Condition 6, it appears to me, put the motorist on notice that no employee save the manager had authority to bind the garage owners to accept responsibility for the safety of the contents of a car. When the plaintiff drove his car into the garage he was met by an attendant who demanded the keys. The plaintiff protested. The attendant stated that it was a rule of the establishment and promised to lock the car himself. The court considered that there was an implied promise by the car attendant purporting to have been given on behalf of the garage owners that the garage owners would see to the safety of the contents. In the outcome the plaintiff lost a suitcase. He sued the garage owners and recovered judgment. It was held that the garage attendant had ostensible authority to make a statement regarding the safety of the contents of the plaintiff's car and therefore ostensible authority to make a promise on behalf of the garage owners to look after the contents. It was held that a promise so made pursuant to the attendant's ostensible authority overrode the written terms of the contract.

Counsel for the defendant company submits that an estate agent has ostensible authority to make representations concerning a property which he has been commissioned to sell. He relies on *Mullens v Miller*[2]. It will be sufficient to read the first paragraph of the headnote which adequately reflects the judgment:

'An agent, commissioned by a vendor to find a purchaser, has authority to describe the property, and to state any fact or circumstance which may affect the value, so as to bind the vendor; and if an agent so commissioned, makes a false statement as to the description or value (though not instructed so to do), which the purchaser is led to believe, and upon which he relies, the vendor cannot recover in an action for specific performance'.

Counsel then steps from that case to the *Mendelssohn* case and argues that the representation made by Willmotts came within the ostensible authority of the auctioneers, though not within their actual authority, and thus condition R(b) is overridden.

I would, for myself, take the view that ostensible authority of an estate agent is dependent on the particular circumstances of the case. I am not convinced that an auctioneer, who is selling a wide range of properties of the sort being sold by Willmotts on 8th November, according to printed particulars such as were distributed in the present case, has any ostensible authority to do more than accept bids. However that may be, in the case before me it is not, in my judgment, possible for the defendant company to assert that Willmotts had ostensible authority to make the representations said to have been made by them, for these reasons – before any contract was made and, indeed, before any representation was made, the defendant company was obviously in possession of a document which, in terms, negatived any such authority. The *Mendelssohn* case in my view was dealing with an entirely different set of circumstances and a different sequence of events. It seems to me that it must be open to a principal to draw the attention of the public to the limits which he places on the authority of his agent and that this must be so whether the agent is a person who has, or has not, any ostensible authority. If an agent has prima facie some ostensible authority, that authority is inevitably diminished to the extent of the publicised limits that are placed on it. When Mr Buckwald telephoned Willmotts he knew, or ought to have known, that Willmotts had no authority to make or give any representation or warranty in relation to this property. When he bid for the property three days later, he did so on the basis that nothing which had been said to him by Willmotts amounted to a representation or warranty binding on the plaintiff company. So, it seems to me that counsel for the defendant company cannot escape from the full implications of condition R(b) notwithstanding the deft use he has made of *Mullens v Miller*[2] and the *Mendelssohn* case.

1   [1969] 2 All ER 1215, [1970] 1 QB 177.
2   (1882) 22 Ch D 194.

19 Jebara v Ottoman Bank [1927] 2 KB 254

Scrutton LJ ... It was argued that if the original contracts were void on the outbreak of war, the bank became agents of necessity and could justify their action in that way. I am not sure that it is not an answer to say that they never thought of themselves in that light, or considered whether it was necessary to act; they thought they were carrying out their contracts. But considerable difficulties arise on the question of agent of necessity in English law. Until recently it was treated as limited to certain classes of agents of whom masters of ships were the most prominent. High authorities had doubted whether it could be extended. I refer to the observations of Lord Esher MR in *Gwillian v Twist*[1]; to the judgment of Parke B in *Hawtayne v Bourne*[2], but especially to the careful judgment of Eyre CJ in *Nicholson v Chapman*[3]. Many of the authorities are collected in a recent judgment of McCardie J in *Prager's* case[4]. He there finds the facts so as not to raise any question of action by an agent of necessity, but discusses what the law would be, if he had found the facts differently. He takes the view that judges should expand the common law to meet the needs of expanding society, and proceeds to expand the doctrine of agent of necessity without clearly defining the limits, if any, of its expansion. The difficulty may be seen by considering the case of the finder of perishable goods or chattels which need expenditure to preserve them. If the finder incurs such expenditure, can he recover it from the true owner when he finds him, as his 'agent of necessity'? Eyre CJ raises this difficulty in the case above cited, and cites *Binstead v Bucks*[5], the case of the pointer dog. The pointer dog was lost, and his finder fed him for twenty weeks, and claimed the cost from his owner when he appeared, but the claim was treated as unarguable. The expansion desired by McCardie J becomes less difficult when the agent of necessity develops from an original and subsisting agency, and only applies itself to unforeseen events not provided for in the original contract, which is usually the case where a ship-master is agent of necessity. But the position seems quite different when there is no pre-existing agency, as in the case of a finder of perishable chattels or animals, and still more difficult when there is a pre-existing agency, but it has become illegal and void by reason of war, and the same reason will apply to invalidate any implied agency of necessity. How can one imply a duty in an enemy to protect the property of his enemy? Will he not be violating his duty to his own country if he takes active steps to preserve an enemy's property? I do not feel strong enough to expand the common law to this extent, and I do not see that McCardie J has considered the effect of illegality and invalidity by reason of war in his doctrine. The principal in *Prager's* case[6] was a Roumanian, and Roumania was an ally of England, though it may be that the principal was in a part of Roumania occupied by the Germans, and was therefore to be treated as an enemy. Compare *Société Anonyme Belge des Mines d'Aljustrel (Portugal) v Anglo-Belgian Agency*[7]. The decision of Greer J in *Ananiadi v Ottoman Bank*[8], to which we were referred, gives more trouble. It is not very clear how the goods in question in that case got to Turkey, but apparently before the war they had got into the hands of the Ottoman Bank at Constantinople as bankers for reward, though the bank there did not know for whom they were acting, and the question who put the goods in bailment with the Ottoman Bank is left in doubt. Then came the war, and the first part of the judgment of Greer J, with which I agree, is that the war invalidated all obligations of the Turkish bank to the English enemy. The bank had not advanced any money on the security of the documents or goods. But having held that the bank were under no obligation as to the goods the learned judge says: 'Now they (the bank) were in a position in which they were bound to do something, otherwise the goods would be entirely lost ... and therefore they were in a position of agents of necessity'. I do not follow the reasoning; if all prior obligations were invalidated by the outbreak of war, how could an implied obligation arise between enemies? How could the bank be 'bound' to an enemy to do anything? How is an enemy bound to take steps to preserve the property of his enemy? So far as I understand the facts in this case, I doubt whether the latter part of the judgment of Greer J can be supported.

1   [1895] 2 QB 84.
2   (1841) 7 M & W 595, 599.
3   (1792) 2 Hy Bl 254, 257.
4   [1924] 1 KB 566.
5   (1777) 2 Wm Bl 1117.
6   [1924] 1 KB 566.
7   [1915] 2 Ch 409.
8   12 March 1923, unreported.

20   Prager v Blatspiel, Stamp and Heacock Ltd [1924] 1 KB 566

McCardie J ... I must refer briefly to several other features of the doctrine of agency of necessity in a case where, as here, the agent has, without orders, sold the goods of his principal. In the first place, it is, of course, clear that agency of necessity does not arise if the agent can communicate with his principal. This is established by all the decisions ... The basis of this requirement is, I take it, that if the principal's decision can be obtained the agent should seek it ere acting. In the present case it is admitted that the agents could not communicate with the principal. In the next place it is essential for the agent to prove that the sale was necessary. What does this mean? In *Cannan v Meaburn*[1], Park J said: 'The master cannot sell except in a case of inevitable necessity'. In *Australasian Steam Navigation Co v Morse*[2], however, Sir Montague Smith said: 'The word "necessity", when applied to mercantile affairs, where the judgment must, in the nature of things, be exercised, cannot of course mean an irresistible compelling power – what is meant by it in such cases is, the force of circumstances which determine the course a man ought to take'. Later on he refers to 'commercial necessity'[3]. In *Acatos v Burns*[4] Brett LJ uses the words 'unless there is an urgent necessity for the sale'. In *Atlantic Mutual Insurance Co v Huth*[5] Cotton LJ says: 'It lies on those who claim title to cargo, as purchasers from the captain, to prove that this necessity clearly existed; further ... it is not sufficient to prove that the master thought he was doing the best for all concerned, or even that the course adopted was, so far as can be ascertained, the best for all concerned'. In *Sims & Co v Midland Rly Co*[6] Scrutton J, as he then was, said that the question was whether 'necessity justified the sale'. In *Springer's* case[7], already quoted, Scrutton LJ said that the defendants must show 'that a sale was in the circumstances the only reasonable business course to take' ... In substance I may say that the agent must prove an actual and definite commercial necessity for the sale. In the third place, I think that an alleged agent of necessity must satisfy the Court that he was acting bona fide in the interests of the parties concerned ... I can now state quite briefly my conclusions of fact after carefully weighing the whole of the evidence, the correspondence and arguments. I hold in the first place that there was no necessity to sell the goods. They had been purchased by the plaintiff in time of war and not of peace. He bought them in order that he might be ready with a stock of goods when peace arrived. He had refused, by letters to the defendants, several profitable offers for some of them before the cessation of correspondence between the defendants and himself. The goods were not perishable like fruit or food. If furs are undressed they may deteriorate somewhat rapidly in the course of a year or two. But these furs were dressed, and not undressed. Dressed furs deteriorate very slowly. They lose somewhat in colour and suppleness year by year. The measure of deterioration is but slight, that is if care is used. The great bulk of the furs here were of the best quality. I see no adequate reason for the sale by the defendants, for I am satisfied that there was nothing to prevent the defendants from putting them into cold storage, and certainly nothing to prevent them from keeping them with proper care in their own warehouse. The expense of cold or other storage would have been but slight compared with the value of the furs. The plaintiff had given nearly 1900*l* for them, and they steadily rose in value. The contra account of the defendants was less than 400*l*. The margin therefore was of the most ample description. The defendants could and ought to have stored the goods till communication with Roumania was restored. I have said that the value of the furs was rising. Broadly speaking, it may be said that from 1917 on to 1919 there was a steady and sometimes a rapid rise in the value of furs. This arose from the shortage of supply. The slight deterioration of the furs was far outweighed by the general and striking increase in market prices. I can see no point of time at which the defendants could honestly and fairly say: 'In the interests of the plaintiff it is imperative that we sell his goods'. That the furs were deteriorating but slightly is, I think, plain, and particularly when I observe the prices at which the defendants sold them. The defendants could not have formed the view at any given time that there was a necessity for sale, for they sold the goods by about seventeen different sales ranging from October 1917, to September 20, 1918. If the defendants honestly believed in the necessity of sale they could at any time have sold the whole. In view of the military position in September 1918, the sales in that month are significant. I hold that there was no commercial necessity for the sale.

In the second place I decide, without hesitation, that the defendants did not act bona fide. I need not repeat the observations I have already made as to the absence of necessity for the sale. But I must add a few further words [His Lordship reviewed the evidence, and continued:] I hold that the defendants were not in fact agents of necessity, that the sales of the plaintiff's goods were not justified, and that the defendants acted dishonestly. In the result I give judgment for the plaintiff for £1822 with costs.

1   (1823) 1 Bing 243 at 247.
2   (1872) LR 4 PC 222 at 230.
3   Ibid, at 231.
4   (1878) 3 Ex D 282 at 290.
5   (1880) 16 Ch D 474 at 481.
6   [1913] 1 KB 103 at 112.
7   [1921] 1 KB 257 at 267.

21 Firth v Staines [1897] 2 QB 70

Wright J ... To constitute a valid ratification three conditions must be satisfied: first, the agent whose act is sought to be ratified must have purported to act for the principal; secondly, at the time the act was done the agent must have had a competent principal; and, thirdly, at the time of the ratification the principal must be legally capable of doing the act himself.

22 Keighley, Maxsted & Co v Durant [1901] AC 240

Lord Macnaghten ... As a general rule, only persons who are parties to a contract, acting either by themselves or by an authorised agent, can sue or be sued on the contract. A stranger cannot enforce the contract, nor can it be enforced against a stranger. That is the rule; but there are exceptions. The most remarkable exception, I think, results from the doctrine of ratification as established in English law. That doctrine is thus stated by Tindal CJ in *Wilson v Tumman*[1]: 'That an act done, *for another*, by a person, not assuming to act for himself, but for such other person, though without any precedent authority whatever, becomes the act of the principal, if subsequently ratified by him, is the known and well-established rule of law. In that case the principal is bound by the act, whether it be for his detriment or his advantage, and whether it be founded on a tort or on a contract, to the same effect as by, and with all the consequences which follow from, the same act done by his *previous* authority'. And so by a wholesome and convenient fiction, a person ratifying the act of another, who, without authority, has made a contract openly and avowedly on his behalf, is deemed to be, though in fact he was not, a party to the contract. Does the fiction cover the case of a person who makes no avowal at all, but assumes to act for himself and for no one else? If Tindal CJ's statement of the law is accurate, it would seem to exclude the case of a person who may intend to act for another, but at the same time keeps his intention locked up in his own breast; for it cannot be said that a person who so conducts himself does assume to act for anybody but himself. But ought the doctrine of ratification to be extended to such a case? On principle I should say certainly not. It is, I think, a well established principle in English law that civil obligations are not to be created by, or founded upon, undisclosed intentions. That is a very old principle. Lord Blackburn, ... traces it back to the year-books of Edward IV (17 Edw 4, 2, pl 2) and to a quaint judgment of Brian CJ: 'It is common learning', said that Chief Justice, ... 'that the thought of a man is not triable, for the Devil has not knowledge of man's thoughts'. ... It is, I think, a sound maxim – at least, in its legal aspect: and in my opinion it is not to be put aside or disregarded merely because it may be that, in a case like the present, no injustice might be done to the actual parties to the contract by giving effect to the undisclosed intentions of a would-be agent.

Lord Shand ... The question which arises on this state of the facts is whether, where a person who has avowedly made a contract for himself (1) without a suggestion that he is acting to any extent for another (an undisclosed principal), and (2) without any authority to act for another, can effectually bind a third party as principal, or as a joint obligant with himself, to the person with whom he contracted, by the fact that in his own mind merely he made a contract in the hope and expectation that his contract would be ratified or shared by the person as to whom he entertained that hope and expectation. I am clearly of opinion, with all respect to the majority of the Court of Appeal, that he cannot. The only contract actually made is by the person himself and for himself, and it seems to me to be conclusive against the argument for the respondents, that if their reasoning were sound it would be in his power, on an averment of what was passing in his own mind, to make the contract afterwards either one for himself only, as in fact it was, or one affecting or binding on another as a contracting party, even though he had no authority for this. The result would be to give one of two contracting parties in his option, merely from what was passing in his own mind and not disclosed, the power of saying the contract was his alone, or a contract in which others were bound with him. That, I think, he certainly cannot do in any case where he had no authority, when he made the contract, to bind any one but himself.

Lord Lindley ... That ratification when it exists is equivalent to a previous authority is true enough (subject to some exceptions which need not be referred to). But, before the one expression can be substituted for the other, care must be taken that ratification is established.

It was strongly contended that there was no reason why the doctrine of ratification should not apply to undisclosed principals in general, and that no one could be injured by it if it were so applied. I am not convinced of this. But in this case there is no evidence in existence that, at the time when Roberts made his contract, he was in fact acting, as distinguished from intending to act, for the defendants as possible principals, and the decision appealed from, if affirmed, would introduce a very dangerous doctrine. It would enable one person to make a contract between two others by creating a principal and saying what his own undisclosed intentions were, and these could not be tested.

1   (1843) 6 Man & G 236 at 242.

23 Bolton Partners v Lambert (1889) 41 Ch D 295

Cotton LJ ... But then it is said that on 13 January 1887, the Defendant entirely withdrew the offer he had made. Of course the withdrawal could not be effective, if it were made after the contract had become complete. As soon as an offer has been accepted the contract is complete. But it is said that there could be a withdrawal by the Defendant on 13 January on this ground, that the offer of the Defendant had been accepted by Scratchley, a director of the Plaintiff company, who was not authorised to bind the company by acceptance of the offer, and therefore that until the company ratified Scratchley's act there was no acceptance on behalf of the company binding on the company, and therefore the Defendant could withdraw his offer. Is that so? The rule as to ratification by a principal of acts done by an assumed agent is that the ratification is thrown back to the date of the act done, and that the agent is put in the same position as if he had had authority to do the act at the time the act was done by him. Various cases have been referred to as laying down this principle, but there is no case exactly like the present one. The case of *Hagedorn v Oliverson*[1] is a strong case of the application of the principle. It was there pointed out how favourable the rule was to the principal, because till ratification he was not bound, and he had an option to adopt or not to adopt what had been done. In that case the plaintiff had effected an insurance on a ship in which another person was interested, and it was held that long after the ship had been lost the other person might adopt the act of the plaintiff, though done without authority, so as to enable the plaintiff to sue upon the policy. Again, in *Ancona v Marks*[2], where a bill was indorsed to and sued on in the name of Ancona, who had given no authority for that purpose, yet it was held that Ancona could, after the action had been brought, ratify what had been done, and that the subsequent ratification was equivalent to a prior authority so as to entitle Ancona to sue upon the bill. It was said by Mr Brice that in that case there was a previously existing liability of the defendant towards some person; but the liability of the defendant to Ancona was established by Ancona's authorising and ratifying the act of the agent, and a previously existing liability to others did not affect the principle laid down.

The rule as to ratification is of course subject to some exceptions. An estate once vested cannot be divested, nor can an act lawful at the time of its performance be rendered unlawful, by the application of the doctrine of ratification. ... The case of *Bird v Brown*[3], which was also relied on by the Appellant, is distinguishable from this case. There it was held that the ratification could not operate to divest the ownership which had previously vested in the purchaser by the delivery of the goods before the ratification of the alleged stoppage *in transitu*. So also in *Lyell v Kennedy*[4] the Plaintiff, who represented the lawful heir, desired, after the defendant Kennedy had acquired a title to the estate by means of the Statute of Limitations, and after the title of the heir was gone, to ratify the act of Kennedy as to the receipt of rents, so as to make the estate vest in the heir. In my opinion none of these cases supports the Appellant's contention.

I think the proper view is that the acceptance by Scratchley did constitute a contract, subject to its being shewn that Scratchley had authority to bind the company. If that were not shewn there would be no contract on the part of the company, but when and as soon as authority was given to Scratchley to bind the company the authority was thrown back to the time when the act was done by Scratchley, and prevented the Defendant withdrawing his offer, because it was then no longer an offer, but a binding contract.

Lindley LJ ... The question is what is the consequence of the withdrawal of the offer after acceptance by the assumed agent but before the authority of the agent has been ratified? Is the withdrawal in time? It is said on the one hand that the ordinary principle of law applies, viz, that an offer may be withdrawn before acceptance. That proposition is of course true. But the question is – acceptance by whom? It is not a question whether a mere offer can be withdrawn, but the question is whether, when there has been in fact an acceptance which is in form an acceptance by a principal through his agent, though the person assuming to act as agent has not then been so authorised, there can or cannot be a withdrawal of the offer before the ratification of the acceptance? I can find no authority in the books to warrant the contention that an offer made, and in fact accepted by a principal through an agent or otherwise, can be withdrawn. The true view on the contrary appears to be that the doctrine as to the retrospective action of ratification is applicable.

Lopes LJ ... An important point is raised with regard to the withdrawal of the offer before ratification in this case.

If there had been no withdrawal of the offer this case would have been simple. The ratification by the Plaintiffs would have related back to the time of the acceptance of the Defendant's offer by Scratchley, and the Plaintiffs would have adopted a contract made on their behalf.

It is said that there was no contract which could be ratified, because Scratchley at the time he accepted the Defendant's offer had no authority to act for the Plaintiffs. Directly Scratchley on behalf and in the name of the Plaintiffs accepted the Defendant's offer I think there was a contract made by Scratchley assuming to act for the Plaintiffs, subject to proof by the Plaintiffs that Scratchley had that authority.

The Plaintiffs subsequently did adopt the contract, and thereby recognised the authority of their agent Scratchley. Directly they did so the doctrine of ratification applied and gave the same effect to the contract made by Scratchley as it would have had if Scratchley had been clothed with a precedent authority to make it.

If Scratchley had acted under a precedent authority the withdrawal of the offer by the Defendant would have been inoperative, and it is equally inoperative where the Plaintiffs have ratified and adopted the contract of the agent. To hold otherwise would be to deprive the doctrine of ratification of its retrospective effect. To use the words of Baron Martin in *Brook v Hook*[5], the ratification would not be 'dragged back as it were, and made equipollent to a prior command'.

I have nothing to add with regard to the other points raised. I agree with what has been said on those points. The appeal must be dismissed.

1   (1814) 2 M & S 485.
2   (1862) 7 H & N 686.
3   (1850) 4 Exch 786.
4   (1887) 18 QBD 796.
5   (1871) LR 6 Exch 89.

24 The Managers of the Metropolitan Asylums Board v Kingham & Sons (1890) 6 TLR 217

Fry LJ ... The case of *Bolton Partners v Lambert* (1889) 41 Ch D 295 has been pressed upon me. In that case an offer by the defendants was accepted by an unauthorised agent on the part of the plaintiffs. The defendant withdrew his offer, and after the withdrawal the plaintiffs ratified the acceptance of the offer by the unauthorised agent. The Court of Appeal held there that the ratification by the plaintiffs related back to the acceptance by the unauthorised agent, and therefore the withdrawal by the defendant was inoperative. I am bound by that decision. It seems to establish that an offer accepted by an unauthorised person can be ratified by letter or by action brought. There are, therefore, two sorts of acceptance – one the ordinary acceptance by a principal or an authorised agent, and the other where there is an acceptance by an unauthorised person subsequently ratified by the principal. ... Accepting, as I am bound to do, that case, there are two sets of circumstances under which the plaintiffs cannot rely on that case. Supposing a person tendering says, 'I will not be bound by an acceptance of any unauthorised person, it must be accepted by the principal', such a condition would be perfectly valid. Further, if ratification is to bind, it must be made within a reasonable time after acceptance by an unauthorised person. That reasonable time can never extend after the time at which the contract is to commence. I have to consider the terms of this offer in the form supplied by the plaintiffs. It says that contractors may learn the result by 24 September. The operative part is that the defendants contract and agree to supply eggs from 30 September 1888, until 30 March 1889. Upon any breach on the part of the contractors the contract may be determined. As to the form of acceptance, it appears to me that the course of business was that tenders must be delivered by 14 September. Meeting of the Board on 22 September. Resolution that common seal should be put to the contract. Two days are allowed the clerk to put the common seal to the contract. The fair meaning is that defendants contracted to supply after seal affixed; then, and then only, they will deliver. Each party has contracted as if the common seal was to be the acceptance of the contract. I do not think that the doctrine in *Bolton Partners v Lambert* applies in this case. The ratification on 8 October was too late. The contract came into force on 1 October, a whole week before the ratification. The defendants could not know whether they were to supply the eggs then or not. I think the ratification was too late, and I dismiss this action with costs.

25 Watson v Davies [1931] 1 Ch 455

Maugham J ... In a case where the agent for one party to a negotiation informs the other party that he cannot enter into a contract binding his principal except subject to his approval, there is in truth no contract or contractual relation until the approval has been obtained. The agent has incurred no responsibility. In *Bolton Partners v Lambert*[1] the decision of the Court was, I think, founded on the view that there was a contractual relation of some kind which could be turned into a contract with the company by a ratification, whilst in the absence of ratification there was a right of action against the agent for breach of warranty of authority. It was admitted that there could be no ratification of a legal nullity. An acceptance by an agent subject in express terms to ratification by his principal is legally a nullity until ratification, and is no more binding on the other party than an unaccepted offer which can, of course, be withdrawn before acceptance.

1   (1889) 41 Ch D 295.

26 Penn v Bristol and West Building Society [1997] 3 All ER 470

Waller LJ … By art 107 of *Bowstead and Reynolds on Agency* (16th edn, 1996) para 9-057 the general principle is stated as follows:

'(1) Where a person by words or conduct, represents that he has authority to act on behalf of another, and a third party is induced by such representation to act in a manner in which he would not have acted if that representation had not been made, the first-mentioned person is deemed to warrant the representation is true, and is liable for any loss caused to such third party by a breach of that implied warranty, even if he acted in good faith, under a mistaken belief that he had such authority.'

Chitty on Contracts (27th edn, 1994) para 31-093 puts it slightly differently as follows:

'One who expressly or impliedly warrants that he has the authority of another is liable in contract for breach of warranty of authority to any person to whom the warranty is made and who suffers damage by acting in the faith of it, if in fact he had no authority. This is a specific type, in fact probably the original type, of collateral contract: the agent offers to warrant his authority in return for the third party's dealing with his principal.'

[Counsel for the appellant] accepts the statements of general principle as far as they go, but submits that in order to found liability, the warranty express or implied must have been given to the plaintiff, and further submits that the transaction into which the plaintiff was induced to enter must have been some form of dealing with the supposed principal. He submits that the whole basis for implying a warranty rests on the fact that the plaintiff has been induced to deal with the purported principal, by the words or conduct of the agent. He gains some support for this second contention from the last sentence of the general principle stated in Chitty, and indeed, so far as I can see, from the text of Chitty thereafter. But Bowstead and Reynolds quote the following passage from Lord Esher MR's judgment in *Firbank's Executors v Humphreys* (1886) 18 QBD 54 at 60 in support of a broader view (para 9-061):

'The rule to be deduced is, that where a person by asserting that he has the authority of the principal induces another person to enter into any transaction which he would not have entered into but for that assertion, and that assertion turns out to be untrue, to the injury of the person to whom it is made, it must be taken that the person making it undertook that it was true, and he is liable personally for the damage that has occurred.'

[Counsel] points out that in *Firbank*'s case the transaction into which the plaintiff was induced to enter was a transaction with the supposed principal, and he suggests accordingly that the case itself falls within the limits that he suggests should be placed on the situations in which a warranty of authority could be established. His difficulty is that there are other authorities where the constraints which he seeks to apply have not apparently been adhered to. In *Starkey v Bank of England* [1903] AC 114 Frederick and Edgar Oliver jointly owned consols and bank stock. Frederick instructed Starkey, a stockbroker, to sell them. Frederick signed the necessary powers of attorney in his own name and forged Edgar's signature. Starkey presented the powers of attorney to the Bank of England, who duly effected the transfer. Once the forgery was established the bank was liable to replace the consols and the stock, and sued Starkey for breach of warranty of authority. Starkey was held liable. The Earl of Halsbury LC described the notion that it was necessary to establish a contract between the purported principal and the plaintiff as illogical, and confusing the question whether the facts established a contractual warranty between plaintiff and defendant, with the question as to whether a contract follows in consequence of a representation. He said (at 118):

'That which does enforce the liability is this – that under the circumstances of this document being presented to the bank for the purpose of being acted upon, and being acted upon on the representation that the agent had the authority of the principal, which he had not, that does import an obligation – the contract being for good consideration – an undertaking on the part of the agent that the thing he represented to be genuine was genuine.'

[Counsel's] submission was that at least the transaction into which the bank was induced to enter related to the assumed principal; but be that as it may, the authority is against [counsel's] basic proposition that what underlies the breach of warranty of authority doctrine is the fact that the plaintiff is induced to transact with the principal.

[Counsel] was also forced to try and explain away the judgment of A L Smith J in *West London Commercial Bank v Kitson* (1883) 12 QBD 157 at 162, on the bases, first, that that case was concerned with a bill of exchange and, second, that A L Smith J was alone of all the judges both at first instance and in the Court of Appeal, in resting his judgment on breach of warranty of authority (see (1884) 13 QBD 360). He furthermore tried to distinguish *V/O Rasnoimport v Guthrie & Co Ltd* [1966] 1 Lloyd's Rep 1 on the basis that the case was concerned with a bill of lading, and (as he submitted), an instrument akin to a negotiable instrument. It is only necessary to look at this latter decision in any detail since the reasoning of A L Smith J was relied on by Mocatta J in reaching the conclusion he did. The facts of the *V/O Rasnoimport* case were that the defendants, as agents of the owners, signed bills of lading stating that 225 bales of rubber had been shipped. In fact, because of a fraud of which the defendants were unaware and totally innocent, only 90 bales were shipped. The plaintiffs were indorsees for value of the bills of lading, and claimed against the defendants for breach of warranty of authority in that it was alleged the defendants only had authority to sign bills of lading for 90 bales.

The argument on behalf of the plaintiffs was not that a warranty had been given to the original holder and transferred to the plaintiffs as indorsees. It was simply that the warranty was given to all persons who might reasonably be expected to rely on the bill of lading in the ordinary course of business (see [1966] 1 Lloyd's Rep 1 at 4).

Mocatta J having quoted the judgment of A L Smith J in *West London Commercial Bank Ltd v Kitson*, and noted that he was alone in holding the views he did, approved that reasoning and took the view that it was not confined to bills of exchange. Mocatta J thus held, having referred to *Carlill v Carbolic Smoke Ball Co* [1892] 2 QB 484, as follows:

'The defendants must be taken as knowing, when they signed the bill of lading, that in the ordinary course of commerce it would be likely to pass from hand to hand and that one or more indorsees from the original shipper would receive the bill, would rely upon the statements in it and would pay money for the goods represented in it to have been shipped which he or they would not otherwise have paid ... I can see nothing extravagant or heterodox in holding that the implied warranty of authority ... was given by the defendants to all whom they could reasonably foresee would become such indorsees and became actionable by such persons on proof of their having acted in reliance upon the warranty and having suffered damage thereby. Common sense and principle alike seem to require this conclusion, and I so hold.' (See [1966] 1 Lloyd's Rep 1 at 13.)

That authority must of course be read in its context in the sense that outside the ambit of bills of exchange or bills of lading, it may be difficult to contemplate the offer or promise of a warranty of authority being given to such a wide number of people. But the authority does supply further support for there not being the constraint contended for by [counsel], that to give rise to the cause of action a transaction between the plaintiff and the would-be principal must have been induced.

In truth, as I see it, the question whether a warranty of authority has been given rests on a proper analysis of the facts in any given situation, and not on any preconceived notions as to what is essential as part of the factual analysis. Of course there is no issue that to establish a warranty of authority, as with any other collateral warranty, there must be proved a contract under which a promise is made either expressly or by implication to the promisee, for which promise the promisee provides consideration. But consideration can be supplied by the promisee entering into some transaction with a third party in a warranty of authority case just as it can in any other collateral warranty case. Furthermore, the promise can be made to a wide number of people or simply to one person, again all depending on the facts. It follows, as [counsel] has submitted, that the plaintiff, whether as one of the wide number of people to whom the offer is made or by virtue of being the only person to whom the offer is made, has to establish that the promise was made to him. There is also no doubt that what he has to establish is that a promise was being made to him by the agent, to the effect that the agent had the authority of the principal, and that he provided consideration by acting in reliance on that promise.

27   Yonge v Toynbee [1910] I KB 215

Buckley LJ ... The interesting and important question in this case is as to the extent to which the principle of *Smout v Ilbery*[1] remains good law after the decision in *Collen v Wright*[2]. In *Smout v Ilbery*[1] Alderson B dealt with the authorities under three heads: first, the case where the agent made a fraudulent misrepresentation as to his authority with an intention to deceive. In such case the agent is, of course, personally responsible. Secondly, the case where the agent without fraud, but untruly in fact, represented that he had authority when he had none, instancing under this head *Polhill v Walter*[3]. In that case A, having no authority from B to accept a bill on his behalf, did accept it as by his procuration, bona fide believing that B would retrospectively approve that which he was doing. In such case again the agent is personally liable, for he induced the other party to enter into a contract on a misrepresentation of a fact within his own knowledge. The third class is where the agent bona fide believes that he has, but in fact has not, authority. This third class the learned Baron seems to subdivide into two heads – the first where the agent never had authority, but believed that he had (eg, when he acted on a forged warrant of attorney which he thought to be genuine), and the second where the agent had in fact full authority originally, but that authority had come to an end without any knowledge, or means of knowledge, on the part of the agent that such was the fact. The latter was the state of facts in *Smout v Ilbery*[4]. I understand *Smout v Ilbery*[4] not to dispute that in the former of these last two cases (that is, where the agent never had authority) he is liable, but to hold that in the latter (namely, where he originally had authority, but that authority has ceased without his having knowledge, or means of knowledge, that it has ceased) he is not liable. The principle is stated in the following words: 'If, then, the true principle derivable from the cases is, that there must be some wrong or omission of right on the part of the agent, in order to make him personally liable on a contract made in the name of the principal, it will follow that the agent is not responsible in such a case as the present. And to this conclusion we have come'. It seems to me that, if that principle be the true principle, then the former of the last two mentioned cases ought to have been resolved in the same way as the latter. I can see no distinction in principle between the case where the agent never had authority and the case where the agent originally had authority, but that authority has ceased without his knowledge or means of knowledge. In the latter case as much as in the former the proposition, I think, is true that without any mala fides he had at the moment of acting represented that he had an authority which in fact he had not. In my opinion he is then liable on an implied contract that he had authority, whether there was fraud or not. That this is the true principle is, I think, shewn by passages which I will quote from judgments in three which I have selected out of the numerous cases upon this subject. In *Collen v Wright*[5] Willes J in giving the judgment of the Court uses the following language: 'I am of opinion that a person who induces another to contract with him, as the agent of a third party, by an unqualified assertion of his being authorised to act as such agent, is answerable to the person who so contracts for any damages which he may sustain by reason of the assertion of authority being untrue. The fact that the professed agent honestly thinks that he has authority affects the moral character of his act; but his moral innocence, so far as the person whom he had induced to contract is concerned, in no way aids such person or alleviates the inconvenience and damage which he sustains. The obligation arising in such a case is well expressed by saying that a person professing to contract as agent for another, impliedly, if not expressly, undertakes to or promises the person who enters into such contract, upon the faith of the professed agent being duly authorised, that the authority which he professes to have does in point of fact exist'. This language is equally applicable to each of the two classes of cases to which I have referred. The language is not, in my opinion, consistent with maintaining that which *Smout v Ilbery*[6] had laid down as the true principle, that there must be some wrong or omission of right on the part of the agent in order to make him liable. The question is not as to his honesty or bona fides. His liability arises from an implied undertaking or promise made by him that the authority which he professes to have does in point of fact exist. I can see no difference of principle between the case in which the authority never existed at all and the case in which the authority once existed and has ceased to exist. In *Firbank's Executors v Humphreys*[7] the rule is thus stated by Lord Esher: 'The rule to be deduced is that, where a person by asserting that he has the authority of the principal induces another person to enter into any transaction which he would not have entered into but for that assertion, and the assertion turns out to be untrue, to the injury of the person to whom it is made, it must be taken that the person making it undertook that it was true, and he is liable personally for the damage that has occurred'.

Lastly, Lord Davey in *Starkey v Bank of England*[8], after stating that the rule extends to every transaction of business into which a third party is induced to enter by a representation that the person with whom he is doing business has the authority of some other person, rejects the argument that the rule in *Collen v Wright*[9] does not extend to cases where the supposed agent did not know that he had no authority, and had not the means of finding out; cites Lord Campbell's language in *Lewis v Nicholson*[10], that the agent 'is liable, if there was any fraud, in an action for deceit, and, in my opinion, as at present advised, on an implied contract that he had authority, whether there was fraud or not'; and concludes by saying that in his opinion 'it is utterly immaterial for the purpose of the application of this branch of the law whether the supposed agent knew of the defect of his authority or not'.

The result of these judgments, in my opinion, is that the liability of the person who professes to act as agent arises (a) if he has been fraudulent, (b) if he has without fraud untruly represented that he had authority when he had not, and (c) also where he innocently misrepresents that he has authority where the fact is either (1) that he never had authority or (2) that his original authority has ceased by reason of facts of which he has not knowledge or means of knowledge. Such last-mentioned liability arises from the fact that by professing to act as agent he impliedly contracts that he has authority, and it is immaterial whether he knew of the defect of his authority or not.

This implied contract may, of course, be excluded by the facts of the particular case. If, for instance, the agent proved that at the relevant time he told the party with whom he was contracting that he did not know whether the warrant of attorney under which he was acting was genuine or not, and would not warrant its validity, or that his principal was abroad and he did not know whether he was still living, there will have been no representation upon which the implied contract will arise. This may have been the ratio decidendi in *Smout v Ilbery*[4] ... . If so, there was no implied contract. The principle, as stated in the words I have quoted, may have been meant to be, but is not in words, rested upon that ground, and, if it is to be understood as it seems to have been understood in *Salton v New Beeston Cycle Co*[11], it is not, I think, consistent with *Collen v Wright*[5]. The true principle as deduced from the authorities I have mentioned rests, I think, not upon wrong or omission of right on the part of the agent, but upon implied contract.

The facts here are that the solicitors originally had authority to act for Mr Toynbee; that that authority ceased by reason of his unsoundness of mind; that, subsequently, they on 30 October 1908, undertook to appear, and on 6 November appeared, in the first action, and, after that was discontinued, did on 21 December undertake to appear, and did on 30 December enter an appearance, in the second action; and that they subsequently, on 22 February 1909, delivered a defence pleading privilege, and denying the slander, and did not until 5 April inform the plaintiff that, as the fact was, their client had become of unsound mind. During all this time they were putting the plaintiff to costs, and these costs were incurred upon the faith of their representation that they had authority to act for the defendant. They proved no facts addressed to shew that implied contract was excluded.

It has been pressed upon us that a solicitor is an agent of a special kind with an obligation towards his client to continue to take on his behalf all proper steps in the action. The particular nature of his agency is not, I think, very material. On the other hand it must be borne in mind that after 21 August, when the defendant Toynbee wrote to the plaintiff's solicitors, referring them to Messrs Wontner & Sons, the plaintiff could not consistently with professional etiquette communicate personally with the defendant. During the period from August 1908 to April 1909 the solicitors had the means of knowing and did not in fact ascertain that the defendant had become of unsound mind. In the interval they did acts which amounted to representations on their part that they were continuing to stand in a position in which they were competent to bind the defendant. This was not the case. They are liable, in my judgment, upon an implied warranty or contract that they had an authority which they had not.

1   (1842) 10 M & W 1.
2   (1857) 8 E & B 647.
3   (1832) 3 B & Ad 114.
4   (1842) 10 M & W 1.
5   (1857) 8 E & B 647.
6   (1842) 10 M & W 1.
7   (1886) 18 QBD 54 at 60.

8   [1903] AC 114 at 119.
9   (1857) 8 E & B 647.
10   (1852) 18 QB 503.
11   [1900] 1 Ch 43.

28 De Bussche v Alt (1878) 8 Ch D 286

Thesiger LJ ... As a general rule, no doubt, the maxim *delegatus non potest delegare* applies so as to prevent an agent from establishing the relationship of principal and agent between his own principal and a third person; but this maxim when analysed merely imports that an agent cannot, without authority from his principal, devolve upon another obligations to the principal which he has himself undertaken to personally fulfil; and that, inasmuch as confidence in the particular person employed is at the root of the contract of agency, such authority cannot be implied as an ordinary incident in the contract. But the exigencies of business do from time to time render necessary the carrying out of the instructions of a principal by a person other than the agent originally instructed for the purpose, and where that is the case, the reason of the thing requires that the rule should be relaxed, so as on the one hand, to enable the agent to appoint what has been termed 'a sub-agent' or 'substitute' (the latter of which designations, although it does not exactly denote the legal relationship of the parties, we adopt for want of a better, and for the sake of brevity); and, on the other hand, to constitute, in the interests and for the protection of the principal, a direct privity of contract between him and such substitute. And we are of opinion that an authority to the effect referred to may and should be implied where, from the conduct of the parties to the original contract of agency, the usage of trade, or the nature of the particular business which is the subject of the agency, it may reasonably be presumed that the parties to the contract of agency originally intended that such authority should exist, or where, in the course of the employment, unforeseen emergencies arise which impose upon the agent the necessity of employing a substitute; and that when such authority exists, and is duly exercised, privity of contract arises between the principal and the substitute, and the latter becomes as responsible to the former for the due discharge of the duties which his employment casts upon him, as if he had been appointed agent by the principal himself. The law upon this point is accurately stated in *Story on Agency*[1]. A case like the present, where a shipowner employs an agent for the purpose of effectuating a sale of a ship at any port where the ship may from time to time in the course of its employment under charter happen to be, is pre-eminently one in which the appointment of substitutes at ports other than those where the agent himself carries on business is a necessity, and must reasonably be presumed to be in the contemplation of the parties; and in the present case, we have, over and above that presumption, what cannot but be looked upon as express authority to appoint a substitute, and a complete ratification of the actual appointment of the Defendant in the letters which passed respectively between *Willis & Son* and the Plaintiff on the one side, and *Gilman & Co* on the other. We are, therefore, of opinion that the relationship of principal and agent was, in respect of the sale of the *Columbine*, for a time at least, constituted between the Plaintiff and the Defendant.

1 Para 201.

29 Parker v McKenna (1874) 10 Ch App 96

James LJ ... I do not think it is necessary, but it appears to me very important, that we should concur in laying down again and again the general principle that in this Court no agent in the course of his agency, in the matter of his agency, can be allowed to make any profit without the knowledge and consent of his principal; that that rule is an inflexible rule, and must be applied inexorably by this Court, which is not entitled, in my judgment, to receive evidence, or suggestion, or argument as to whether the principal did or did not suffer any injury in fact by reason of the dealing of the agent; for the safety of mankind requires that no agent shall be able to put his principal to the danger of such an inquiry as that.

30 Boston Deep Sea Fishing and Ice Co v Ansell (1888) 39 Ch D 339

Cotton LJ ... If a servant, or a managing director, or any person who is authorised to act, and is acting, for another in the matter of any contract, receives, as regards the contract, any sum, whether by way of percentage or otherwise, from the person with whom he is dealing on behalf of his principal, he is committing a breach of duty. It is not an honest act, and, in my opinion, it is a sufficient act to shew that he cannot be trusted to perform the duties which he has undertaken as servant or agent. He puts himself in such a position that he has a temptation not faithfully to perform his duty to his employer. He has a temptation, especially where he is getting a percentage on expenditure, not to cut down the expenditure, but to let it be increased, so that his percentage may be larger. I do not, however, rely on that, but what I say is this, that where an agent entering into a contract on behalf of his principal, and without the knowledge or assent of that principal, receives money from the person with whom he is dealing, he is doing a wrongful act, he is misconducting himself as regards his agency, and, in my opinion, that gives to his employer, whether a company or an individual and whether the agent be a servant, or a managing director, power and authority to dismiss him from his employment as a person who by that act is shewn to be incompetent of faithfully discharging his duty to his principal.

Bowen LJ ... I will, first of all, deal with what is the cardinal matter of the whole case; whether the Plaintiffs were justified or not in dismissing their managing director as they did. This is an age, I may say, when a large portion of the commercial world makes its livelihood by earning, and by earning honestly, agency commission on sales or other transactions, but it is also a time when a large portion of those who move within the ambit of the commercial world, earn, I am afraid, commission dishonestly by taking commissions not merely from their masters, but from the other parties with whom their master is negotiating, and with whom they are dealing on behalf of their master, and taking such commissions without the knowledge of their master or principal. There never, therefore, was a time in the history of our law when it was more essential that Courts of Justice should draw with precision and firmness the line of demarcation which prevails between commissions which may be honestly received and kept, and commissions taken behind the master's back, and in fraud of the master ...

Now, there can be no question that an agent employed by a principal or master to do business with another, who, unknown to that principal or master, takes from that other person a profit arising out of the business which he is employed to transact, is doing a wrongful act inconsistent with his duty towards his master, and the continuance of confidence between them. He does the wrongful act whether such profit be given to him in return for services which he actually performs for the third party, or whether it be given to him for his supposed influence, or whether it be given to him on any other ground at all; if it is a profit which arises out of the transaction, it belongs to his master, and the agent or servant has no right to take it, or bargain for it, or to receive it without bargain, unless his master knows it. It is said if the transaction be one of very old date, that in some way deprives the master of his right to treat it as a breach of faith. As the Lord Justice has pointed out, the age of the fraud may be reason in the master's mind for not acting on his rights; but it is impossible to say that because a fraud has been concealed for six years, therefore the master has not a right when he discovers it to act upon his discovery, and to put an end to the relation of employer and employed with which such fraud was inconsistent. I, therefore, find it impossible to adopt Mr Justice Kekewich's view, or to come to any other conclusion except that the managing director having been guilty of a fraud on his employers was rightly dismissed by them, and dismissed by them rightly even though they did not discover the fraud until after they had actually pronounced the sentence of dismissal.

31 Logicrose Ltd v Southend United Football Club Ltd [1988] 1 WLR 1256

Millett J ... The principal whose agent has received a bribe from the other party to the transaction is entitled to recover the amount of the bribe from the agent, whether he affirms or repudiates the transaction itself. As against the other party to the transaction, he is entitled to treat the benefit obtained by or promised to the agent as part of the consideration which should have been received by the principal (if he is a vendor) or as excess consideration provided by the principal (if he is a purchaser). In either case, if he elects to affirm the transaction, he is entitled to recover the amount of the benefit from the other party as money had and received to his use, but must give credit for anything already recovered from the agent: *Hovenden & Sons v Millhoff* (1900) 83 LT 41 at 42, 43; *Mahesan s/o Thambiah v Malaysia Government Officers' Co-operative Housing Society Ltd* [1979] AC 374 at 383 and *Armagas Ltd v Mundogas SA* [1986] AC 717 at 743.

It is thus clearly established that a principal whose agent has been bribed is *entitled*, as against the other party to the transaction, to treat the bribe as part of the consideration. It does not, however, follow that he is *bound* to do so, and I can see no ground upon which he should be. He makes no such assertion as against the agent; he recovers as against him because it is a secret profit, not because it is part of the consideration. The other party, having paid it secretly to the agent as a gift to him instead of openly to the principal as part of the consideration, cannot be heard to say (though only when it comes to light) that it was part of the consideration after all. In my judgment, a principal who elects to rescind is bound to return the benefits he has received under the contract, but no more; and he is not bound to treat money paid to his agent otherwise than under the contract as if it were paid under it.

32 Keech v Sandford (1726) Sel Cas Ch 61

Lord Chancellor ... I must consider this as a trust for the infant: for I very well see, if a trustee, on the refusal to renew, might have a lease to himself, few trust estates would be renewed to *cestui que* use; though I do not say there is a fraud in this case, yet he should rather have let it run out, than to have had the lease to himself. This may seem hard, that the trustee is the only person of all mankind who might not have the lease: but it is very proper that rule should be strictly pursued, and not in the least relaxed; for it is very obvious what would be the consequence of letting trustees have the lease, on refusal to renew to *cestui que* use. So decreed, that the lease should be assigned to the infant, and that the trustee should be indemnified from any covenants comprised in the lease, and an account of the profits made since the renewal.

33 Marcan Shipping (London) Ltd v Polish SS Co; The Manifest Lipkowy [1989] 2 Lloyd's Rep 138

May LJ ... In cases where an agent is employed to bring together a potential seller and a potential buyer so that a binding contract of sale, or a sale itself may be effected, such as, for instance, the shipbroker in the instant case, or estate agents in another well-known field, it is quite usual to provide in the contract of employment of the agent that if he is successful in achieving the object for which he is employed, then he will be paid substantial remuneration. In some circumstances, to some people, it may appear that the remuneration provided for is excessive. Be that as it may, the other side of the coin is that if the agent's work is not successful and does not achieve a binding sale, then even if he has done a great amount of work, brought the parties within inches perhaps of a binding agreement, if the transaction falls through the agent receives no remuneration at all.

In such a case, where the agent is employed by only one of the potential contracting parties, it is well established that there will be implied into the agent's contract of employment a term to the effect that when the agent has achieved that which he was employed to do and upon the achievement of which his entitlement to remuneration depends, his principal will not fail to perform the arranged contract with the third party, arranged by the agent, so as to deprive that agent of the remuneration due to him under the agency contract. Authorities to this effect go back a long time ...

Bingham LJ ... Before the judge and, albeit unwillingly, before the court the agents founded their claim solely on a term to be implied into this agreement between them and the sellers. I take it to be well-established law that a term will be implied only where it is necessary in a business sense to give efficacy to a contract, or where the term is one which the parties must obviously have intended.

The authorities establish two relevant propositions:

(1) If A, the agent, acting on behalf of P, the principal, has negotiated a contract with TP, a third party, under which A is entitled to payment of commission periodically during the performance of the contract, a term is not to be implied into the agency contract between P and A that P will not, in a manner involving no breach of contract, make a further agreement with TP which will prevent the first contract running its full course and so deprive A of the commission he would otherwise have received. Such is, I think, the ratio of *French & Co Ltd v Leeston Shipping Co* [1922] 1 AC 451, (1922) 10 L1 L Rep 448.

(2) If A, acting on behalf of P, has negotiated a contract with TP under which A is entitled to payment of commission when the contract is performed, it may be proper to imply a term that P will not break his contract with TP and thus deprive A of the commission A would otherwise have received. That is, as I understand it, the ratio of *Alpha Trading Ltd v Dunnshaw-Patten Ltd* [1981] QB 290, [1981] 1 All ER 482.

The present case is not the same as either (1) or (2). It differs from (1) because there has been a breach of contract, whereas in (1) there was not. It differs from (2), because the breach in (2) was by P, whereas here the breach was by TP, whose agent A was not. So put in the same terms the question here may be expressed thus: if A acting on behalf of P has negotiated a contract with TP under which A is entitled to commission when the contract is performed and TP has agreed with A that the commission may be deducted from the contract price otherwise payable to TP, is a term to be implied into that second agreement that TP will not fail to perform the contract and thus deprive A of the commission he would otherwise have received?

On the facts found here I have no hesitation in answering that question No. If one applies the test of business efficacy, one must ask what business end the implied term must be efficacious to produce. The agents here would answer: the business end of ensuring that the agents were duly remunerated if, as a result of the sellers' breach of contract, no sale proceeds ever became payable. But that is a boot strap argument. I find nothing in the wording of the agreement relied on to suggest that the parties – that is, the agents and the sellers – did intend the agents to be remunerated if there were never, because of the sellers' default, any sale proceedings from which the commission could be deducted. The language of the agreement suggests otherwise and, put at its very lowest, the evidence before the judge did not suggest that buyers' agents were customarily remunerated in such circumstances.

If, alternatively, one asks whether the term contended for is one which the parties must obviously have intended, the answer is, I think, the same. It is by no means obvious to me that the sellers would have intended to pay nearly a quarter of a million dollars in hard currency to the other party's agents even if, albeit through their own fault, they never received any proceeds of the sale of the vessel. As for the agents, the fact that they did not agree the term expressly must throw doubt on the proposition that they intended it, because this eventuality cannot be one they never thought of.

Every case turns on its own facts and this is not a field in which hard and fast rules can be laid down, but on the facts here I am satisfied that the judge's conclusion was right and I also agree that the appeal should be dismissed.

34 George Trollope & Sons v Martyn Bros [1934] 2 KB 436

Scrutton LJ ... Maugham LJ takes the view, as I understand his judgment, that although the implied term that the employer must not 'prevent' the agent from earning his commission is too wide, it is 'necessary' to imply a term that the employer shall not 'without just cause' prevent the agent from earning his commission, and as a corollary that if he 'arbitrarily' (by which phrase I understand him to mean 'without alleging any just excuse') refuses to sell, he is in default, though in an agreement subject to contract he breaks no contract with the purchaser by refusing to complete without giving any reason. I cannot agree with this view, which seems to make the subsidiary matter, the remuneration of the agent who is to obtain a contract of sale, as of more importance than the sale itself, which without breach of any contract with the purchaser has not been completed or materialised. It does not seem to me that a vendor taking an attitude towards the purchaser which by his contract he is entitled to adopt, if he gives no reason why he so acts except that it is in the bond, is acting arbitrarily and therefore in some unspecified default. Every man who receives and refuses without giving a reason an offer which he is not bound to accept, may be said to act arbitrarily, but I cannot understand why he is in default.

35 Luxor (Eastbourne) Ltd (in liquidation) v Cooper [1941] 1 All ER 33

Viscount Simon LC ... The implied term upon which the respondent relies, following *Trollope (George) & Sons v Martyn Bros*[1], amounts to saying that, once he has introduced his duly qualified nominee, the appellants must look in no other direction for a purchaser, but are bound, in the absence of 'just excuse', to do their best to sell to that nominee. It appears to me that this proposition leads to great difficulties in its application, and to great uncertainty as to what might amount to a just excuse. In the present case, the respondent was not appointed sole agent, and there might have been half-a-dozen competitors for the proffered commission. If the respondent's introduction of his nominee had been immediately followed by a better offer through another agent, would the appellants have been bound to refuse the latter, or to accept it only with the consequence of paying two commissions? If, after receiving the respondent's 'name', and before becoming bound by contract of sale, the appellants sold the property to another purchaser without the intervention of any agent at all, would this expose the appellants to a claim by the respondent for damages? The contrary has been held, I think correctly, by McCardie J, in *Bentall, Horsley & Baldry v Vicary*[2]. Again, what would be the rights of the agent if he were employed on precisely corresponding terms to find a tenant for a house at a named rent? Can it be that the owner would be bound to accept the first tenant so offered to him who was willing to pay the rent? How would matters stand in such a case where the house was to be let furnished and the selection of a suitable tenant was, therefore, of particular concern to the landlord?

I find it impossible to formulate with adequate precision the tests which should determine whether or not a 'just excuse' exists for disregarding the alleged implied term, and this leads me to consider whether there really is any such implied term at all. The matter may be tested in this way. If such an implied term must be assumed, then this amounts to saying that, when the owner gives the agent the opportunity of earning commission on the express terms thus stated, the agent might have added: 'From the moment that I produce a duly qualified offeror, you must give up all freedom of choice, and carry through the bargain, if you reasonably can, with my nominee'. The vendor must reply: 'Of course. That necessarily follows'. However, I am by no means satisfied that the vendor would acquiesce in regarding the matter in this light. I doubt whether the agent is bound, generally speaking, to exercise any standard of diligence in looking for a possible purchaser. He is commonly described as 'employed', but he is not 'employed' in the sense in which a man is employed to paint a picture or to build a house, with the liability to pay damages for delay or want of skill. The owner is offering to the agent a reward if the agent's activity helps to bring about an actual sale, but that is no reason why the owner should not remain free to sell his property through other channels. The agent necessarily incurs certain risks, eg, the risk that his nominee cannot find the purchase price, or will not consent to terms reasonably proposed to be inserted in the contract of sale. I think that, upon the true construction of the express contract in this case, the agent also takes the risk of the owner not being willing to conclude the bargain with the agent's nominee. This last risk is ordinarily a slight one, for the owner's reason for approaching the agent is that he wants to sell.

If it really were the common intention of owner and agent that the owner should be bound in the manner suggested, there would be no difficulty in so providing by an express term of the contract, but, in the absence of such an express term, I am unable to regard the suggested implied term as 'necessary' ... . In concluding his judgment in *Trollope (George) & Sons v Caplan*[3]. Sir Wilfrid Greene MR expressed the view, at 401, that the case law as to the rights and obligations of house-agents and their clients with regard to the sort of questions then under discussion was not in a very satisfactory condition, and that it was desirable that the whole position should be reviewed, if opportunity offered, in the House of Lords ... There is, I think, considerable difficulty, and no little danger, in trying to formulate general propositions on such a subject, for contracts with commission agents do not follow a single pattern, and the primary necessity in each instance is to ascertain with precision what are the express terms of the particular contract under discussion, and then to consider whether these express terms necessitate the addition, by implication, of other terms. There are some classes of contract in which an implied term is introduced by the requirements of a statute – for example, under the Sale of Goods Act or the Marine Insurance Act. There are other contracts where an implied term is introduced by the force of established custom – for example, the necessity of a month's notice in the case of hiring a domestic servant. In contracts made, however, with commission, there is no justification for introducing an implied term unless it is necessary to do so for the purpose of giving to the contract the business effect which both parties to it intend that it should have. It may be useful to point out that contracts under which an agent may be occupied in endeavouring to dispose of the property of a principal fall into several classes. There is the class in which the agent is promised a commission by his principal if he succeeds in introducing to his principal a person who makes an adequate offer, usually an offer of not less than the stipulated amount. If that is all that is needed in order to earn his reward, it is obvious that he is entitled to be paid when this has been done, whether his principal accepts the offer and carries through the bargain or not. No implied term is needed to secure this result. There is another class of case in which the property is put into the hands of the agent to dispose of for the owner, and the agent accepts the employment, and, it may be, expends money and time in endeavouring to carry it out. Such a form of contract may well imply the term that the principal will not withdraw the authority he has given after the agent has incurred substantial outlay, or, at any rate, after he has succeeded in finding a possible purchaser. Each case turns on its own facts, and the phrase 'finding a purchaser' is itself not without ambiguity. *Inchbald's* case[4] might, I think, be regarded as falling within this second class. However, there is a third class of case, to which the present instance belongs, where, by the express language of the contract, the agent is promised his commission only upon completion of the transaction which he is endeavouring to bring about between the offeror and his principal. As I have already said, there seems to me to be no room for the suggested implied term in such a case. The agent is promised a reward in return for an event, and the event has not happened. He runs the risk of disappointment, but, if he is not willing to run the risk, he should introduce into the express terms of the contract the clause which protects him.

Lord Russell of Killowen ... A few preliminary observations occur to me. (1) Commission contracts are subject to no peculiar rules or principles of their own. The law which governs them is the law which governs all contracts and all questions of agency. (2) No general rule can be laid down by which the rights of the agent or the liabilities of the principal under commission contracts are to be determined. In each case, these must depend upon the exact terms of the contract in question, and upon the true construction of those terms. (3) Contracts by which owners of property, desiring to dispose of it, put it in the hands of agents on commission terms are not (in default of specific provisions) contracts of employment in the ordinary meaning of those words. No obligation is imposed on the agent to do anything. The contracts are merely promises binding on the principal to pay a sum of money upon the happening of a specified event, which involves the rendering of some service by the agent. There is no real analogy between such contracts and contracts of employment by which one party binds himself to do certain work and the other binds himself to pay remuneration for the doing of it ... My Lords, in my opinion there is no necessity in these contracts for any implication, and the legal position can be stated thus. If, according to the true construction of the contract, the event has happened upon the happening of which the agent has acquired a vested right to the commission (by which I mean that it is *debitum in praesenti*, even though only *solvendum in futuro*), then no act or omission by the principal or anyone else can deprive the agent of that right. Until that event has happened, however, the agent cannot complain if the principal refuses to proceed with, or carry to completion, the transaction with the agent's client. I have already expressed my view as to the true meaning of a contract to pay a commission for the introduction of a purchaser at a specified or minimum price. It is possible that an owner may be willing to bind himself to pay a commission for the mere introduction of one who offers to purchase at the specified or minimum price, but such a construction of the contract would, in my opinion, require clear and unequivocal language.

Lord Wright ... What is in question in all these cases is the interpretation of a particular contract. I deprecate in general the attempt to enunciate decisions on the construction of agreements as if they embodied rules of law. To some extent decisions on one contract may help by way of analogy and illustration in the decision on another contract, but, however similar the contracts may appear, the decision as to each must depend on the consideration of the language of the particular contract, read in the light of the material circumstances of the parties in view of which the contract is made. I shall, therefore, in the first instance, examine the particular contract in question in the light of the material facts ... It is important to simplify as far as possible the problem of construing commission agency agreements, especially in regard to the sale of houses and land. These are of common occurrence among all classes of the community, and it is most undesirable that subtleties and complications of interpretation calculated to lead to disputes should be allowed to confuse what is *ex facie* a plain and simple agreement ... It may be said that, in the view of Scrutton LJ[5], ... the prospect of the agent getting his reward is speculative, and may be defeated by the arbitrary will of the principal. That may perhaps be so in some cases, but it is clear, I think, that, under a contract like the present, the agent takes a risk in several respects. Thus, for instance, the principal may sell independently of the agent to a purchaser other than the purchaser introduced by him, or, where the employment is not as sole agent, he may sell through another agent. Why should not the agent take the chance also of the employer changing his mind and deciding not to sell at all? It is said that, according to the term which it is suggested should be implied, he can change his mind if he has a reasonable excuse or just cause. Is it to be decided from the point of view of the owner or from the point of view of the commission agent? It is just the difficulty of applying these vague phrases which has already led to so much litigation on this question. In my opinion, the implied term is unworkable. Even in this case Branson J has taken one view and the Court of Appeal another. If the suggested implied term is discarded, a contract such as the present will be simple and workable. Commission agents may sometimes fail to get the commission they expect, but they will be relieved from disputes and litigation, and they can always, if they desire, demand what they consider a more favourable form of contract.

1   [1934] 2 KB 436.
2   [1931] 1 KB 253.
3   [1936] 2 All ER 842.
4   *Inchbald v Western Neilgherry Coffee, Tea and Cinchona Plantation Co Ltd* (1864) 17 CBNS 733.
5   *Trollope & Sons v Martyn Bros* [1934] 2 KB 436.

36 Midgley Estates Ltd v Hand [1952] 1 All ER 1394

Jenkins LJ ... Contracts of agency between owners of property and estate agents have been many times before these courts. We have been referred to a large number of authorities including, in particular, the well-known case in the House of Lords of *Luxor (Eastbourne) Ltd v Cooper*[1], and *James v Smith* (1921)[2]. I hope I will not be thought disrespectful to the careful judgment of the learned judge or to the very full argument which has been presented to us if I refrain from referring to the numerous authorities in detail. As has been pointed out over and over again in the reported cases, an agency contract of this sort, just like any other contract, must be construed according to its terms. One has to look at the contract and see whether, according to its terms, construed in accordance with the ordinary principles of construction, the event has happened in which the commission is expressed to be payable. So far as any general principle is deducible from the authorities, their effect may, I think, be thus summarised. The question depends on the construction of each particular contract, but, prima facie, the intention of the parties to a transaction of this type is likely to be that the commission stipulated for should only be payable in the event of an actual sale resulting. The vendor puts his property into the hands of an agent for sale, and, generally speaking, he contemplates that, if a completed sale results, and not otherwise, he will be liable for the commission, which he will then pay out of the purchase price. That is, broadly speaking, the intention which, as a matter of probability, the court should be disposed to impute to the parties. It follows that general or ambiguous expressions, purporting, for instance, to make the commission payable in the event of the agent 'finding a purchaser' or 'selling the property' have been construed as meaning that the commission is only to be payable in the event of an actual and completed sale resulting, or, at least, in the event of the agent succeeding in introducing a purchaser who is able and willing to purchase the property. That is the broad general principle in the light of which the question of construction should be approached, but this does not mean that the contract, if its terms are clear, should not have effect in accordance with those terms even if they do involve the result that the agent's commission is earned and becomes payable although the sale in respect of which it is claimed for some reason or another turns out to be abortive.

1   [1941] 1 All ER 33.
2   [1931] 2 KB 317n.

37 Danziger v Thompson [1944] KB 654

Lawrence J … I am of opinion that this evidence is admissible. The description 'tenant' does not imply that the person so described is not acting as an agent or nominee. As Lord Haldane pointed out in *Fred Drughorn Ltd v Rederiaktiebolaget Trans-Atlantic*[1], the description of a party to a contract as owner or proprietor of certain property does imply that at the time of entering into the contract he is the owner or proprietor of the property and evidence that that party is the agent of the owner or proprietor and not the owner or proprietor himself contradicts the written contract. It is, as Lord Haldane says, not a question of agency, but one of property, and as Lord Sumner pointed out[2], a question of property, not after the contract has been entered into but before the time it is entered into. It is true that Lord Haldane contrasts a charterparty with a lease[3], but, as he was there dealing with a charterer and with the right of a principal to the benefit of a charterparty made by his agent, he must, I think, have been referring to a lessor and the description 'lessor' does imply an antecedent interest in the property, whereas the description 'lessee' or 'tenant' does not. In my opinion, the description 'tenant' no more negatives agency than would the description 'contracting party'. As Lord Sumner said about the description 'charterer', the description 'tenant' means the person 'who by this contract becomes liable to the obligations and entitled to the rights, which this contract allots to the tenant', and, as Lord Sumner and the House of Lords held, such a description is not inconsistent with a person so described being an agent. For these reasons, I am of opinion that the evidence was admissible and I give judgment for the plaintiff against RJ Thompson with costs.

1   [1919] AC 203 at 206–207.
2   Ibid, at 210.
3   Ibid, at 207.

38 Fred Drughorn Ltd v Rederiaktiebolaget Trans-Atlantic [1919] AC 203

Viscount Haldane ... My Lords, by the law of England if B contracts with C prima facie that is a contract between these two only, but if at the time B entered into the contract he was really acting as agent for A, then evidence is generally admissible to show that A was the principal, and A can take advantage of the contract as if it had been actually made between himself and C. ... But, my Lords, the principle is limited by (a) consideration, about which ... there is no doubt, and the applicability of which to the present case is beyond question. In *Humble v Hunter*[1] it was approved, although it was not necessary to give a decision on the point, and also in *Formby Bros v Formby*[2] and in other cases. These are authorities for the proposition that evidence of authority of an outside principal is not admissible, if to give evidence would be to contradict some term in the contract itself. It was held in *Humble v Hunter*[1], that where a charterer dealt with someone described as the owner, evidence was not admissible to show that some other person was the owner. That is perfectly intelligible. The question is not before us now, but I see no reason to question that where you have the description of a person as the owner of property, and it is a term of the contract that he should contract as owner of that property, you cannot show that another person is the real owner. That is not a question of agency – that is a question of property.

My Lords, in the same way in *Formby Brothers v Formby*[2] the term was 'proprietor', and 'proprietor' was treated in the opinion of the Court of Appeal as on the same footing as the expression 'owner'. But, my Lords, we are not dealing with that case here. The principle remains, but the question is whether the principle applies to a charterparty where the person who says that he signed only as agent describes himself as the charterer.

My Lords, there may be something to be said from the heading of the charterparty in this case, and the reference to the company which claims to have been his principal, for the proposition that, reading the document as a whole, there is evidence that he intended to convey that he was acting as agent for somebody else; but whether that is so or not the term 'charterer' is a very different term from the term 'owner' or the term 'proprietor'. A charterer may be and prima facie is merely entering into a contract. A charterparty is not a lease – it is a chattel that is being dealt with, a chattel that is essentially a mere subject of contract; and although rights of ownership or rights akin to ownership may be given under it prima facie it is a contract for the hiring or use of the vessel. Under these circumstances it is in accordance with ordinary business commonsense and custom that charterers should be able to contract as agents for undisclosed principals who may come in and take the benefit of the charterparty.

But, my Lords, it is said in this charterparty the terms are such as to exclude that notion. Why is that said to be so? Because the term 'charterer' is used. Well, I have already commented upon that. It is said that the term 'charterer' was meant simply to describe a particular person who is to carry out the nomination of arbitrators and everything else which is contained in the charterparty – to give orders which can only be given by one person, and that for the working out of the charterparty it is essential to treat the person so contracting as designated as a person whose identity cannot be varied or contradicted.

My Lords, the answer is that the principal may take that place, and that the company, in this case acting through its agent, whoever that agent may be, will be in the same position as the charterer contracting originally. There is nothing in that position inconsistent with the stipulations of this charterparty, and therefore it appears to me that the qualifying principle of *Humble v Hunter*[1], that you shall not contradict the instrument by giving evidence of agency, has no application in this case.

1   (1848) 12 QB 310.
2   (1910) 102 LT 116.

39 Asty Maritime Co Ltd and Panagiotis Stravelakis v Rocco Giuseppe and Figli SNC, The Astyanax [1985] 2 Lloyd's Rep 109

Kerr LJ … The common law doctrine of the undisclosed principal is now a settled part of our law of contract, although its basis is somewhat obscure and open to some criticism … It entitles an unnamed and undisclosed third party to sue and to be sued on a contract in certain circumstances. But a number of conditions must be satisfied before it can apply. One of these may be that the personality of the alleged agent as a contracting party is (not) a matter of importance to the other party, either in the sense that the latter intended to contract with the alleged agent alone or that he would (not) have contracted with the alleged principal …

The present case is concerned with the question whether either or both of two settled requirements for the application of the doctrine are satisfied. The first concerns the relationship between the alleged principal (P) and the alleged agent (A). P can only claim to sue, or be sued, on the contract if A contracted on behalf of P and with P's express or implied authority to do so. In other words, there must, at the time of the contract, be an actual or subsisting principal/agent relationship between P and A pursuant to which the contract by A is made with X. If this is not so, then P cannot claim to take the benefit of the contract subsequently: *Keighley, Maxsted & Co v Durant* [1901] AC 240. Nor can P do so where A contracts with his knowledge or approval, with the mutual intention of conferring some subsequent advantage on P, but acting himself as a principal and not as P's agent.

The second requirement concerns the relationship between A and X. If the terms of the contract or the circumstances are inconsistent with agency because they show that A was in fact acting or purporting to act as a principal in contracting with X, then the doctrine and P's right of intervention are again excluded.

We must briefly mention some of the authorities to which we were referred. In each of them the first of the above requirements was satisfied, ie A in fact contracted on behalf of and with the authority of P. The issues turned on the second of these requirements and in each case on A's description in the contract with X. In *Humble v Hunter* (1848) 12 QB 310, a son chartered out a vessel owned by his mother but signed the charterparty in his own name with the addition 'owner'. It was held that she could not enforce it as undisclosed principal on the basis that she was in fact the shipowner, since the description of her son as owner was inconsistent with this. In *Fred Drughorn Ltd v Rederiaktiebolaget Trans-Atlantic* [1919] AC 203, *Humble v Hunter* and a later decision were distinguished: an agent was described as 'charterer', and it was held that this description was neutral in the sense that it did not preclude evidence showing that the undisclosed principal was in fact the charterer on whose behalf the agent had contracted. In *Epps v Rothnie* [1945] KB 562, Lord Justice Scott expressed the view at 565 that *Humble v Hunter* could no longer be regarded as good law, but for present purposes it is unnecessary to decide whether this statement was obiter or not, since nothing turns on that case as such.

The owners' sheet-anchor on this issue was the decision of Mr Justice Morris (as he then was) in *O/Y Wasa Steamship Co Ltd and NV Stoomschip, Hannah v Newspaper Pulp & Wood Export Ltd* (1949) 82 L1 L Rep 936. The first plaintiffs, a Finnish company, owned a vessel called *Elle*, and their managing agents were the second plaintiffs, a Dutch company. The latter had express authority to perform any acts on behalf of the former, including the chartering out of the vessel on their behalf. They did so under a charter with the defendants in which they were described as 'disponent owners' and which they signed as 'disponents'. Furthermore, a letter was attached to the charter which expressly described the Dutch company as 'Managers' for the Finnish company. It was submitted that due to the enemy occupation of Holland the Dutch company could not enforce the charter and that the Finnish company could also not do so as undisclosed principals, because their claim to do so was inconsistent with the Dutch company's description in it as 'disponent owners'. Not surprisingly, this submission was rejected in the circumstances. The Dutch company had in fact contracted as agents, and their description as disponent owners was not necessarily inconsistent with agency. As already mentioned, we think that this is the only reported instance of a person chartering out as 'disponent owner' when that person was in fact only an agent for the shipowner and not – as has since become usual – the charterer under a head charterparty. If the position in that case had been that the Dutch company had contracted under a head charter from the Finnish company, then the decision on that aspect would obviously have been different, because it would have been inconsistent with their contracting as agents for the shipowners.

We therefore do not consider that the *O/Y Wasa* case is of any assistance to the owners here. The description of Mr Panagiotis (the purported agent) as 'disponent owner' was admittedly in itself neutral. But the surrounding circumstances and the course of the negotiations clearly show that the intention was that he would conclude a time charter with the registered owners and that it was on this basis that he was described in the sub-voyage charter as 'disponent owner'. This was inconsistent with his contracting in the capacity of a mere agent on behalf of the registered owners, with the result that they cannot contend that they were in fact his undisclosed principals.

40 Thomson v Davenport (1829) 9 B & C 78

Lord Tenterden CJ ... I take it to be a general rule, that if a person sells goods (supposing at the time of the contract he is dealing with a principal), but afterwards discovers that the person with whom he has been dealing is not the principal in the transaction, but agent for a third person, though he may in the mean time have debited the agent with it, he may afterwards recover the amount from the real principal; subject, however, to this qualification, that the state of the account between the principal and the agent is not altered to the prejudice of the principal. On the other hand, if at the time of the sale the seller knows, not only that the person who is nominally dealing with him is not principal but agent, and also knows who the principal really is, and, notwithstanding all that knowledge, chooses to make the agent his debtor, dealing with him and him alone, then, according to the cases of *Addison v Gandassequi* (1812) 4 Taunt 574, and *Paterson v Gandasequi* (1812) 15 East 62, the seller cannot afterwards, on the failure of the agent, turn round and charge the principal, having once made his election at the time when he had the power of choosing between the one and the other. The present is a middle case. At the time of the dealing for the goods, the plaintiffs were informed that M'Kune, who came to them to buy the goods, was dealing for another, that is, that he was an agent, but they were not informed who the principal was. They had not, therefore, at that time the means of making their election. It is true that they might, perhaps, have obtained those means if they had made further enquiry; but they made no further enquiry. Not knowing who the principal really was, they had not the power at that instant of making their election. That being so, it seems to me that this middle case falls in substance and effect within the first proposition which I have mentioned, the case of a person not known to be an agent; and not within the second, where the buyer is not merely known to be agent, but the name of his principal is also known. The point insisted upon by the learned counsel at the trial was, that it ought to have been part of the direction to the jury, that if they were satisfied the plaintiffs, at the time of the order being given, knew that M'Kune was buying goods for another, even though his principal might not be made known to them, they, by afterwards debiting M'Kune, had elected him for their debtor. The point made by the defendant counsel, therefore, was, that if the plaintiffs knew that M'Kune was dealing with them as agent, though they did not know the name of the principal, they could not turn round on him. The recorder thought otherwise: he thought that though they did know that M'Kune was buying as agent, yet, if they did not know who his principal really was, so as to be able to write him down as their debtor, the defendant was liable, and so he left the question to the jury, and I think he did right in so doing. The judgment of the Court below must therefore be affirmed.

41 Clarkson, Booker Ltd v Andjel [1964] 3 All ER 260

Russell LJ ... The defendant having contracted as agent for an undisclosed principal, the plaintiffs were entitled to enforce the contract either against the defendant on the footing that he was contracting and liable as principal, or against the principal on the footing that the defendant was not liable, being merely an agent. The plaintiffs could not enforce the contract against both. Their right against the defendant and their right against the principal were inconsistent rights. At some stage the plaintiffs had to elect to avail themselves of one of those inconsistent rights and to abandon the other. The question is whether the correct conclusion from the facts of this case is that, prior to the issue of their writ against the defendant, the plaintiffs had so elected. If they had, the election crystallised their rights, and they could not sue the defendant ... It was reluctantly (though rightly) accepted by counsel for the defendant that the service of a writ against the principal per se does not show an election; statements by Lord Blackburn in *Scarf v Jardine*[1] cannot be taken as establishing that position in law. It would be in some respects convenient if that were so, as tending to certainty in the application of the law; but even that would not resolve the problems that would arise in the case of a single writ against the principal and agent claiming in the alternative, or in the case of simultaneous or substantially simultaneous writs. The position is that in every case the external acts of the third party must lead to the conclusion, as a matter of fact, that the third party has settled to a choice involving abandonment of his option to enforce his right against one party. I have no doubt that in a given case this may be shown without his proceeding to the length of obtaining a judgment; indeed, if judgment is obtained against either principal or agent, this is more than election, though frequently referred to as election; the judgment supersedes the contractual right against either, and if obtained against the agent precludes action against the principal even if the plaintiff was ignorant of his existence, and therefore unable to elect. Further, I have no doubt that, in assessing the facts of a particular case in pursuit of a conclusion on the question of election, the fact of the service of a writ against one and not against the other points significantly towards a decision to exonerate the other. A letter may assert a claim and demand satisfaction, but it is not capable of bearing fruit even if wholly ignored by the recipient, whereas service of a writ is the first step in actual enforcement of the claim, to be ignored by the recipient at his peril. On the other hand, it is in terms a statement that the plaintiff makes a claim against the defendant. As I have said, it does not necessarily involve abandonment of a similar alternative claim against another possible defendant. It would not do so if there were a simultaneous writ against the other. Nor would it do so if the plaintiff were simultaneously expressly informing the other that the alternative claim was not abandoned. Nor would it do so if simultaneously the plaintiff was maintaining vis-à-vis the other the attitude that he might be looked to for liability on the contract.

1   (1882) 7 App Cas 345 at 360, [1881–85] All ER Rep 651 at 658.

42 L C Fowler & Sons Ltd v St Stephens College Board of Governors [1991] 3 NZLR 304

Doctrine of election

Thomas J ... Numerous decisions were cited to me in argument, but I do not propose to canvass them all. As Professor Reynolds has said 'though the English cases (which are comparatively few) show a vague uniformity of practice, they contain mutually inconsistent dicta and do not clearly accept any one view of the basis of the doctrine' (see 'Election Distributed' (1970) 86 LQR 318, at 320). I therefore consider that it is largely open to me to approach the matter on the basis of principle.

The doctrine of election is said to apply where the plaintiff could seek to hold either the principal or agent liable and elects to sue one and not the other. His election to sue one bars his remedy against the other. This doctrine is generally distinguished from that of merger which applies where judgment is given against one party jointly liable with another. The obligation or cause of action is then said to be 'merged' in the judgment and this prohibits the possibility of any further action against the other party arising out of that joint obligation.

The first point I wish to make is that the doctrine of election is frequently misnamed. Rather, it is to be regarded as being an instance of waiver (or estoppel or release). The plaintiff, by adopting a certain course of conduct, waives his right to sue a particular party. But nothing arises out of the election as such; the recognised requirements of waiver must be present. In order to amount to an 'election', therefore, the decision not to sue must be deliberate and unequivocal and based on a full knowledge of all the relevant facts (see eg, *Clarkson Booker Ltd v Andjel* [1964] 2 QB 775, [1964] 3 All ER 260, per Willmer LJ at 792–793). Thus, the waiver may range from explicit assurances to a party that he or she will not be sued to the implication to be drawn from the plaintiff's conduct where it is inconsistent with the maintenance of the right to sue that party. In such cases the right to sue has been abandoned.

It is essential, as has been observed by Lord Atkin, to bear in mind the distinction between choosing one of two alternative remedies and choosing one of two inconsistent rights (see *United Australia Ltd v Barclays Bank Ltd* [1941] AC 1, at 29). Although there have been restrictions in the past, a plaintiff today suffers no impediment in choosing between alternative remedies. It is otherwise with inconsistent rights. If the plaintiff has, with full knowledge of the relevant facts, unequivocally acted in such a way as to show that he has chosen to pursue one of those rights, he cannot then pursue the other. By reason of the inconsistency, the second choice is no longer his to choose (ibid, p 30).

It follows, therefore, that to constitute an 'election' in this sense, the plaintiff need not obtain a judgment against the other party. Any conduct indicating a waiver of his or her right to sue the party concerned may fall short of that. Similarly, the cases which suggest that an election is conclusively proved once the plaintiff has obtained judgment against either the principal or the agent are to be read with caution (see eg, *Davidson v Donaldson* (1882)

9 QBD 623, and *Irvine & Co v Watson & Sons* (1880) 5 QBD 414). Founded on the principle of waiver, the requirement that the plaintiff must have known the relevant facts and have made an unequivocal decision must still be present. I would find it unacceptable that a plaintiff who might have been misled into suing, say, the agent, through to judgment should be held to have waived his or her right to sue the principal simply because a judgment had been obtained. (I deal with merger later.)

The doctrine of election in its more chaste state is appropriately invoked where a third party has entered into a contract with an agent who is acting for an *undisclosed* principal. On discovering the existence of the principal, the third party may continue to hold the agent with whom he or she thought they were contracting liable under the contract, or they may elect to hold the principal liable (see *Priestly v Fernie* (1865) 3 H & C 977; *Kendall v Hamilton* (1879) 4 App Cas 504; and *Clarkson Booker Ltd v Andjel*). In such cases the third party has made one contract with one party. Upon the revelation of the undisclosed principal, the law allows him or her to enforce liability against that person, but it is clear that at some point they must choose between the two as to whom they will hold liable. Only one person can be liable on the one obligation under the one contract.

The reasoning is not entirely persuasive. I would think that it could be possible, by virtue of the terms of a contract entered into with an agent for an undisclosed principal, for both the newly discovered principal and the agent to be liable under the contract. It would depend on the construction of the contract. Be that as it may, the same reasoning has been inappropriately and unnecessarily extended to contracts where the agent enters into an agreement for a *disclosed* principal. It is asserted that the third party cannot hold both the agent and the disclosed principal liable (see eg, *Calder v Dobell* (1871) LR 6 CP 486, at 489; and *Benton v Campbell, Parker & Co* [1925] 2 KB 410, at 414).

A moment's reflection, however, will suffice to confirm that this reasoning can only be applicable if the liability of the agent and principal are in the alternative. In other words, the terms of the contract must be such that only one or the other can be held liable. Only then can it be said that there is an inconsistency in the plaintiff maintaining a right of action against both parties as in the case of the undisclosed principal. In such circumstances, his or her decision to sue one or the other amounts to an 'election' to sue that person to the exclusion of the other. This situation, however, clearly does not arise where liability is not in the alternative, but joint and several. The plaintiff is then free to sue either through to judgment.

To my mind, notwithstanding dicta to the contrary, the same position pertains where the liability of the principal and agent is a joint liability and not joint and several. The plaintiff is not then obliged to sue one or the other; he or she may sue both. It is open to him or her to discontinue against the one and sue the other or to amend the proceeding by adding the other. Both may thus be held liable by way of judgment although, of course, the plaintiff may obtain satisfaction only the once.

With joint and several liability each debtor is liable on his separate promise as well as on his joint promise, so that there are several causes of action. With joint liability there is one joint promise and only one cause of action. But once it is appreciated that the question in issue is really one of waiver rather than 'election' as such, the distinction is not critical. Certainly, where liability is joint and several it is untenable to suggest that the mere act of suing one of the debtors amounts to a waiver of the right to sue the other. Where the liability is a joint liability, and therefore there is only one cause of action against both principal and agent, the action of suing one to the exclusion of the other may add some credence to the claim that the plaintiff has waived his right to sue the other person. But it will not be decisive. The answer will still depend on the circumstances and whether the plaintiff made a deliberate and unequivocal decision based on a full knowledge of all the relevant facts.

The principle of merger

… In the case of a contract where the principal is disclosed but the liability is a joint liability, the creditor should be able to sue both debtors and obtain judgment against both, although of course the debt or obligation could be satisfied only once. For the plaintiffs to be told that his or her claim is barred because they did not sue the co-debtors at the same time, or after they have chosen to sue and obtain judgment against the one who has turned out to be insolvent, is an irony which would discredit the law. In essence, two parties have jointly promised performance of the contractual obligation and the plaintiff must be able to look to both for that performance. To my mind, therefore, the principle must focus on the satisfaction of the debt rather than the entry of judgment.

While it is acknowledged that on a proper analysis of a joint debt there is only one cause of action, there are nevertheless two or more possible and proper defendants, and the fact that judgment may have been obtained against one is not necessarily inconsistent with subsequently pursuing judgment against the other on the same cause of action. Nor is there anything incongruous (however procedurally undesirable) in joint debtors being sued in separate proceedings on the same cause of action rather than in the one proceeding. The difference is temporal, not substantive. Consequently, as there is no essential inconsistency, the reasoning which underlies the principle of merger when applied to situations involving an undisclosed principal is not applicable where the principal is disclosed and the liability is a joint liability.

Some doubt that this is the case may arise, as pointed out by McGechan J in *R J Bowling Motors Ltd v Kerr* (Palmeston North, A 112/85, 8 July 1988), because of the terms of article 86 and the accompanying text in *Bowstead on Agency* (15th Edn, 1985) at 346–348. While observing that the doctrine is exceptionally difficult to justify in the disclosed principal situation, *Bowstead* suggests that it cannot be reversed short of reconsideration of the problem by the House of Lords.

The House of Lords' decision thought to require review is undoubtedly *Kendall v Hamilton* (1879) 4 App Cas 504. In that case, the plaintiff secured judgment against two members of a three-person partnership to which he had lent money. The judgment remained substantially unsatisfied. The plaintiff then discovered the existence of a third partner and he brought a fresh action against that person. His plea failed on the basis that the earlier judgment had extinguished the cause of action. Admittedly, the decision is not easy to distinguish. However, it is clear, in my view, that their Lordships were concerned with a factual situation in which the defendant had been an *undisclosed* principal (see Earl Cairns, the Lord Chancellor, at 513, Lord Hatherley at 519, Lord Penzance at 524–525, Lord O'Hagan at 533, and Lord Blackburn at 541). It was essentially a case where the right of action which the plaintiff pursued against the other partners could not co-exist with the right of action on the same facts against the undisclosed principal (see especially Earl Cairns LC at 514–515). Moreover, when considering the nature of the contract (which was one of joint liability between the two known principals and the undisclosed principal) their Lordships rejected the proposition that there was a principle of equity to the effect that a liability which is joint in law is, in respect of a partnership, to be regarded as joint and several. This issue was dealt with at length. The question of whether a contract which gives rise to a joint liability contemplates that both co-debtors may be held liable on the joint obligation until such time as the debt is satisfied (without the obligation being construed as joint and several) was not explicitly addressed. As suggested above, there is no necessary reason why judgment against one should be taken to have extinguished the liability of the other ...

... For these reasons, and apart altogether from the intervention of statute, I do not consider that the principle of merger is to be extended to cases where the liability of the principal and agent is a joint liability. In enacting s 94 (of the New Zealand Judicature Act 1908) (as with the enactment of s 3 of the Civil Liability (Contribution) Act 1978 in the United Kingdom) the legislature simply anticipated the development of the common law.

Furthermore, I do not consider that the doctrine of merger is to be applied today where the judgment is the outcome of a flawed election to sue the agent and not the principal. Thus, if the plaintiff's decision to sue the agent (or principal) was the result of fraud or duress (which are not, I hasten to add, present in this case) it would be harsh to suggest that the liability of the principal (or agent) is merged in the judgment. Again, where the initial election is made by a plaintiff who is not in possession of all the relevant facts or whose decision is equivocal for one reason or another, I doubt that it could properly be held that the cause of action is merged in the judgment. Some limited support for this view is provided by *Isaacs & Sons v Salbstein* [1916] 2 KB 139 where it was held that a judgment against a firm (Salbstein Bros), which was never shown to exist or to be liable, was no bar to a subsequent action on the same facts against a person (H Salbstein) who is liable.

Such a view accords with both principle and logic. It would more often than not be unfair to deprive a plaintiff of the right to sue on a valid cause of action when his or her claim remains unsatisfied, whether against a defendant who is liable in the alternative or jointly, unless their decision to obtain judgment against the other party is the result of an informed and deliberate decision. Thus, the factors which I have enumerated above relating to the defence of election would apply in respect of the defence of merger. In such circumstances, the cause of action simply survives the judgment. Alternatively, on facts of the kind which exist in this case, the defendant will be estopped from relying upon the defence. In all, it must now be accepted that, in virtually all circumstances other than where an *undisclosed* principal becomes known to the plaintiff before he or she elects to sue the agent or principal, the question of whether the plaintiff's claim remains unsatisfied, and not whether judgment has been obtained, will be determinative of their right to sue the other party.

43 Cooke & Sons v Eshelby (1887) 12 App Cas 271

Lord Halsbury LC … My Lords, in this case a merchant in Liverpool effected two sales throug'i his brokers. The brokers effected the sales in their own names. The appellants, the merchants with whom these contracts were made, knew the brokers to be brokers, and that it was their practice to sell in their own names in transactions in which they were acting only as brokers. They also knew that the brokers were in the habit of buying and selling for themselves. The appellants with commendable candour admit that they are unable to say that they believed the brokers to be principals; they knew they might be either one or the other; they say that they dealt with the brokers as principals, but at the same time they admit that they had no belief one way or the other whether they were dealing with principals or brokers.

It appears to me that the principle upon which this case must be decided has been so long established that in such a state of facts as I have recited the legal result cannot be doubtful. The ground upon which all these cases have been decided is that the agent has been permitted by the principal to hold himself out as the principal, and that the person dealing with the agent has believed that the agent was the principal, and has acted on that belief. With reference to both those propositions, namely, first, the permission of the real principal to the agent to assume his character, and with reference to the fact whether those dealing with the supposed principal have in fact acted upon the belief induced by the real principal's conduct, various difficult questions of fact have from time to time arisen; but I do not believe that any doubt has ever been thrown upon the law as decided by a great variety of judges for something more than a century. The cases are all collected in the notes to *George v Clagett*[1].

In *Baring v Corrie*[2], in 1818, Lord Tenterden had before him a very similar case to that which is now before your Lordships, and although in that case the Court had to infer what we have here proved by the candid admission of the party, the principle upon which the case was decided is precisely that which appears to me to govern the case now before your Lordships. Lord Tenterden says of the persons who were in that case insisting that they had a right to treat the brokers as principals: 'They knew that Coles & Co acted both as brokers and merchants, and if they meant to deal with them as merchants, and to derive a benefit from so dealing with them, they ought to have inquired whether in this transaction they acted as brokers or not; but they made no inquiry'. And Bayley J says: 'When Coles & Co stood at least in an equivocal situation, the defendants ought in common honesty, if they bought the goods with a view to cover their own debt, to have asked in what character they sold the goods in question. I therefore cannot think that the defendants believed, when they bought the goods, that Coles & Co sold them on their own account. And if so, they can have no defence to the present action.

I am therefore of opinion that the judgment of the Court of Appeal was right. The selling in his own name by a broker is only one fact, and by no means a conclusive fact, from which, in the absence of other circumstances it might be inferred that he was selling his own goods. Upon the facts proved or admitted in this case the fact of selling in the broker's name was neither calculated to induce nor did in fact induce that belief.

Lord Watson ... I do not think it necessary to enter into a minute examination of the authorities, which were fully discussed in the arguments addressed to us. The case of *George v Clagett*[1] has been commented upon and its principles explained in many subsequent decisions, and notably in *Baring v Corrie*[2]; *Semenza v Brinsley*[3], and *Borries v Imperial Ottoman Bank*[4]. These decisions appear to me to establish conclusively that, in order to sustain the defence pleaded by the appellants, it is not enough to shew that the agent sold in his own name. It must be shewn that he sold the goods as his own, or, in other words that the circumstances attending the sale were calculated to induce, and did induce, in the mind of the purchaser a reasonable belief that the agent was selling on his own account and not for an undisclosed principal; and it must also be shewn that the agent was enabled to appear as the real contracting party by the conduct, or by the authority, express or implied, of the principal. The rule thus explained is intelligible and just; and I agree with Bowen LJ that it rests upon the doctrine of estoppel. It would be inconsistent with fair dealing that a latent principal should by his own act or omission lead a purchaser to rely upon a right of set-off against the agent as the real seller, and should nevertheless be permitted to intervene and deprive the purchaser of that right at the very time when it had become necessary for his protection.

Lord Fitzgerald ... I concur with my noble and learned friend in adopting at once the decision and the reasons of the Court of Appeal. I have, however some hesitation in accepting the view that the decisions rest on the doctrine of estoppel. Estoppel in pais involves considerations not necessarily applicable to the case before us. There is some danger in professing to state the principle on which a line of decisions rests, and it seems to me to be sufficient to say in the present case that Maximos did not in any way wilfully or otherwise mislead the defendants (Cooke & Sons) or induce them to believe that Livesey & Co were the owners of the goods or authorised to sell them as their own, or practice any imposition on them. The defendants were not in any way misled.

1   (1797) 7 Term Rep 359 cited in Sm LC (8th Edn) 118.
2   (1818) 2 B & Ald 137.
3   (1865) 18 CBNS 467.
4   (1873) LR 9 CP 38.

44 Central Newbury Car Auctions Ltd v Unity Finance Ltd [1956] 3 All ER 905.

Hodson LJ ... The mere handing over of a chattel to another does not create an estoppel, and there will be no estoppel unless the doctrine of ostensible ownership applies, as, eg, when the owner gives the recipient a document of title or, as has often been said, invests him with the indicia of ownership. This doctrine was first applied by a common law court to a commercial transaction by Ashhurst J, who pronounced in *Lickbarrow v Mason* (1787) 2 Term Rep 63 at 70, the famous dictum:

'We may lay it down as a broad general principle, that, whenever one of two innocent persons must suffer by the acts of a third, he who has enabled such third person to occasion the loss must sustain it'.

This dictum has been said to be too wide for general application. See the observations of Lord Lindley in *Farquharson Brothers & Co v King & Co* [1902] AC 325 at 343, where he pointed out that it could not be relied on without considerable qualification. The noble Lord thought (ibid, at 343), that the word 'enable' introduced an element of error. The Earl of Halsbury LC, in the same case, speaking of the word 'enabled' as used by an American judge (Savage CJ), in the context, said (ibid, at 332):

'... in one sense every man who sells a pistol or dagger enables an intending murderer to commit a crime: but is he, in selling a pistol or a dagger to some person who comes to buy in his shop, acting in breach of any duty?'

As Donovan J pointed out in *Jerome v Bentley & Co* [1952] 2 All ER 114 at 118 everything depends on the construction of the word 'enabled' in Ashurst J's dictum, for, if I carelessly leave my front door open so that a thief walks in and steals my silver, I have in a sense enabled him to steal it by not locking my door; but that does not prevent my recovering it from some innocent purchaser from the thief ...

In *Lickbarrow v Mason*, the facts were that an unpaid vendor of goods shipped them to the purchaser and indorsed to him the bill of lading. The purchaser transferred the bill of lading to a sub-purchaser and became insolvent before the arrival of the goods. The vendor asserted a right to stop the goods in transit, but it was held that he could not assert this right against the sub-purchaser because, by his conduct in indorsing over the bill of lading to the purchaser, the vendor had enabled the purchaser to represent himself as the owner of the goods and so to deceive the sub-purchaser. The word 'enabled' was therefore not apparently used in any extended sense by Ashhurst J.

It is said that the negligence of the plaintiffs in parting with the registration book was a breach of a general duty owing to the whole of the public or at any rate that section of it who might become purchasers of motor cars, for, as Blackburn J said in *Swan v North British Australasian Co* (1863) 2 H & C 175 at 182, there

'... must be the neglect of some duty that is owing to the person led into that belief, or, what comes to the same thing, to the general public of whom the person is one, and not merely neglect of what would be prudent in respect to the party himself, or even of some duty owing to third persons, with whom those seeking to set up the estoppel are not privy ...'.

This conception of duty was accepted by the Privy Council in *Mercantile Bank of India Ltd v Central Bank of India Ltd* [1938] 1 All ER 52 where the topic of estoppel was discussed at length.

The plaintiffs do not deny that, by negligently allowing the registration book to fall into the hands of the thief, they facilitated his fraudulent conduct, but they deny that they were in breach of any duty owing to the general public any more than the man who leaves his house unlocked as in the example given by Donovan J. In my judgment the case falls to be determined, not on a consideration of negligence, but on what is the nature of the representation made by the delivery of the registration book. The book itself is not a document of title; its terms negative ownership and it contains no representation by the plaintiffs or anyone else that the thief was entitled to deal with the car as his own. I think that counsel for the plaintiffs was right in saying that, while a person in possession of a chattel may reasonably be thought to be the owner when he offers it for sale the case of a person in possession of a motor car does not differ in kind, although the absence of the registration book detracts from the signification of possession.

45 Eastern Distributors Ltd v Goldring [1957] 2 All ER 525

Devlin J ... There are many cases of sale of goods where an agent has been held out or represented to have an authority to sell which he has not in fact got and the solution of the difficulty so created might no doubt have been found by the application of the doctrine of estoppel, but in fact the courts of common law approached the problem of the unauthorised sale from a different angle. They began with the principle that no one could pass a better title than that which he had: *nemo dat quod non habet*. To this general principle they admitted a number of exceptions, simply on the ground of mercantile convenience. The best known exceptions relate to transfers of currency and negotiable instruments. Sales in market overt afford another example. In these cases, as is well known, a transferee may acquire a better title than that of his transferor. In the same way, and for the same reason of mercantile convenience, the courts of common law allowed a good title to a buyer who bought in good faith from a man who had apparently been given by the true owner the right to dispose of the goods. Such a buyer did not merely acquire a title by estoppel, based on the implied representation by the owner that there was a right of disposition and vulnerable at the suit of anyone who was not bound by that representation. He acquired in the same way as the transferee of a negotiable instrument or the buyer in market overt a good title against all the world.

The doctrine of apparent authority was most clearly laid down by Lord Ellenborough CJ in *Pickering v Busk* (1812) 15 East 38 at 43. As we have said, he based it, not on estoppel, but on mercantile convenience:

'Strangers can only look to the acts of the parties, and to the external indicia of property, and not to the private communications which may pass between a principal and his broker: and if a person authorise another to assume the apparent right of disposing of property in the ordinary course of trade, it must be presumed that the apparent authority is the real authority. I cannot subscribe to the doctrine, that a broker's engagements are necessarily and in all cases limited to his actual authority, the reality of which is afterwards to be tried by the fact. It is clear that he may bind his principal within the limits of the authority with which he has been apparently clothed by the principal in respect of the subject matter; and there would be no safety in mercantile transactions if he could not'.

The case in which this principle was then most commonly applied was that of a factor, the nature of whose position was to be taken as giving him an implied authority to sell goods entrusted to him; he was able to pass a good title to a buyer even if, by reason of a special limitation put by the principal on his powers, he had no actual authority to do so. But the courts held that, although a factor must be taken to have general authority to sell, it could not be assumed that he had the same authority to pledge; and consequently that, unless he was specially held out as having authority to pledge, he could not, without actual authority, create a valid pledge. It was this ruling which gave rise to the Factors Acts, the first of which was passed in 1823.

All this is expounded by Willes J in *Fuentes v Montis* (1868) LR 3 CP 268 at 276 where he refers to

'... the class of questions which relate to how far a person who is not the real owner of goods, but who appears to the world, or rather to those who deal with him, as owner, and who deal with him on the faith of his apparent ownership, should be allowed to confer upon a third person a greater title than he himself has'.

He then refers to transfers of currency and negotiable instruments and sales in market overt and continues as follows (ibid, at 277):

'A third case in which a man may convey a better title to goods than he himself had, and one which is more apposite to the present is, where an agent who carries on a public business deals with the goods in the ordinary course of it, though he has received secret instructions from his principal to deal with them contrary to the ordinary course of that trade. In that case he has what has been sometimes called an apparent authority, or, as my brother Byles more accurately calls it, an ostensible authority, to deal in such a way with the goods as agents ordinarily deal with them; and, if he deals with them in the ordinary ways of the trade, he binds his principal. These instances, however, are exceptional to the rule that no man can give a better title to goods than he has himself, and that the real owner is not bound except to the extent of an interest which he has parted with or an authority which he has given. Now, the result of that state of the law with respect to agents employed to sell, led to the course of legislation which is known by the general description of the Factors Acts; because it was held by the courts of law that the case of a pledge of goods by a factor intrusted with the possession of goods, and authorised to sell them, fell within the general rule to which the instances above enumerated are exceptions, and that it did not fall within the exceptions by reason of a pledge being an ordinary and accustomed transaction to be entered into by a person intrusted as agent to sell, or perhaps more properly by reason of the courts of law having treated a pledge as being out of the scope of an authority to sell'.

There has been a series of Factors Acts ... The legislation which now governs the position of factors, or 'mercantile agents', is the Factors Act 1889, s 2. There can be no doubt that these sections are based on and supplement the common law, and the language which they employ, which in this respect has been the same from the first, is not the language of estoppel. The Factors Act 1889, s 2, for example, says that a sale, pledge or other disposition which is within its terms 'shall ...be as valid as if he were expressly authorised by the owner of the goods to make the same'.

The Factors Act 1889, and the example given by Willes J in *Fuentes v Montis* apply to an agent who is entrusted with goods. No doubt cases in which the only evidence of apparent authority is the possession of goods must now be treated as being governed by the Factors Act 1889, which in this respect codifies as well as amplifies the common law; and it does not apply in this case since (the dealer) was not put into possession of the van. But there are other ways besides the possession of the goods in which a man can be clothed with apparent ownership or apparent authority to sell. The common law principle is, as it has always been, wide enough to govern this. This is shown by the early cases on pledges. Because the factor was not held out merely by virtue of his position as having apparent authority to pledge, the doctrine of apparent authority did not apply at common law if nothing more than possession could be shown. It was otherwise if there was other evidence of holding out. Thus, in *Martini v Coles* (1813) 1 M & S 140, 150 Bayley J said:

'A factor has authority to sell, but not to pledge; and therefore a person who takes a pawn of a factor takes it at his peril. If the principal does any thing to induce the person to believe the factor really the principal, that would be a different case'.

Similarly, in *Boyson v Coles* (1817) 6 M & S 14, the headnote reads:

'A factor cannot pledge, unless the owner of the goods arm him with such indicia of property as to enable him to deal with it as his own ...'

Abbott J, in particular, said (ibid, at 27):

'... possession alone is not a sufficient emblem of authority to entitle a factor to pledge, so as to enable the pawnee to hold the goods against the real owner. In the present case, it does not appear that the defendant was misled by any act or document with which the plaintiffs were concerned, other than such as regarded possession ...'

In many cases since then common law principle has been considered concurrently with the Factors Acts; for example, *Vickers v Hertz* (1871) LR 2 Sc & Div 113; *Johnson v Crédit Lyonnais Co* (1877) 3 CPD 32; *Lowther v Harris* [1927] 1 KB 393. The apparent ownership or authority has generally taken the form of arming the agent with some indicia which made it appear that he was either the owner or had the right to sell. In our judgment the principle applies to any form of representation or holding out of apparent ownership or the right to sell. It is embodied in s 21(1) of the Sale of Goods Act 1893, which provides:

'... where goods are sold by a person who is not the owner thereof, and who does not sell them under the authority or with the consent of the owner, the buyer acquires no better title to the goods than the seller had, unless the owner of the goods is by his conduct precluded from denying the seller's authority to sell'.

This section expresses the old principle that apparent authority to sell is an exception to the maxim *nemo dat quod non habet*; and it is plain from the wording that if the owner of the goods is precluded from denying authority, the buyer will in fact acquire a better title than the seller.

We doubt whether this principle, which is sometimes referred to – eg, by Wright J in *Lowther v Harris* – as common law estoppel, ought really to be regarded as part of the law of estoppel. At any rate it differs from what is sometimes called 'equitable estoppel' in this vital respect, that the effect of its application is to transfer a real title and not merely a metaphorical title by estoppel.

46 Lloyds and Scottish Finance Ltd v Williamson [1965] I All ER 641

Salmon LJ ... When Mr Marshall expressly authorised Peerless to sell the motor car he knew that they might (and indeed probably would) sell as principals and implicitly authorised them to do so. Acting on his mandate, they clearly held themselves out as principals to the defendant Mr Lunt and sold to him as apparent principals. The plaintiffs, who authorised Peerless to sell the motor car as apparent principals, and put them in a position to do so, cannot now be heard to say that Peerless were in reality only agents and had no authority to act as they did, or that the defendant Mr Lunt acquired no title from them. This to my mind is well settled. In *Eastern Distributors Ltd v Goldring (Murphy, Third Party)*[1], Devlin J, who delivered the judgment of this court, said:

'The Factors Act 1889, and the examples given by Willes J, in *Fuentes v Montis*[2] [a case much relied on by the counsel for the plaintiffs] apply to an agent who is entrusted with goods. No doubt cases in which the only evidence of apparent authority is the possession of the goods must now be treated as being governed by the Factors Act 1889, which in this respect codifies as well as amplifies the common law ... But there are other ways besides the possession of the goods in which a man can be clothed with apparent ownership ... The common law principle is, as it has always been, wide enough to govern this ... Because the factor was not held out merely by virtue of his position as having apparent authority to pledge, the doctrine of apparent authority did not apply at common law if nothing more than possession could be shown. It was otherwise if there was other evidence of holding out. Thus in *Martini v Coles*[3], Bayley J said: "A factor has authority to sell, but not to pledge; and therefore a person who takes a pawn of a factor takes it at this peril. If the principal does anything to induce the person to believe the factor really the principal, that would be a different case" '.

This must mean if the principal does something more than merely put the factor in possession of the goods. In the present case the principal did much more than merely put Peerless in possession of the motor car. He did what he could to induce any person buying the car from Peerless to believe that Peerless were the owners of the motor car by authorising Peerless to sell it as owners. As a result, the defendant Mr Lunt obtained a good title at common law. This is not because of the operation of a true estoppel, for the defendant Mr Lunt obtained a real title which he could properly transfer. The plaintiffs are not merely estopped as between themselves and the defendant Mr Lunt from calling evidence to show that they are the true owners of the grey Jaguar.

Counsel for the defendants relied on the line of cases culminating in *Montagu v Forwood*[4] in which it was held that if A authorises B to sell A's goods as their apparent owner, C, the buyer, if sued for the price by A (as an undisclosed principal) may set off against the price any debt due to C from B. Counsel for the plaintiffs rightly points out that there is a real distinction between that class of case and the present in as much as there the plaintiffs are repudiating the contract entered into by their agent. Counsel for the plaintiffs accordingly argued that the true basis of the decisions in the cases on which the defendants rely is the doctrine that no one can at the same time approbate and reprobate a contract. This may be so, but it does not appear to have been so stated or understood by any of the judges who decided them. In *Montagu v Forwood*, Bowen LJ says[5]:

'If A employs B as his agent to make any contract for him ... and B makes a contract with C ... if B is a person who would be reasonably supposed to be acting as a principal, and is not known or suspected by C to be acting as an agent ... A cannot make a demand against C without the latter being entitled to stand in the same position as if B had in fact been a principal. If A has allowed his agent B to appear in the character of a principal, he must take the consequences'.

This is certainly so if A has expressly authorised B to sell as principal.

Bowen LJ says that this is not only a rule of law but of justice and common sense. I respectfully agree.

In cases in which the true principal not only puts an agent in possession of the goods and the indicia of title, but also expressly authorises him to sell as principal, the question whether the factor sold in the ordinary course of business can, in my judgment, be relevant only in so far as it throws light on the bona fides of the buyer. In the present case there is no suggestion against the defendant Mr Lunt's bona fides, nor is it suggested that he ought to have suspected that Peerless were selling as agents. The transaction in question was one which Peerless, had they been principals, could properly have made. In these circumstances, the fact that the transaction between Peerless and the defendant Mr Lunt was an unusual transaction and may not have been in the ordinary course of an agent's business is, in my view, irrelevant.

The defendants are amply protected by the common law, and no question arises under the Factors Acts which, whilst they codified and amplified the common law so far as it applied to mercantile agents, certainly did not derogate from it; see s 13 of the Factors Act 1889. If the same authority as was given to Peerless had been given to a person who was not in business at all, the plaintiff's case would not have been even apparently arguable. In such a case no question of the agent's ordinary course of business could have arisen, yet he would undoubtedly have passed a good title to anyone buying in good faith from him as the apparent owner of the motor car.

1   [1957] 2 All ER 525, [1957] 2 QB 600 at 609, 610.
2   (1868) LR 3 CP 268 at 277.
3   (1813) 1 M & S 140 at 150.
4   [1893] 2 QB 350.
5   [1893] 2 QB 350 at 355, 356.

47 Staffs Motor Guarantee Ltd v British Wagon Co Ltd [1934] 2 KB 305

MacKinnon J ... The plaintiffs put their claim on one or other of two alternative grounds. The first of these alternative grounds is that this case falls within the Factors Act 1889, s 2, sub-s 1: 'Where a mercantile agent is, with the consent of the owner, in possession of goods or of the documents of title to goods, any sale, pledge, or other disposition of the goods, made by him when acting in the ordinary course of business of a mercantile agent, shall, subject to the provisions of this Act, be as valid as if he were expressly authorised by the owner of the goods to make the same; provided that the person taking under the disposition acts in good faith, and has not at the time of the disposition notice that the person making the disposition has not authority to make the same'. The plaintiffs say that the defendants entrusted the possession of the lorry to Heap, who was a mercantile agent for the sale of second-hand lorries, and that they, the plaintiffs, in good faith and without any notice of his want of authority entered into a contract with him for the purchase of the lorry, and, therefore they claim that they have a good title to the lorry as against the defendants pursuant to the provisions of that section. There was no doubt some evidence that Heap did deal in second-hand motor vehicles as an ordinary seller of them. I will suppose that, if an ordinary owner of a motor-car had brought his car to Heap and asked him to sell it for him and Heap had sold it to someone at a lower price than that authorised by the true owner or otherwise not in accordance with his instructions, the purchaser from Heap would be entitled under the section which I have quoted to claim as against the true owner. I think, however, that it has rightly been pointed out on behalf of the defendants that there would be this difficulty in the way of the plaintiffs' assertion of that claim, that if the transaction between the defendants and Heap was a genuine transaction – and the plaintiffs' claim in this respect arises on that basis – then the lorry had been sold by Heap to the defendants and had been entrusted by the defendants to Heap not as a mercantile agent dealing in or selling motor vehicles, but to Heap as a hirer of the car and therefore as its bailee. In these circumstances I do not think that it is open to the plaintiffs to say that the defendants entrusted the car to Heap as a mercantile agent. In *Oppenheimer v Frazer and Wyatt*[1] Channell J, in examining the meaning of the Act of 1889, said[2]: 'It seems to me that the true rule is that where there is a consent of the owner of the goods to the possession of the goods by the mercantile agent as a mercantile agent – and that is the important part of the matter – that then the statute applies, provided the other conditions are fulfilled'. I observe that Sir Mackenzie Chalmers, the learned draftsman of the Sale of Goods Act 1893, in his comment on this section, makes the same suggestion and illustrates it by what seems to be a very forcible example: 'Suppose a house were let furnished to a man who happened to be an auctioneer. Could he sell the furniture by auction and give a good title to the buyers? Surely not'[3]. That, of course, is an extreme case, but, I think, the same principle applies here. Because one happens to entrust his goods to a man who is in other respects a mercantile agent, but with whom he is dealing not as a mercantile agent but in a different capacity, I do not think that it is open to a third party who buys the goods from that man to say that they were in his possession as a mercantile agent and that therefore he had power to sell them to a purchaser and to give him a good title to them. The claimant must be able to assert not only that the goods were entrusted by the owner to him as a mercantile agent. As Channell J said, it is the consent of the owner of the goods to the possession of them by the mercantile agent as a mercantile agent that is the important part of the matter. I therefore think that this ground of the plaintiffs' claim fails.

1   [1907] 1 KB 519, [1907] 2 KB 50.
2   [1907] 1 KB 519 at 527.
3   Chalmers *Sale of Goods Act 1893* (11th Edn, 1931), p 176.

48 Oppenheimer v Attenborough & Son [1908] 1 KB 221

Lord Alverstone CJ ... When you are dealing with a person who is a mercantile agent, you have to find out whether in the customary course of his business as such agent he has authority to sell or consign for sale or buy or raise money on goods. It is clear, therefore, why the words 'in the customary course of his business as such agent' were inserted in sub-s 1 of s 1 of the Factors Act 1889. There are many kinds of agents who receive possession of goods, such, for instance, as carriers, and yet it is no part of the customary course of business of such agents to sell them or consign them for sale or raise money on them. Therefore, when you are dealing with an agent in possession of goods, you have, no doubt, to consider what kind of agent he is, and what his customary course of business would be when he is acting in the capacity of agent. Mr Rawlinson pressed upon us the case of an auctioneer, which is undoubtedly one of some difficulty. He suggested that under sub-s 1 of s 2, unless it be read as he wishes to read it, an auctioneer would have power to pledge goods entrusted to him for sale. It seems to me that there may be particular agents, such as auctioneers, with regard to whom a pledge by them of goods entrusted to them would be such a departure from the ordinary course of their business as to put the pledgee upon notice. No question of that kind arises in this case. Having got the class of mercantile agents whose transactions are to be validated in the interests of a pledgee, as contemplated by the preamble of the Factors Act 1842, we come to sub-s 1 of s 2, which deals with the circumstances under which the transaction must be carried out. I think that the sub-section means that the transaction is to be validated, if the agent has acted in the transaction as a mercantile agent would act. That, no doubt, includes limits that have been suggested, such as that the sale, or whatever the transaction is, must not take place outside business hours, or under circumstances under which a mercantile agent in the trade would not ordinarily transact business. The view I take of the law is really that which was taken in two of the cases cited to us. In *Lamb v Attenborough*[1] a clerk who was authorised by his employer to sign delivery orders per procuration, and who by so doing obtained possession of dock warrants, was held not to be an agent entrusted with the possession of documents of title to goods within the meaning of 5 & 6 Vict c 39. Blackburn J in that case said: 'The agent contemplated by the statute is an agent having mercantile possession, so as to be within the mercantile usage of getting advances made. In this case Bryant's possession was that of servant, not of agent: and when the documents were created by the dock company, they belonged to the plaintiff, and he had a right to demand them back from the defendant'. In the case of *Hastings v Pearson*[2] a man employed at a salary of 30s per week and a commission to take small articles of jewellery to private houses to sell, instead of selling them for his employers, pawned them for his own benefit. Mathew J said: 'There is no such business as that of an agent to pledge with pawnbrokers small articles of jewellery for the purpose of raising money for the employer of the agent. The Factors Act therefore does not apply'. Mathew J therefore dealt with the case on the basis that it could not fairly be said that the agent, who was employed only to sell small articles of jewellery, was a person who, in carrying out the transaction of pledge, was acting in the ordinary course of business of a mercantile agent. It may be possible to take another view of the facts, but that is the way in which the case was decided by Mathew J, and it does not seem to me to go far enough for Mr Rawlinson's argument. In my opinion the words 'acting in the ordinary course of business of a mercantile agent' mean that the person must act in the transaction as a mercantile agent would act if he were carrying out a transaction which he was authorised by his master to carry out.

Buckley LJ ... There is a difference of expression between s 1, sub-s 1, and s 2, sub-s 1. In the one case the expression used is 'customary course of his business', while in the other it is 'the ordinary course of business of a mercantile agent'. I think I see the reason. Section 1, sub-s 1, is speaking of the arrangements made between the owner of the goods and his agent. It contemplates that the principal has given possession of the goods to the agent in the customary course of the business which the principal knows, or believes, the agent carries on as a mercantile agent. It deals with the circumstances under which the agent gets his authority; to satisfy the definition he must get it in the customary course of his business as a mercantile agent. Section 2, sub-s 1, deals with another matter. It has to do with the stage at which the agent is going to deal with the goods in his possession with reference to some other person, and the form of the expression is here altered to 'when acting in the ordinary course of business of a mercantile agent'. The plaintiff's argument involves our reading there 'of such mercantile agent', or 'of a mercantile agent in such a trade as that in which he carries on business'. I do not think that is the meaning of the expression. I think it means, 'acting in such a way as a mercantile agent acting in the ordinary course of business of a mercantile agent would act'; that is to say, within business hours, at a proper place of business, and in other respects in the ordinary way in which a mercantile agent would act, so that there is nothing to lead the pledgee to suppose that anything wrong is being done, or to give him notice that the disposition is one which the mercantile agent had no authority to make. Dealing with it in that way, it seems to me that there is no great difficulty in the Act of Parliament.

1   (1862) 31 LJQB 41.
2   [1893] 1 QB 62.

49 The Swan [1968] I Lloyd's Rep 5

Brandon J ... Where A contracts with B on behalf of a disclosed principal C, the question whether both A and C are liable on the contract or only C depends on the intention of the parties. That intention is to be gathered from (1) the nature of the contract, (2) its terms and (3) the surrounding circumstances: see *Bowstead on Agency* (12th Edn, 1959), at 257 and 258, para 113, and the authorities there cited. The intention for which the court looks is not the subjective intention of A or of B. Their subjective intentions may differ. The intention for which the court looks is an objective intention of both parties, based on what two reasonable businessmen making a contract of that nature, in those terms and in those surrounding circumstances, must be taken to have intended.

Where a contract is wholly in writing, the intention depends on the true construction, having regard to the nature of the contract and the surrounding circumstances, of the document or documents in which the contract is contained. Where, as in the present case, the contract is partly oral and partly in writing, the intention depends on the true effect, having regard again to the nature of the contract and the surrounding circumstances, of the oral and written terms taken together.

Many of the decided cases on questions of this kind relate to contracts wholly in writing. But it seems to me that, in principle, there can be no difference in the approach to the problem, whether the contract concerned is wholly in writing or partly in writing and partly oral. In either case the terms of the contract must be looked at and their true effect ascertained ... A distinction has been drawn between cases in which a person contracts expressly as agent and those in which, although he describes himself as an agent, he does not contract expressly as such. Where it is stated in the contract that a person makes it 'as agent for', or 'on account of', or 'on behalf of', or simply 'for', a principal, or where words of that kind are added after such person's signature, he is not personally liable: *Gadd v Houghton* (1876) 1 Ex D 357; *Universal Steam Navigation Company Ltd v James McKelvie & Co*, [1923] AC 492; *Kimber Coal Company Ltd v Stone and Rolfe Ltd* [1926] AC 414.

Where such words are not used but the person is merely stated to be an agent, or the word 'agent' is just added after his signature, the result is uncertain, because it is not clear whether the word is used as a qualification or merely as a description: see *Gadd v Houghton, sup*, per James LJ at 359; and *Universal Steam Navigation Company Ltd v James McKelvie & Co sup*, per Lord Sumner at 501. In general it would seem that in such a case the person does not avoid personal liability, although there may be exceptions to this general rule depending on the other terms of the contract or the surrounding circumstances.

Where a person contracts as agent for a company and does nothing more than add the word 'director' or 'secretary' after his signature, it seems that he does not avoid personal liability: *Brebner v Henderson* 1925 SC 643. This was a Scottish Appeal to the Court of Session which turned on the construction of s 26 of the Bills of Exchange Act 1882, but I think the reasoning is applicable to a similar situation at common law.

Bearing in mind the distinctions drawn in the authorities to which I have referred, I return to an analysis of the facts in the present case. It seems to me that the defendant did not ever contract expressly as agent in the sense of saying either orally or in writing that he was acting 'as agent for', or 'on account of', or 'on behalf of', or 'for' the company. What he did was to describe himself to both plaintiffs at an earlier stage as 'Mr Rodger, of J D Rodger Ltd', and later to write the written orders on the company's notepaper and add the word 'Director' to his signature. On the other hand, the plaintiffs' subsequent conduct shows that they understood clearly that the bills for their work were to be sent to the company. It has been argued with force for the defendant that this shows that the plaintiffs understood the defendant to be contracting 'on account of' the company and it was to the company alone that they were giving credit. I am not sure, however, that this is the only interpretation to be put on the facts, for it is possible for a person to give credit to a principal without at the same time giving exclusive credit to him.

50 Teheran-Europe Co Ltd v S T Belton (Tractors) Ltd [1968] 2 All ER 886

Diplock LJ ... Reliance is placed on the observations of Blackburn J in *Elbinger Act für Fabrication von Eisenbahn Material v Claye*[1] of which the relevant part is as follows:

'I quite agree that a man may, as agent, make a contract upon such terms as not only to bind himself but also so as to bind the principal; in other words, so that the principal shall be party to the contract, and may then either sue or be sued ... But although such a contract may be where the principals are English; yet where a foreigner has instructed English merchants to act for him, I take it that the usage of trade, established for many years, has been that it is understood that the foreign constituent has not authorised the merchants to pledge his credit to the contract, to establish privity between him and the home supplier. On the other hand, the home supplier, knowing that to be the usage, unless there is something in the bargain showing the intention to be otherwise, does not trust the foreigner, and so does not make the foreigner responsible to him, and does not make himself responsible to the foreigner'.

Blackburn J was really dealing with two usages which he considered (for the suggestion came from him, not from counsel) were current in 1873: the first a usage existing between English merchants and foreign principals, viz that foreign principals did not authorise English merchants to enter into contracts on their behalf. The second usage, which was a consequence of the knowledge by English merchants of the first, is a usage between English merchants that unless an English merchant states the contrary, he is not willing to enter into a contract with a foreigner through an English agent.

I agree entirely with Donaldson J[2] that commercial usages are far from immutable. For my part I find it difficult to see how even in 1873 there can have been the first usage. For the authority conferred on the English merchant must have depended on the terms of the contract of agency made between him and his foreign principal of which the proper law may be other than English law. Conflict of laws was not, however, in the forefront of the judicial mind in 1873. Anyway I am confident that there is no such usage today. The reason for the second usage has accordingly vanished, and I have no doubt that it too has disappeared. I agree with Donaldson J[3], that the fact that the principal is a foreigner is one of the circumstances to be taken into account in determining whether or not the other party to the contract was willing, or led the agent to believe that he was willing, to treat as a party to the contract the agent's principal, and, if he was so willing, whether the mutual intention of the other party and the agent was that the agent should be personally entitled to sue and liable to be sued on the contract as well as his principal. It is, however, only one of many circumstances, and as respects the creation of privity of contract between the other party and the principal its weight may be minimal, particularly in a case such as the present where the terms of payment are cash before delivery and no credit is extended by the other party to the principal. It may have considerably more weight in determining whether the mutual intention of the other party and the agent was that the agent should be personally liable to be sued as well as the principal, particularly if credit has been extended by the other party; but we are not concerned with that issue here.

Sachs LJ ... In determining the intention of the parties on this point the modern approach was aptly stated by Pritchard J in *J S Holt & Moseley (London) Ltd v Sir Charles Cunningham & Partners*[4] where he said:

'The intention of the parties can only be ascertained from the facts as proved in evidence, and the nationality and whereabouts of the principal is no more and no less than one of the facts to which such weight will be given as in any particular case the court thinks proper'.

As the years go by many factors change in relation to estimating the intention of the parties. For instance, the system of credits is constantly changing, as my Lords have already stated: and as reciprocity in the enforcement of judgments between nationals of this country and nationals of the other country develops and becomes more effective, the weight of the fact that the principal is foreign has diminished and no doubt will continue to diminish further as new factors, such as the scope of Government-inspired guarantees, evolve. In any given case it may, as Donaldson J said[2], already be minimal but it is not always necessarily minimal. For instance, the weight may vary according to the country in which the principal carries on his business. There may be differences between cases where the country is one with little civilisation or no really effective legal system, and cases concerning countries such as those which are members of the EEC. Suffice it to say that in the present case the weight to my mind to be attached to the principals being from Persia was minimal. It did not in any shape or sense outweigh the other factors which have been mentioned by my Lords; and for that reason I agree that the appeal on that issue should be dismissed.

1   (1873) LR 8 QB 313 at 317.
2   [1968] 1 All ER 585 at 590.
3   [1968] 1 All ER 585 at 591.
4   (1949) 83 Ll L Rep 141 at 145.

51 Sika Contracts Ltd v B L Gill & Closeglen Properties Ltd (1978) 9 BLR 11

Kerr J ... A person who is in fact an agent, in the sense that he has somebody standing behind him, such as an employer or a principal, can nevertheless enter into a contract in such a way that, although in fact an agent, he becomes personally liable to the other contracting party. It therefore follows that the fact that Mr Gill was not acting beneficially for his own account, as would be the position if he had been asking somebody to carry out repairs to his own property, but that he was professionally engaged on behalf of a client, does not exclude the possibility of his being personally liable to a third party on a contract concluded by him in his own name.

... Where the contract in question is in writing, as it is here, then the question whether or not a signatory has contracted personally or only as agent is a question of construction. One has to consider the signature and the contents in their context ... The position here is that the acceptance of the quotation was signed by Mr Gill in his own name without any qualification to suggest that he was contracting as agent for anybody else. The body of the letter of acceptance contains no such reference. The only words which Mr Gill's counsel could rely on in this connection are the words 'Chartered Civil Engineer' after the signature.

As already explained, the fact that Mr Gill was acting in a professional capacity does not by any means necessarily exclude his personal liability ... It would have been open to him (though I accept that it would have been unusual) to have added to his signature and to the words 'Chartered Civil Engineer' words such as 'as agent only', or even, 'acting for building owner' with or without the owner's name and address. I appreciate that this is not commonly done. But whether or not it is done may be crucial when the building owner unexpectedly goes into liquidation as here.

On the basis of this correspondence it is impossible, in my view, for Mr Gill to say that on its true construction he only acted as agent. The plaintiffs are perfectly entitled to say, quite apart from the law which is in their favour, that they relied on the credit of Mr Gill and on no one else's credit, since no other person was named in the correspondence. That appears to me to be the end of the case.

52 Universal Steam Navigation Co Ltd v J McKelvie & Co [1923] AC 492

Lord Sumner ... It has sometimes been said that when 'agents' is the word added to the signature, it is a mere word of description, and so does not qualify the liability which the act of signing imports. I question this explanation. One's signature is not the place in which to advertise one's calling, nor is 'agent' ordinarily used to describe a trade, as 'tailor' or 'butcher' would be. I have no doubt that, when people add 'agent' to a signature to a contract, they are trying to escape personal liability, but are unaware that the attempt will fail. The result, however, is the same. When words added to a signature in themselves qualify liability, it is because, as words, they can be so construed in conjunction with the contract as a whole.

In construing the words 'as agents', there is a distinction to be taken. Though it may be somewhat subtle, it has been mentioned in the older cases. Do the words 'as agents' mean 'and as agents', or 'only as agents'? The positive affirmation, that I sign 'as agent' – that is, for another – is formally consistent with my signing for myself as well. If the act of signing raises a presumption of personal assent and obligation, which has to be sufficiently negatived or qualified by apt words, are the words 'as agent' apt or sufficient to exclude personal liability? For myself, I think that, standing alone, they are. To say 'as agent', meaning thereby 'also as agent' for someone undisclosed, is substantially useless. If the agent refuses to disclose, the opposite party is no better off. If the statement is true, the rights and liabilities of the principal can be established at any time by proof. The statement only acquires a business efficacy as distinct from a formal content, if it means 'I am not liable but someone else is and he only', and this is what I think it does mean.

Unless, then, something is to be found to the contrary in the earlier part of this charter, the qualification 'as agents' appears to me to relieve Messrs McKelvie & Co from personal liability on the contract.

53 Higgins v Senior (1841) 8 M & W 834

Parke B ... The question in this case, which was argued before us in the course of the last term, may be stated to be, whether in an action on an agreement in writing, purporting on the face of it to be made by the defendant, and subscribed by him, for the sale and delivery by him of goods above the value of £10, it is competent for the defendant to discharge himself, on an issue on the plea of non assumpsit, by proving that the agreement was really made by him by the authority of and as agent for a third person and that the plaintiff knew those facts, at the time when the agreement was made and signed. Upon consideration, we think that it was not: and that the rule for a new trial must be discharged.

There is no doubt, that where such an agreement is made, it is competent to shew that one or both of the contracting parties were agents for other persons, and acted as such agents in making the contract, so as to give the benefit of the contract on the one hand to, and charge with liability on the other, the unnamed principals: and this, whether the agreement be or be not required to be in writing by the Statute of Frauds: and this evidence in no way contradicts the written agreement. It does not deny that it is binding on those whom, on the face of it, it purports to bind; but shews that it also binds another, by reason that the act of the agent, in signing the agreement, in pursuance of his authority, is in law the act of the principal.

But, on the other hand, to allow evidence to be given that the party who appears on the face of the instrument to be personally a contracting party, is not such, would be to allow parol evidence to contradict the written agreement; which cannot be done.

54 Hutchinson v Tatham (1873) LR 8 CP 482

Brett J ... It does seem a strange thing, when a person expressly says to another, in a written document, that he is not contracting with him as principal, and in signing that writing states the same thing again, to hold that it can by any evidence afterwards be established that he is liable, not as agent but principal. On the authority of what was said by Cockburn CJ in *Fleet v Murton*[1], and Hill J in *Deslandes v Gregory*[2], it is clear that without evidence of custom the defendants would not be liable as principals. So strong do I consider the terms of this contract in this respect, taking the terms in the body and the signature together, that, were evidence offered to shew that from the beginning the defendants were liable as principals, I should be prepared not to admit it; but the cases have lately gone very far as to the admissibility of evidence of custom. It is clear, however, that no such evidence can be admitted to contradict the plain terms of a document. If evidence were tendered to prove a custom that the defendants should be liable as principals under all circumstances, that would contradict the document; but it has been decided that, though you cannot contradict a written document by evidence of custom, you may add a term not inconsistent with any term of the contract. What, I apprehend, it is here attempted to add, is, not that the defendants would be liable as principals in the first instance or under all circumstances, but that, though prima facie and in most cases the brokers are mere agents, yet, if they fail to disclose the name of the principals within a reasonable time, they, the agents, may on the happening of this contingency, be principals. This is not, I think, on the whole, inconsistent with the contract, and therefore, though with some doubt, I think the evidence was admissible, and the rule must be discharged.

1   (1871) LR 7 QB 126.
2   (1860) 2 E & E 602 at 607.

55 N & J Vlassopulos Ltd v Ney Shipping Ltd, The Santa Carina [1977] 1 Lloyd's Rep 478

Lord Denning MR ... The Judge held that the brokers who ordered the fuel were personally liable. He was much influenced by the cases where a person gives a written order for goods or signs a written contract when he is known to be acting as an agent. Nevertheless, although he is known to be acting as an agent, he will be liable on that order or liable on that contract if he signs in his own personal name without qualification. That is settled by cases both in this Court and in the House of Lords: see *H O Brandt & Co v H N Morris & Co Ltd* [1917] 2 KB 784 at 796 per Lord Justice Scrutton, and *Hichens, Harrison, Woolston & Co v Jackson* [1943] AC 266 at 273 per Lord Atkin. In order to exclude his liability he has to append to his signature some such words as 'as agent only' or 'for and on behalf of' or such exclusion must be apparent elsewhere in the document. That is clear from *Universal Steam Navigation Co v James McKelvie & Co* [1923] AC 492 at 505–6.

The Judge thought that those cases on written orders and written contracts should be applied to the present case of an oral contract ...

I have no doubt that those cases on written orders and written contracts arose out of the old rule of evidence whereby it was not permissible to admit oral evidence to alter or contradict a written contract. Those cases still apply today to written orders and written contracts. But they do not apply to oral orders or oral contracts. At any rate not so rigidly. In many cases if a man, who is an agent for another, orders goods or makes a contract by word of mouth, but does not disclose the name or standing of his principal (so that his credit is unknown to the other contracting party) the agent himself is liable to pay for the goods or to fulfil the contract. It may be that the other contracting party knows that the man is only an agent, but, as he does not know who the principal is, it is to be inferred that he does not rely on the credit of the principal but looks to the agent. That, I think, is the thought underlying the dictum of Mr Justice Salter in *Benton v Campbell, Parker & Co Ltd* [1925] 2 KB 410 at 414 ... But in other cases that may not be the proper inference. There are cases where, although the man who supplied the goods knows that the other is an agent and does not know his principal, nevertheless he is content to look to the credit of that principal whoever he may be. This is something which Lord Justice Diplock contemplated in the case of *Teheran-Europe Co Ltd v S T Belton (Tractors) Ltd* [1968] 2 Lloyd's Rep 37, [1968] 2 QB 545. He said that

.'... he may be willing to treat as a party to the contract anyone on whose behalf the agent may have been authorised to contract ...'

This applies particularly to the case of a broker. As Mr Justice Blackburn said in *Fleet v Murton* (1871) LR 7 QB 126, at 131:

'... I take it that there is no doubt at all, in principle, that a broker, as such, merely dealing as broker and not as purchaser of the article, makes a contract from the very nature of things between the buyer and the seller and he is not himself either buyer or seller'.

It seems to me that the present case falls into that second category. It was known to both sides that the agents, Ney Shipping Ltd, were only brokers. They were brokers ordering bunkers for a vessel. It was obvious that they were only agents, and they were ordering bunkers for the time charterers or the owners of a vessel. They had often done it before. The accounts for the fuel had always been paid by the principals either directly or through the brokers. It cannot be supposed that the brokers were ever intended to be personally liable. The suppliers would look to the time charterers or the owners, whoever they might be, they being the people to be relied upon. Although they were not named or specified or disclosed, they would be the people to whom the suppliers would look for payment of the oil.

It is just the same, it seems to me, as if the brokers had given a written order for the bunkers and added to their signatures 'as agents only'. In that case they would not have been personally liable. Nor should they be liable in this case when it was done by word of mouth and when the inference from the conduct and the whole of the circumstances was that they were ordering the fuel as agents only.

56 Maritime Stores Ltd v H P Marshall & Co Ltd [1963] 1 Lloyd's Rep 602

Roskill J ... Mr Staughton also referred me to a recent decision of Mr Justice Pearce, as he was then, in the case of *Rusholme Bolton & Roberts Hadfield Ltd v S G Read & Co (London) Ltd* [1955] 1 WLR 146. The actual facts do not matter, but I think I should read a passage from the learned judge's judgment (ibid, at 150) where he quotes from the judgment of Lord Justice Scrutton in *H O Brandt & Co v H N Morris & Co Ltd* [1917] 2 KB 784:

'The fact that a person is agent and is known so to be does not of itself prevent his incurring personal liability. Whether he does so is to be determined by the nature and terms of the contract and the surrounding circumstances. Where he contracts on behalf of a foreign principal there is a presumption that he is incurring a personal liability unless a contrary intention appears; and similarly where he signs in his own name without qualification. In *Brandt (H O) & Co Ltd v Morris (H N) & Co Ltd* (sup, at 796) Scrutton LJ said: "Later in *Gadd v Houghton* (1876) 1 Ex D 357, which may perhaps be called the leading case, Mellish LJ stated the same principle (ibid, at 360) 'As is said in the notice to *Thomson v Davenport* (1829) 9 B & C 78, when a man signs a contract in his own name he is prima facie a contracting party and liable, and there must be something very strong on the face of the instrument to show that the liability does not attach to him'. When I find in this contract the words 'We have this day bought from you', and the signature 'H O Brandt & Co', in my view something very strong is needed to show that Brandt & Co have not contracted personally". He added later (*sup*, at 797): "The other fact which I take into account is that Messrs Sayles Bleacheries are foreigners, and while I think that one cannot at the present day attach the importance which used to be attached forty or fifty years ago to the fact that the supposed principal is a foreigner, it is still a matter to be taken into account in deciding whether the person said to be an English agent has or has not made himself personally liable" '.

I respectfully adopt that statement of law of Lord Justice Scrutton, and I take into account, as I am enjoined to do, the fact that the principals here behind the defendants were foreigners. Nevertheless, that is no more than a fact which I have to take into account.

57 Bickerton v Burrell (1816) 5 M & S 383

Lord Ellenborough CJ ... In the ordinary transactions of commerce, a man may sell or purchase in his own name, and yet it does not follow that the contract is his, but the transaction is open to explanation, and others who do not appear as parties to the contract are frequently disclosed, and step in to demand the benefit of it. But where a man assigns to himself the character of agent to another whom he names, I am not aware that the law will permit him to shift his situation, and to declare himself the principal, and the other to be a mere creature of straw. That, I believe, has never yet been attempted ... It was proposed to call Mrs Richardson to prove that she had no interest in the transaction, and a reason was assigned why her name appeared in it, viz that the purchase was intended for her benefit. Admitting this to be so, yet the question still occurs, whether a man who has dealt with another in the character of agent is at liberty to retract that character without notice, and to turn round and sue in the character of principal. As to which, it appears to me that the defendant ought at least to have an opportunity of knowing by means of a specific notice, before he is dragged into a court of justice, the real situation in which the plaintiff claims to stand, in order that he may judge how to act. In the present case, *non constat* but that the defendant would have tendered the money. It was the plaintiff's fault originally that he misled the defendant, by assuming a situation which did not belong to him, and therefore he was bound to undeceive the defendant before bringing an action. This seems to follow from a consideration of what the common principles of justice demand, which accord with the cases decided upon this subject.

58 Rayner v Grote (1846) 15 M & W 359

Alderson B ... At the time when this contract was made, the plaintiff was himself the real principal in the transaction; and although the contract on the face of it appeared to have been made by him as agent for another party, there was evidence given at the trial, tending strongly to shew, that when the first parcel of the goods was delivered to and accepted by the defendants, the name of the plaintiff as the principal was then fully known to the defendants: and we think that it was then properly left to the jury to infer from the evidence, that the defendants, with the full knowledge of the facts, had received that portion of the goods, and that all parties then treated the contract as one made with the plaintiff as the principal in the transaction. The defendants' counsel, in the argument, contended against this view of the case, and cited the case of *Bickerton v Burrell* as an authority that the plaintiff could not sue in such a case in his own name. That case is indeed in one respect stronger than the present, inasmuch as that was an action for money had and received, whereas this is a case of an executory contract. If, indeed, the contract had been wholly unperformed and one which the plaintiff, by merely proving himself to be the real principal was seeking to enforce, the question might admit of some doubt. In many such cases, such as, for instance, the case of contracts in which the skill or solvency of the person who is named as the principal may reasonably be considered as a material ingredient in the contract, it is clear that the agent cannot then shew himself to be the real principal, and sue in his own name; and perhaps it may be fairly urged that this, in all executory contracts, if wholly unperformed, or if partly performed without the knowledge of who is the real principal, may be the general rule. But the facts of this case raise a totally different question, as the jury must be taken to have found, under the learned Judge's direction, that this contract has been in part performed, and that part performance accepted by the defendants with full knowledge that the plaintiff was not the agent, but the real principal. If so, we think the plaintiff may, after that, very properly say that they cannot refuse to complete that contract, by receiving the remainder of the goods, and paying the stipulated price for them. And it may be observed that this case is really distinguishable from *Bickerton v Burrell*, on the very ground on which that case was decided; for here, at all events, before action brought and trial had, the defendants knew that the plaintiff was the principal in the transaction.

Index